Loose Space

In cities around the world people use a variety of public spaces to relax, to protest, to buy and sell, to experiment and to celebrate. *Loose Space* explores the many ways that urban residents, with creativity and determination, appropriate public space to meet their own needs and desires. Familiar or unexpected, spontaneous or planned, momentary or long-lasting, the activities that make urban space loose continue to give cities life and vitality.

This book examines physical spaces and how people use them. Contributors discuss a wide range of recreational, commercial and political activities; some are conventional, others are more experimental. Some of the activities occur alongside the intended uses of planned public spaces, such as sidewalks and plazas; other activities replace former uses, as in abandoned warehouses and industrial sites.

Following an introduction to the concept of looseness, the book is organized around four themes: Appropriation, Tension, Resistance and Discovery. The thirteen case studies, international in scope, demonstrate the continuing richness of urban public life that is created and sustained by urbanites themselves.

Karen A. Franck is a Professor in the School of Architecture and the Department of Humanities at the New Jersey Institute of Technology.

Quentin Stevens is a Lecturer in urban design at the Bartlett School of Planning, University College London.

Loose Space

Possibility and Diversity in Urban Life

Edited by
Karen A. Franck and Quentin Stevens

Routledge
Taylor & Francis Group
LONDON AND NEW YORK

Superstudio, still from film series *Five Fundamental Acts*, from act entitled "Life" (1972–1973)

First published 2007 by Routledge
2 Park Square, Milton Park, Abingdon, Oxon, OX14 4RN

Simultaneously published in the USA and Canada by Routledge
270 Madison Avenue, New York, NY10016

Routledge is an imprint of the Taylor & Francis Group, an informa business

Typeset in Univers by Keystroke, 28 High Street, Tettenhall, Wolverhampton

British Library Cataloguing in Publication Data
A catalogue record for this book is available from the British Library

Library of Congress Cataloging-in-Publication Data
Franck, Karen A.
Loose space : possibility and diversity in urban life / Karen A. Franck and Quentin Stevens.
p. cm.
Includes bibliographical references.
ISBN 0-415-70116-3 (hardback : alk. paper) — ISBN 0-415-70117-1 (pbk. : alk. paper) — ISBN 0-203-79957-7 (ebook) 1. City and town life. 2. City and town life—Case studies. 3. Public spaces. 4. Sociology, Urban. I. Stevens, Quentin, 1969– II. Title. III. Title: Possibility and diversity in urban life.
HT119.F73 2006
307.76—dc22 2006015099

ISBN10 0-415-70116-3 (hbk)
ISBN10 0-415-70117-1 (pbk)
ISBN10 0-203-79957-7 (ebk)

ISBN13 978-0-415-70116-7 (hbk)
ISBN13 978-0-415-70117-4 (pbk)
ISBN13 978-0-203-79957-4 (ebk)

Contents

Illustration Credits vii

Notes on Contributors viii

1 Tying Down Loose Space 1
Karen A. Franck and Quentin Stevens

Part I Appropriation **35**

2 Found Spaces: Freedom of choice in public life 38
Leanne G. Rivlin

3 Open-Ended Space: Urban streets in different cultural contexts 54
Nisha A. Fernando

4 Betwixt and Between: Building thresholds, liminality and public space 73
Quentin Stevens

Part II Tension **93**

5 Urban Appropriation and Loose Spaces in the Guadalajara Cityscape 96
Bernardo Jiménez-Domínguez

6 Urban Slippage: Smooth and striated streetscapes in Bangkok 113
Kim Dovey and Kasama Polakit

7 Transforming Public Space into Sites of Mourning and Free Expression 132
Karen A. Franck and Lynn Paxson

8 Central Park, the Aesthetics of Order and the Appearance of Looseness 154
Julia Nevárez

Part III Resistance **171**

9 Heterotopias and the Experience of Porous Urban Space 174
Stavros Stavrides

10 Stalker *on* Location 193
Peter T. Lang

11 Dead Zones, Outdoor Rooms and the Architecture of Transgression 210
Gil M. Doron

Part IV Discovery **231**

12 Social Practices, Sensual Excess and Aesthetic Transgression in Industrial Ruins 234
Tim Edensor

13 Unruly and Robust: An abandoned industrial river 253
Lynda H. Schneekloth

14 Patterns of the Unplanned 271
Urban Catalyst (Philipp Oswalt, Philipp Misselwitz, and Klaus Overmeyer)

Annotated Bibliography 289
Index 296

Illustration Credits

Amy Cash © 11.6
Arena Berlin © 14.2
Bernardo Jiménez-Domínguez © 5.1, 5.2, 5.3, 5.4, 5.5, 5.6
Buffalo and Erie County Historical Society © 13.2
Darryl Jarvis © 11.7
David Baltzer/Zenit © 14.7, 14.8, 14.9
Emiliano Zapatero © 9.4
Gil M. Doron © 10.2, 11.1, 11.2, 11.3, 11.4, 11.5
Julia Nevárez © 8.1, 8.2, 8.3, 8.4, 8.5, 8.6
Karen A. Franck © 1.1, 1.4, 1.7, 1.10, 2.4, 7.2, 7.5, 7.7, 7.8
Kasama Polakit © 6.1, 6.3, 6.5, 6.7
Kim Dovey © 6.2, 6.4, 6.6, 6.8
Klaus Overmeyer © 14.1, 14.3, 14.4, 14.5
Leanne G. Rivlin © 2.1, 2.2, 2.3
Lorenzo Romito, Stalker © 10.1
Lynda H. Schneekloth © 13.1, 13.3, 13.4, 13.5, 13.6, 13.7
Lynn Paxson © 7.1, 7.4
Mira Engler © 7.3, 7.6
Nimal Peiris, Telepix, Kandy © 3.8
Nisha A. Fernando © 3.1, 3.2, 3.3, 3.4, 3.5, 3.6, 3.7
Peter T. Lang © 10.3
Pia Livia di Tardo, Stalker © 10.4, 10.5
Quentin Stevens © 1.2, 1.3, 1.5, 1.6, 1.8, 1.9, 1.11, 1.12, 4.1, 4.2, 4.3, 4.4, 4.5, 4.6, 4.7, 4.8
Romolo Ottaviani, Stalker © 10.3
Stavros Stavrides © 9.3, 9.5, 9.6
Superstudio © cover image
Tim Edensor © 12.1, 12.2, 12.3, 12.4, 12.5, 12.6, 12.7
Urban Catalyst © 14.6

Contributors

Gil M. Doron, writer and artist, is the founder of Transgressive Architecture, a group of artists and architects who work on multi-media projects to create multi-cultural, inclusive public spaces. He has been a design tutor at Greenwich University School of Architecture and has taught history and theory of architecture at the University of East London and University of North London. He has lectured widely on dead zones and the architecture of transgression; his article on that topic appeared in the *New Babylonians* (Wiley-Academy, 2000). Currently he is completing a PhD at the Bartlett School of Architecture, London.

Kim Dovey is Professor of Architecture and Urban Design at the University of Melbourne. He has a PhD in architecture from the University of California, Berkeley, and has published widely on social issues in architecture and urban design. His recent work includes *Framing Places: Mediating Power in Built Form* (Routledge, 1999) and *Fluid City: Transforming Melbourne's Urban Waterfront* (Routledge, 2005).

Tim Edensor teaches Cultural Geography at Manchester Metropolitan University. He is the author of *Tourists at the Taj* (1998), *National Identity, Popular Culture and Everyday Life* (Berg, 2002) and *Industrial Ruins: Space, Aesthetics and Materiality* (Berg, 2005). He also has two websites on British Industrial Ruins. He has written widely on tourism, space and place, walking and driving and the film *Braveheart.*

Nisha A. Fernando is currently an Assistant Professor of Interior Architecture, University of Wisconsin-Stevens Point, and a PhD candidate in architecture (environment-behavior studies) at the University of Wisconsin-Milwaukee. Her dissertation is on cultural aspects of urban streets of Chinatown, New York City. Other research interests include culture and space, multi-sensory aspects of built environments and the meaning of space in cross-cultural contexts. Nisha is a registered architect in Sri Lanka where she practiced and taught part-time at the University of Moratuwa.

Karen A. Franck is a Professor in the New Jersey School of Architecture and the Department of Humanities at the New Jersey Institute of Technology in Newark. She has published several books in the field of architecture and design, most recently *Architecture Inside Out*, with Bianca Lepori (Wiley-Academy, 2000). Her book most closely related to *Loose Space* is *Ordering Space: Types in Architecture and Design*, co-edited with Lynda Schneekloth (Van Nostrand Reinhold, 1994). She has guest-edited two issues of *Architectural Design*: *Food and Architecture* (2003) and *Food and the City* (2005). Professor Franck has a PhD in environmental psychology from the City University of New York.

Bernardo Jiménez-Domínguez has a PhD in social psychology and is Professor in the Urban Studies Center of the University of Guadalajara, Mexico. He teaches social psychology in the psychology BA program and environmental psychology in the MA Program in Urbanism and Development. He has written widely in these fields. His most recent articles have appeared in the journal *Piso* and in the book *Psychology of Sustainable Development*, edited by P. Schmuck and N. Schultz (Kluwer, 2002). His research interests include: urban culture, identity and appropriation, public space, participation and housing.

Peter T. Lang is currently an Assistant Professor at the College of Architecture at Texas A&M with the Santa Chiara Student Center in Tuscany. He is a licensed architect and holds a PhD in Italian history and urbanism from New York University. He has edited two anthologies, *Mortal City* (1995) and *Suburban Discipline* (1997). He is co-editor of the September 2003 issue of *Architectural Design* "Urban Flashes Asia" and of the book catalog, *Superstudio: Life Without Objects* (2003) that accompanies the exhibition he co-curated. He is an active member of Stalker ON, the international urban research group based in Rome.

Philipp Misselwitz is an architect and writer based in Tel Aviv and Berlin and studied at Cambridge University and the Architectural Association in London. He is one of the founding members of the architecture research group Urban Catalyst in Berlin. In 2003, he initiated the trilateral European, Israeli and Palestinian project "Grenzgeografien" (border geographies) which included international workshops and conferences and is being published as a book. His other research includes "Shrinking Cities" and ongoing investigation into development strategies for the informal urbanism of refugee camps, in cooperation with the UN.

Julia Nevárez obtained her PhD in Environmental Psychology from the City University of New York. She is currently an Assistant Professor in the Sociology and Anthropology Department at Kean University, New Jersey. Her research interests are related to urban issues, research and methods including aspects of the urban experience, urban safety, urban development, globalization, public space and, most recently, technoculture.

Philipp Oswalt, architect and writer and a founding member of Urban Catalyst, studied architecture at the Technical University of Berlin and the University of Fine Arts in Berlin. He worked for the Office of Metropolitan Architecture and MVRDV, served as editor of the journal *Arch+* and is the author of *Berlin: Stadt ohne Form* (2000). In 1998, he won the international competition for the memorial site of the Former Women's Concentration Camp at Ravensbruck (with Stefan Tischer and Stefanie Oswalt). He served as project director and chief curator for the "Shrinking Cities" project and curator of the Volkspalast 2004 (with Amelie Deufhard and Mathias Lilienthal).

Klaus Overmeyer is a landscape architect with his own practice in Berlin. He is one of the founding members of Urban Catalyst, the architecture research group in Berlin that serves as a platform for research activities, exhibitions, publications and debates, including the international conference "Fun Palace Berlin 200X," held in October 2004. He is the 2003 prize winner of the national award for landscape architecture.

Lynn Paxson is an Associate Professor of Architecture at Iowa State University. An architect and a doctoral candidate in environmental psychology at the City University of New York, she worked in corporate architectural practice in New York City before joining the ISU faculty. Her research is varied and often focuses on open and public space issues, especially as they relate to participation, contestation, sacred space or First Nation issues. Lynn is a co-author, with Mark Francis and Lisa Cashdan, of *Community Open Spaces: Greening Neighborhoods through Community Action and Land Conservation* (Island Press, 1984).

Kasama Polakit is Visiting Professor in the Department of Urban and Regional Planning at Florida Atlantic University in Fort Lauderdale. Previously she taught at Kasetsart University in Bangkok where she also practiced architecture. Her chapter is based in part on the fieldwork for her completed PhD dissertation in urban design at the University of Melbourne, entitled "Bangkok Streetlife: Transformations of Place in Three Communities."

Leanne G. Rivlin is a Professor of Environmental Psychology at the City University of New York Graduate Center. Her early work centered on studies of psychiatric institutions that yielded information that helped to formulate concepts useful to environmental psychology. Other institutions that she has examined include schools and day care centers. She has also conducted research on homeless shelters as well as the lives of urban squatters. Her interests in the public realm led to research on parks, plazas and playgrounds as well as found spaces. She is one of the co-authors of *Public Space* (Cambridge University Press, 1993). Much of her writing in recent years has addressed socio-spatial conflicts and terrorism and their impacts on local, national and international levels.

Lynda H. Schneekloth, ASLA, is a Professor at the School of Architecture and Planning, University at Buffalo/SUNY. Her scholarly research is focused on the idea of placemaking, that is, how people transform the world, including natural processes and built form. Recently funded projects include research on the historic Buffalo grain elevators, watershed planning on the Buffalo and Niagara Rivers, and participation in the development of a bi-national heritage corridor along the Niagara River. She is the author of *Placemaking: The Art and Practice of Building Communities*, with R. Shibley; *Ordering Spaces: Types in Architecture and Design*, with K. Franck, and *Changing Places: ReMaking Institutional Buildings*, with M. Feuerstein and B. Campagna.

Stavros Stavrides is a lecturer in the School of Architecture, National Technical University of Athens, Greece, where he teaches graduate and postgraduate courses. He has published four books in the field of spatial theory: *The Symbolic Relation with*

Space (Athens: Kalvos, 1990), *Advertising and the Meaning of Space* (Athens: Stachy, 1996), *The Texture of Things* (in collaboration with the photographer Evi Kotsou, Athens: Iris, 1996) and *From the City-as-Screen to the City-as-Stage* (Athens: Ellinika Grammata, 2002, winner of the national book award). He has a PhD in architectural theory from the Aristoteleion University of Thessaloniki and continues his research on the social meaning of space, emphasizing forms of emancipating spatial practices.

Quentin Stevens is a lecturer in urban design at the Bartlett School of Planning, University College London. He has a PhD in urban design from the University of Melbourne and also studied in Berkeley, Chicago and Berlin. His research examines unplanned uses of public spaces and the ways that social interactions are framed by urban spatial form. His other research interests include sensory perceptions of space, urban waterfronts, domed cities and human settlements in Antarctica. His book, *The Ludic City: Exploring the Potential of Urban Public Spaces*, will be published by Routledge in 2007.

Chapter 1

Tying Down Loose Space

Karen A. Franck and Quentin Stevens

A young man hangs one more pair of faded jeans on the fence next to two other pairs, a worn leather jacket and several shirts. Displayed on the sidewalk below are bits of kitchen equipment, miscellaneous plates and glasses, a stack of CDs and several pairs of men's shoes. He leans on the fence, smiling at passers-by on their way to Saturday errands and activities. On a different stretch of sidewalk, a painter sits at his easel painting, facing the street. Finished oil paintings lean against the wall of the building, on display. Drivers stop and ask how much a painting costs and he explains he only paints on commission. On the lamppost nearby small signs advertise a stoop sale the following day, a block party, a missing dog.

Two skateboarders swing into the open plaza, now empty of office workers, aiming directly for a low wall where a couple sits talking intently. Just before reaching the wall, they veer quickly to the right, skateboards and bodies tilting as they aim for the steps, reaching the sidewalk below and zipping by a hot dog vendor before the security guard has reached the middle of the plaza. Along the sidewalk, wooden barriers await the next day's parade.

About 100 bicyclists head out together from Union Square on a chilly Friday evening. The first ride since a state judge rejected the city's effort to shut down the monthly Critical Mass rides, riders are curious what the police will do this time. In the years before the National Republican Convention, police aided the riders, even stopping car traffic at some intersections to let the riders through. But since the sometimes brutal arrest of more than a quarter of the riders who participated in a ride during the convention, the police have interfered with each ride, arresting 30 to 40 participants every month, often for "parading without a permit." This time, only three are arrested, two for riding the wrong way on Broadway. Others receive summonses for traffic violations.

In urban public spaces around the world people pursue a very rich variety of activities not originally intended for those locations. Sometimes these activities occur along with the primary, intended uses, as on the sidewalk, in the street or in the plaza. In other places a fixed use no longer exists, as in a ruined factory, or possibly never existed at all, as next to a railroad track. In all such cases, through people's activities, spaces become "loose." Accessibility, freedom of choice and physical elements that occupants can appropriate all contribute to the emergence of a loose space, but they are not sufficient. For a site to become loose, people themselves must recognize the possibilities inherent in it and make use of those possibilities for their own ends, facing the potential risks of doing so.

The possibility that looseness will occur varies with place (or building) type, types being the categories cultures have developed to organize the world, their beliefs and activities (Schneekloth and Franck 1994). Some types are purely imaginary (heaven, hell, utopia); others refer to kinds of places found on the earth (beach, river, forest, desert); and others result from human manipulations and constructions (field, house, park, street, sidewalk, plaza, playground, library, factory, prison). Types order activities and the manner of carrying them out. What one does and how one does it differ significantly according to the type one is occupying, with some types allowing for more freedom of choice of activities and more means of carrying them out. This is a key theme of Robert Sommer's (1974) book, *Tight Spaces*, in which he contrasts the "hard architecture" of classrooms which have chairs bolted to the floor in rows and the teacher's desk at the front with the "soft architecture" of classrooms which have movable chairs, often arranged in clusters, and the teacher's desk in among the pupils' desks.

One way to think of a type is as an interconnected set of features of form, use and meaning, often particular to a specific culture and historic period (Franck 1994). It is partly these interrelated features that make some types of places more restrictive of people's behavior than others and hence limit the possibilities that looseness will emerge. When a prison is fulfilling its regular, intended use, the physical aspects and enforcement of rules exert a strong constraint on what can take place there, largely controlling behavior and freedom of choice. In contrast, sidewalks and plazas are typically both more physically open and subject to less control and regulation, thus offering more freedom of choice of what to do, where and when. However, when the prisoners take over the prison, the intended use is disrupted, and they have, for the period of the rebellion, loosened the space of the prison. While some types of places are, by definition, looser than others, it is people's actions which make a space loose, with or without official sanction and with or without physical features that support those actions. Similarly, possibilities for looseness may be curtailed through official constraints on activities, as in forbidding "loitering" or playing ballgames, imposing a curfew or restricting large gatherings on sidewalks.

Cities are composed of a great variety of place types. In between the more constraining ones, the private and enclosed places of the city (houses, apartment buildings, office towers, shops, churches, libraries), lie public spaces, often outdoors, where definitions and expectations are less exclusive and more fluid, where there is greater accessibility and freedom of choice for people to pursue a variety of activities. Here is the breathing space of city life, offering opportunities for exploration and discovery, for the unexpected, the unregulated, the spontaneous and the risky.

Many of the activities that generate looseness are neither productive (like traveling to work) nor reproductive (like buying necessities), being instead a matter of leisure, entertainment, self-expression or political expression, reflection and social interaction—all outside the daily routine and the world of fixed functions and fixed schedules. As importantly, loose space is a space apart from the aesthetically and behaviorally controlled and homogeneous "themed" environments of leisure and consumption where nothing unpredictable must occur. The retail activities of buying and selling food, drink and consumer items in urban public space often lie outside the formal economy.

The activities that make a space loose may be impromptu or planned in advance. They may occur only once or they may take place on a regular schedule. They may be unfamiliar, even strange, to passers-by or regular occurrences in the urban scene. They may be disruptive or unruly. But, invariably, they are temporary, whether they last only a few minutes or months or years. Even if they are long-lasting, they occur without official sanction and assurance of continuity and permanence from those in authority.

1.1
Filipino maids, working in Hong Kong without their families, gather in public spaces all over the city on their weekly day off. They chat, eat, play cards, read magazines and try out make up and nail polish

Sometimes official permission is required and license given: vendors purchase licenses to sell their wares and organizers of parades and demonstrations apply for permits weeks or months ahead. Often, however, the activity requires no official sanction, or it may be transgressive, occurring against accepted norms or stated laws, and possibly camouflaged except to those in the know. In some places citizens have greater freedom to pursue the activities they choose than in other more restricted places; sometimes they simply assert that freedom, facing the sanctions that may ensue. Because the activities that make a space loose are different from the primary, intended ones (or occur in the absence of them), there is often some uncertainty about what is legal or socially acceptable.

Loose spaces give cities life and vitality. In loose spaces people relax, observe, buy or sell, protest, mourn and celebrate. Loose spaces allow for the chance encounter, the spontaneous event, the enjoyment of diversity and the discovery of the unexpected. Many writers have pointed out the increasing privatization, commodification and sanitization of public and quasi-public space in cities (Davis 1990; Sorkin 1992a; Deutsche 1996; Lofland 1998; Kayden 2000; Mitchell 2003; Kohn 2004). These forces do indeed prescribe and homogenize urban activities and identities, placing people in the role of passive consumer rather than active creator or participant. They pose serious threats to the continued existence of loose space but they have not eradicated it. The diverse contributions to this book explore the possibility and diversity that urban public life still offers.

Where Space Becomes Loose

Loose space is most likely to emerge in cities since, traditionally, it is there that certain and social and physical conditions that encourage looseness exist. Free access to a variety of public open spaces, anonymity among strangers, a diversity of persons and a fluidity of meaning are all urban conditions that support looseness. For such reasons, the city is a "place of desire, permanent disequilibrium, seat of the dissolution of normalities and constraints, the moment of play and of the unpredictable" (Lefebvre 1991b: 129). The variety of open spaces in cities includes those that are planned for certain assigned functions but that, both legally and physically, accommodate other activities as well; it also includes other kinds of spaces currently without assigned functions that accommodate unintended and unexpected activities. Many of these spaces possess particular physical features that invite people to appropriate them for their own uses.

The urban public realm

Cities comprise a variety of public spaces that are open to all and, in the best cases of urbanity, extend the right to carry out one's desired actions while recognizing the presence and rights of others (Lynch 1981; Carr *et al.* 1992). What Lefebvre calls

1.2
Spanish tourists emerge from the crowd and start dancing in response to African drummers, Leicester Square, London

the "right to the city" encompasses the "right to freedom, to individualization, to habitat and to inhabit" (1996: 173) as well as rights to participation and appropriation.

The sense of freedom and the inclination to engage in actions one might not elsewhere arise partly from the anonymity of urban public space. The positive side of the blasé detachment that Simmel noted is that strangers in public urban space are less likely to constrain our behavior (Simmel 1903; Greenbie 1981). In public we can escape the constraints which are typically connected with known social positions and roles or with smaller communities where residents know each other. In cities people are, mostly, politely inattentive to each other's activities in public spaces: encounters are risky, and so in principle, strangers require a reason to engage with each other (Goffman 1980). For many people, the sense of being free from judgment is one of the main pleasures of being out in public (Lofland 1998).

"Strangers" include those who are biographically unknown to each other but otherwise similar and those people who are socially and culturally different. Being exposed in public oneself engenders civility towards the diversity of strangers who share public space, leading to more relaxed and inclusive behavioral rules and standards. Thus there are two ways strangers help establish the looseness of public space: because they avoid us and because they accept us.

The diversity of urban residents is most visible in its public spaces (Young 1991a) where people of different classes, sexes, ages and cultures intermingle. Possibilities are expanded and space is loosened by the wide diversity of activities pursued (Whyte 1988; Low 2000) and the number of unplanned, unregulated encounters any one person may have. Given the density and mixing of people, such encounters, however fleeting, are unavoidable: people must encounter many others different from themselves. The discretion and conviviality this requires help people to be, paradoxically, more free: the diversity and the density of urban space demand measures of social flexibility and acceptance that we call "tolerance" (Sennett 1971).

Some users of public space are more likely to become engaged in unplanned, unstructured social encounters than others. The presence of available, "open persons," including children and the elderly, provides a catalyst for the loosening of space (Goffman 1980). The barriers to interacting with such strangers are reduced. Others may also approach us and force us into engagements: foreigners who are lost, drunks, charity collectors, as well as those who merely bump into us in crowds. Part of the looseness of the public realm is not being able to control social distance or choose how and when we will interact.

Locations and types of loose space

Looseness depends in part on the overall structure of the urban environment. Some kinds of urban layouts generate more complex spatial interconnections and interrelations and more choices than others. A greater variety of streets and land uses stimulate the emergence of loose space. Mixed-use neighborhoods with buildings of different sizes and ages and short blocks are robust and long-lasting because they do not have a tight, singular relation of form to function; they are loose and adaptable (Jacobs 1961). Street blocks with many separate building frontages and numerous entrances bring strangers into contact more frequently, diversifying the uses of the street spaces and squares onto which they open. Neighborhoods built at human scale encourage people to walk. Urban environments which are composed of many different, densely interconnected and overlapping circulation loops ("ringy" spaces) provide more opportunities to turn when moving through the city and allow individual spaces and people to be encountered in different sequences, undermining the possibility of strict control over movement (Alexander 1965; Dovey 1999). Such formal conditions encourage "the messy vitality of the metropolitan condition, with its unpredictable intermingling of classes, races, and social and cultural forms" (Boddy 1992: 126). While "redundant" urban layouts are in one sense not optimally utilized, they also provide spaces which remain available for unknown future uses.

Loose space emerges in a variety of types of urban locations, some planned for specific uses (planned public open space) and others without assigned functions (leftover and abandoned spaces). They are all accessible to the public. They are not typically buildings, except in cases where buildings have been abandoned. The range of sites overlaps somewhat with Lynch's "open space," which has "no necessary relation to ownership, size, type of use, or landscape character" and can include all "the negative (i.e. unbuilt), extensive, loose, uncommitted" space in the city (Lynch 1965: 396–397). Crawford's "everyday urban space" includes vacant lots, sidewalks, front yards, parks and parking lots that have been appropriated for new and often temporary uses, that possess "multiple and shifting meanings rather than clarity of function" (Crawford 1999: 28).

1.3
Vegetable gardens planted in front of the imperial palace in Vienna as a temporary memorial to remember food shortages at the end of World War II

Urban streets, sidewalks, plazas and squares—publicly-owned, designed and maintained to serve particular kinds of activities and actively overseen by municipal authorities—are usually open to a variety of uses beyond the ones intended. It is primarily in these spaces that the city exhibits the key features of urbanity: access, freedom of choice, density and the intermixing of different kinds of people and activities. Over recent decades other types of so-called "public space" have emerged, including corporate plazas, corporate atria, gallerias and festival market places (Carr *et al.* 1992). Although they are privately owned and accessibility and freedom of action are curtailed, they still offer opportunities for unexpected actions.

Leftover spaces, usually publicly owned but without any assigned function, are often located right next to spaces with fixed and delimited functions. Examples include the spaces under bridges and next to highways and railroad tracks. These exist beyond the boundaries of organized social space, having no intended use and often lacking conventionally appealing features. Tightness of programming suddenly unravels, heightening the contrast with the adjacent space with its clearly defined function (the highway, the railroad track) and allowing the insertion of activities in search of a home. Such spaces may be oddly shaped or difficult to get to, they may lack a name or be secret; yet they become places of expression and occupation—often because of these very characteristics. Bishop describes the underside of the bridge: "Bridges gather to them an underside; they have an underworld. They are outside the rush and flow taking place above, over the bridge" (1988: 96).

Empty lots, abandoned buildings, piers, waterfronts and tunnels—spaces that once had assigned functions but no longer do—possess similar qualities. Here the previously established uses have become detached from the space leaving it open for new uses and new meanings—for a community garden, for inhabitation by homeless people or runaways, for transgressive activities that require remoteness and seclusion. Sometimes the spaces have been completely abandoned by their owners; sometimes ownership is not enforced, is unclear or is under dispute. In the case of ruined structures, there may be clues of the former use. These intimations and the air of decay together invite a kind of reverie, offering an invitation to imagine what this place could be.

Lacking officially assigned uses, leftover spaces and abandoned spaces lie outside the "rush and flow" as well as the control of regulations and surveillance that come with the established uses of planned urban public space. They are the negative or void to the city of named and fixed types of open space (park, plaza, street, sidewalk)—the "other" places, what Ignasi de Solá-Morales calls *terrain vague* (1995). Calling them "superfluous landscapes," Nielsen (2002) sees abandoned spaces as the "backsides" of the designed, "primary" spaces of public life, which he sees as controlled and scripted, following the model of the theme park and the mall. Also called "no man's lands," "indeterminate spaces" and "free zones" (Groth and Corijn 2005), abandoned and leftover spaces, temporarily free of official planning and commodification, are appropriated for other uses. Abandoned mines in Tyneside, England, become places for bird watching, parachuting and clay pigeon shooting (Lonsdale 2001); an abandoned railroad maintenance building in Denver becomes an unofficial "museum of graffiti" (Ferrell 2001); former railway sheds in Helsinki are occupied by artists' collectives, startup businesses and a flea market (Groth and Corijn 2005). La Varra calls these spaces and their uses Post-It City: "a fragile and fragmentary network which filters into the tightly woven structures of urban public space" (2001: 428).

Physical features of loose space

Through their actions people make use of the physical features they find in public space; many fixed elements intended for one purpose can easily serve another (Whyte 1988). Walls, fences and ledges, which are often supposed to delimit space and behavior, can be sat upon, climbed onto and used to display banners or items for sale; their looseness is a product of affordances which such boundaries provide (Gibson 1979). Niches, stairs and recesses located at the edges of public spaces encourage people to linger. An overhang or bridge becomes the roof of a temporary home; lampposts can be used to lean against while sitting or standing. A hard and expansive surface, free of objects or structures, such as a parking lot or plaza, allows for a variety of behavioral possibilities: teenagers or others may gather to hang out; protests can be held.

1.4
Vendor uses steps to display vegetables for sale, Noryangjin fish market, Seoul

Props can be brought in to make spaces more useful, if only temporarily. Tents and tables support markets for farmers and craftspeople; closing a space to cars and placing a number of "jumps" and other fixtures offers an afternoon of skate-boarding and inline skating for children. Elements that are moveable, flexible or malleable can be appropriated, for example, chairs or plants, but also parts of ruins or junk left behind in abandoned spaces. These provide tools that assist in active, bodily exploration of new actions.

A certain amount of physical disorder can encourage new and inventive uses, not only because it indicates lower surveillance and lack of regulation but also because it provides spaces and materials that expand the potential scope of actions (Lynch 1990). Physical deterioration can make complex the layout of the terrain, opening up new links and thus new opportunities.

The potential of a space to become loose may lie in its relationship to other spaces. When the edge is porous, one can see and move easily between spaces or easily straddle the barrier between them as people sit on a wall around a plaza, watching the scene. Building thresholds, often appropriated as loose space, are spaces between. They are clearly enclosed on their private side, but they generally offer graduated transitions into the public realm. For some kinds of activities, people seek spaces that are less open, more enclosed and more hidden from view.

Physical qualities of urban public spaces can frame opportunities for expression and for social engagement. Elevated stages, intersections and doorways are examples of sites that performers can use to capture the attention of others in public, as a way of changing people's attitudes. The appearance of spaces can also directly communicate a variety of religious and political beliefs and commercial and artistic agendas. Symbolism can either stimulate or inhibit actions by affecting potential users' interpretations and feelings, persuading them that a space is sacred or accommodating or private, that it provides or denies roles to certain individuals, that it is a place for escapism or grieving or work or protest.

Meaning is not only conveyed by what the environment looks like. The touch, sound and smell of a place also shape people's perceptions of it. These experiences of urban space are typically intense, sudden, random, fleeting and mysterious—in other words, loose (Latham 1999). Urban spaces, in all their density and complexity, generally provide mixed messages. A public space might look "bureaucratic," smell "bad," and yet be filled with "celebratory" music and "mysterious" foreign languages. The periphery of an airport may seem "overgrown," "noisy" and "caustic" but at the same time be "invigorating" and "untrammeled." Lefebvre notes that "urban spaces are . . . 'over-inscribed': everything therein resembles a rough draft, jumbled and self-contradictory" (1991b: 142). One of the freedoms of public space is that the sensations encountered there are often loosened from their conventional contexts and are brought into new relationships of ambiguity and confusion. The city is delirious; such de-familiarization of space promotes loose and playful responses, a re-discovery of spaces' potential (Gilloch 1996).

Whether the physical and representational qualities of a space are a support or a hindrance depends so much on what people want to do. A large expanse of flat open space may be good for demonstrations but only if it is centrally located and in public view. And to be a market, such a space may require tables and possibly tents. Too much openness limits activities to those that can be performed in a void or requires users to introduce additional elements. A smooth, flat surface does not necessarily have more potential than a rough or sloping one. Ruins and flights of stairs are desirable for some uses even though these terrains may be difficult to negotiate.

How Space Becomes Loose

Two young girls have drawn a series of colored squares in chalk for a game of hopscotch that extends along the sidewalk, up the stoop and onto the landing in front of the door to a brownstone. The children, like many other creators of loose space, went beyond the intended use of a public space, improvising their own use. In the physical features of the space—the change in levels, the difference in the size of the spaces and the hard surfaces—they discovered a new set of possibilities, extending and complicating an established game by using the opportunities at hand, using a space of circulation in their own way.

People create loose space through their own actions. Many urban spaces possess physical and social possibilities for looseness, being open to appropriation, but it is people, through their own initiative, who fulfill these possibilities. The emergence of a loose space depends upon: first, people's recognition of the potential within the space and, second, varying degrees of creativity and determination to make use of what is present, possibly modifying existing elements or bringing in additional ones. In these ways, unlike the passive consumers of prepackaged activities and experiences in the themed environments of malls and festival market places, citizens actively fashion public settings to satisfy their own basic needs as well as their desires.

People's belief in the general freedom of public space is an essential prerequisite to their acting out that freedom through use. Physical barriers and locks provide the most obvious controls on the use of space, but an individual's behavior is also constrained by what they think is appropriate, admissible or possible (Bourdieu 1977). People with different backgrounds have varied beliefs, expectations, aspirations and skills. Because urban settings gather a diversity of people together, including many from other places, there are always some who misread cues, who are willing to break rules, who find a space that specially motivates them to action. A diversity of users translates into more prospects of loosening.

People often seek out spaces that will support the actions they wish to pursue. They may have clear functional objectives—to play hide-and-seek, to take a nap, to publicize the services they provide—and they find spaces where such actions are possible though unintended. Conversely, people's actions may be "triggered" by specific physical contexts and social situations they encounter (Lerup 1977; Wortley 2001), such as spontaneously starting to dance when music is heard, splashing in a fountain on a hot day, touching a sculpture or starting a conversation with a stranger about something witnessed on the street.

1.5
People of various ages enjoying the sun and varied opportunities offered by street furniture, Christchurch, New Zealand

In some cases, the stimulations may arouse subconscious or forbidden desires. Without warning, without thinking and contrary to good sense, we may begin following a passing stranger, picking flowers, preening ourselves in a store window or walking on the grass. Thus looseness includes going beyond the limits of what an individual expects themselves to do in public or in general. Our actions may even be dangerous: sliding down a smooth handrail, balancing on a narrow ledge, having an emotional argument in the middle of the street, taking a shortcut through the red-light district.

People's behavior may also be more broadly transgressive. Selling counterfeit goods, under-age drinking and public sex may be novel uses of a particular setting, but more significantly they also test the limits of what is socially acceptable behavior. Sometimes transgressions establish new standards of acceptability for the use of urban space, as with public protests in a society emerging from dictatorship or the increasing openness of homosexuality. Sometimes space is loosened as a result of someone's intention to merely use a space differently, sometimes spatial conditions inspire people to act in new ways, and sometimes loosening pushes against society's ideas about "good" behavior.

Activities

Some of the activities that make a space loose are, in Gehl's (1987) terms, necessary while others are optional. People address their economic need to make a living when, for instance, street vendors sell fresh produce and prepared foods in public urban spaces on sidewalks and in squares. Or they may be selling art works, handicrafts, "designer" watches, jewelry and sunglasses, souvenirs or handbags. Musicians and mimes give street performances; artists offer their skills in drawing portraits or sell their own works. Homeless people find shelter in all kinds of urban spaces.

Physical recreation is one broad category of voluntary action that characterizes loose space. Public spaces of all kinds offer opportunities for daring physical feats—climbing up lampposts, dirt biking in empty lots. Games may also be more sedentary, such as cards and chess. People find places for reading, drawing, sun bathing, dancing, gardening, chatting with others, having a meal or a snack or just relaxing, lost in their own thoughts or studying the passing scene. Art installations and art festivals may gather many people, stimulating spin-off events and vending. As importantly, loose space can be sites for loose living: forbidden behaviors for which no one ever intentionally makes room and which may require privacy, if not secrecy, occurring in places that are not easily accessible or visible. People who want to enjoy stolen treasure, messy paint-ball games, drug use or sexual encounters find a wide range of urban sites where they are able to do so.

Expressive activities are also common in loose space. Spaces where the public gathers provide opportunities for people to communicate with others. Political activities are frequent: protests, rallies and speeches, leafleting and petitioning and voter registration drives. Private emotions are also expressed in public settings,

1.6
People leave bouquets, cards and notes in Russell Square, London, close to the site where a bomb exploded on a bus, July 2005. A succession of individual acts of remembrance builds a formal circular arrangement.

through the creation of spontaneous shrines and graffiti written and drawn on pavements and walls, and when people stand in public and kiss or argue. Public streets and squares host cultural and religious rituals, festivals and parties, including those connected with particular events such as New Year's Eve or the Millennium, the end of a war or the success of a sports team. People's unregulated and sometimes unexpected actions loosen up the dominant meanings which characterize the "representational spaces" of specific sites and monuments: "This is the space which the imagination seeks to change and appropriate" (Lefebvre 1991b: 39). Changing meanings give rise to new perceptions, attitudes and behavior.

Movement

Just as people may break free of intended uses and established meanings, they may also break free of restricted forms of comportment and movement. This means overcoming physical constraints—as a skateboard leaps off a wall or bench—or it may be a matter of relaxed social norms. Stretching out in the sun or sitting on the ground surface are postures seldom adopted, or accepted, in the tighter spaces of the city. The same is true of singing or dancing or calling out for people's attention. Postures and movements may be transgressive: when homeless people sleep and cook and occupy public space as their homes; when people engage in public sex.

In loose space, the actions of others may be quite unpredictable, as can be the speed and direction of their movement. Immediate negotiation is often required when cyclists, runners and skateboarders mingle with pedestrians. Sidewalks have little of the strict order and pattern of the highway. Often just being in a loose space, with this variety and unpredictability of movement, requires careful attention and negotiation; yet at other times and places, loose space allows for a reduction in attention and a chance to reflect or to shift attention beyond one's immediate environs.

Skateboarding illustrates how the looseness of a space is both produced and experienced through action. Mundane features such as concrete sewer pipes and curbs do not change physically when they are skated upon. What is loosened is the user's understanding of how the physical environment can be combined with "body, image, thought and action" to produce new spatial experiences (Borden 2001a: 33). The design of modern urban spaces is dominated by the framing of spectacular imagery set at a distance from the viewer/consumer, but skaters come to know space primarily through the other senses, up close, through the body and in motion through space. Against the spectacle of well-managed, "functional" urban space and its passive, sedate patterns of use, skating illustrates the potential of the human body to perceive, imagine and act in original and unintended ways.

People's active appropriation of public space and their willingness to overcome or ignore physical or social constraints are well captured by the evocative verbs researchers have employed to describe activities that create looseness. Borden (2001a) describes how skateboarders adopt, take over, colonize, emulate, repeat, work within, work against, re-imagine, re-temporalize, reject, edit and recompose the spaces of the city. In Shields's (1989) study of shopping malls, his verbs highlight the possibly radical nature of activities in loose space: rebel, ignore, defy, evade, deflect, question, mock, disrupt, subvert, parody, recode, critique, mediate, recuperate, reverse, destabilize, intervene, exploit, highjack, transform and contradict.

When Is Space Loose?

The looseness of spaces varies across time. Many spaces are only called upon to serve their primary functions at particular times of the day, week and year. At other times, these functions are in abeyance, as are the management practices and user groups that maintain them. Then the space becomes available for other, more informal activities. Many city streets are, for example, closed to vehicles at certain times. Nighttime in particular is a period of escapism and deviance (Nasaw 1992; Cresswell 1998; Schlör 1998), although in the evening space also tightens up, as gates are locked, lights are switched off and security systems are switched on. City sidewalks are usually physically open and authorities usually allow a great variety of activities and events. However, under particular circumstances, such as curfews, martial law or closing specific streets for security reasons, the sidewalk becomes much tighter by force of law, and use changes.

Looseness may serve as a "time-out" from everyday routines, as is apparent in spontaneous and optional activities, which are typically irregular in timing, duration and structure. Lynch and Carr suggest there is potential behavioral openness "wherever people do not have other overriding purposes (in transit, . . . in bars and hangouts, for example)" (1968: 425). Defining the characteristics of such "third places" which sustain informal public socializing, Oldenburg first identifies "the escape or time out from life's duties and drudgeries" (1991: 21).

When everyday functions or controls are suspended, looseness may be very temporary, perhaps lasting only a few minutes. Other zones of looseness can be very long-lasting, even permanently so. Parks, garbage dumps and derelict buildings may have fixed owners and names, but physically and socially they remain very loose. The constant movement of people, vehicles and materials through sites such as roadways, railway corridors, doorways, floodplains and storm drains thwarts the prospect of any long-term occupation, but this also guarantees they remain available for unintended, short-term uses.

The timing of people's exploratory and transgressive actions often illustrates their conscious reaction to the periodic looseness or tightness of a space. The bicycle protesters of Critical Mass specifically choose to block major city street intersections during the Friday evening rush hour. During Carnivale, people really let their hair down although the timing of this activity is carefully regulated. People create looseness but not always according to a timetable of their own choosing.

Different social groups have different perceptions of when a given space is loose and available to them. Urban spaces are "shared . . . across time by different

1.7
Elderly residents dance to music from a boom box, outside a YM-YWCA on a wintry afternoon in Brighton Beach, Brooklyn, New York

publics" (Iveson 1998: 30). People achieve inclusivity and flexibility by carefully structuring the timing of their different activities to avoid unnecessary conflicts, through a constantly re-negotiated and improvised "place ballet" (Jacobs 1961).

Time is not only cyclic, especially in cities, and looseness also changes over historical time. Ideal, pure, utopian environments are those where the potential for ongoing change and development has been removed. Loose space constantly changes; tight also means static (Sibley 1988). Changes in the form, regulations and use of a given space sometimes start out temporary or unpredictable but then, over time, become regular and anticipated; their looseness can fade away. Nighttime again offers the clearest illustration. Developments in technology, morality and policing opened up new times and spaces for new work and leisure activities, after which these activities themselves have become subject to control and instrumentalization (Nasaw 1992; Bianchini 1995).

Spaces that start out tight may become loose through use and over time—in some cases, lots of time—as their original use is gone and their physical features change. This includes unkempt and derelict spaces where, through destruction or mere neglect, parts, surfaces or boundaries have come loose or become soft or slack.

Other spaces may start off loose and, for various reasons, become more controlled regarding appearance and acceptable uses. A derelict waterfront, no longer used for shipping, becomes the site of exploring, art installations, fishing, picnics, and then is redesigned to be a public park, still loose but less so than previously (Campo 2002).

Benefits and Risks of Loose Space

This book focuses on the virtues of loose space, virtues arising largely from the qualities of possibility, diversity and disorder. These qualities stand in direct opposition to qualities of public space that many people value: certainty, homogeneity and order. Whether a given quality is considered an asset or a liability depends on the needs of the viewer and, just as importantly, upon one's assumptions about what is good about public space.

Given different assumptions about the value of public space, it is unlikely that a consensus on benefits and risks can be reached. Even when some benefits can be agreed upon, citizens and municipal authorities often overestimate risks or decide that potential risks outweigh those benefits. Precisely because the activities occurring in loose space are varied and unpredictable, there is always a degree of uncertainty which, in and of itself, may be seen by some as a substantial risk. Differing interests play a role as well. Calls for order and beautification may belie intentions to prevent social change or to redevelop property and attract wealthier residents and patrons to an area. The existence of loose space is continuously threatened by these and other interests, making it all the more important to state one's assumptions and, from the perspective of those assumptions, to weigh the leading benefits with the perceived risks of loose space.

Possibility

Loose space is characterized by an absence or abeyance of the determinacy which is common in place types with assigned and limited functions (Schneekloth and Franck 1994). The indeterminacy of loose space, along with free access, opens the space to other possibilities: to activities not anticipated, to activities that have no other place, to activities that benefit from a relative lack of control and economic constraints. Freedom is a prerequisite of loose space for people to be able to pursue possibilities of their choice. Freedom is also a consequence of loose space as people's actions generate more possibilities, possibilities of a political, commercial or experimental nature.

Political groups are able to make their points, to spread their messages, when they have free access to a wide and diverse public, including those who may not wish to hear their message, in places where the message is not controlled by others (Kohn 2004). Historically, streets, sidewalks, squares and parks have been such places, with and without the permission of authorities. In these spaces groups have been able to represent themselves and their interests for political as well as cultural purposes (as in festivals and parades). It was by taking over and transforming Tiananmen Square that the mass movement of students in China in 1989 made themselves and their concerns visible to the world (Mitchell 2003), risking their lives in the process. Without concrete spaces within which it is enacted, society remains a meaningless abstraction (Lefebvre 1991b); for a society to be free requires public spaces which are in various ways open, unregulated and visible to many others.

Possibilities are commercial as well. Many public urban spaces offer opportunities for individual vendors to conduct their own businesses with minimal overhead costs or to work for larger businesses that provide the carts and the items for sale. A study of vending of street food in nine developing countries shows that it is a growing phenomenon in urban areas, that most vendors are micro-entrepreneurs, not dependent workers, that many are women and that many earn as much as school teachers or government clerks (Tinker 1997). Immigrants from rural areas or from other countries find a source of earning money without having to rely on an employer, fluency in a new language or capital investment. Buyers benefit from the easy accessibility and lower prices of food and goods the vendors sell. In times of war or other social disorder, the chance to buy and sell in public space provides both jobs and necessities, as in Belgrade, during a UN embargo on imported goods in 1991, when market stands, cars and vans, straw mats and cardboard boxes replaced conventional shops (Djura *et al.* 2003), eventually expanding to 10,000 "shopkeepers." The informal and often robust economy observable in loose space sustains small-scale, independent and local entrepreneurship, all in sharp contrast to businesses owned by multinational corporations. And they help sustain a local, place-specific culture through the kinds of things they sell and their ways of doing so.

Possibilities to experiment may arise from a lack of choice: that is, loose space offers locations for activities that have no other place. Those without housing may sleep in a park, under a bridge, next to a railroad track or a highway. Without formally assigned plots to farm, urban residents appropriate empty lots to grow fruits and vegetables: hundreds of community gardens flourish in New York City (Englander 2001). In abandoned industrial buildings artists, musicians, small start-up businesses and cultural groups find a place to work (Groth and Corijn 2005). Within the fabric of fixed place types, with their assigned functions and regulations, their financial costs and controlled public exposure, there is much less opportunity for innovation and experimentation. Experimentation in abandoned buildings may take more transgressive forms as well, such as raves (Multiplicity 2003), paint wars, experimentation with drugs and sex. What starts out as a single and possibly temporary innovation may become more firmly established or more widely adopted. The first farmers market in New York City started in one square in 1976; such markets now take place all over the city and in other parts of the country (Project for Public Spaces 2003).

The possibilities offered by loose space generate risks. Despite all good intentions, political demonstrations and other large gatherings of people in public spaces can lead to more disruptive behavior and/or arrest and possibly brutal

1.8
Risky bodily exploration of a complex terrain, Memorial to the Murdered Jews of Europe, Berlin

interventions by police. The mere possibility of disruption often leads authorities to forbid such gatherings, severely restricting the opportunities that should be available in public space and undermining rights to free speech. In finding adventure and testing out physical skills in loose space, people expose themselves, through their own freely chosen actions, to risk of physical injury. Freedom, however, includes opportunities of choosing to undertake actions that confront danger, court it even, of going beyond what we can be sure of—of adventuring (Simmel 1911). The physical dangers of open space are often overestimated, and often in the design of contemporary environments such risks are too closely and too bluntly managed (CABE Space 2005), reducing the possibilities of personal control, freedom and adventure.

Diversity

The myriad possibilities available in many public spaces attract a variety of people and generate a great variety of activities. In loose spaces people encounter people like themselves and others who are extremely different, activities they may expect and ones unanticipated. Contact with what is different, new and unexpected is a source of learning both for children and adults. When people encounter others unlike themselves, they grow accustomed to difference, are encouraged to accept it; they may learn more about themselves as well. Lofland suggests that learning tolerance, a sign of cosmopolitanism, depends on a certain amount of controlled "anarchy," absent in "Disneyland cities" that are "cleaned-up, tidy, purified . . . where nothing shocks, nothing disgusts" (1998: 243). Young also holds that differences are a resource for learning (1991a, 1997) and suggests that encounters with difference can be "erotic" as well: in the "pleasure and excitement of being drawn out of one's routine to encounter the novel, the strange, the surprising" (1991a: 239).

The easy availability of different kinds of places and people, doing what they choose, gives people the chance to enact particular individual and collective identities, to learn and to find others like themselves.

> When others act more freely, we learn about them, and thus about ourselves. The pleasure of an urban space freely used is the spectacle of those peculiar ways . . . It is an opportunity for the expression of self and group, unfettered by routine constraints of workplace and home.
>
> (Lynch and Carr 1979: 415)

The opportunity to explore an identity is particularly important for those who rely on public space to do so and to interact with others like themselves. Teenagers of both sexes use a variety of public urban spaces to explore and display self-identity (Toon 2000). The chance to meet others either briefly or for longer relationships is important for gay men, who depend on specific public places for such opportunities (Binnie 2000; Brown 2004). Both groups find themselves excluded when public spaces are tightened through the installation of surveillance cameras, the removal of shrubbery and limitations on access.

These and other measures, intended to increase order in public space, reduce the diversity of activities and occupants. Some restrictions on people's use of public space curtail the right to free speech and can be contested in court (Kohn 2004). Other initiatives that curtail diversity of actions and actors—ostensibly to improve safety in public space—are more complicated because they are intended to increase freedom *from* fear and *from* violent crime, but at the same time these measures decrease freedom *to*—freedom to engage in activities that may seem threatening to social order or that require privacy and freedom from surveillance cameras (Dovey 1999; Lees 2004). The questions always need to be asked: Whose freedom is increased?, To do what?, And whose freedom is curtailed?, To do what? Increased freedom for some should not mean, inevitably, the curtailed freedom of others. Public space can be seen as the setting used by *multiple* publics, suggesting a normative model of public space that is equitable and non-exclusionary (Iveson 1998).

Loose space encompasses a rich variety of settings with widely different physical and social conditions. This variety allows different kinds of people to find the kinds of public space that will meet their particular needs and desires. This multiplicity of people and places are all under threat when a universal model of "the public" or "the community" or "the common good" is adopted (Deutsche 1996). Such terms suggest a commonality and an homogeneity among citizens that do not exist (Young 1991b). The adoption of this language and the goals they represent in the design, management and evaluation of public space implicitly (but forcefully) excludes those considered marginal and, as intended, reduces difference.

Through the diversity of actions and actors it invites, loose space nurtures particularity in the urban public realm, sustaining local practices and allowing the

1.9
Vendors preparing food and setting up tables for the evening meal that breaks the day's fast, at sundown, during the month of Ramadan, Place Jemaa el Fna, Marrakesh

identity of place and culture to flourish. These practices may change over time as cultures change or as immigrants bring their customs with them, but in all cases differences between places arise from the actions of the occupants themselves. In Florence, Singhalese immigrants play football in the Piazza Indipendenza and also sell their wares on streets along the Arno; South American families dance on summer evenings in the Piazza dell Repubblica; and Peruvian religious processions move through the city, reviving an earlier Florentine custom (Allegretti 2004). In Jemaa el Fna, the main square of Marrakesh, snake charmers, musicians, acrobats and food vendors draw crowds day and night, and a few elderly professional storytellers still tell dramatic tales of ancient battles and romance (Simons 2006). Often commercial interests and the pressures of urban development threaten the culturally-shaped activities that loose space supports. At Jemaa el Fna several development projects have been stopped; traffic has been banned from the square; and in 2001 UNESCO designated it a site in its program of "Oral and Intangible Heritage of Humanity." The continued survival of loose space may often require measures to protect and preserve.

Disorder

The mixture of diverse activities and people, the occurrence of unexpected events and actions, apparent disarray and physical deterioration all create a certain amount of disorder in loose space, as illustrated by many of the images in this book. Disarray and deterioration have benefits: they invite people to take the initiative in imagining and creating their own arrangements of space and finding alternative uses, as, for instance, in empty lots and other abandoned sites. Visual disorder suggests an absence or lessening of control, the presence of possibilities for intervention and appropriation. Some people, however, see in visual disorder threats to social order. City officials and property investors have vested interests in a homogeneous, predictable and well-ordered environment where use and appearance are controlled. The unregulated movements and actions of people, the ill-defined boundaries, the unkempt landscapes and damaged structures become reasons for tightening up space. The imposition of visual order onto space, however, does not always suit everybody's interests. The appearance of harmony may constrain the use of space or it may mask chaos behind the scenes. Conversely, messy appearances are sometimes the product of a strong underlying social order which an outsider does not notice or understand.

There is a difference between an aesthetic preference and consequential dangers. Lynch and Carr warn us that "new activities" in public space may "seem dangerous without being so." They recommend that we refrain from exerting social control until real dangers emerge (1968: 427–428). Real risks, if they arise, come from specific actions. Loose space, with its relaxation of constraints, does provide a haven for many activities that are legally defined as crimes. Some—dumping toxic waste, assault—pose threats for everyone, wherever they occur, and it may be necessary to tighten space to reduce these dangers. Other activities, however, such as ball playing, loitering or drinking alcohol, are unpleasant rather than dangerous. They pose relatively little harm to other people and are tolerated in some locations but not in others. In response to fears about these kinds of risks, the potentials of space and action are often inordinately tightened. This tightening often merely displaces risky activities somewhere else and, at the same time, unnecessarily restricts the opportunity for a great many legal and desirable activities.

Loose space also harbors the risk that people might behave in legal ways which other people find objectionable or offensive, including unselfconscious displays of identity such as homosexuals kissing, cross-dressing or body piercing. Encounters with what is shocking or troublesome can be a benefit, resulting in greater acceptance, tolerance and personal growth. In *The Uses of Disorder*, Sennett (1971) argues that social conflicts that can arise in face-to-face encounters in cities encourage the development of maturity and the capacity to recognize and deal with conflict, in contrast to the need to avoid it and withdraw into a myth of solidarity, so prevalent in suburban settings. In a similar vein, Lofland (1998) suggests that a certain amount of anarchy and mild fear must be experienced in public space to learn tolerance. The opposite view—that public space should be harmonious—requires that differences be transcended or suppressed (Young 1991b). Such an ideal runs counter to the very idea of a democratic society.

The lack of order in loose space is often seen as inefficient. The density of activities and the overlap of intended activities with unintended ones can cause congestion and slow the passage of pedestrians and vehicles. Everyday routines and instrumental tasks may be disrupted, time lost—or so it is believed. Such concerns have led to attempts to remove vendors from sidewalks (Whyte 1988) and to the

1.10
Critical Mass's regular bicycle demonstration explores a gentrified café precinct, to the amusement of onlooking cappuccino sippers, Hardware Lane, Melbourne

complete abolition of traditional street systems, removing outdoor public space for gathering, forcing it indoors (Holston 1998). In abandoned sites, space is believed to be "wasted" because it is not generating its "highest and best" use. Such an instrumental, functionalist view of space ignores the benefits to economic development of temporary, experimental, changing and shifting economic activity. Orderly, controlled space is efficient from the viewpoint of monopolies and government regulators. Congestion, underutilized spaces and uneven spatial development are risky and perhaps wasteful, at least in the short term, but they are also a key source of sociability, inclusiveness, diversification and growth. "An environment for growth . . . would not be the most efficient and safe environment. Nor would it offer maximum stability and security. It would certainly not be extremely comfortable, nor even very beautiful" (Lynch and Carr 1968: 425).

Relationships between Loose and Tight Space

The looseness and tightness of space are related conditions, emerging from a nexus of the physical and the social features of a space. It is possible, within this general characterization, to consider different possible relationships between loose and tight and, with these approaches, to explore different ways people create and experience looseness.

Looseness vs. tightness

It is tempting to see looseness and tightness as opposite conditions and to dichotomize urban spaces accordingly. Over the past decades we have witnessed the emergence of new kinds of "public spaces" that discourage or actively forbid the kinds of unplanned activities that make a space loose. Often privately owned, such as malls and corporate plazas and atria, or privately maintained, as parks or sidewalks in Business Improvement Districts in US cities, these are places of public gathering but restrict many of the activities that have long characterized truly public urban space. Boddy, for example, contrasts "the analogous city" of "filtered, prettified, homogeneous" indoor pedestrian environments as a substitute for "the messy vitality of the metropolitan condition, with its unpredictable intermingling of classes, races, and social and cultural forms" (1992: 126). The impermeable boundaries, secured entries and sign-posted rules of private skyways, shopping malls and gated communities give concrete form to a clear conceptual opposition between tight and loose spaces, as *kinds* of spaces.

Apparent looseness

Urban public spaces often appear to be loose, both to users and to researchers, even when there are significant restrictions in place. Vision and formal qualities dominate other ways of understanding space; this draws attention away from what people are actually doing in a space and from constraints on use. Large public open spaces such as Tiananmen Square and the forecourt of Australia's Parliament House are deceptively "open" because behavior is tightly regulated by non-spatial means (Dovey 1999). People often presume they have the freedom to use public open spaces as they wish. They may find, however, that actions which are generally acceptable are prohibited in certain public spaces or at certain times. Two graduate students playing chess on a laptop in New York City's Bryant Park were told by a private security guard (paid by the Conservancy corporation that funds this public park's maintenance) that they could not do so. Although the theme park Disneyland is promoted as escape from everyday routine, it is in fact "anti-carnivalesque," involving "celebrations of the existing order of things in the guise of escape from it" (Sorkin 1992b: 208).

Simulations of looseness may actually be agents of discreet tightening. Crawford (1992) suggests that "free" time spent "informally" in a shopping mall has in fact been carefully scripted to provide a simulation of the variety and spontaneity of the real city, while encouraging consumption and eliminating other distractions: very little about the consumption experience is accidental. As modern life becomes more and more routinized and predictable, people's desire for adventure increases, even though escapism itself is often incredibly formulaic (Lyman and Scott 1975; Cohen and Taylor 1976). Many loose occasions and places can be seen as merely licensed "safety valves," harmless ways to release tension which are carefully regulated in time, space and intensity (Turner 1969). But controlled and pre-programmed "looseness" is not loose; people can only appropriate spaces for their own uses if they have full access and freedom of choice.

Looseness as relative and adjustable

Looseness, the appropriation of public space for unplanned uses, results from freedom of choice, but no public space is absolutely free, and some spaces may be too free. Even in settings where everyday taboos regarding modes of dress or the justification for interacting with strangers are generously relaxed, such as beaches and carnivals, escape involves the invocation of other norms (Shields 1989). In other cases, design and regulation only make particular actions or expressions more difficult, rather than preventing them completely.

One space is looser than another to the extent to which particular behavioral patterns, controls and expectations are peeled away or resisted and unanticipated activities are pursued. Our discussion of the temporal variability of looseness highlighted that various kinds of social and physical controls can be turned on or off, increased or decreased, for example, the locking of gates. Decay over time usually increases looseness. Loose parts contribute significantly to the flexibility of use of a space; moving these parts around can significantly alter the level of looseness. Moveable chairs allow people to vary their separation and orientation. Police barricades are mostly used to restrict movement, but even these can provide opportunities for expressive action. New ways of loosening are always being discovered.

1.11
A security barricade is appropriated for display during a protest against taxation of tampons, Bourke Street Mall, Melbourne

There are situations where the tightening of space is needed to ensure the safety of those who have no choice but to use the space, including places that become the sites of violent crime because of their openness and lack of apparent control. For example, the wide open expanses of space in low-income public housing developments in the US became "no-man's lands"—the sites of life-threatening crimes, places residents themselves avoided when they could. Measures for making such spaces safe and useable have included limiting access, making their intended uses much clearer and more fully supported by physical features and improving their appearance (Newman 1972), all ways of tightening that have allowed residents to enjoy the re-designed spaces (Vale 1996). The line between spaces that offer opportunities for people to choose their own uses and spaces that restrict those opportunities by virtue of people's justified fear is a fine and variable one, depending much on the location, specific features and local perceptions of a particular space.

Loosening/tightening as a dialectical process

Even within very "tight" institutional settings such as prisons, hospitals, schools and the family home, where rules, meanings and physical structure are explicit and relatively fixed, people appropriate spaces for their own purposes and actively resist established routines and regulations. This suggests the necessity of a more complex approach: understanding looseness within a dialectic where loosening and tightening are in a dynamic relation, where each continually develops in relation to the other. Defining looseness in specific spatial, temporal or behavioral terms fixes its form, purpose and meaning. Such is the case with "themed" environments and purified enclaves (Foucault 1997). Yet looseness is exactly that which cannot be tied down. It may arise as an immediate and unexpected response to specific constraints; it develops and changes over time.

Viewing looseness as a dialectical process reveals its development through tensions: between intended and established activities, rules and meanings and those that are unanticipated and may create conflict. Loose use of urban space often shows people's conscious reaction against rules, expectations and constraints. The familiar habits and expectations of everyday life give shape to the new kinds of desires, actions and interpretations which loosen rules and spaces.

Conflicting actions of loosening and tightening do not remain locked at odds with each other in a perpetual stand-off; nor does one force typically simply obliterate all trace of the other. They form, instead, a synthesis, reaching a resolution—a new state of play which draws from two opposing perspectives but which also transcends and modifies both, so that new definitions of "possible," "desirable," "acceptable," "strange" and "transgressive" behavior and expression emerge (Bourdieu 1977). Struggles are continuous, transformed as the terrain shifts, as new sites, rules and meanings are discovered and appropriated; tensions constantly arise as new controls come into being, which are themselves resisted and challenged (Ferrell 2001; Mitchell 2003; Kohn 2004).

The means and loci of tightening also constantly change. Although restrictions on public open space use are sometimes broadly pre-emptive, the majority of controls and rules for spaces are introduced to combat specific challenges to the status quo, both material and ideological. Any new form of looseness generates social contradictions, bringing forth other agents who counteract and restrict it. Skateboarders who frequent the perimeter of London's South Bank Centre (SBC) have been able to gain, over time, the "tacit" approval of place managers who have simply been unable to prevent them. The relationship of SBC to the skaters "has evolved from one of hostility to cohabitation" (CABE Space and CABE Education 2004). Despite the "publicness" of public space, the right to pursue activities other than those which are acceptable, expected and predetermined is by no means guaranteed; it is often hard won. Spatial, representational and behavioral limits and opportunities are the product of continual negotiation and contestation as people pursue the activities they choose and as authorities allow or curtail those activities (Mitchell 2003; Dovey 1999). There is usually some uncertainty about what is legal or socially acceptable in loose space. Actions that may be generally acceptable can result in sanctions in certain public spaces or at certain times or can lead to conflict with other users. People are constantly exploring possible degrees and kinds of looseness, whether the activity is minor (sitting on the sidewalk or standing around) or overtly political, while at the same time other people are trying to tighten space up.

1.12
Unexpected use becomes regular and accepted: a tolerant relation between promenading tourists and local teenagers, undercroft of Queen Elizabeth Hall, South Bank, London

Looseness—and thus diversity, change and risk—is still possible in public and quasi-public spaces where designers and managers attempt to control behavior. Moreover, it is often the efforts at tightening that give rise to loosening—as reaction or resistance—and give it form. As an example, the tightly-bounded liminal fantasy space of the shopping mall has been shaped specifically to promote consumption. Looseness is still evident when users receive and mediate the comforting signals and behavioral controls produced by the mall environment in unanticipated ways. In Calgary's "tight," quasi-public skyway system, prostitutes and poor black men gain entry by dressing in expensive fashions, meeting expectations but at the same time bending the rules and opening up boundaries (Boddy 1992). Similarly, teenagers make use of the mall for *flânerie*, displaying themselves and socializing—without making any purchases. They sit on the floor rather than the provided benches and pretend to be drunk just to aggravate the security guards. They rescript this themed space by defying its implied behavioral codes (Shields 1989).

Through their actions, people can loosen the physical conditions of spaces as well as the social and representational conditions. An example is the handrails adjacent to steps, objects designed with a "precise and imperative utilitarianism." The handrail is "a highly functional object whose time and use are highly programmed," but the skateboarder who leaps up and slides rapidly down a handrail "targets something to do with safety and turns it into an object of risk. The whole logic of the handrail is turned on its head" (Borden 2001a: 191–192). In this example, the tightness of design aims to aid bodily stability and loosening is about conscious engagement with risk. A different dialectic can be seen when features added to public spaces which are intended to restrict skating, such as projecting metal angles set into benches and ledges, stimulate the discovery of new possible actions: skaters develop their skills by jumping, sliding and weaving between these constraints (Stevens and Dovey 2004). Skating that damages such features is itself a form of spatial production that loosens. Skaters do not skate because it's safe or easy; most forms of tightening are, to them, welcome challenges.

Organizing Looseness: Four Parts

The contributions to this book are arranged into four parts: Appropriation, Tension, Resistance and Discovery. These themes and their sequence indicate different kinds of relations between acts of looseness and their wider social context: that is, their relation to the more orderly, and expected uses of various public settings. This cycle also plots a course over the lifetime of a space's designed life. The creation of a brief for a given site and the prime uses for which it is designed are the absent prelude to the cycle of loosening or re-use which is charted in this book. At the beginning, uses are carefully conceived and defined. Then things start to loosen up.

Appropriation

Loose space is, by definition, space that has been appropriated by citizens to pursue activities not set by a predetermined program. Appropriation is therefore a defining feature of all loose space. The first chapters in the book illustrate this appropriation in some of its clearest, most straightforward and easily observable forms since they occur in familiar public settings. The activities described are part of everyday life but amongst those aspects of everyday life that are often overlooked because they are unintended, transient or impractical. The opportunities to pursue them are largely physical and often obvious; in later sections of the book, opportunities are not so readily apparent.

These appropriations are, on the whole, benign additions to public life; they are not combative or controversial; they are only mildly transgressive if at all. People in their ordinary everyday activities simply occupy and make use of spaces that allow for a variety of actions not officially directed or intended. Cultural and social differences among actors provide a first lens for looking at how people recognize different opportunities in spaces and use them differently. This is only possible in public settings where there are not tight regulations on use, such as sidewalks and public staircases.

Tension

The second group of chapters explores the complexity of urban life. The authors reveal the various kinds of tightness that are socially coded into the public realm: expectations about decorum, ownership and social meanings and values that often go unspoken. People find a way to pursue desired activities within or around the existing order and controls; the latter do not prevent looseness from emerging. Rules may be relaxed at certain times, or they may be negotiated or even subverted.

Tension is not always conflictual. In the four case studies in this part, loose uses of space bounce off the more regular uses and off each other, often in very creative and productive ways, contributing to a dialectical development of social life (Simmel 1917; Lefebvre 1991a, 1991b). Tension is not necessarily bad. Through the tensions generated by informal activities, we are made aware of the ways in which public space mediates the relations between different groups of people and different ideas of the public interest. Various forces, ideals and actions give shape to space. In many cases in these chapters, we see the introduction of new people, objects or ideas into spaces that are already occupied. The theme of tension emphasizes that spaces are neither completely empty and without structure nor completely structured.

Resistance

In the third part of the book, things get tighter. Through a variety of mechanisms, behaviors and meanings in social space are locked down. Municipal authorities are often the agents of this fixing, often in concert with wider economic, social and political forces. Spaces themselves are rebuilt or demolished as a means of regulating use or erasing meanings. In this part we see looseness arising as a response. The city itself—its citizens—resist. In many of these cases, the physical tightening or erasure of space is the catalyst that inspires and gives rise to acts of resistance. These loosening acts are conscious and overt. In contrast to pragmatic appropriations that are convenient, innocuous and easy to tolerate, resistant activities have wider political and ideological contexts and consequences. Behavior becomes tactical; looseness is engaged to achieve particular ends.

Acts of resistance illustrate how inelastic space can be; they test its tolerance levels. In some of these case studies, the looseness of the public realm is clearly under threat; space even becomes oppressive. What this section emphasizes is some of the triumphs of looseness over such adversity, showing that control is not necessarily inevitable or total. Looseness continues.

Discovery

In one sense, discovery is the first experience of all loose space: one has to find a space in order to put it to use. What distinguishes the chapters in this final section from other chapters is that they all present spaces currently without any formal, official uses. The uses for which they were designed are now gone. What is discovered is not just the space but a new purpose for it. The ruinous conditions of some of the industrial sites described show how time itself can loosen urban form, creating new possibilities.

Urban spaces, produced through myriad social acts, nevertheless remain available for new forms of practice and new meanings. Urban spaces continue to be physically transformed but transformations do not put an end to looseness. Quite the contrary, transformations may generate new possibilities. Looseness is relative rather than absolute. As shown in all the following chapters, it arises from the unfolding of social encounters in public, whether they are forms of commerce, expression, adventure, escape or innovation.

The themes represented by the four parts of *Loose Space* highlight different conditions observable in urban public space. Tension emerges when occupants' uses and preferences compete with each other or come into conflict with authorities. Similarly, resistance occurs when and where agents seek to limit or deny looseness to others. There are, however, certain elements of discovery and appropriation in any public space. There is so much yet to be known, no end to possibility and diversity.

References

Alexander, C. (1965) "The City Is Not a Tree," *Architectural Forum*, 122(1): 58–62 and 122(2): 58–61.

Allegretti, G. (2004) "Urban Transgression Beyond the Geography of Transgressive Spaces," in R. Paloscia (ed.) *The Contested Metropolis: Six Cities at the Beginning of the 21st Century*, Berlin: Birkauser.

Bianchini, F. (1995) "Night Cultures, Night Economies," *Planning Practice and Research*, 10: 121–126.

Binnie, J. (2000) "Cosmopolitanism and the Sexed City," in D. Bell and A. Haddour (eds) *City Visions*, London: Longman.

Bishop, P. (1988) "The Soul of the Bridge," *Sphinx: A Journal for Archetypal Psychology and the Arts*, 1: 88–114.

Boddy, T. (1992) "Underground and Overhead: Building the Analogous City," in M. Sorkin (ed.) *Variations on a Theme Park: The New American City and the End of Public Space*, New York: Hill and Wang.

Borden, I. (2001a) *Skateboarding, Space and the City*, Oxford: Berg.

Borden, I. (2001b) "Another Pavement, Another Beach: Skateboarding and the Performative Critique of Architecture," in I. Borden, J. Kerr and J. Rendell (eds) *The Unknown City: Contesting Architecture and Social Space*, Cambridge, MA: MIT Press.

Bourdieu, P. (1977) *Outline of a Theory of Practice*, Cambridge: Cambridge University Press.

Brown, G. (2004) "Sites of Public (Homo)Sex and the Carnivalesque Spaces of Reclaim the Streets," in L. Lees (ed.) *The Emancipatory City?: Paradoxes and Possibilities*, London: Sage.

CABE Space and CABE Education (2004) *Involving Young People in the Design and Care of Urban Spaces: What Would You Do with This Space?* London: Commission for Architecture and the Built Environment.

CABE Space (2005) *What Are We Scared Of? The Value of Risk in Designing Public Space*, London: Commission for Architecture and the Built Environment.

Campo, D. (2002) "Brooklyn's Vernacular Waterfront," *Journal of Urban Design*, 7: 171–199.

Carr, S., Francis, M., Rivlin, L. and Stone, A. (1992) *Public Space*, Cambridge: Cambridge University Press.

Cohen, S. and Taylor, L. (1976) *Escape Attempts: The Theory and Practice of Resistance to Everyday Life*, London: Routledge.

Crawford, M. (1992) "The World in a Shopping Mall," in M. Sorkin (ed.) *Variations on a Theme Park: The New American City and the End of Public Space*, New York: Hill and Wang.

Crawford, M. (1999) "Introduction," in J. Chase, M. Crawford and J. Kaliski (eds) *Everyday Urbanism*, New York: The Monacelli Press.

Cresswell, T. (1998) "Night Discourse: Producing/Consuming Meaning on the Street," in N. Fyfe (ed.) *Images of the Street*, London: Routledge.

Davis, M. (1990) *City of Quartz: Excavating the Future in Los Angeles*, New York: Verso.

Deutsche, R. (1996) *Evictions: Art and Spatial Politics*, Cambridge, MA: MIT Press.

Djura, A., Djuric, M., Kucina, I., Neelen, M. and Topalovic, M. (2003) "The Invasion of Commerce," in Multiplicity (ed.) *USE: Uncertain States of Europe*, Milan: Skira.

Dovey, K. (1999) *Framing Places: Mediating Power in Built Form*, London: Routledge.

Englander, D. (2001) *New York's Community Gardens: A Resource at Risk*, New York: Trust for Public Land.

Ferrell, J. (2001) *Tearing Down the Streets: Adventures in Urban Anarchy*, New York: Palgrave.

Foucault, M. (1997) "Of Other Spaces: Utopias and Heterotopias," in N. Leach (ed.) *Rethinking Architecture: A Reader in Critical Theory*, London: Routledge.

Franck, K. A. (1994) "Types Are Us," in K. A. Franck and L. H. Schneekloth (eds) *Ordering Space: Types in Architecture and Design*, New York: Van Nostrand Reinhold.

Gehl, J. (1987) *Life Between Buildings*, New York: Van Nostrand Reinhold.

Gibson, J. (1979) *The Ecological Approach to Visual Perception*, Boston: Houghton Mifflin.

Gilloch, G. (1996) *Myth and Metropolis: Walter Benjamin and the City*, Cambridge: Polity Press.

Goffman, E. (1980) *Behavior in Public Places*, Westport, CT: Greenwood Press.

Greenbie, B. (1981) *Spaces: Dimensions of the Human Landscape*, New Haven, CT: Yale University Press.

Groth, G. and Corijn, J. (2005) "Reclaiming Urbanity: Indeterminate Spaces, Informal Actors and Urban Agenda Setting," *Urban Studies*, 42: 503–526.

Holston, J. (1998) "Space of Insurgent Citizenship," in L. Sandercock (ed.) *Making the Invisible Visible: A Multicultural Planning History*, Berkeley, CA: University of California Press.

Iveson, K. (1998) "Putting the Public back into Public Space," *Urban Policy and Research*, 16: 21–23.

Jacobs, J. (1961) *The Death and Life of Great American Cities*, New York: Vintage.

Kayden, J. S. (2000) *Privately Owned Public Space: The New York City Experience*, New York: John Wiley & Sons.

Kohn, M. (2004) *Brave New Neighborhoods: The Privatization of Public Space*, New York: Routledge.

Latham, A. (1999) "The Power of Distraction, Tactility and Habit in the Work of Walter Benjamin," *Environment and Planning D*, 17: 451–473.

La Varra, G. (2001) "Post-It City: The Other European Spaces," in R. Koolhaas, S. Boeri, S. Kwinter, N. Tazi and H. U. Obist (eds) *Mutations*, Bordeaux: ACTAR.

Lees, L. (2004) "'The Emancipatory City': Urban (Re)Visions," in L. Lees (ed.) *The Emancipatory City?: Paradoxes and Possibilities*, London: Sage.

Lefebvre, H. (1991a) *Critique of Everyday Life*, vol. 1, 2nd edn, trans. J. Moore, London: Verso.

Lefebvre, H. (1991b) *The Production of Space*, trans. D. Nicholson-Smith, Oxford: Blackwell.

Lefebvre, H. (1996) *Writings on Cities*, trans. and eds E. Kofman and E. Lebas, Oxford: Blackwell.

Lerup, L. (1977) *Building the Unfinished: Architecture and Human Action*, Beverley Hills, CA: Sage.

Lofland, L. (1998) *The Public Realm: Exploring the City's Quintessential Social Territory*, New York: Aldine de Gruyter.

Londsdale, J. (2001) "Tyneside (Inertia)," in R. Koolhaas, S. Boeri, S. Kwinter, N. Tazi and H.U. Obist (eds) *Mutations*, Bordeaux: ACTAR.

Low, S. (2000) *On the Plaza: The Politics of Public Space and Culture*, Austin, TX: University of Texas Press.

Lyman, S. and Scott, M. (1975) *The Drama of Social Reality*, New York: Oxford University Press.

Lynch, K. (1965) "The Openness of Open Space," reprinted in T. Banerjee and M. Southworth (eds) (1995) *City Sense and City Design: Writings and Projects of Kevin Lynch*, Cambridge, MA: MIT Press.

Lynch, K. (1981) *Good City Form*, Cambridge, MA: MIT Press.

Lynch, K. (1990) *Wasting Away*, San Francisco: Sierra Club.

Lynch, K. and Carr, S. (1968) "Where Learning Happens," reprinted in T. Banerjee and M. Southworth (eds) (1995) *City Sense and City Design: Writings and Projects of Kevin Lynch*, Cambridge, MA: MIT Press.

Lynch, K. and Carr, S. (1979). "Open Space: Freedom and Control," reprinted in T. Banerjee and M. Southworth (eds) (1995) *City Sense and City Design: Writings and Projects of Kevin Lynch*, Cambridge, MA: MIT Press.

Mitchell, D. (2003) *The Right to the City: Social Justice and the Fight for Public Space*, New York: The Guilford Press.

Multiplicity (ed.) (2003) *USE: Uncertain States of Europe*, Milan: Skira.

Nasaw, D. (1992) "Cities of Light, Landscapes of Pleasure," in D. Ward and O. Zunz (eds) *The Landscape of Modernity: Essays on New York City, 1900—1940*, New York: Russell Sage Foundation.

Newman, O. (1972) *Defensible Space*, New York: Macmillan.

Nielsen, T. (2002) "The Return of the Excessive: Superfluous Landscapes," *Space and Culture*, 5: 53–62.

Oldenburg, R. (1991) *The Great Good Place: Cafes, Coffee Shops, Community Centers, Beauty Parlors, General Stores, Bars, Hangouts, and How They Get You Through the Day*, New York: Paragon.

Project for Public Spaces (2003) *Markets as a Vehicle for Social Integration and Upward Mobility*, New York: Project for Public Spaces.

Schlör, J. (1998) *Nights in the Big City*, London: Reaktion.

Schneekloth, L. H. and Franck, K. A. (1994) "Type: Prison or Promise?" in K. A. Franck and L. H. Schneekloth (eds) *Ordering Space: Types in Architecture and Design*, New York: Van Nostrand Reinhold.

Sennett, R. (1971) *The Uses of Disorder: Personal Identity and City Life*, Harmondsworth: Penguin.

Shields, R. (1989) "Social Spatialization and the Built Environment: The West Edmonton Mall," *Environment and Planning D*, 7: 147–164.

Sibley, D. (1988) "Survey 13: Purification of Space," *Environment and Planning D*, 6: 409–421.

Simmel, G. ([1903] 1997) "The Metropolis and Mental Life," trans. E. Shils, in N. Leach (ed.) *Rethinking Architecture: A Reader in Cultural Theory*, London: Routledge.

Simmel, G. ([1911] 1965) "The Adventure," in G. Simmel, trans. K. Wolff, *Essays on Sociology, Philosophy, and Aesthetics*, New York: Harper and Row.

Simmel, G. ([1917] 1950) "Sociability (An Example of Pure, or Formal, Sociology)," in G. Simmel, trans. K. Wolff, *The Sociology of Georg Simmel*. Glencoe, IL: Free Press.

Simons, M. (2006) "Keeping a Moroccan Tradition Alive, One Tale at a Time," *New York Times*, February 27, 2006: A4.

Solá-Morales, I. (1995) "Terrain Vague," in C. Davidson (ed.) *Anyplace*, Cambridge, MA: MIT Press.

Sommer, R. (1974) *Tight Spaces: Hard Architecture and How to Humanize It*, Englewood Cliffs, NJ: Prentice Hall.

Sorkin, M. (ed.) (1992a) *Variations on a Theme Park: The New American City and the End of Public Space*, New York: Hill and Wang.

Sorkin, M. (1992b) "See You in Disneyland," in M. Sorkin (ed.) *Variations on a Theme Park: The New American City and the End of Public Space*, New York: Hill and Wang.

Stevens, Q. and Dovey, K. (2004) "Appropriating the Spectacle: Play and Politics in a Leisure Landscape," *Journal of Urban Design*, 9: 351–365.

Tinker, I. (1997) *Street Foods: Urban Food and Employment in Developing Countries*, New York: Oxford University Press.

Toon, I. (2000) "Find a Place in the Street: CCTV Surveillance and Young People's Use of Urban Public Space," in D. Bell and A. Haddour (eds) *City Visions*, London: Longman.

Turner, V. (1969) *The Ritual Process: Structure and Anti-Structure*, Harmondsworth: Penguin.

Vale, L. (1996) "Public Housing Redevelopment: Seven Kinds of Success," *Housing Policy Debate*, 7: 491–534.

Whyte, W. H. (1988) *City: Rediscovering the Center*, New York: Doubleday.

Wortley, R. (2001) "A Classification of Techniques for Controlling Situational Precipitators of Crime," *Security Journal*, 14: 63–82.

Young, I. M. (1991a) "City Life and Difference," in I. M. Young, *Justice and the Politics of Difference*, Princeton, NJ: Princeton University Press.

Young, I. M. (1991b) "The Ideal of Impartiality and the Civic Public," in I. M. Young, *Justice and the Politics of Difference*, Princeton, NJ: Princeton University Press.

Young, I. M. (1997) "Communication and the Other," in I. M. Young, *Intersecting Voices: Dilemmas of Gender, Political Philosophy and Policy*, Princeton, NJ: Princeton University Press.

Part I

Appropriation

People create loose space through their own actions. With their bodies they lay claim to public spaces, pursuing activities of their choice, activities not intended in the design or program of these spaces. To do so, they use the physical features of their surroundings when they find those features helpful, and overcome or ignore them when they are constraining. The authors in this section explore the more benign forms of appropriation for commercial, leisure and cultural purposes: namely, activities that occur in planned public spaces that generate little if any tension, that constitute the everyday life commonly associated with a city's streets and squares. All three following chapters focus on particular kinds of spaces and the activities that occur there; each author explores the opportunities afforded by those spaces and the ways people exploit those opportunities.

Leanne Rivlin, in Chapter 2, notes the kinds of places that people in New York City find to engage in their own, often recreational, pursuit of public life—places that are designed for one purpose but, once chosen and appropriated, serve another. Freedom of choice is both a condition and a consequence of their discoveries of "found space." In Chapter 3, Nisha Fernando observes the vibrant street life created by commercial and cultural activities that occur on and adjacent to sidewalks, as shopkeepers, vendors, restauranteurs and consumers make full use of the "open-ended" qualities of urban streets in New York's Little Italy and Chinatown and in cities in Sri Lanka. Drawing upon the concept of liminality, in Chapter 4, Quentin Stevens recounts the playful ways both young people and adults occupy public space in Melbourne, London and Berlin as they step out, possibly just for a moment, from their daily routines, enjoying the freedom that in-between spaces and in-between times offer. Many of the leisure time activities Rivlin and Stevens describe arise from a freedom of choice. The commercial, social and ceremonial uses that Fernando outlines arise more from cultural circumstances; she is the only author in the book to examine cultural similarities and differences.

Each author describes a diversity of users and uses, focusing on access and opportunity and revealing how everyday appropriation of urban space is inclusive.

Each pays close attention to the ways people use everyday features of public space to support desired activities, often in very creative ways, and bring additional props with them. The activities making the spaces loose occur in addition to their intended functions, which are typically the circulation of pedestrians and vehicles. The intended and the unintended occur side by side or they overlap and intermingle, creating moments of congestion and possibilities for tension and conflict. As recounted in these chapters, however, these circumstances help generate the density, diversity and vitality of urban public life.

Some acts of appropriation in these chapters are fleeting, others are longer-lasting, sometimes extending over the course of an entire day. They may be spontaneous and unexpected or they may occur on a regular schedule, possibly every day. Thus, while actions that make space loose are not originally intended in its design, they may become expected aspects of life in particular urban neighborhoods, even contributing to the identity of those neighborhoods.

Sidewalks, streets, steps and building entryways figure prominently in this section. These kinds of spaces are fully and easily accessible, open to public view and generally perceived as safe. While people may take physical risks in them, they are not inherently dangerous places. They are reasonably well maintained and in good condition. Since the spaces are intended for circulation, or immediately adjacent to spaces of circulation, no special effort is required to discover or locate them; they appear on many people's routes through the city. They are right there—convenient places to take a break from the everyday routine or to make a purchase, either spontaneously or pre-planned. Given their locations, the spaces in this section are generally occupied by many people and host a variety of activities. The mixing of uses is synergistic: commercial activities of buying and selling create opportunities for contact and communication and offer opportunities, as Fernando describes, for maintaining and displaying cultural identity and community ties.

In these chapters, users of loose space choose locations precisely for their density and their close relationships to other spaces and other activities, seeking the liveliness, the adjacencies and the overlaps a city offers. Vendors find locations where there will be many pedestrians; so do street performers and others offering their services. Those who wish to watch the passing scene seek good vantage points, often at a boundary or junction between spaces. Activities spill over from one space to another—from interior to exterior, from building entry to stairway, from sidewalk to street. Shops, services and restaurants extend their business out onto adjacent streets and sidewalks. Like sidewalk vendors, they blur the boundary between spaces of commerce and spaces of circulation. People enjoy occupying the boundary as they sit on a wall or hang items for sale on a fence. Only Stevens refers directly to the concept of liminality but it is applicable to many of the cases presented.

The city of loose spaces is not only seen but felt. The overlapping of different activities and the softening of boundaries between one space and another create visually and sensually rich experiences: the smell of food from a street vendor or an outdoor restaurant; the sound of music from an arcade, a restaurant, or a street performance; the texture of the step or wall one is sitting on. The density and mixing of uses, the encounters between those people who are moving along and those who are standing (or sitting) all require negotiation. Loose spaces in this section are places of constant movement and change as the crowd ebbs and flows, as vendors come and go, as lunchtime is over or the street festival comes to an end.

Chapter 2

Found Spaces

Freedom of Choice in Public Life

Leanne G. Rivlin

In the panoramic peasant scenes depicted in the works of Peter Bruegel the Elder, the sixteenth-century painter, and in William Hogarth's paintings of eighteenth-century street life, the vitality of the public spaces and their many different functions is displayed. The public arena has long contained marketplaces, vendors of various kinds of merchandise, entertainers, children playing, rituals and celebrations, casual and arranged meetings and a much enjoyed activity—gazing at the passing scene. After the development of designed spaces for public life, especially marketplaces, commons areas, squares and plazas in the seventeenth and eighteenth centuries and parks in the nineteenth century, many of these activities occurred in settings specifically designed to accommodate them. However, some of these same activities and others, spontaneous and *ad hoc*, occur in "found spaces," places intended for other uses that people have occupied to meet their public life needs. By looking closely at contemporary found spaces and their uses and users, we can discover much about public behavior and come closer to understanding what people are seeking in their use of the public domain.

The research on found spaces that provides evidence for this analysis of public life began in the mid-1980s, during a time when there was considerable dissatisfaction with public spaces. Architects, landscape architects, planners and users criticized their design and management for their failure to meet people's needs, for their commercial rather than human qualities, for their non-use, misuse and abuse (Carr *et al.* 1992). New York City, for example, experienced a plague of "bonus plazas" following the city's "incentive zoning" passed in 1961. During the 1960s, 1970s and into the 1980s bland, barren, windswept plazas were built in many parts of Manhattan such as Sixth Avenue (Avenue of the Americas). They were attached to high-rise office buildings whose developers received permission from the city to increase the bulk or height of their constructions if they provided these outdoor areas. Incentive zoning of this form spread to other urban areas where similar plazas were created. The plazas were considered threats to public life for their increasing privatization of public space (Whyte 1988; Kayden 2000).

Although bonus plazas still exist in New York, many have been modified under the guidance of William H. Whyte who offered an alternative plan, adopted by the city in 1975. This required that developers providing privately owned public space in return for more floor space include specific amenities that Whyte advocated, especially seating surfaces such as the edges of planters and low walls and benches. The city also has allowed developers to provide indoor atria and concourses rather than the outdoor plazas which were more difficult to monitor and maintain. In fact, Whyte (1988) believed that managers of buildings that included bonus spaces were more concerned with excluding certain types of users than with issues of aesthetics. Found spaces offer alternative to these problematic spaces and to public parks.

Found Spaces

Found spaces are a neglected area in the study of public spaces and public life yet they constitute a large portion of the outdoor urban places used by children and adults. They contrast with tight spaces (Sommer 1974) that are heavily programmed places with extensive rules and prescribed ways of being used. In the case of bonus plazas, many have limited resources available to users. Found spaces, a term that I have used to distinguish them from sites designed as public spaces, offer a sense of discovery and serendipity that is special to their functions (Rivlin 1986).

It became clear in my observations of public spaces and public life that the conventional public places designed to accommodate people, such as parks, plazas, squares, and playgrounds, were not the only settings used by people for their leisure-time activities. The other outdoor public settings are "found" in the sense that users locate and appropriate them for uses that they serve effectively but which they were not originally designed to serve. The found nature of these spaces contrasts with the planned nature of other public spaces and together they form the outdoor settings used by people. Found spaces offer alternative places for public life since their uses spring from a complex matrix of needs brought to them by users. We see people in found spaces all the time—neighbors chatting on a street corner, a vendor selling things on a city block, children playing in an empty lot. These activities do not differ dramatically from those occurring in spaces designed for leisure activities, but they do differ in their origins, their diversity and often in the physical qualities of their sites.

Although found spaces can be seen in many local neighborhood areas, people often travel a distance to reach them. They can become a favorite place to be alone or simply the location of a special street vendor selling fruit. The spaces meet the needs of people in a casual manner. Unlike designed spaces, it is the users themselves who locate and program found spaces although the traffic of the passing pedestrians and performances of street entertainers are qualities that can contribute to making the site a found space. Performers also are drawn to areas with potential audiences since they rely on donations for their work.

After the attack on the World Trade Center on September 11, 2001, a number of found spaces appeared in Lower Manhattan. Some of them displayed efforts to locate missing people, with names and photographs placed on walls, construction sites and outside hospitals. Others were memorials with flowers, flags and diverse mementos—silent tributes to a tragic loss. People passing by stopped to look at the displays, and to add their own contributions, sharing the sadness and the power of the event.

Primarily, found spaces are places that enable people to exercise their freedom of choice (Proshansky *et al.* 1970), allowing them to be active pursuers of their own interests. Rather than being captive audiences, passive consumers in a designed world that mandates what happens in a site, freedom of choice offers a different kind of opportunity. It allows people to be "cognizing and goal-directed organisms," making active attempts to satisfy their needs in their "interactions and exchanges" with the physical environment (ibid.: 174). As a result, people make an effort to organize the environment so that it maximizes their freedom of choice. The freedom allows people to manipulate the environment and to add resources to it, which are ways they can create opportunities for privacy, deal with density, reach out to others to form a social environment, and satisfy other personal needs.

Freedom of choice is at the core of people's ability to discover possibilities in the environment and thereby to make use of found spaces. Although this capacity may develop as the individual matures, it is especially evident in pre-school children who have not yet been socialized to filter out their desires. One example observed in the study of found spaces was a group of three children playing at the edge of a parking lot outside a restaurant. They had discovered a corner where the asphalt had broken, exposing the earth below. They were digging enthusiastically using sticks (found tools) in a tiny area containing what Nicholson (1971) has identified as "loose parts." These are elements within a site that are amenable to manipulation and change and have the potential to lead to creativity and discovery. This is the essence of found spaces: people finding possibilities in available public spaces and appropriating and adapting them for their own purposes.

Another useful perspective on found spaces comes from the concept of "affordance" expressed in J. J. Gibson's (1979) work. As the components of environments change, affordances emerge from the changing nature of the environment and the opportunities opened to people observing these settings. Gibson viewed affordance as cutting across "the dichotomy of subjective–objective and helps us to understand its inadequacy. It is equally a fact of the environment and a fact of behavior" (1979: 129). From the affordances offered through perception, people pick up visual cues that suggest possible uses of settings, which can vary across perceivers. Affordances enable the discovery of possibilities, an important dimension of public space that helps to satisfy people's needs.

Identifying Found Spaces

The study of found space grew out of research on public space that led to a subsequent book (Carr *et al.* 1992) and to my curiosity about this alternative form of public life. There were two stages to the study: first, a survey was undertaken to identify specific places, and then a focused study was undertaken of a selected number of them.

In 1984, survey forms were sent to 80 environmental psychologists and urban planners who lived in New York City. They were asked to provide the locations of found spaces, if they knew of any. The criteria for these spaces were described: (1) the space had not been designed with its main function as a public space, a place for public activities; and (2) people in the space were involved in one or more activities such as resting, eating, watching, talking, reading, writing, contemplating, playing games, sports or other forms of recreation. The 30 surveys that were returned identified 84 different places in New York City that qualified as found spaces (Rivlin and Windsor 1986). The kinds of places mentioned ranged from a forbidden area of a garage where children delighted in playing to street corners, building and store fronts, sidewalks and intersections where people gathered.

Prior to selecting places for in-depth study, we visited a number of the sites to identify their physical features and to observe how they were being used. Some were segments or strips of sidewalks; some were isolated from other areas and uses; and others were "spillovers" from places receiving steady or heavy use such as restaurants, shops or clubs, where people were lingering outside. Others were steps in front of public buildings and stoops or stairs in front of residences which formed natural amphitheaters for observing the urban or neighborhood scene. There also were islands or squares, often parts of intersections that were geographically set off from the surrounding space. These were appropriated for selling things or hanging out.

Fences or low walls appeared in a range of settings, offering an amenity that could be used in unusual ways. The fence or wall around a school or park provided a convenient place to hang merchandise to be sold or was a comfortable backdrop for vending booths. Low walls became sitting ledges that enabled people to rest and watch, eat, read and linger in the site. There were places with greenery or water in areas with beaches, waterfronts, abandoned piers, or community gardens created out of empty lots, all of which attracted users for their "natural" elements. Some places had historic or artistic elements, public art, sculpture, or monuments, drawing attention to the area's potential as a public space, and marking that space as special or distinctive.

Times of use also differentiated the spaces that were nominated. Some were places of weekday use, generally during lunchtime, in the location of office buildings. Others were largely used on weekends when recreational crowds in residential, entertainment and shopping areas populated the spaces. There were some spaces that functioned all week long although rarely at the same level of density during every time period.

Eleven places were selected for focused study from the 84 sites that had been nominated. An effort was made to cover the range of sites that had been identified in the surveys. They were located in two of the boroughs of New York City—Brooklyn and Manhattan. Two of the places selected were staircases in front of grand public buildings: the New York Public Library located between 40th Street and 42nd Street on Fifth Avenue in mid-Manhattan, and the main post office on Eighth Avenue between 31st and 33rd Streets on the west side of Manhattan.

Four places were identified as "perching places," where people lingered to wait for friends, spend time, or look at the passing scene. One was in a Brooklyn neighborhood, largely residential, outside a medical building. Two, in Manhattan, were outside churches: St. Thomas Church on Fifth Avenue and 53rd Street in an active business area and Trinity Church in lower Manhattan with a cemetery adjoining a church that had public art. One site in Manhattan's Columbus Circle was a place where people lingered near a sculpture located there.

Two sites were identified as "spillover" places, with some people inside buildings and others standing outside. One was a sidewalk area adjacent to the northernmost building of the World Trade Center, with office workers and tourists present. The other was a variety of sidewalk locations in the East Village in lower Manhattan. The remaining three sites were places where vendors were present. One was a weekend flea market set up in the playground of an elementary school on a shopping street in the Park Slope, Brooklyn neighborhood (Fig. 2.1). Another was a pedestrian bridge, a walkway that crossed a highway in a Brooklyn residential area. The third was a weekly crafts fair along the 42nd Street fenced border of Bryant Park in mid-Manhattan.

2.1
Flea market at Brooklyn elementary school

All the sites were studied by informal observations with field notes and formal interviews undertaken with occupants. The steps of the 42nd Street library were divided into sections and observed using a time sampling procedure that produced behavioral maps (Ittelson *et al.* 1970) that identified the kinds of users and their activities in different segments of the steps. This site was studied over a two-year period and formed an in-depth case study.

The kinds of people interviewed varied according to the nature of the site. Interviewers approached vendors and their customers in places where selling and buying took place. In other places we identified "users," people who came to the space to spend some time. Street entertainers performed in a few places but they were rarely disturbed for interviews. In some places, such as the steps of the New York Public Library, all types of users were present. Within each user group interviewers were told to make an effort to represent the different kinds of people present in terms of age, gender, and clothing (conventional, casual and unusual or disheveled). Interviewers were instructed to select roughly the same number of males and females. However, males were the predominant users of most sites. An exception was the Brooklyn elementary school flea market where women outnumbered men (60 percent of those interviewed). Unlike the other sites that were studied, the flea market was a weekend event. Observations of the library steps, an individual case study, also identified more male users than female.

Uses of Found Spaces

Passing time was a popular use observed and described in the interviews. People were waiting for someone or watching the passing parade of pedestrians. The central locations of the sites near major urban crossroads or heavily trafficked areas made them particularly popular for these activities.

Most selling and buying as well as looking over the goods for sale took place where pedestrians could easily see the display of items and stop to investigate them. However, in one place, on a pedestrian bridge in Brooklyn, the buying and selling was more of a neighborhood amenity. Street performances by musicians, magicians and mimes also drew users' attention and were especially popular on the sidewalk in front of the steps of the New York Public Library.

Eating and drinking was another common activity in many of the sites. At times the food was purchased at the found space from nearby vendors but these places also attracted people carrying their own food who sat, leaned, or stood while consuming their lunches and snacks.

Socializing in a found space included casual chatting as well as intense involvement with another person or a group of people. In some areas the chance meeting with a friend or neighbor or casual conversation with someone nearby led to longer interactions. These activities were observed at the neighborhood flea market, the neighborhood street corner, and the steps of the New York Public Library.

Qualities of Found Spaces

Findings from the content analysis of the interviews, the informal field notes and the behavioral maps for the library steps demonstrate that found spaces have multiple, overlapping qualities. First, they serve people's varied needs offering comfort, a place to rest and the opportunity to be outdoors. For some, going to the site fit in well with other planned activities for the day so that they slipped in a visit, sometimes scheduling it in advance.

The reasons given for coming to the sites ranged from time to reflect to those involving engagement with the ongoing scene. Although the explanations were not that different from those for designed areas such as parks and plazas (Carr *et al.* 1992), they were offered for a diversity of places and each site generated its own pattern of reasons for their users' presence. This is an important consideration when addressing the question of why these particular sites were used rather than more conventional settings.

Found spaces offer an openness that appeals to people, one that is casual and spontaneous and where they find possibilities that are not available in conventional sites. Unlike other public spaces such as parks and bonus plazas that have lists of rules for their use, found spaces offer relative freedom. Their open-ended qualities such as edges on which to sit or lean supported a range of different uses. Areas large enough to set up tables were appropriated by vendors to sell things.

Generally, found spaces are located in convenient places, often at crossroads. They require small investments of time and effort to arrive there. However, not all the users we interviewed came from the local area. Some people had traveled from distant places, and the found spaces became a valued part of their trip, a resource available for them. In the case of found spaces in Manhattan, some of the visitors were from other boroughs, suburban areas and other states. They used the proximity of found spaces such as the steps of the library or the post office as an opportunity to rest or have something to eat before heading to their destinations.

In some places, particular qualities of the site had drawing power. The weekend flea market at the school in Brooklyn was a definite attraction for many local residents and others who learned about it in the course of shopping in the area. People enjoyed meeting neighbors there as well as the serendipity of discovering the different merchandise that was available each week. The central location and the amphitheater created by the cascade of steps at the New York Public Library made this site a favorite space. Local workers, occasional visitors and tourists enjoyed sitting on the stairs, watching the passing pedestrian scene and the street performers when they were there.

The anonymity described by Westin (1967) as a component of privacy is present in public places, including found spaces, especially on the library and post office steps. The assurance of anonymity is a powerful factor influencing the kinds of behaviors seen in some found spaces. People could go there and sit in a sea of strangers, unknown to others. We observed people deeply engaged in their own thoughts, with bowed heads in their hands, a few quietly crying. They were able to engage in these very personal behaviors because they had a sense of privacy amidst a crowd.

People also experienced the entertainments of the street which ranged from street performers to pedestrians moving along. People-watching was an activity that the urban critic William H. Whyte greatly valued. He advocated for the provision of ample public sitting places which could be benches or the tops of planters or low walls that were wide enough for sitting (Whyte 1980). The Danish urban designer, Jan Gehl, also notes the importance of people-watching and points particularly to the activities of construction workers who draw the attention of both children and adults (Gehl 1987).

Found spaces can be occupied for varying lengths of time. The research identified a range of times people spent in the places. Some stopped by for a few minutes to rearrange packages or other belongings or to rest, while others remained for the better part of a day. These alternatives are also created by the open borders of found spaces and their availability for use at any time of day. This freedom of use draws people to sites that become some of the many resources of the city.

Found spaces stimulate open-mindedness, another consequence of having options. This can lead to diverse uses as people creatively take advantage of available street furniture—steps, walls, flat surfaces—to accommodate their needs. In some cases the built portions of a site open up possibilities to hang things or to put things down. A fence around a building became a display space for the sale of used clothing. A flat surface was used as a seat or a table for having a meal, or a space for re-arranging papers. A sculpture can become a leaning post for tired walkers, as well as an aesthetic experience for people in the site and for pedestrians walking by. People bring things to found spaces—food, reading and writing materials, radios, items to make their stays there pleasant and interesting, also expanding what can be done on the site.

The flea market on a neighborhood shopping street in Brooklyn is a found space that began on weekends with people bringing things they wanted to sell and hanging them on the outside of the fence around the playground, along the sidewalk in front of an elementary school. After a precedent was established for using the site for selling things, the Parent Teacher Association of the school invited vendors into the play area for a small fee that went towards funds for the school's arts program. The vendors could bring their own tables or use the play elements as display areas. This has been a successful, weekend market since 1982.

Found spaces offer people freedom of use and freedom from intrusion. The combination of the possibilities to do things and the absence of rules make these sites appealing to people, much like the empty lot for children's play or the street corner for casual conversations. For vendors, the particular location, whether a heavily used pedestrian street or an open stretch of sidewalk near a cemetery, offered a place that could be temporarily altered by opening up a folding table or by hanging things on a ledge. This transformed the space into a small bazaar that appealed to a number of people who liked the convenience of this form of shopping as well as the low prices of the merchandise.

Found spaces provide freedom of choice (Proshansky *et al.* 1970). People generally look for particular opportunities to do what they need to do, searching in very quick and automatic ways for sites that maximize their choices and select the ones that offer them alternatives. From interviews with users of the library steps, the free entertainment on some days (with voluntary contributions if they were so inclined), the available seating if they wanted to rest and the general view of the passing pedestrian scene made the site appealing. In contrast, designed spaces such as bonus plazas had a tighter set of restrictions that could be imposed by management (Carr *et al.* 1992). In Greenacre Park, a small, vest-pocket park in Manhattan, managed by a private foundation, users were restricted from feeding pigeons and from dozing, rules enforced by the supervisors who were present.

Finally, found places were viewed as safe, an essential requirement of public spaces (Rivlin and Windsor 1986; Carr *et al.* 1992). Given the multiple threats to public life, including various forms of violence, crime and harassment, the opportunity to spend a lunchtime or afternoon at a site demanded that the place be free of sources of personal abuse. For women, whose access to public life has been subjected to multiple challenges, safety in public places is central to their public lives (Franck and Paxson 1989). The choices offered by the library steps reveal some of the elements that support public safety.

2.2
Steps in front of the New York Public Library

The Library Steps: A Closer Look at Found Spaces

The steps of the New York Public Library face Fifth Avenue between 40th and 42nd Streets in Manhattan (Fig. 2.2). They are part of an architectural landmark, a major research library in the city. The two marble sitting lions that flank its entrance are notable examples of New York City's public sculpture and evoke affection from many people.

The white marble neo-classical building, designed by Carrere and Hastings and built on the site of the Croton Reservoir, was completed in 1911. The library now has two kinds of resources. One is a public circulating library in a building across the street on Fifth Avenue. The other, in the main library building, consists of a number of major research collections available for use in the library itself. The library also regularly mounts exhibitions in various sections of its building. These two functions account for some of the traffic up the stairs. Bryant Park is behind the library; at the time of our research it had some serious problems, including drug dealing. There were occasional spillovers of this activity onto the rear, side areas of the library steps.

The library steps consist of a series of segments, each one containing steps and a landing (Fig. 2.3). The lowest segment has three steps and a small flat area with a stone bench on either side. The marble statues of lions flank either side of the entrance where five steps lead to a large terrace that has both a central section and

side sections. Flowering plants and other greenery decorate the front and back edges of the terrace. Most of the steps are in the section leading up to the entrance of the library, in a series of 3 steps, 11 steps and 6 steps, each one separated by a small landing. After the period of our observations a kiosk was placed on either side of the large landing. Noontime observations there in 2005 found no kiosks but the plateau was covered with moveable chairs and tables which were filled with people eating their lunches.

We studied the library steps more closely than the other ten places because it contained a varied collection of found spaces and an interesting mix of people. We divided the site into 15 different sectors so that detailed observations could be made of the users and uses in each portion of the steps (Fig. 2.3). Observations were made on weekdays between 10 a.m. and 4 p.m. when the temperature fell within a tolerable range. One set of observations was completed in July and August, the other between November and early December. Interviews with users were undertaken during both these time periods.

Different densities, different activities, and in some cases different types of users were observed in different sections of the steps. On some days the areas along the street (areas 1 and 2) were filled with a crafts fair which attracted many people. At other times street performers, generally mimes, magicians and musicians, drew large audiences. The landings at the top of the upper stairs (areas 13, 14, 15) leading to the library entrance, also showed high levels of use. It was an excellent

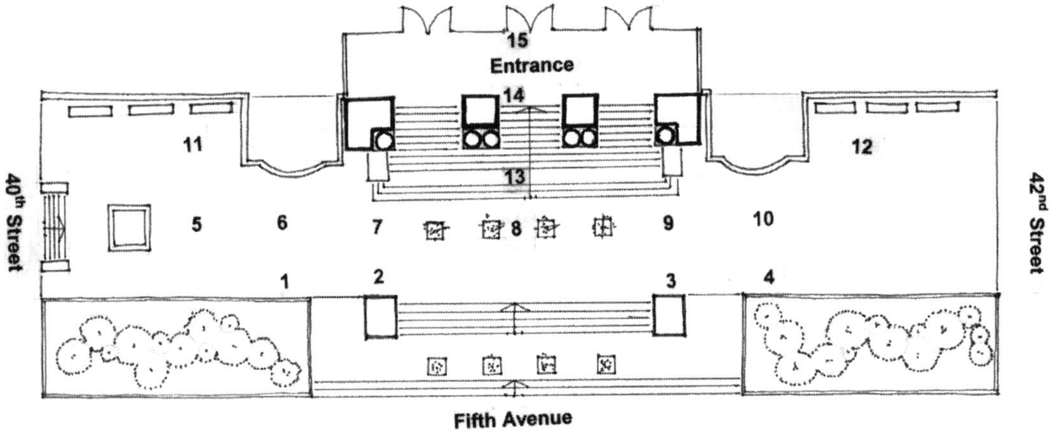

2.3
Plan showing areas of observation on the New York Public Library steps

viewing post for the panoramic scene below. When asked why they chose the places where they were positioned, people mentioned that they were trying to be in the best position for looking at what was going on. Other areas drew fewer people and they tended to be in less central portions of the site (areas 11 and 12), where the activities were less visible than other portions of the site. It was in these sectors that we observed a few instances of drug dealing.

Analysis of user types by their clothing revealed that the majority of users, 65 percent, were dressed in sports clothes, casual dress, with 33 percent in conservative clothing (suits and ties and a similar style for women). The remaining 2 percent were construction workers, street people and a few police officers, the latter using the steps while on a break. The kinds of people observed covered the range likely to be found in any midtown business area and they co-existed peacefully on the library steps.

When the 15 sectors of the steps were examined for differences in types of users, we found that more conservatively dressed people than other clothing types occupied the most central space (area 8). There was a spillover of this user type into the adjoining areas on one side (area 10). The peripheral and side areas (areas 11 and 12) drew casually-dressed types as well as small numbers of unusually-dressed persons, some in the worn clothing characteristic of some homeless street people. The casually and conservatively dressed people occupied the more visible areas of the site, having selected, according to interviews, places where they felt comfortable (Fig. 2.4). In the majority (98 percent), these two groups positioned themselves in the central areas although they sometimes had to wait for a preferred spot to be available. They were largely regular users, coming from local office buildings and were dressed in ways characteristic of those places.

When we looked at what people did on the site, other patterns emerged. Activities recorded on the steps were influenced by the weather, by planned events and by the presence of street performers, vendors, and people handing out flyers in support of particular causes. Crafts fairs and performers affected the location and

2.4
People sitting on New York Public Library steps, mostly office workers eating lunch

types of behaviors observed as well as the number of people on the site. The most frequent activity recorded in all areas of the steps was observing the scene, highest when street performers were present. Looking at objects occurred when there was a crafts fair and was restricted to the display tables. Talking and pedestrian movement were also frequently observed, with pedestrians mainly walking on the terraces and up the steps. Conversations were observed on the steps where people were sitting together or leaning against the walls.

The predominant activities on the library steps were passive ones—looking at the passing scene, watching activities taking place, and less frequently, reading, writing, sleeping, sunning, contemplating and listening to a radio. People used the physical attributes of the site to pursue these activities, with steps on which to sit and columns and walls against which to stand and lean.

Despite their infrequency, the more active behaviors offered an indication of what can occur when people are given the freedom to play out their lives in a public territory. Some were enthusiastically engaged in conversations, lunching together, often from bags brought to the site, sometimes purchased from the local vendors who sold frankfurters, sodas, pretzels, chestnuts and other New York street food. Transactions with the vendors on the pavement in front of the steps were regular activities, as were street performances. Less frequent were people feeding the pigeons, playing their own musical instruments, and photographing the scene.

In the interviews, people were asked to identify the origin and the final destination of their visit to the library steps. Most were coming from work, with others coming from their homes or hotels, shopping or entertainment, school, appointments, or were messengers delivering packages. This variety underlines the ways the steps function as a lunchtime destination for local workers, as a landmark building interesting to tourists and as a stopping point for people on their way to other parts of the city. Most had come from the immediate area or within easy walking distance but others had traveled a distance to reach the steps.

In the 1990s, after our data collection, food kiosks and chairs and tables were placed on both sides of the top portico, transforming these sites into busier and less private areas. It is interesting to speculate whether the kiosks were added to the side areas to discourage the drug-dealing we had observed there. The freedom of use offered by found spaces may also attract drug dealing and other illegal activities. However, the research on found spaces identified little of this, actually restricted only to a few observations on the library steps. This contrasts with Nager and Wentworth's (1976) study of Bryant Park which found that the abundant vegetation there at that time made the park a delightful respite, screening out hectic mid-Manhattan. However, the physical qualities that attracted users also led to persistent drug dealing that discouraged many local people from using the park.

Most of the people interviewed on the steps had very positive feelings about the site (83 percent). Set at a major crossroads in Manhattan, the steps drew passers-by and local workers in the vicinity, many of whom went there on a regular basis. The site enjoys a dual status as an urban landmark building and an office workers' amenity; in both its roles it attracts large numbers of users, even in the colder months. The users of the library steps found the space to be comfortable and safe, qualities they stressed as being very important.

The Found Space Freedoms

The 11 different sites studied illustrate the ways that found spaces offer freedom of use and in the process meet people's needs. Found spaces have impacts on people, some quite obvious, others more subtle. Based on the catalogue of found spaces and observations and interviews in the subset of 11 sites, it is clear how they served the needs of users. We could easily observe the obvious ones, for example, opportunities to sit down and rest, but interviews uncovered strong feelings about the sites and the conveniences they offered. They served these needs with minimal commitment on the part of users since most of the spaces are close to workplaces and homes, becoming regular parts of people's lives. Many are located at the intersection of major streets in dense parts of the city. They fit into people's lives in an easy, casual manner and may not be considered to be important until something threatens their use. Managers of spaces that are designed for outdoor leisure activities can learn much from the popularity of found spaces and provide greater freedom of choice in their sites.

Found spaces offer a form of freedom in public life, freedom to enjoy, to find a sanctuary, to engage with others or to be alone. This freedom emerges from the reality that the sites are chosen by users and serve functions that people desire in their public lives. Adapting Gibson's (1979) term "affordance," there are two interacting sources of affordances in found spaces: the alternatives offered by the setting and those perceived by people who are able to imagine uses that are possible. The affordances of places are aspects of a site that are viewed as adaptable and amenable to change and are available for particular uses. The fences around spaces can be seen as restricting entry or as good places to hang or lean items for sale or display. People's open-mindedness and creativity are required to identify the possibilities offered by the physical qualities embedded in a site.

The freedoms of found spaces include freedom to engage with others, to retreat, to do what people need to do and to do it at times convenient for them. They illustrate the spatial rights that Kevin Lynch (1981: 205–207) defined as integral to control, especially the "right of presence," "use and action," "appropriation" and "modification." They enable people's freedom to engage in activities and freedom from intrusion and threat.

Found spaces offer opportunities for people in cities to find, among other qualities, the peace and solitude that others search for in wilderness areas (Stankey 1989). In found spaces people are able to create invisible boundaries that appear to partition spaces. In places such as the steps of the library or the post office, people reported that they were able to screen out the sounds of traffic and their close proximity to others. Users of these sites regroup their resources in ways that suggest the availability of a sanctuary that offers a form of urban solitude that is possible when people look for it. In contrast to many designed public spaces such as the bonus plazas in the midtown of Manhattan, found spaces can supply this essential aspect of urban life because they do not have restrictions and rules that shape what can and cannot be done. They offer a freedom that expands public life possibilities for people and, in the process, help them personalize cities and customize them to fit their needs. They open up possibilities for creative uses of diverse sites. In this sense they contribute to people's place identity (Proshansky *et al.* 1983), allowing them to endow the public realm with personal meanings that are invisible to others, and in the process, weave a web of familiar urban areas.

The perception of safety expressed by many users reflects the very nature of found spaces—their centrality within residential and commercial neighborhoods and their frequent adjacency to highly trafficked spaces. The traffic and visibility around them offer the protection of "eyes on the street" that Jane Jacobs described (1961), something that is not always available in parks, plazas and malls.

Found spaces are open spatial niches that support two opposite possibilities. They can be stimulus shelters (Wachs 1979), safe havens in the midst of urban intensity, offering respites to regroup resources and to rest. At other times found spaces are stimulus inducers, sources of entertainment and distraction. A single site can be both a stimulus shelter for some people while serving as a stimulus inducer for others. One person may be deeply engrossed in the passing scene or engaged in conversation with a companion while another person, nearby, is lost in thought. An individual may go to a site frequently and find the opportunities for different activities at different times. These spaces enable a range of services and relationships, some of which may be available in other public spaces, but without the immediacy and easy accessibility of the found space.

The spontaneity and casualness of use make the qualities of found spaces difficult to translate into principles for designed spaces. Found spaces are at once simple and complex. Their simplicity comes from the basic human needs they serve—to rest, to nourish oneself, to relax, to retreat, to engage with other human beings, all functions that we heard our interviewees express. But they also are complex in their physical qualities and their evolution, in their affordance qualities and the ways they fit into the urban mosaic.

Further studies are needed on found spaces in other cities. This extended research could provide additional clues, including cultural ones, to their functions. In the end, the networks of freedoms that enhance the publicness of the found public realm could be seen more clearly and the poetics of public life could truly emerge.

Acknowledgments

This chapter draws upon a study conducted with support from a Faculty Research Award of the City University of New York Graduate Center. Ahuva Windsor assisted in the development of research instruments, coordinated the field research and participated in all phases of the work. Interviewers were Basima Ahmad, Eric Glunt, Nava Lerer, Ruth Rae, Dale Schneider, Ahuva Windsor, and Amy Wolfe. Nava Lerer provided valuable assistance in the analysis of data. Zeynep Turan prepared the photographs and the graphic for the chapter.

References

Carr, S., Francis, M., Rivlin, L. G. and Stone, A. M. (1992) *Public Space*, New York: Cambridge University Press.

Franck, K. A. and Paxson, L. (1989) "Women and Urban Public Space: Research, Design and Policy Issues," in I. Altman and E. Zube (eds) *Public Places and Spaces*, New York: Plenum Press.

Gehl, J. (1987) *Life Between Buildings*, New York: Van Nostrand Reinhold.

Gibson, J. J. (1979) *The Ecological Approach to Visual Perception*, Boston: Houghton-Mifflin.

Ittelson, W. H., Proshansky, H. M. and Rivlin, L. G. (1970) "The Use of Behavioral Maps in Environmental Psychology," in H. M. Proshansky, W. H. Ittelson, and L. G. Rivlin (eds) *Environmental Psychology: Man and His Physical Setting*, New York: Wiley.

Jacobs, J. (1961) *The Death and Life of Great American Cities*, New York: Vintage.

Kayden, J. S. (2000) *Privately Owned Public Space: The New York Experience*, New York: John Wiley.

Lynch, K. (1981) *A Theory of Good City Form*, Cambridge, MA: MIT Press.

Nager, A. R. and Wentworth, W. R. (1976) "Bryant Park: A Comprehensive Evaluation of its Image and Use with Implications for Open Space Design," unpublished paper, City University of New York, Center for Human Environments.

Nicholson, S. (1971) "How Not to Cheat Children: The Theory of Loose Parts," *Landscape Architecture*, 62: 30–34.

Proshansky, H. M., Fabian, A. K., and Kaminoff, R. (1983) "Place-identity: Physical World Socialization of the Self," *Journal of Environmental Psychology*, 3: 57–82.

Proshansky, H. M., Ittelson, W. H., and Rivlin, L. G. (1970) "Freedom of Choice and Behavior in a Physical Setting," in H. M. Proshansky, W. H. Ittelson, and L. G. Rivlin (eds) *Environmental Psychology: Man and His Physical Setting*, New York: Wiley.

Rivlin, L. G. (1986) *Final Report: A Study of Found Public Spaces*, New York: City University of New York Graduate Center.

Rivlin, L. G. and Windsor, A. (1986) "Found Spaces and Users' Needs," paper presented at the 21st International Congress of Applied Psychology, Jerusalem, Israel, July.

Sommer, R. (1974) *Tight Spaces*, Englewood Cliffs, NJ: Prentice Hall.

Stankey, G. H. (1989) "Solitude for the Multitudes," in I. Altman and E. H. Zube (eds) *Public Spaces and Places*, New York: Plenum Press.

Wachs, T. D. (1979) "Proximal Experience and Early Cognitive Intellectual Development: The Physical Environment," *Merrill-Palmer Quarterly*, 25: 3–41.

Westin, A. F. (1967) *Privacy and Freedom*, New York: Atheneum.

Whyte, W. H. (1980) *The Social Life of Small Urban Spaces*, Washington, DC: Conservation Foundation.

Whyte, W. H. (1988) *City: Rediscovering the Center*, New York: Doubleday.

Chapter 3

Open-Ended Space

Urban Streets in Different Cultural Contexts

Nisha A. Fernando

Active public spaces enrich public life in cities. They act as breathing spaces where people may relax, socialize, purchase food and other goods, engage in various public events or simply enjoy being in an urban setting and absorbing the everyday life surrounding them. In some cultures, urban streets are such active public spaces, providing a stage for the variety of commercial, political, social and cultural activities that create lively urban scenes and enhance experiences of public life.

Some public spaces, however, are not used to their full potential. One reason for this is the strict regulations governing what activities can or cannot take place. While some regulations are useful to maintain security and safety, excessive control can result in empty public spaces devoid of life. Overly controlled urban open spaces tend to repel people and eventually become underused. Various physical features also tighten public spaces, limiting the possibilities to invite people in and to generate activities. Fences, bollards with chains and locked gates around public plazas, lack of places to sit in public squares and socio-fugal seating arrangements in parks are some examples. Sidewalks, another type of public space, are increasingly being privatized for aesthetic allure or to express the prestige of nearby buildings, inhibiting their potential for public use.

This chapter examines how urban streets in three different cultural milieus enrich public life by being open to a variety of uses over relatively short periods of time. Open-ended streets enable a wide range of commercial and social activities that contribute to public life in cities without significant modifications to their overall physical fabric. As most outdoor public activities occur at street level adjacent to buildings, sidewalks play a significant role in public life. Open-ended streets offer opportunities for manipulating sidewalk spaces and organizing various physical features to accommodate a wide variety of activities without changing the overall architectural appearance of the street.

Amos Rapoport first coined the term "open-endedness" in relation to residential environments where residents can exert control over and easily personalize spaces in dwellings (Rapoport 1968). He defined the concept as the overall capacity of a space to accommodate a wide range of user needs and wants, at one time or over time (Rapoport 1990). The concept also includes changes in meanings corresponding to changes in user needs, as these are critical in residential buildings. According to Rapoport, open-endedness links two commonly used terms—adaptability and flexibility (Rapoport 1990; Oxman 1977; Pikusa 1983). Adaptability refers to the potential of a space to accommodate different uses without any significant modifications to its physical attributes, while flexibility refers to a space that accommodates different uses by being easily changed. The former involves no change to the physical form, scale or character, while the latter does involve such changes. Rapoport suggests that open-endedness inherently includes both adaptability and flexibility, as some degree of change to accommodate new uses is present in both.

Although Rapoport (1990) considers open-endedness as applicable to all environments, he does not discuss its specific usefulness for analyzing urban public environments. What are the attributes of an open-ended urban space? Do adaptability and flexibility play equal roles in an open-ended urban environment? Unlike residential spaces, one may not be able to change the physical form, architectural features or scale of a public space to render it flexible to meet user needs. On the other hand, public spaces may easily be adapted to a number of uses without requiring any changes to their form or scale.

An open-ended urban space possesses several qualities that allow for a wide range of possible uses without changing the existing physical characteristics or altering the primary function of the space. For example, the main function of public plazas in many southern European and Latin American cities is to provide open "breathing spaces" in the city center where people spend their leisurely afternoons. But urban plazas may also frequently be used for religious activities, political rallies, private social functions and entertainment (Low 1997).

Any outdoor urban public space—be it a plaza, square, piazza or a street—can be open-ended. It may accommodate a wide variety of activities at one point in time. As Edensor (1998) demonstrates, one small section of an urban sidewalk in India is used for food vending, socializing, people watching, haircutting and even cooking, all at the same time. Physical features of a public space, especially those that are easily arranged and rearranged, play a key role in making a street adaptable to diverse uses. By organizing and manipulating tables, chairs, planters, sign boards and ornamental items, an urban commercial street can change from a busy retail space to a festive activity space and then back to a retail space within a single day (Fernando 2000).

The following sections describe the open-ended qualities of urban commercial streets in three different cultural contexts: Chinatown in New York City,

Little Italy in New York City and Colombo and Kandy in Sri Lanka. The open-ended qualities are explored at the street level, focusing on activities occurring on sidewalks and in ground floor spaces of buildings that open onto the sidewalk. All observations are drawn from field research conducted in the respective cities.

Chinatown, New York City

Chinatown was established in the Lower East Side of Manhattan in the late nineteenth century. It was a place of refuge and safety for the Chinese immigrant workers who were fleeing racial discrimination and violence in the western states of the US. Prior to this period, the neighborhood had been occupied by a sequence of Irish, German, Jewish and Italian immigrants (Riis [1890] 1971). Once the first few Chinese residents settled in and their small-scale businesses in laundry services and restaurants started to grow, the area of Chinatown began to expand rapidly. More retail, financial, industrial and other businesses steadily increased in number and size. Today the neighborhood comprises more than 50 blocks, loosely bounded by Broadway, Broome Street, the Manhattan Bridge, Madison Street, Park Row and Worth Street. These boundaries of Chinatown, however, are not physically marked. Unlike many other Chinatowns in the US, there are no arches, gateways or welcome signs that clearly distinguish the neighborhood from the surrounding areas. The boundaries are only implied by the presence of numerous Chinese business establishments.

Chinatown is zoned for mixed commercial and residential land use. Streets are generally crowded, teeming with various retail activities, attracting large numbers of tourists and generating high revenue year around. For this reason, Chinatown is considered a vital economic and political space (Zhou 1992; Kwong 1996). In addition to economic aspects, the streets are important community and social spaces, playing a vital role in Chinese-Americans' everyday life and in establishing the cultural identity of the neighborhood.

Four streets constitute the commercial and social core of Chinatown: Canal Street (between Broadway and The Bowery); Mott Street (south of Canal Street); Mulberry Street (south of Canal Street); and Hester Street (between Mulberry and The Bowery). Typically, these streets are lined with a large number of gift stores, jewelry shops, grocery and dry good stores, fish and meat stores, restaurants and religious establishments. On some streets, such as Canal Street, gift and curio shops, fresh seafood stores, banks, restaurants, pharmacies and flower shops exist side by side. Retail spaces at street level are mostly similar in size and design, but they have been adapted to accommodate an array of different retail activities. A jewelry shop selling expensive items operates next to an open fresh fish store and a small niche between an international bank and a fake flower shop is used to sell phone cards and cheap cell phones. On one side of a single block on Canal Street, 18 different kinds of retail activities were observed.

The architecture of the buildings in Chinatown is generally uniform: almost all buildings are five to six stories tall with an approximate 25-foot building frontage.

3.1
Miscellany of stores and visual complexity at street level, Bayard Street, Chinatown

The majority of buildings were constructed in the nineteenth century with red brick façades, uniformly repeated small windows and external wrought-iron fire escapes. A few select buildings, however, have been modified with some characteristics of Chinese traditional architecture which add a particular character to the streetscape. The Charles Schwab building on Canal Street, the McDonald's restaurant on Bowery Street and the HSBC Bank building in Chatham Square are three examples. On these buildings, the up-curved and colorful clay tile roofs, brightly colored columns, painted windows and intricately carved traditional motifs readily convey the cultural identity of Chinatown. Façades of Buddhist temples, such as the one on the corner of Bowery and Canal Streets, display many Chinese motifs and decorations in red and gold (indicating good luck and prosperity, respectively). Cement lion statues adorn the doorways of banks, expensive restaurants and apartment buildings, implying a higher social status.

A single building may accommodate multiple uses at street level. On Mott Street, the ground floor of one five-storey building contains a clothing store, a curio shop, a wholesale gift store, a DVD and music store and a Buddhist temple along with an entry stairway to a prominent Chinese community association on the upper level. The upper floors of such buildings are less diverse in use type; they house mainly apartment units, garment factories or offices. Building spaces at street level provide a larger number and a wider array of possibilities for different commercial uses; this variety demonstrates the adaptability of a single building at street level. The multiplicity of uses also adds a rich and vibrant visual texture to the streetscape (Fig. 3.1).

While some streets in Chinatown have diverse retail uses, three to four blocks of other streets have distinctive clusters of specific uses. Dry food and herbal medicine stores are abundant on Hester Street and expensive jewelry stores outnumber other commercial establishments on the north side of Canal Street. Community activities are more prevalent at the south end of Mulberry Street. The Columbus Park area is frequently used by elderly Chinese for relaxing, exercising, practicing tai-chi, playing Chinese chess, socializing and people-watching. The sidewalks adjacent to the park are often occupied by female astrologers, palm readers and musicians playing traditional Chinese instruments. The space next to the park provides an open court for different ball games and a playground for children. These small social spaces exhibit another form of open-endedness: they support hubs of culture-specific retail or community activities.

Uses of the sidewalk are both numerous and diverse in Chinatown. Many types of street vendors, selling an array of fruits, vegetables, snacks, clothes, handbags, gifts, hair accessories, herbal medicine and prepared meals occupy the sidewalks on almost every street. On some streets, salespersons offer various products and services to pedestrians from vans and small trucks parked by the curb. Within a single day, several vehicles on Canal Street provided a postal service, offered a health insurance service, sold music and video disks and distributed religious pamphlets. Small vans stationed behind fruit and vegetable vendors provide storage space for additional supplies of goods.

Vendor activities are not correlated to what is being sold in the nearby stores. Fruit vendors may be stationed by gold jewelry stores, clothing vendors by restaurants. Artists sitting by a multi-storey bank building paint the names of customers on long pieces of paper and people distribute flyers and coupons by the entrances to restaurants and Buddhist temples.

Although on first glance most activities on the streets of Chinatown appear to be purely commercial, many social activities also take place. The sidewalks are spaces for informal socializing, people watching, gossiping, and for informal chats about business (Fig. 3.2). They are meeting places for people of all ages, gender and social status; they are places where everyone mixes seamlessly with others. Some retail activities promote other types of activities: while selling fruits and vegetables on the sidewalk, vendors chat with each other and share gossip with regular customers. After their shopping is complete, Chinese residents use the streets as a venue to meet friends, socialize and people-watch. The street corners are also places where restaurant chefs and other workers come to take breaks and eat their lunch. Spontaneous commercial and social activities alike seem to be the norm on the streets of Chinatown. Gehl (1996) points out that when the quality of an outdoor space is desirable, not only necessary activities but also optional activities take place there. As optional activities draw people into the space, the number of social activities tends to increase in that space. A parallel is present in Chinatown; the variety of retail activities draws in optional activities which in turn support informal social activities.

3.2
A common scene in Chinatown: males socializing at the corner of Center and Canal Streets

Although the streets are crowded and are seemingly chaotic with numerous vending activities and pedestrians, there is a certain order in how space is appropriated. Generally, street vendors set up their wares either in front of buildings facing the sidewalk or on the curbside edge of the sidewalk facing the buildings, creating a corridor in the center for pedestrian movement (Fig. 3.3). Entrances to buildings and alleyways are kept free. Within the limited space available, vendors organize their merchandise in a wide variety of ways. Some set up their merchandise under the awnings of buildings while others use umbrellas or tarpaulin covers to create temporary shelters. On street corners, some vendors are grouped together so that one vendor can draw the attention of customers shopping at another vendor. Observations show that some street peddlers also move from one place to another on different days, selecting the most suitable spots based on the number of potential customers.

Some vendors settle for rather unlikely spaces for their business. A shoe repairman, an artist and several astrologers frequently use the narrow, unpaved space under a construction scaffolding on Mulberry Street. These vendors choose this section of the street for several reasons. First, the scaffolding provides a good shelter from the weather. Second, vendors sit on the sidewalk and the entrance steps to buildings while using window ledges and the scaffolding structure to set up

3.3
A sidewalk space used by vendors and stores, Canal Street, Chinatown

merchandise and hang signs. Finally, the location is close to the community area of Columbus Park. Residents visiting the park and from the nearby centers for the elderly frequently stop by to chat with the vendors. The fortune readers, shoe repairmen, cosmetics and accessories vendors and artists all stationed under the scaffolding seem to find the space appealing as it is in close proximity to community activities.

Street vendors in Chinatown use numerous "semi-fixed" elements (Hall 1969; Rapoport 1977) to set up spaces to sell their wares. These easily moveable physical items include folding tables and chairs, pushcarts and umbrellas, wooden tables, wooden boards, clothing racks, shelves, stools, cardboard boxes, plastic crates and buckets. Name artists typically use ironing boards to spread out long pieces of paper to paint on. Many signboards in Chinese and English, colorful awnings and banners in various sizes create a complex visual character. These semi-fixed features and the fluidity of the patterns of use provide excellent versatility in spatial organization and result in a plethora of commercial activities. They play a significant role in transforming an otherwise rigid and somewhat monotonous urban landscape into one that is changeable and vibrantly diverse.

Many shopkeepers use the sidewalk as an extension of the interior space of their stores (Fig. 3.4). Dry food stores display many boxes and buckets immediately outside the store on the sidewalk. These are filled with dried fish, seafood, mushrooms, vegetables and herbal products, names and prices conspicuously marked in Chinese. Signboards are set up on the sidewalk next to the building and dry food products are hung from the awnings. Pedestrians on the sidewalk can easily see what is for sale without having to go inside the store, while the display within reach invites the consumer to touch, smell, taste and evaluate the price from the sidewalk.

3.4
Sidewalk space is essentially part of a Chinese dry food store, Grand Street, Little Italy

Diverse and numerous commercial activities are common on traditional urban streets in China. Streets there are also commonly used as social and cultural spaces where people spend time relaxing and engaging in culturally-specific activities. A strikingly similar ambiance is present in Chinatown in New York City where urban scenes familiar to the Chinese immigrant residents are continually recreated. The streets are adaptable for a range of spatial functions and expressions that depict the socio-cultural identity of the Chinese community.

Little Italy, New York City

The neighborhood of Little Italy is located primarily on Mulberry Street immediately north of Canal Street and is rapidly decreasing in size as Chinatown expands. Remnants of the neighborhood still exist on sections of Grand, Hester and Mott Streets. Despite being in close proximity to each other and being flanked by similar buildings, the streets of Little Italy are very different from those of Chinatown proper. In Little Italy, streets are abundant with restaurants offering Italian cuisine, a feature that creates the unmistakable ambience of Little Italy.

When there is an outdoor section in a restaurant, tables, chairs, umbrellas, awnings and other decorative elements create a variety of possibilities for organizing the outdoor space. Tables and chairs may be set up on the building side of the sidewalk, either under wide awnings or in the open air. Or tables and chairs are spread out on the sidewalk under wide umbrellas. The variety and flexibility of seating arrangements present both small and medium-sized dining spaces. Often the outdoor dining spaces are only loosely demarcated from the rest of the sidewalk, separated from the pedestrian area either by a short metal railing, a step, a row of planters or a carpet.

Menu stands, planters, statues and similar decorative elements are often set up along the curb side of the sidewalk. Although this spatial arrangement leaves barely sufficient space for pedestrians to walk, it generates interest in those who pass by. The open cafés and restaurants attract pedestrians with food served on the sidewalk immediately next to where they walk. This proximity allows food smells to linger in the air enticing passers-by. In some cases, the dining space occupies the entire width of the sidewalk (Figs 3.5, 3.6). This arrangement invites pedestrians to walk into the space, meander in between the tables and closely experience the sensory aspects of food and drink.

With the predominance of restaurants and cafés, Little Italy lacks the diversity of retail businesses characteristic of Chinatown (except near Canal Street where Chinese stores have been established). Nonetheless, the streets in Little Italy display great variety resulting from the colors and the diversity of the semi-fixed elements of furniture, umbrellas, signs, plants, lights and other decorations. Some restaurant spaces can be distinguished from each other only by the colors of tables, chairs and umbrellas used.

Although the primary uses of the streets in Little Italy are food-related, social and cultural activities are also common. Cafés and restaurants act as regular meeting places for the Italian-American community, especially for elderly residents, families, businessmen and visitors from other areas who frequent the neighborhood for dining, socializing, shopping and celebrating cultural events. Close ties among the older residents in the neighborhood are often maintained through the cafés and ethnic

3.5
Loose boundaries of an outdoor café, Hester and Mulberry Streets, Little Italy

3.6
Café and pedestrian spaces intermingle on Mulberry Street, Little Italy

grocery stores where they regularly meet each other. Small family-owned businesses like bakeries and tobacco shops—some of them dating back to the nineteenth century—are places where residents frequently run into each other. Cafés, restaurants, stores and bakeries are not only business establishments but generate a sense of community and place identity for Italian-American residents and visitors.

Mulberry Street becomes an important cultural space during the annual religious feast of San Gennaro. Early immigrants who settled on Mulberry Street were originally from Naples and the tradition of celebrating San Gennaro (Saint Januarius), the patron saint of Naples, has been followed every September since 1926. During the festival, the statue of the saint is carried in a procession along Mulberry Street. Cordoned off from vehicular traffic, the street becomes a lively hub of celebrations and social activity. Many food stalls offer sausage sandwiches, pizza, drinks and gelato, while kiosks with games and souvenirs attract crowds of people. The street is transformed into a vibrant and festive environment with colorful flags, hanging lights and signs with red, white and green (i.e. the colors of the national flag of Italy), while Italian music plays in the background. People meet with friends, eat, drink, socialize and watch people throughout the day and evening. During such events, the everyday ambience of the streets created predominantly by restaurants is quickly transformed into a temporary but intense center of both entertainment and religious observance. The food stalls, gift and souvenir vendors and live music attract throngs of pedestrians, generating a very lively social and cultural environment. Some outdoor restaurants extend their outdoor dining spaces into the pedestrianized street, transcending the boundary between the sidewalk and street and adding to the mixture of activities. When the festival is over, Mulberry Street springs back to the previous order with the street opening for vehicular traffic and the restaurants operating on the sidewalk.

Colombo and Kandy, Sri Lanka

Urban streets in Sri Lanka are generally filled with many types of commercial activity. On a typical street, one may find a grocery store next to an informal eatery or a teashop; next to it a pharmacy adjacent to a used bookstore and a shoe store. Outdoor fruit and vegetable markets, movie theaters, electronic shops, stores selling household items, dental clinics, churches and many other types of uses can be observed within a single block (Fernando 2000), making it easier for the consumer to buy goods and use various services in one single stop. Outdoor fruit and vegetable markets are also places where people meet, chat and gossip. Contiguous buildings on a segment of Kotugodella Vidiya in Kandy house a school, a Roman Catholic church, a restaurant, a house, a hardware store, an electronics store and a pharmacy. Sidewalks in front of buildings are filled with a miscellany of stationary vendors, peddlers, flyer distributors, panhandlers, consumers, people waiting for buses and taxis, pedestrians and people meeting with others. Urban streets in Sri Lanka act as a nexus for both retail and social activities.

On some streets, such as Galle Road in Colombo and Kotugodella Vidiya in Kandy, spice shops exist alongside jewelers, clothing stores next to temples. This seemingly unrelated combination of space use is sometimes determined by certain cultural and social forces. Stores selling jewelry and traditional clothing specific to the Tamil Hindu culture are located near Hindu temples to attract the Tamil clientele likely to buy such products. Restaurants serving ethnic foods are also located nearby. Members of the Tamil community also treat these spaces as informal social places.

Street-level shops are typically wide open to the sidewalk. Shopkeepers put their merchandise on view for the pedestrians by organizing them next to the shop entrance and outside on the sidewalk (Fig. 3.7). Many storekeepers use the entire width of the entrance space and even the steps to stack up their wares such as large bags of rice, flour, sugar, dry fish, onions, spices, potatoes and other food items. Clothes hang from racks and awnings in front of textile shops, while bunches of bananas, candy, cigarettes and newspapers are on display on the sidewalk in front of small fast food restaurants. Windows, if there are any, act as display spaces advertising the variety of goods inside. Although they appear disorganized, the adaptability of sidewalks optimizes the use of space without relying on many permanent structures. The stores are interchangeable for different uses without requiring major physical alterations. A restaurant at present can easily change into a pharmacy or a hardware store with no major modification to the façade. Storefronts are neither tightly regulated by city ordinances nor designed in one particular way, making the variability of uses possible.

Vendors sell a range of goods: fresh produce, lottery tickets, used books, clothes, kitchen utensils, tools, newspapers, flowers, incense, candy and cosmetics. Some vendors also provide small repair services for shoes, umbrellas and electronics. Most vendors do not operate at a single permanent location; they often move from one spot to another on a street, depending on what and to whom they may sell. Vendors also relocate to other streets while new vendors take their place. Use of space for street vending is not predetermined but flexible and loose. There are also street performers, people-watchers, police officers, and depending on the time of the day, school children, nannies, office workers and fast food vendors. Sidewalk

3.7
A small sidewalk space is used for a number of activities: walking, buying and selling, parking bicycles, advertising, meeting and waiting, Galle Road, Colombo

activities also change over the course of the day. Fruit and vegetable vendors, for example, are more common in the morning hours and on weekends. Towards mid-afternoon, vending activities decrease in number except in areas with some shade. In the evenings, vendors sell fast food for dinner from vans parked by the curb while others sell spicy snacks and cigarettes for those who come out from nearby taverns.

Another change in use occurs during frequent political activities when streets become the stage for activist rallies and protests. Vehicular traffic is blocked during such events, allowing people to march along the streets and hold demonstrations, while onlookers congregate on the sidewalks. These occasions last a few hours to half a day, at the end of which the street is open again for vehicles, business and social activities. Another significant transformation takes place during frequent Buddhist, Hindu and Christian religious festivals. In an annual Buddhist procession, featuring elite Buddhist officials in colorful attire, traditional dancers, drummers, musicians, traditional torch bearers and many elephants, the sacred relic of the Tooth is carried along designated streets of the city of Kandy as a mark of blessing and prosperity to its residents (Fig. 3.8). These streets metamorphose from busy retail and social spaces to important holy places filled with Buddhists, tourists and spectators crowded together on the sidewalks.

The transformation of the physical environment for these rituals is noteworthy; the building façades, electricity and telephone poles and trees become adorned with Buddhist flags, garlands of lights and other symbolic decorations. Sidewalks are arranged with rows of chairs, tents and other make-shift furniture as

3.8
A street is transformed into a place of celebration with decorated elephants and lights during an annual Buddhist procession in Kandy

seating for observers. These physical features, along with many sounds of Buddhist chants and music through speakers hung on trees, create a rather spiritual ambience. Although the event typically takes place at night, towards the end of the festival the procession becomes a daytime event as well. When the procession is over for the day the vending and social activities spring back to life, and when the few weeks of the religious festival are over, the streets return to complete normalcy with their typical retail and social activities. Brown (1995) describes a similar event in Mexico where street activities shift between the secular and sacred over the course of a single day. The ability of these urban streets to accommodate activities of the worldly and the sacred in a relatively short time signifies their open-endedness for expressing different meanings.

Common Characteristics of Open-Ended Urban Streets

Urban streets in Chinatown, Little Italy and Sri Lanka display similarities as well as differences in the qualities of open-endedness they possess. The following section describes the ways streets in the three cultural milieus are open-ended.

Diversity of uses

With commercial activities, social interaction, people-watching, community activities and religious celebrations, a wide spectrum of uses of streets is present in all three settings. A large number and a great variety of retail activities can be observed on the sidewalks in Chinatown and Sri Lanka. Even though a single use dominates the sidewalks in Little Italy, the spatial qualities and decorative elements of the restaurants create a significant level of diversity. In addition to commercial uses, urban streets in all three contexts are places for formal cultural functions and many informal social activities. The streets are neither strictly zoned for a single use, nor are they inhibited from readily accommodating a range of uses. The possibilities for diverse activities indicate a high level of open-endedness of streets in all three cultural contexts.

A great variety of uses in the interior spaces at street level is common in Chinatown and Sri Lanka. Instead of one specialized use, the ground-level space of a single building may be sub-divided to contain many different activities. Upper levels of the same building typically exhibit less diversity; they contain either offices or apartment units. The variety of uses of individual buildings at street level reflects another form of the open-ended quality of streets.

Adaptability to different uses

Sidewalk spaces are adaptable for varying uses in all three cultural contexts. They afford a wide range of activities: selling and buying, taking breaks from work, reading newspapers, sitting, walking, window-shopping, people-watching, meeting, socializing and waiting for transportation. One may also find people simply idling, as in the case of the elderly both in Chinatown and Little Italy, and young and old alike in Sri Lanka. Sidewalks can also be adapted to express different cultural identities through the use of various physical features. Although sidewalks have a common primary purpose (as a pedestrian thoroughfare and an entry space to buildings), they are easily adapted to accommodate very different uses, to express cultural identity and to enhance public life.

Building spaces at street level in Sri Lanka and Chinatown are adapted for different retail activities without modifications. The building frontage is usually kept open to the street to allow retailers to display their merchandise in the most suitable way. Clothing merchants can hang clothes on racks, on folded entry doors and from the awnings; gift and curio retailers display items on open shelves in front of the store; fishmongers display an array of seafood in crates and tanks flowing out to the sidewalk; jewelers display items in secured but transparent glass cases facing the street; and other retailers place fresh produce and dry foods in boxes and buckets immediately in front of the store. The entry spaces of stores, restaurants, banks and religious establishments are also places for socializing, waiting, people-watching and carrying out business transactions. Some street vendors set up their stalls in front of a store drawing the attention of customers visiting the store. Storefronts are not fixed in design, style or in the way they are intended to be used. They are open-ended and can be manipulated easily to suit the specific type of business.

In all three contexts the sidewalk is intensively used but with differing spatial organization. Commercial activities in buildings at the street level extend out onto the sidewalk: in Chinatown and Sri Lanka storekeepers use sidewalks to display their merchandise and in Little Italy restaurants use the sidewalk for dining space. Street vendors and restaurants alike may occupy the entire width of a sidewalk. While their use is a common trait, the ways sidewalks are spatially ordered and the degree to which the curb is incorporated as part of the sidewalk are different across the three cultural contexts. Vendors in Chinatown typically use both the building side and the curb side of the sidewalk to set up their wares while pedestrians use the corridor space in the center. The curb is sometimes used for parking vehicles to store additional supplies for vendors or to offer various mobile services. The restaurants in Little Italy often occupy the sidewalk immediately next to buildings, directing pedestrians to the middle and edge of the sidewalk. When restaurants take up the entire space of the sidewalk, pedestrians must walk in between the tables. In Little Italy, the curb is rarely used except during festivals when vehicular traffic is absent. In Sri Lanka, the spatial boundaries of the sidewalk are much more blurred than in the other two contexts. Both vendors and pedestrians use the entire width of the sidewalk without any pre-determined pattern; vendors are scattered on the building side, in the center or on the edge of the sidewalk, while pedestrians skirt around or walk in between the vendor stalls. Both vendors and pedestrians often use the curb as an extension of the sidewalk. Some vendors sell their goods from the curb facing the buyers on the sidewalk while pedestrians frequently walk in the curb space to avoid the crowded sidewalks.

Fixed and semi-fixed elements

With the single exception of the added architectural details on a few buildings in Chinatown, fixed physical elements commonly remain unaltered in all three cultural contexts. Instead of being physically altered, building façades are used to attach many semi-fixed elements such as flags, banners and signboards.

In all three contexts many moveable physical elements are commonly used on the sidewalk to accommodate various uses and to create specific cultural identities. They also aid in changing the streets to accommodate different types of activities over time. The significance of semi-fixed components is three-fold. First, by their very nature of being moveable, semi-fixed physical components allow sidewalk spaces to be easily arranged and rearranged. Semi-fixed elements such as push carts, tables, stools, umbrellas and signs, also allow different types of street vending activities to take place. Second, the large number and variety of semi-fixed elements create visually complex and culturally specific streetscapes. This visual complexity indicates the degree of open-endedness of the streets: that they accommodate a diverse range of uses. Third, semi-fixed elements readily convey the cultural meanings associated with the specific uses. This is important where the cultural identity of a neighborhood needs to be communicated to visitors and tourists.

Multi-sensory qualities

As a result of diverse activities and assortments of physical elements, open-ended streets in the three contexts possess multi-sensory complexity. While the visual complexity is created by the colors, shapes and sizes of physical elements (especially semi-fixed elements), other sensory experiences are created by various sounds, smells and textures. As a result of the significant variety of sensory experiences, the streets are both distinctive and noticeable.

Such sensory stimuli in urban environments are critical for communicating a specific socio-cultural identity (Hall 1969). Certain cultural groups use the types and intensities of specific smells to demarcate different social spaces. Olfactory and auditory experiences are important socio-cultural factors that translate into organization of space. Pred (1963) describes how neighborhoods in Chicago can be easily distinguished from each other (high vs. low economic areas, synonymous with White vs. Black business areas) at street level by the types of sounds (traffic, jazz music, loud songs) or their absence, and by the types of colors (brightly colored shop fronts and signs in Black business areas vs. less imposing exteriors in White areas).

Changes in ambience on a single urban street in Sri Lanka result from changes in the sensory qualities: the sounds of music and drums around a Buddhist temple and the sounds of Islamic prayers from loudspeakers in a mosque create very different atmospheres. The scent of fresh fish, dried food and herbal medicine from the stores, of burning incense from temples, of Chinese food from restaurants and the sounds of Chinese language and music all help define the identity of Chinatown, while nearby the Italian food and opera music help establish the identity of Little Italy. These sensory experiences are a direct result of activities related to each culture. Multi-sensory qualities also indicate the looseness of urban streets: when streets are open-ended, the diversity of uses gives rise to a variety of sensory experiences.

Socio-cultural identity

Open-ended streets in each cultural context express a socio-cultural identity associated with that context. They do so by accommodating the culturally-specific activities of festivals and routines of everyday social life. Cultural identity is also expressed through the organization of sidewalk space. The choice of locations for vendors, pedestrians and others indicate cultural differences, which in turn suggest a specific cultural identity. The types of semi-fixed elements used for activities also indicate particular cultural identities. Signs in different languages, colors of flags and banners, the types of street furniture used in vending and in restaurants are marks of cultural specificity. Streets that are typically similar in superstructure easily accommodate modifications to create distinctive cultural characteristics, as seen in Chinatown and Little Italy The variations are an important indicator of the degree of open-endedness in streets.

Significance of Open-ended Urban Spaces

Open-endedness in urban environments needs in-depth discussion, especially at a time when there is a growing concern about embracing socio-cultural differences in multicultural cities (Appleyard 1976; Burayidi 2000). Large cities, increasingly defined as multi-social and multi-cultural entities, face the challenge of offering more choices (Franck 1994). Yet the range of choices is increasingly being reduced through the privatization of urban public spaces, including sidewalks (Kayden 2000). Although people may have visual access to public spaces, the lack of physical access (through the use of fences, bollards, etc.) and the control imposed on certain activities can limit people's ability to actually use a space (Carr *et al.* 1992). Open-ended urban streets, on the other hand, offer diverse possibilities for public uses, enable cultural activities and create more choices for public life.

Although they accommodate spontaneous and diverse activities and generate sensory-rich experiences, open-ended urban streets are not necessarily open-ended for any type of public activity or to suit all types of users. Instead, they are influenced to a great degree by the socio-cultural and behavioral requirements of specific user groups in a particular context. Within a given context, open-ended streets can contain many possibilities for uses and many varieties of sensory experiences that signify the respective socio-cultural aspects. Open-ended streets play an important role in creating culturally-specific urban environments.

When urban streets are open to multiple public uses, they create a certain vitality and an inviting quality. In his study of small-scale urban public spaces, Whyte (1980; 1988) demonstrates how a single activity can draw in others, often in a spontaneous manner. In a plaza with a fountain, one person takes his lunch sitting on the fountain ledge and this may invite others to sit there and enjoy the sun. In the presence of others, children may feel safe to come in to the plaza to touch and play in the water while parents following the children will use the space to sit and relax. People-watchers, in turn, are attracted to the space. Eventually the fountain area becomes filled with people and activities, as an urban public space should be. The street artists in Chinatown first attract a few people and then small crowds, while others watch the people and the activities from afar. People begin to comment on the artist's work which leads to brief conversations among strangers. The lack of a fixed program in urban public spaces enables a great degree of spontaneity in space use and creates opportunities for a variety of activities to take place and for expressing specific cultural identities.

Designers and urban planners play a key role in offering such open-ended urban public spaces. In cities where different cultural groups live, single land use zoning and restrictive codes for public spaces may lead to empty public spaces. Some sidewalks in the CBD of Colombo, Sri Lanka, are devoid of public uses as a result of municipal restrictions on vending and social activities. If sidewalks are kept open for activities, they may be easily appropriated by a wide range of public users including vendors, customers, school children, office workers, people-watchers and people meeting people. This notion is applicable to any type of urban space where social activities are deemed important to urban public life overall. Whyte's studies (1980; 1988) of public spaces corroborate this.

It is also important not to over-design sidewalks with permanent fixtures such as benches, fences, planters, kiosks and other structures that may obstruct spontaneous activity and the easy movement of people. When sidewalks are physically open, vendors, performers and others have the opportunity to shape and organize the spaces to suit their activities, especially by utilizing a variety of temporary, moveable elements. Sidewalks in both Chinatown and Sri Lanka do not contain any fixed street furniture. As a result, sidewalks are not limited to one particular group and allow different user groups over time to appropriate the spaces as necessary. Clear examples of this resilience are seen in Chinatown and Little Italy, where in a very similar physical environment, the two groups have altered the street-level spaces and their uses in very different ways.

The empirical evidence from open-ended streets in the three cultural contexts suggests that adaptability plays a more significant role than flexibility. While incorporating some changes, the physical environment of streets, especially the sidewalk space, is highly adaptive to a great variety of uses without significant physical modifications. This is an important aspect to consider when planning urban public spaces. Designs and decisions that predetermine space organization are likely to thwart the variety of user needs so evident in open-ended streets, especially when user needs are not particularly well known to the design professionals in advance. It is thus necessary to allow for a wide range of possibilities for public activities in public spaces. In addition, public spaces should not be over-controlled by administrative agencies in cities. When kept open to possibilities, urban public spaces can thrive in spontaneity and diversity, enlivening and enriching the experiences of urban public life.

References

Appleyard, D. (1976) *Planning a Pluralist City: Conflicting Realities in Ciudad Guayana*, Cambridge, MA: MIT Press.

Brown, D. F. (1995) "Un Spacio Construido Efimero: Las Alfombras de Aserrin en Huamantala, Tlaxcala," in M. Amerlinck (ed.) *Hacia una Antropologia Arquitectonica*, Guadalajara, Mexico: Universidad de Guadalajara.

Burayidi, M. A. (ed.) (2000) *Urban Planning in a Multicultural Society*, Westport, CT: Praeger.

Carr, S., Francis, M., Rivlin, L. G. and Stone, A. M. (1992) *Public Space*, Cambridge: Cambridge University Press.

Edensor, T. (1998) "The Culture of the Indian Street," in N. R. Fyfe (ed.) *The Images of the Street: Planning, Identity and Control in Public Space*, London: Routledge.

Fernando, N. (2000) "An Analysis of the Changing Character of an Urban Street: A Case Study on Galle Road, Colombo, Sri Lanka," *Built Environment Sri Lanka*, 1/2: 25–37.

Franck, K. A. (1994) "Types Are Us," in K. A. Franck and L. H. Schneekloth (eds) *Ordering Space: Types in Architecture and Design*, New York: Van Nostrand Reinhold.

Gehl, J. (1996) *Life Between Buildings: Using Public Space*, Copenhagen, Denmark: Arkitektens Forlag.

Hall, E. T. (1969) *The Hidden Dimension*, Garden City, NY: Doubleday.

Kayden, J. S. (2000) *Privately Owned Public Space: The New York City Experience*, New York: John Wiley & Sons.

Kwong, P. (1996) *The New Chinatown*, New York: Hill & Wang.

Low, S. M. (1997) "Urban Public Spaces as Representations of Culture: The Plaza in Costa Rica," *Environment and Behavior*, 29: 3–33.

Oxman, R. (1977) "Flexibility in Supports: An Analysis of the Effect of Selected Physical Design Variables upon Flexibility of Support Type Housing Systems," DSc dissertation, Technion-Israel Institute of Technology, Haifa.

Pikusa, S. (1983) "Adaptability," *Architecture Australia*, 72: 62–67.

Pred, A. (1963) "Business Thoroughfares as Expressions of Urban Negro Culture," Economic Geography, 39: 217–233.

Rapoport, A. (1968) "The Personal Element in Housing: An Argument for Open-ended Design," *RIBA Journal*, 75: 300–307.

Rapoport, A. (1977) *Human Aspects of Urban Form*, Oxford: Pergamon Press.

Rapoport, A. (1990) "Flexibility, Open-endedness and Design," keynote paper presented at People and Physical Environment Research Conference, Brisbane, Australia.

Riis, J. A. ([1890] 1971) *How the Other Half Lives*, New York: Dover Publications Inc.

Whyte, W. H. (1980) *The Social Life of Small Urban Spaces*, Washington, DC: The Conservation Foundation.

Whyte, W. H. (1988) *City: Rediscovering the Center*, New York: Doubleday.

Zhou, M. (1992) *Chinatown: The Socioeconomic Potential of an Urban Enclave*, Philadelphia, PA: Temple University Press.

Chapter 4

Betwixt and Between

Building Thresholds, Liminality and Public Space

Quentin Stevens

A threshold is a point where the boundary between inside and outside can be opened; space loosens up, and a wide range of perceptions, movements and social encounters become possible. As Norberg-Schulz notes, "the opening is the element that makes the place come alive, because the basis of any life is interaction" (1971: 25). A threshold is also a restricted space; its design always constrains people's behavior and their perceptions (Hillier and Hanson 1984). Because of these in-between, both–and, inside–outside qualities, thresholds are always loose for playful possibilities. Many different architectural elements distinguish inside from outside and mediate people's passage between them: doorways, turnstiles, colonnades, marquees, porches, terraces, stairways and stoops. Each provides distinctive perceptual, behavioral, social and symbolic affordances. Observations of a diversity of playful social activities around the exterior thresholds of buildings in Melbourne, Berlin and London reveal a multiplicity of ways in which thresholds, even though they are designed as control mechanisms, are actually surprisingly loose.

Liminality and Liminal Spaces

Thresholds, though designed for practical function, are also sites where a great variety of playful and liminal social behavior occurs. Liminality, from the Latin word for threshold, is an anthropological term for the intermediate stage in rituals of progression from one social status to another, "rites of passage" (van Gennep 1960; Turner 1982). Examining this concept of ritual liminality can tell us much about how threshold spaces are liminal, and about how they shape playful aspects of social life.

Ritual performances of liminality are crucial to identity formation through the discovery and development of new understandings of the self. During the liminal stage, normal, serious social roles, rules and status relations are temporarily suspended or inverted. Boundaries may become blurred, allowing for the combining of "the ordinarily uncombinable" (Lyman and Scott 1975: 151), the bridging of binary oppositions that often define social life. People, symbols and objects are encountered outside cultural frames of reference and normal instrumental relations (Spariosu 1997).

Liminality is akin to play: it frames escape from social convention and the exploration of new possibilities. The dissolution of social order in the liminal process is usually temporary: "forms of reversal . . . occur during interstices between periods of intense or serious activity" (Stevens 1991: 238). In contemporary society, liminal experience is closely associated with everyday leisure (Cohen and Taylor 1978; Lefebvre 1991; Shields 1992; Rojek 1995). Certain actors and times of life also exemplify liminality: children, teenagers and elderly people as well as those getting married; rush hour and smoking breaks as well as public holidays, celebratory parades and other special occasions.

Thresholds, like rituals, create conditions of intensity, transformation, the elevation of status and the blurring of social categories and rules. These physical conditions create liminal moments in everyday life which often give rise to playful behavior. At building thresholds which mediate between different behavioral settings, between public and private realms and between indoor and outdoor space, people experience release from the limitations and order of spaces where they have defined roles and commit their attention to specific tasks. Some actions and dispositions may carry over from this setting into the public realm, but interstitial thresholds are sites of significant shifts in people's status, their perceptions and their actions. At thresholds, people may experience sudden exposure to new stimuli and new possibilities, to freedom, anonymity and risk. The physical and temporal constriction of thresholds further heightens their complexity. Despite the constraints, they are sites where conventions get loosened through people's diverse playful behavior. While buildings often provide a sense of order (Markus 1993; Dovey 1999), when one steps out onto the threshold, one is on the loose.

Although most of the observations in this chapter focus directly on physical activity and concrete spatial conditions, social liminality is also experienced and produced through representations. People communicate many potential meanings of a threshold through formal wedding photographs, which are frequently taken on thresholds in downtown Melbourne during the liminal ritual of marriage. The liminal properties of thresholds can be appreciated when wedding couples act them out. Wedding photographers often capture the betrothed crossing the thresholds of buildings. In doing so, they employ the physical and experiential qualities of thresholds as metaphorical expressions of the social distinctions framing marriage, representing the specific liminal social status of the couple (Shields 1991). The threshold has become a symbol of this particular liminal rite of passage, carrying collective memories of its own material conditions (see Chapter 9 by Stavrides in this volume); people's uses of a threshold reflect and contribute to this metaphoric potential. People's poses in wedding photos are often transgressive of everyday behavioral codes. Such poses are ritualized inversions of the proper, practical, decorous uses of public spaces such as thresholds; they highlight the power people have to create new social discourse through their actions within the built environment.

The taking of wedding photographs, often thought of as a highly formal social event, actually helps to loosen up the meanings of quite formal spaces. These photographs use urban space as a symbolic landscape which helps constitute identity. Through their wedding photographs, people seek out and perform a variety of social meanings which lie latent in the spatial properties of thresholds: intimacy and publicity; progression and irreversibility; transgression, security and permanence; distinction and grandeur. By gathering such meanings together within the picture frame, wedding photographs help constitute the liminality of the wedding. Through their playful actions, wedding couples are not just acknowledging, but actually producing social meanings, and inscribing them within built form. The theatricality of wedding parties' performances suggests that the photographs are not necessarily a reflection of identities whose nature is already well understood, but rather an important means of discovering new selves, through encounters with space and with the urban public.

The observations that follow illustrate six distinct ways that thresholds can mediate experience, spatially, perceptually and socially. The threshold is a constrained site which gathers people together, channeling their movement, focusing their attention and forcing them into close contact with others. It is a passage, a transitional place where people spend time. The passage also frames people's emergence from private spaces into the public realm; it is a site of new stimulations. The threshold is a complex setting in its own right with distinctive physical properties. It is a space set apart from the wider public realm where people can control their level of exposure to others. And yet it is both–and, between inside and outside, a loose mix of two different environments.

Convergence

Four thresholds in central Melbourne where a great number of playful events were observed were the entries of major public buildings: Flinders Street Railway Station, the General Post Office, the State Library and Parliament House. Each has a large formal façade fronted by a wide staircase, with a grand arch or colonnade marking the entry. It is hardly surprising that much playful activity occurs in front of such buildings. A great number and variety of people use these buildings. Even though their entries are often small and crowded, the generously-scaled forecourts which they open onto make them likely settings for informal use.

In front of the wide staircase of Melbourne's main railway station, skateboarders roll back and forth, sometimes trying to jump up the steps. Even though

4.1
Maori man dances a *haka* (war dance) at the turnstile entry to Melbourne's main railway station, Flinders Street

the luxurious width of the stairs allows skaters to avoid conflict with practical users, friction does exist. One skateboarder races across unexpectedly in front of oncoming pedestrians and grinds along a step's edge. Inside the station vestibule, a Maori man does a brief informal version of the *haka* war chant and dance in front of the turnstiles, symbolically blocking the path of commuters leaving the city (Fig. 4.1).

London's Leicester Square is fronted by the thresholds of numerous entertainment venues: three major cinemas that screen world premieres, a nightclub and the city's half-price theater ticket booth. Nearby lie the Shaftsbury Avenue theater district, the National Gallery and the Royal Opera. These permanent spectacles attempt to capture tourists' imaginations for commercial gain, but on the way in and out of such venues, tourists have to pass through an extraordinarily busy, distracting pedestrian zone. The entertaining ambience spills over the thresholds of buildings and into the public square itself. The entertainment spectacle which attracts the crowds gives rise to derivative forms of performance, which ultimately help nourish it. Street performers dress up and stand on pedestals, pretending to be statues of film characters (Fig. 4.2). This theater-on-the-threshold results from the strong local demand for professional actors. An audience, on its way toward the venues and keen to consume fanciful performances, encounters these figures, as characters (almost) stepping down from the screen. Onlookers can walk up to and around these actors and even touch them.

4.2
Street performer pretending to be a statue of a character from a blockbuster film which had recently opened in one of the cinemas fronting onto Leicester Square, London

One Saturday evening in Berlin, a touring troupe performs a piece entitled "The Bells" to hundreds gathered in front of the Stella-Musicaltheater on Marlene-Dietrich-Platz, near Potsdamer Platz. The bellrope-tugging actors lunge out into their audience, leaning perilously close to the spectators. Behind the performers, above the building's entry, is a massive billboard for the current show: Disney's *The Hunchback of Notre Dame* (Fig. 4.3). As the act finishes, program sellers emerge from the Musicaltheater, its doors just opening for the evening show. The representational link is purely accidental. However, the slope of the plaza toward the doorway and the building's awning roof are not. The temporal link from street theater to indoor theater amplifies the intentional spatial connection.

These events highlight the distinctive spatiality of social relations at thresholds. They are natural gathering points, bottlenecks where many people's paths must converge (Lynch 1960). In such settings, chance and risk are always present (Goffman 1982). What's distinctive about social encounters on major thresholds is their frequency and intensity. Particularly when strangers have to negotiate doorways and queues, they are unexpectedly forced into close proximity, increasing bodily exposure and thus tension. Spatial convergence also offers the potential for more dramatic or confrontational encounters. Thresholds are scaled and designed to serve flows of pedestrians. Playful practices such as the war dancer, singers and skateboarders interrupt this instrumental function.

4.3
Street theatre *The Bells* (left) preceding performance in indoor theatre (right), Marlene-Dietrich-Platz, Berlin

People are sometimes forced to converge at thresholds, but they also often gather at thresholds willingly. Urban leisure settings are typically the scenes of dense flows of people who are already outside their serious work role. People heading into London's and Berlin's theaters appear to enjoy being intercepted by free, informal, more physically engaging performances which take place outside their doors. These events extend people's escapist, liminal experience in time and space, beyond the controlled conditions of the venue. In the case of "The Bells," there is a symbolic link between the performances on the threshold and the stage as well as a functional one.

The thresholds of major urban railway stations serve as thresholds at the scale of the city as a whole (Lynch 1960). One's arrival in the metropolis is a dramatic rite of passage. Large numbers of strangers who are engaged in quite unrelated activities find themselves gathered together here according to the rhythms of the trains. Exposure to new experiences and heightened sensations is likely, and this can stimulate playful opportunities:

> Railway stations are characteristic places for dense and varied as well as anonymous and fleeting encounters, in other words, for the type of interactions which were to mark the atmosphere of life in big cities, described by Benjamin as overflowing with excitement.
>
> (Habermas 1997: 229)

Regardless of the physical tightness of such places in terms of bodily movement, the sheer number of people and phenomena they contain establishes a threshold condition in the sense of testing people's tolerance for new perceptions (Simmel 1997).

Another dimension of the liminality of urban thresholds becomes apparent when we zoom out from single building entries to the scale of the urban block. A city street which provides views and access onto a wide variety of activities is most stimulating to the senses and generates the richest urban life (Gehl and City of Melbourne 1994). For urban space to provide a concentration of the city's symbols and experiences requires constraining the width of individual thresholds. When the thresholds of many buildings with different uses are pressed close together in the street, new experiences and unplanned juxtapositions of social groups and behaviors are more likely (Jacobs 1961). Street blocks in Melbourne with a greater number of separate frontages are also generally the sites of more numerous play activities. Skateboarders move along streets where they can find new physical challenges on every doorstep. In Leicester Square and Marlene-Dietrich-Platz, it is not just one attraction, but the variety and collective intensity of the theaters, cinemas and nightclubs which make these squares so lively, drawing a great number and mix of people at different times.

Sometimes closed, unused thresholds of buildings can sustain playful behavior. On Melbourne's waterfront Southbank Promenade, the entry to the Esso Headquarters is locked to the public; this blank backdrop provides an ideal stage for street performers. But this lifeless threshold only comes alive because constant flows of people are drawn past it to a variety of other adjacent attractions, including a casino, art gallery, aquarium and exhibition center (Stevens and Dovey 2004).

The Passage of Time

Most people use doorways and stairs only to get from one place to another. Thresholds are often planned for only fleeting occupation, yet people often spend time on them. Some instances of play at thresholds highlight the temporal dimension of behavior, as people occupy and modulate this brief time in transition by playing. It is interesting to consider the reasons why they linger, the ways they extend their visit and the distinctive behaviors associated with moving across a threshold.

After a morning tea break outside a Melbourne office building, a worker heading back inside with colleagues accidentally drops his balled-up paper bag. He slides forward to grab it and feigns a basketball shot before stepping through the revolving door. This play is a last attempt to use up excess energy and live more intensely, before returning to the physical passivity and mental discipline of desk work.

The Europacentre shopping complex sits on one corner of West Berlin's Breitscheidplatz. One Sunday evening a rock band performs outside the building, next to its main entry doors. Hundreds of people watch, either standing or sitting at adjacent café tables. The performance is very polished and energetic. Some people dance enthusiastically. Their liberation from the passivity of watching reflects one of the band's selections: "I want to break free." Similarly at Alexanderplatz, Berlin's historic center, Christian evangelist youth groups often sing and dance in front of the Galeria Kaufhof department store. One sunny Saturday there are thousands in the plaza, and a group plays African drums near the doorway. Two couples exit the Kaufhof together; one man does a few little rumba steps to the beat. In these examples, someone occupies a strategic position between pedestrians and their destination, encouraging the passers-by to extend the time they spend at the threshold. In the interests of play, an opportunity to escape everyday responsibilities, someone getting in the way of the door can be a good thing.

A crowd of thousands gathers at Alexanderplatz to view a major solar eclipse in the summer of 1999. Some people are compelled to keep working during the eclipse, though even for them the threshold can become a site of escape. A youth working in a fast-food restaurant facing onto Alexanderplatz steps out of its front door, whips the special glasses out of his pocket and takes a quick look at the eclipse. A co-worker rushes out after him, grinning, and also has a quick look. The first youth conscientiously looks around to retrieve used food trays: he finds a legitimate pretext to come outside and momentarily join the throng in their admiration of the natural spectacle. He manages to ever-so-slightly bend the rules of his employment, creating a free space-time, using instrumental demands on his time and location as leverage for an escape from instrumentality.

A great variety of playful behavior can be observed outside leisure-oriented facilities such as cinemas, theaters, nightclubs, casinos, cafés and churches. When entering, crowds must converge and wait for a programmed event. Afterwards, although people can quickly disperse, they often linger outside in groups. There is a close relationship between highly structured, instrumentalized consumption indoors and unregulated, liminal activities immediately outdoors. After a prolonged period of mental and bodily discipline and passivity, where attention is carefully directed to indoor performances and physical interaction is minimal, people may emerge with their bodies restless and their perceptual faculties highly stimulated, keen to release pent-up energies. It is in the liminal times and spaces after these events that people interact freely. Spontaneous, active forms of play often arise: games of tag, running, jumping on each other and similar kinds of horseplay.

Extended, repetitive, "unproductive" uses of thresholds challenge the minimal, instrumental conception of urban space (Gilloch 1996). The activities observed show great variation in the temporality of people's experiences of thresholds. Because they are points of necessary convergence, thresholds are places where people often have to pause, reflect and change direction. For these very functional reasons, people can find themselves unexpectedly distracted or delayed at thresholds. Musicians outside Berlin's shopping centers stimulate people's obvious interest in escaping the practicalities of their everyday tasks. They are not blocking the entry, but stand in close proximity to the portal, hoping people in the flow will be distracted and will extend their necessary activity of shopping into an optional one

(Gehl 1987), as when the man's stride takes on a rumba beat. In Jacobs's (1961) terms, playful, disruptive acts are secondary, derivative "uses" which rely on the primary use inside a building's doorway for their vitality.

The Act of Passage

One crucial reason for the loose timing of threshold use is that most thresholds form an interface between two quite different spatial, perceptual and social realms: public space outside, where people are exposed to diverse stimuli and to unstructured encounters with strangers, and more private spaces inside where ambience is regulated and social behavior and encounters are more carefully structured (Norberg-Schulz 1971). The office worker playing basketball with his rubbish underscores the sharp opposition between work and play. He marks the end of a special time on the threshold through his liminal behavior. He recognizes the threshold as a point where a space and time apart from instrumentality end. People play at thresholds because it is their first and last chance to act upon the freedoms and inspirations which urban public space provides, where they have the opportunity to "be themselves." At the moment when people cross thresholds between private and public space, they often make the most of the experiences which are possible there. Their actions can be exuberant, expressive of freedom, of escape from controls on their use of time and space.

This exuberance is also manifest in some ritualistic forms of behavior which occur at thresholds. Wedding photographs framed in doorways emphasize the liminal, transformative nature of the wedding ritual. The couple emerge from the private realm and present themselves to the public gaze. This action is symbolic of the new couple's respectability. The doorway frames a dialectical transition between the personal and the social. Wedding photos are commonly taken in the doorways of old buildings. This shows the partners stepping out of the past, underscoring the evolutionary nature of the marriage ritual. The thresholds of old buildings draw together a sense of a liminal moment and a sense of historical progression.

Many wedding photos in front of buildings show the couple on their way somewhere. The threshold is a place of movement, and flights of steps outside doorways dramatize this sense of flow, leading the eye across the picture (Fig. 4.4). Sometimes the groom stands one or two steps ahead of the bride, suggesting he is leading her into the public sphere. Steps emphasize that the couple is in a directional movement, symbolizing a social progression. It is "a place where there's just no turning back," as the couple's new status becomes sealed (Shields 1991: 144). Long flights of stairs cascade ahead of the couple; getting married is indeed a big step. Newlyweds are generally pictured heading away from buildings and down steps, down into the everyday, public world of the city streets.

The popular use of the grand staircase fronting Melbourne's Parliament House, which on weekends is often the site of simultaneous wedding shoots, frames couples on the precipice of a huge incline, exposed to the excitement and

licentiousness of the city which stretches out below (Fig. 4.4). A comparison can be drawn with Shields's (1991) observations on newlyweds' visits to Niagara Falls. Both are liminal initiation rites where the couple's exposure on the threshold of a sublime, intoxicating setting serves as a test of their passions.

4.4
Getting married is a big step; wedding photos outside Parliament House, Melbourne

A Special Geography

People often linger at thresholds which are distinct spaces in their own right: spaces in front of doorways but separated from the street, such as terraces and flights of steps, which provide for particular forms of occupation and use. The physical dimensions of thresholds, their widths and heights, shape playful opportunities. Sheer size is necessary for certain actions to become possible. In the case of large buildings with wide frontages, reduced pedestrian flows at certain times of day provide a surfeit of public space which is then open to appropriation for various uses. Skateboarders are seldom interested in going inside the buildings whose thresholds they frequent. They tend to choose thresholds which are not in use by pedestrians, especially office buildings after hours. They often explore and test the special physical characteristics of the intermediary space of thresholds: their material, their height, their inclination and the potential this provides for generating speed and risk. They discover new ways of moving across them (Borden 2001). One important factor in such playful exploration is choice. Steps, ledges and handrails of various heights allow skaters to regulate the level of risk they are exposed to, to gradually push the limits of their skills (Caillois 1961; Huizinga 1970). Sloping ground in front of one office building provides an inclined ledge, and skate marks starting and ending at different points along it reveal different levels of speed, strength, control and confidence among users.

The threshold is a complex geography of inclines, drops, barriers and smooth ledges which the body can negotiate in many different ways. Late at night, novice in-line skaters do slow circles on the terrace in front of Melbourne's State Library, at the top of a long cascading staircase. More experienced skaters glide down this inclined, directional surface, a liminal phase of accelerating under the tug of gravity, riding out the difficult terrain at high speed. Their smooth form of movement loosens up the physical striation of the steps. One skater even leaps backward from the top terrace, lands half-way down the first flight, continues backward, swivels at the landing and then rolls forward down the second flight (Fig. 4.5). A beginner rolls to the edge of the terrace and looks down, gauging the difficulty and danger of this feat. She, like the office workers and the eclipse viewers, wants to be able to manage her exposure, to time it, to choose her angle of attack.

These steps at the building entry are a region of looseness and risk within a surrounding urban terrain which is flat and open. Spaces of relatively easy movement exist both in front of and beyond the threshold. The delight of this loose space is bracketed within a context of control. The "safe" open space at the top of the steps is used to prepare, to accelerate and orient oneself for takeoff. The depth of flat, open space at the bottom is also important, particularly because skaters do not always land safely. It means the risk is of limited duration and that it will be possible to regain controlled movement. The bottom of the threshold is a place to enjoy the momentum that comes from the descent, to decelerate, to be among the public and on display.

Raised steel angles installed along most steps and ledges outside Melbourne's State Library are intended to deter skateboarders from playing there. Rather than closing the threshold to use, such changes merely bring new challenges to the terrain. This restriction has engendered a creative response: skaters develop new ways of transgressing the space's limits. They invent new games on the stairs,

4.5
Skating backwards down steps at night outside the State Library, Melbourne

risking injury by jumping off landings and flipping their boards in mid-air, or jumping their boards up the stairs.

Skaters' transgressive acts contradict and loosen the straightforward functionality of stairs, finding new potential for play within them. Rather than moving slowly through the threshold and down the stairs, they roll down quickly, jump off them or up them, or slide across them, suspended within the liminal zone.

A Space Apart

In contrast to the intensity, speed and risks of skating, threshold spaces which are comfortable and expansive can also facilitate a range of more relaxed behaviors. Thresholds are often designed to make the transition between inside and outside gradual and leisurely, sometimes including several intermediary spaces such as semi-private foyers, doorways, wide landings and generous steps. People have space, as well as time, for a gradual transition, for lingering and for non-instrumental social interaction (Gehl 1987).

At Melbourne's Flinders Street Railway Station, people often sit to rest or to meet friends on the stairs outside the main entry. This includes many who have not traveled by train. Those gathered here watch playful events on the open paved area in front of the steps: an accordion or bagpipe player, or people kicking a Hacky Sack. Sometimes strangers sitting and watching become active participants in these activities. Informal performances also occur on the steps themselves, which people use as a stage. University students going through an initiation ritual form a choir spread up the steps to sing "Jingle Bells" (Fig. 4.6).

In the doorway on an inner-Melbourne laneway three office workers take a cigarette break. This doorway has a thick stone frame, with a deep landing at the top of five steps. A woman standing against one side of the entry talks animatedly to two colleagues opposite. Meanwhile a man passes by on the footpath below, heading away from her. After he passes, the woman comments to her colleagues, then steps down to the footpath and mimics his walk. Continuing the parody, she looks fixedly ahead, serious; then coming abreast of the doorway, she suddenly swivels her head to view where she herself had been standing and puts an exaggerated beaming smile on her face. All three laugh. One colleague re-enacts his own version. The threshold space frames the interaction among these three workers, but the public realm is the necessary ingredient that triangulates, providing novelty that arouses playful action (Whyte 1980). The doorway shapes her encounter with the stranger. This threshold provides a "back" region where the performer can reliably expect that "no member of the audience will intrude" as well as a "front" region "where the performance is presented" (Goffman 1959: 98). As the man moves along the street, the constrained views both in and out of the doorway, which protect the back region, suddenly expand, heightening the spatial and temporal compression of the two individuals' contact and increasing its dramatic tension. The passer-by unexpectedly notices the

4.6
Informal choir singing on steps of Flinders Street Railway Station, Melbourne

woman as he passes the building entry, and reacts spontaneously to this close engagement. Stepping out of his normal role as a plodding, detached pedestrian, his overstated smile is a small impromptu performance for her.

Within the threshold, people are able to strike an acceptable balance between exposure to the unfamiliar and relative seclusion and safety. During the 1999 eclipse in Berlin, a number of distinct social groups seem unaccustomed to and somewhat uncomfortable with spending much time in open, undefined public settings such as Alexanderplatz. These groups tend to occupy particular parts of the plaza. Businesspeople stand together in clumps close to the entries of buildings from which they have emerged. Dressed in fine suits, they would not sit down in the open, paved landscape. Although they all purchase special viewing glasses, they spend little time looking at the eclipse. Mostly they just socialize, taking advantage of the unusual mid-day freedom. The elderly also tend to cluster along the edges of the space, but as far away as possible from busy doorways. In particular they crowd against the display windows of the Galeria Kaufhof department store, a space otherwise seldom used. Less confident in their occupation of public space, they find a refuge from which to view the event (de Jonge 1967), without the risk of being bumped into by anyone, being in anyone else's way, being robbed or being exposed to the weather.

Many people also gather along the upper balcony of the Galeria. This is a restful place, with a rail to lean on. Both threshold sites allow people to be in the public event but also separate from it. They do not have to make a clear commitment to unregulated public encounter. The people on the balcony are also making a symbolic gesture, attempting to be closer to the sun when it disappears. As with most thresholds, this balcony also affords a better view over the plaza, to experience the sense of being in a massive crowd witnessing an historic event.

These examples illustrate the use of thresholds as a "space apart," physically distinguished from both inside and outside, available for play (Huizinga 1970). The examples also show that movement across threshold spaces involves gradations of perception, regulation and exposure. They are complex micro-geographies that structure a great range of social and bodily relations. The busiest thresholds in the city can be sites of relatively uncontrolled encounters with strangers. At thresholds, an observer is "likely to experience a sudden rush of information—a sudden dilation of his view and exposure too—which may (or may not) suit his intentions" (Benedikt 1979: 58). Playful events which spill across thresholds show that people do not always minimize their contact with others. But thresholds allow people to regulate their exposure to the unfamiliar and to risk in a number of ways, to manage the problem of overstimulation. People have different attitudes and desires in relation to the freedom of public space. Not all individuals want to take themselves to the limit.

Staircases and landings outside thresholds provide a space apart, separated horizontally and vertically from both the regulated indoors and the constant movement of the street (Huizinga 1970). The brownstone stoop has long been an important setting for informal socializing and play (Dargan and Zeitlin 1990). Raised thresholds also offer a good overview of the bustle of public space. Visibility works both ways: staircases can become stages or seating. Stairs thus frame relations between audiences and actors which add to the tension of the latter's performances (Caillois 1961; Whyte 1988). Wedding couples photographed standing within doorways, porches and at the tops of steps are framed on public display to passers-by. Steps structure social distances between strangers: each tread is an increasingly-engaged threshold. When people choose where to sit on flights of stairs in public, they are able to adjust how close they are to public scrutiny, challenge and unpredictability. Stairs also provide for an easy transition between seated audience member and player.

Blurred Space In-between

Play around some thresholds is diverse because the physical and social conditions prevailing at them are so varied. Some thresholds are clearly demarcated and controlled, but in other cases play arises precisely because the threshold is quite nebulous and ill-defined.

On Melbourne's Bourke Street Mall, loud pop music spills from an open storefront, saturating public space and distracting people's attention away from their conscious objectives. An athletic old man dances energetically just outside, for fun (Fig. 4.7). Here the body's exposure to sound arouses a playful exploration of the body's capacities. By remaining in public space, the man remains free to respond to the music however he wishes. He generally has his back to the store. Rather than yielding his attention to the merchandise which the store is trying to promote, the man

4.7
Stimulus spills over the threshold; man dancing in front of music store, Bourke Street Mall, Melbourne

makes use of the sound to draw attention to himself. He invites passers-by to join him, and several do. His enthusiasm rubs off.

The video game arcade is another private leisure environment which extends beyond its threshold and contributes to the atmosphere of play in public. Pedestrians passing one Melbourne arcade at lunchtime stop to watch two players dance on sensor pads, following a disco beat which keeps accelerating. The video screens show little: the competitors' attention is on the music, the onlookers' attention is on the competitors. The youths finish with a synchronized jump. The large audience applauds, then suddenly dissolves and moves on. This wide, open façade on a busy pedestrian route provides good views of the action, temporarily distracting passers-by. Other game screens are large and turned toward the street, to attract players but also spectators (Fig. 4.8). The barrier between watching and playing is highly permeable. Energetic players provide vicarious pleasure to adult pedestrians. Watching crowds spill both into and out of the private space, an audience which spurs the players' efforts.

In both these examples, open façades frame public performances which are stimulated by sound and motion generated inside private spaces. The old man dancing oriented himself to the music store's threshold to receive and mobilize specific kinds of sensory and social stimuli in his play: music from within a private realm and exposure to a public audience. The threshold of a video game arcade exposes playful possibilities and provides little regulatory function; it offers the possibility of distraction. Such thresholds are liminal in the sense suggested by Zukin (1991): there is a seamless, frictionless possibility of entry into the pleasure zone, a blurring which allows people to "forget" that a social boundary exists. People often seek the tension of such sites which are "defined and yet not too defined" (Alexander *et al.* 1977: 349).

4.8
Distraction across an open threshold; video game arcade, Melbourne.

The design of the video arcade's threshold frames peripheral views which can stimulate playful behavior. Glass walls provide a preview of what will be seen and felt up close at the entrance. The game screens fall within the normal cone of vision of even those pedestrians whose gaze remains fixed directly ahead. The passer-by's response is similar to the "Gruen transfer" in shopping malls: "the moment when a 'destination buyer,' with a specific purchase in mind, is transformed into an impulse shopper, a crucial point immediately visible in the shift from a determined stride to an erratic and meandering gait" (Crawford 1992: 14). In shopping malls, adjacent attractions, such as handbag shops near shoe shops, are never a matter of chance; the shopping experience is carefully scripted (ibid.). Yet on urban streets with many thresholds, with relatively unregulated juxtapositions of uses and styles, one can never be sure what will come into view through the next display window or doorway.

These observations show that the social liminality of thresholds can arise from a softening of distinctions between inside and outside which is made possible by wide, transparent and open frontages, floor surfaces continuous with the footpath, advertising and merchandise placed in the street and awnings and verandas which extend the interior out over the footpath. Publicly-accessible thresholds of stores do not neatly separate public from quasi-public settings. Such open thresholds cannot filter sensations according to the practical needs of passers-by. Views, music, smells, breezes and actions from both realms extend across the threshold and overlap. Passers-by become aware of the escapist atmosphere spilling out from these thresholds. The flashing lights and music at both the arcade and the music store are highly stimulating because of their intensity and variability. The dancers provide movement and actively encourage others to participate. Whether such sensations are distractions or attractions depends on the changeable attitudes of individuals; they merely offer options to respond.

The Negotiation of Thresholds

Thresholds at all scales are places of movement, but that movement is not as straightforward as we might imagine. Observations show that people's uses of thresholds are tremendously varied and not always efficient or practical. The flows of people across thresholds vary in their rate and direction; there are also significant differences in the ease with which people move and the risks involved; thresholds frame careful exposures as well as unexpected ones. Just as social liminality brings ambiguity, disorder and heightened awareness, the passage across a threshold between private and public space can generate new and unfamiliar perceptions and can frame new relations with the other people who share public space. Building thresholds, like weddings, are special settings for the play of meaning because they are between social categories. By framing liminal spatial conditions of transformation, intensity, contrast, escape and risk, they support a "culture of negotiation" (Stavrides 2001), where identity can be reconfigured. Liminal, playful practices test the boundaries of what is acceptable and what is desirable about social life in threshold spaces.

Taken together, the diverse observations outlined here suggest that thresholds allow people to constantly adjust the balance between public exposure and personal control. At the threshold, a controlled space meets an unregulated, disordered space full of strangers and unfamiliar phenomena. The frequency with which people linger at building thresholds suggests that people savor the overlap of roles and sensations between the private and public realms which are available there.

People use the architecture of the threshold to adjust both their own perceptions and the extent to which they are perceived by others in public. Using various threshold conditions, through small-scale movements, individuals can readily and subtly calibrate their exposure to others on a variety of registers: visual, auditory and bodily. This control over gradients of perception and exposure gives people the freedom which is a necessary prerequisite to play (Simmel 1950; Lefebvre 1991). The space apart offers choice, expanding the range of users and uses that come out in public. The woman smoking concealed in the doorway shows how a threshold can structure physical encounters between strangers from different realms, public and private. She uses the threshold's depth to balance her level of stimulation and risk from public exposure against the control and security offered by the private realm. She has a close view of people passing by, but is unthreatened by their glances because of her separation within a distinct, defensible space.

People pursuing clandestine, proscribed play behavior often take advantage of the seclusion of edges—the "edge effect" (de Jonge 1967)—just as do the elderly and the shy for their leisure activities because for them the public realm also presents a wide variety of threats and hazards. Entering into public life is a liminal process. It means moving from a controlled setting into a more open and risky setting. Hence generally "activities grow from the edge toward the middle" (Gehl 1987: 152). Play situations begin in a similar context, as the individual steps beyond the threshold of comfort, toward the unknown.

And yet people's engagement with thresholds is not always so tightly under their control; this complex social and physical geography often requires hesitation and negotiation. The diversity of uses of urban thresholds is not without difficulties or conflicts. Spontaneous, exploratory, impractical and dangerous uses of thresholds can be a bodily threat to people's instrumental need for passage. Security officers often chase away those who play and ask those sitting to move aside and keep the threshold clear. Yet because building thresholds are generally only designed for momentary, fleeting occupation, and because they must provide access directly from a public space, they will always remain open to appropriation by various members of the public for new uses.

The Wider Liminality of Public Space

This examination of thresholds sheds light on the liminal conditions of public space generally, and on the ways that people, through their everyday play, discover and engage with the transformative potentials that public spaces offer.

Newlywed couples and skating teenagers who use thresholds are actors in well-defined liminal stages of the life cycle. Their actions are often publicly tolerated because these actions are not seen by others as lasting or dangerous; indeed, it can be argued that these liminal stages of release and transformation are necessary for the stable reproduction of the wider society (Turner 1982; Bakhtin 1984). But these examples also illustrate a general condition intrinsic to urban social experience: encounters with difference and the unexpected in public space are in themselves adventures or escapes from the everyday which can transform our sense of self (Cohen and Taylor 1978).

This general liminality of the city has physical, representational and social dimensions. Analysis of the convergence of strangers at thresholds shows that sensory intensity, overlaps of people's activities in time and space and unexpected juxtapositions of action or meaning all help to constitute liminality. The threshold's transitional function and its physical separateness highlight people's ability to compress or stretch spatial experience and action, to choose and to control how and when to step outside the everyday and the expected. Threshold spaces can, at least temporarily, be manipulated as distinct settings and enjoyed for their unique behavioral opportunities. Other parts of the public realm are similarly available for playful appropriation.

Wedding photographs show how people's behavior brings new meanings to thresholds. The sanctity of the meanings of marriage gives justification to unusual actions. Though not what thresholds were planned for, playful activities loosen up the rules and expand our common understanding of the value of these places. Such creative, performative action is not limited to thresholds or to rituals (Thrift 1997). The street performers in Leicester Square who become statues extend the meanings and significance of the theater out into public space, as does the man dancing outside the music store. New uses and interpretations of parts of the urban environment are always there as potential. The scope of liminal possibilities depends on the affordances (Gibson 1979) which a particular site offers for human perception and action, practical or otherwise, including the different configurations of other people who are moving through it, who become actors or audience. The social context of actions in public is always shifting, and always unpredictable.

The liminality of public spaces does not provide freedom in any absolute sense. People's appropriation of space does not necessarily give them a high degree of control, and many playful uses of public space have uncertain outcomes. Perfectly flat, open, unregulated spaces may seem loose, but there are limits to what people can do there because such settings lack both variety and choice. Conversely, both unexpected encounters in doorways and the risks of skating down staircases demonstrate that physical constraint can in fact serve as the stimulus for many novel, unexpected experiences. It is the diversity and variability of interpretation and action that are possible in urban spaces that make them liminal sites where a wide range of play happens. Public spaces offer both opportunity and risk largely because of their blurred, indeterminate in-betweenness. Rojek notes that at the heart of leisure experience is "a constant vacillation between tension and release" (1995: 87). Under conditions of liminality, social distinctions and controls still exist, but they are negotiated. Public space is constantly being opened up and transformed and thus remains "in play."

References

Alexander, C., Ishikawa, S., Silverstein, M., Jacobson, M., Fiksdahl-King, I. and Angel, S. (1977) *A Pattern Language: Towns, Buildings, Construction*, New York: Oxford University Press.

Bakhtin, M. (1984) *Rabelais and His World*, Bloomington, IN: Indiana University Press.

Benedikt, M. (1979) "To Take Hold of Space: Isovists and Isovist Fields," *Environment and Planning B*, 6: 44–69.

Borden, I. (2001) *Skateboarding, Space and the City: Architecture and the Body*, Oxford: Berg.

Caillois, R. (1961) *Man, Play and Games*, New York: Free Press of Glencoe.

Cohen, S. and Taylor, L. (1978) *Escape Attempts: The Theory and Practice of Resistance to Everyday Life*, Harmondsworth: Pelican.

Crawford, M. (1992) "The World in a Shopping Mall," in M. Sorkin (ed.) *Variations on a Theme Park*, New York: Hill and Wang.

Dargan, A. and Zeitlin, S. (1990) *City Play*, New Brunswick, NJ: Rutgers University Press.

de Jonge, D. (1967) "Applied Hodology," *Landscape*, 17: 10–11.

Dovey, K. (1999) *Framing Places: Mediating Power in Built Form*, London: Routledge.

Gehl, J. (1987) *Life Between Buildings: Using Public Space*, New York: Van Nostrand Reinhold.

Gehl, J. and City of Melbourne (1994) *Places for People*, Melbourne: City of Melbourne.

Gibson, J. (1979) *The Ecological Approach to Visual Perception*, Boston: Houghton Mifflin.

Gilloch, G. (1996) *Myth and Metropolis: Walter Benjamin and the City*, Cambridge: Polity Press.

Goffman, E. (1959) *The Presentation of Self in Everyday Life*, New York: Anchor.

Goffman, E. (1982) "Where the Action Is," in E. Goffman (ed.) *Interaction Ritual*, New York: Pantheon.

Hillier, B. and Hanson, J. (1984) *The Social Logic of Space*, New York: Cambridge University Press.

Huizinga, J. (1970) *Homo Ludens: A Study of the Play Element in Culture*, London: Temple Smith.

Jacobs, J. (1961) *The Death and Life of Great American Cities*, New York: Vintage.

Lefebvre, H. (1991) *Critique of Everyday Life*, vol. 1, 2nd edn, London: Verso.

Lyman, S. and Scott, M. (1975) *The Drama of Social Reality*, New York: Oxford University Press.

Lynch, K. (1960) *The Image of the City*, Cambridge, MA: MIT Press.

Markus, T. (1993) *Buildings and Power: Freedom and Control in the Origin of Modern Building Types*, London: Routledge.

Norberg-Schulz, C. (1971) *Existence, Space and Architecture*, New York: Praeger.

Rojek, C. (1995) *Decentring Leisure: Rethinking Leisure Theory*, London: Sage.

Shields, R. (1991) *Places on the Margin: Alternative Geographies of Modernity*, London: Routledge.

Shields, R. (1992) "Spaces for the Subject of Consumption," in R. Shields (ed.) *Lifestyle Shopping: The Subject of Consumption*, London: Routledge.

Simmel, G. (1950) "Sociability (An Example of Pure, or Formal, Sociology)," in G. Simmel (ed.) *The Sociology of Georg Simmel*, Glencoe, IL: Free Press.

Simmel, G. (1997) "The Metropolis and Mental Life," in N. Leach (ed.) *Rethinking Architecture: A Reader in Cultural Theory*, London: Routledge.

Spariosu, M. (1997) *The Wreath of Wild Olive: Play, Liminality and the Study of Literature*, Albany, NY: SUNY Press.

Stavrides, S. (2001) "Spatiotemporal Thresholds and the Experience of Otherness," *The Journal of Psychogeography and Urban Research*, 1. http://www.psychogeography.co.uk/spatiotemporal_thresholds.htm (accessed November 1, 2001).

Stevens, P. (1991) "Play and Liminality in Rites of Passage: From Elder to Ancestor in West Africa," *Play and Culture*, 4: 237–257.

Stevens, Q. and Dovey, K. (2004) "Appropriating the Spectacle: Play and Politics in a Leisure Landscape," *Journal of Urban Design*, 9: 351–365.

Thrift, N. (1997) "The Still Point: Resistance, Expressive Embodiment and Dance," in S. Pile and M. Keith (eds) *Geographies of Resistance*, London: Routledge.

Turner, V. (1982) *From Ritual to Theatre: The Human Seriousness of Play*, New York: Performing Arts Journal Publications.

van Gennep, A. (1960) *The Rites of Passage*, London: Routledge and Kegan Paul.

Whyte, W. H. (1980) *The Social Life of Small Urban Spaces*, Washington, DC: Conservation Foundation.

Whyte, W. H. (1988) *City: Rediscovering the Center*, New York: Doubleday.

Zukin, S. (1991) *Landscapes of Power: From Detroit to Disney World*, Berkeley, CA: University of California Press.

Part II

Tension

People appropriate public space for different purposes, purposes that may conflict with each other or with the objectives of those who exert authority over the space. The free movements of people and goods in public space and the encounters which can result are inherently complex and unpredictable. The actions of some users may also be defined as unattractive, offensive or criminal by others. Appropriation of public space is not always easy; it often requires negotiation to resolve or avoid conflict. The tense spatial relations observed in this section illustrate various ways different actors manage the risks of looseness.

In Chapter 5, Bernardo Jiménez-Domínguez shows how tensions between the interests of global businesses and local citizens are played out on street corners in Guadalajara and in its public plazas. In Chapter 6, Kim Dovey and Kasama Polakit focus on one neighborhood in Bangkok to reveal how social, economic and cultural tensions there are managed through a constant, complex slippage of physical arrangements and social practices and meanings. These two chapters demonstrate how a wide variety of small, informal commercial enterprises compete to take advantage of urban spaces, to try to maximize their commercial potential. To the outsider, informal commerce may seem disorderly, unsafe, unsanitary and illegitimate, but it meets many local needs and sustains local customs and traditions. To those in power, the loosening of control also means lost profits. These authors show that the locations and equipment of commercial enterprise are both loose and contested. Informal commerce looks as if it escapes control. But controls do not only come from above; there are many negotiations between actors; there are patterns within the disorder.

The multifarious local economic activities which make these spaces loose are not purely instrumental, commercial transactions. They are also shaped by particularities of culture and place; they provide opportunities for socializing and for expressing identity; they are linked to patterns of religious belief. It is in part for such reasons that tensions arise: the economy of urban space is not frictionless and efficient. There are also different opinions about which kinds of uses are productive, which are not and who should profit.

Both case studies bear witness to how the space of the local—formed by and filled with the customs and practices of people who use a space to serve their life needs—is confronted by the space of the global—more abstract, anonymous and technical, designed to optimize one kind of function: the smooth circulation of cars, goods, brands, capital or social power. The local and the global rub up against each other. Part of the looseness of these urban spaces is that new groups of residents, visitors and authorities continue to arrive, bringing their customs and values with them, becoming local.

While the first two chapters focus largely on commercial activities, the second two chapters address representational aspects of public space and in particular the management of disorderly, unpredictable appearances. Franck and Paxson in Chapter 7 examine memorials spontaneously created by members of the public near the sites of sudden, tragic events, focusing on the attack on the World Trade Center, the bombing in Oklahoma City and the assassination of Yitzhak Rabin in Tel Aviv. In Chapter 8, Julia Nevárez looks at New York's Central Park as an example of how managers enforce an "aesthetics of order" in public open space through a regime of beautification, maintenance and surveillance. What Franck and Paxson describe is a loosening of public space; what Nevárez profiles is a tightening. Each involves tension.

Spontaneous memorials allow people to express differing opinions related to the tragic event, making tensions visible to all. Contributors to some spontaneous memorials disagree over what kinds of statements and artifacts are suitable and engage in editing items others have left. Sometimes, after municipal authorities have removed spontaneous memorials, largely because of what is considered their disorderly appearance, members of the public continue to leave items or statements. It is precisely the appearance of order and evidence of control that the enforcement of an "aesthetics of order" seeks to achieve, in what is, at the same time, an apparently open and benign leisure environment. The tensions here between loose and tight may be masked or they may emerge as people encounter the enforcement of limitations on their actions.

The chapters in this part illuminate the nature of authority: how it is enacted in public spaces, how it is confronted and whether it is effective. Authority can vary in form, from being covert to being negotiated (e.g. through bribes) to being persuasive (e.g. through aesthetics), to outright force and disappropriation. These chapters show that control by the state, civil institutions or big business does not put an end to looseness: it merely requires that agents adapt. Users' responses to authority are not necessarily uniform, focused and organized. The emphasis in all four chapters is on the importance of negotiation, whether frank or tacit. People need to choreograph their activities as they overlap in loose space, to maximize opportunity and minimize disruption, conflict or waste. The tensions in these chapters are always being resolved: there is little overt opposition; it seldom comes to confrontation or conflict. And yet it is not completely harmonious either. It seems to get worked out.

The loosening and tightening of space is not a zero-sum game; people win a little and they have to give a little. Conflicting uses create opportunities to strategize; to develop new kinds of defiance, evasion or graft; to advance one's own interests through creative engagement with difference. Space is often in high demand—in Dovey and Polakit's study, everything seems to overlap—but spatial conditions are fluid in the sense that they change over time: rules, roles and boundaries continue to shift according to balances of power, with changing spatial needs and alliances. New détentes are reached, and new forms of compliance, oppression and subterfuge emerge.

In this section we see the introduction of new people, objects or meanings into spaces that are already occupied, reshaping them, although often only temporarily. These meanings and objects are typically introduced without permission or contrary to accepted practice. They help create new opportunities but in many cases create new tensions, as a wide range of actors ensure that public spaces are constantly loosened. The complex social interactions and negotiations documented in these chapters illustrate how loosening is a dialectical process, constantly unfolding.

Chapter 5

Urban Appropriation and Loose Spaces in the Guadalajara Cityscape

Bernardo Jiménez-Domínguez

The current socio-economic and political pressures reshaping space in most Latin American cities are producing an increasing number of cases of urban disappropriation as part of the local–global process that is transforming the cityscape. This process of dualization has occurred as a result of restructuring and the impact of new information and communications technologies. High tech industries have created new industrial landscapes on the model of Silicon Valley which are affecting cities all over the world. At the same time, these industries have intensified existing social and economic inequalities. The security-obsessed urbanism of walled and guarded neighborhoods and privatized public spaces is also creating new tensions and conflicts in urban landscapes.

The globalized markets of production bring to Latin America only the appearance of advanced high-tech manufacturing: the productive activities which have relocated here are largely low-skilled, low-paid and low value-added. The globalization of consumption is altogether more complete and more pervasive. It brings global competition to the retail sector from the largest marketplaces all the way down to the scale of the local street corner. The replacement of public spaces with enormous shopping malls and multinational shops and supermarkets is destroying local neighborhood businesses, creating tensions between formal and informal, and between emerging global and local retail activities.

This chapter charts creative strategies of local resistance to this two-pronged assault on the economic life and space of a Latin American city. In the interstices between global and local, or "glocalized" logic, specific activist interests—and even unexpected interests—run counter to prevailing modes of thought, as activists encounter spaces that are loose. These loose spaces are spaces of possibility and spontaneous cultural resistance that give life, enjoyment and diversity to cities.

The public is often viewed as passive, but in fact people are active as they pursue diverse goals and express their urban identities. In doing so, they resist the assaults on local economies and local traditions as they keep looking for daily life alternatives and a means of economic survival. They give different uses to the unilaterally-planned urban spaces that they appropriate through daily urban life.

The Reshaping of Latin American Cities

Latin American cities are increasingly fragmented by an urban duality that consists, on the one hand, of a network of homogenized, sanitized, commodified, privatized, global spaces, and, on the other, a city that is more and more invisible, possessing an informal urban economy, growing heterogeneity and intense polarization of space, but also great variety and unpredictability. According to Borja and Castells (1996), urban dualization reflects an urban social structure based on the interaction between opposite and dynamic poles of the informational economy, which polarizes society and segregates the uses of a metropolitan space shared by different classes, groups and functions. Globalization is being translated into practices that transform physical spaces, as well as social and cultural traditions. These transformations enable local and global trends to penetrate each other and to diverge from each other at the same time. Globalization consists of geographic, social, cultural and psychosocial developments that are unequal; they form a geography of power (Harvey 1996). But, as Lash and Urry (1994) state, the contemporary global economy produces a de-centered set of sign economies in space; there are multiple structures of flows that operate simultaneously. At the same time, many men and women are becoming increasingly critical of and reflexive about the changes brought about by globalization. Globalization entails a compression of time and space, reflexive modernization, intermingled landscapes, and a society of risk and fear.

We can identify the underside of globalization in statements made by people who are excluded by global–local contradictions. They are the inhabitants of the invisible part of the city, the part of the city which is not profitable for global processes, where the poorest live, the ones who never held regular jobs or only junk-jobs, with no welfare safety net. Most of these people are self-employed, part of the underground economy. However, each Latin American city presents differences in its specific evolution in the context of globalization. In cities like Mexico City, Bogotá and Montevideo, the deep social fragmentation co-exists in dense and fluid urban spaces, while in Santiago de Chile, fragmentation presents a radial shape which gives rise to several different Santiagos growing in different directions and exacerbating the deep social fragmentation. In Guadalajara the tendency is towards a consolidated, polarized housing pattern and growing social segregation and functional fragmentation in which privatized development seeks to adjust the social and physical borders of urban space. This means, in practice, that to the inequalities deriving from the current economic system we have to add physical and symbolic exclusions. The urban sprawl grows with no restrictions, destroying natural resources of the seven metropolitan municipalities in an unsustainable way. The gated communities are fashionable even in social housing projects. In the 1990s, the luxurious ones, where just 2 percent of the metropolitan population live, already covered 10 percent of the urban fabric (Cabrales 2005).

Guadalajara and the Illusion of Silicon Valley

In the city of Guadalajara, Mexico's second largest city, the introduction of a globalized electronics industry has allowed the region to create its own local version of Silicon Valley. The state of Jalisco, of which Guadalajara is the capital, offers one of the most advanced examples of digitalization and the use of virtual resources in Mexico. Guadalajara is no longer "La Perla de Occidente" ("The Pearl of the West"); today it is a computer and telecommunications manufacturing center. From 1994 to 1999, the number of electronics-related businesses increased from 25 to 112 (Palacios 2001). Some of these businesses are located in "high-tech islands" surrounded by squatter settlements, antiseptically separated by security barriers. Like spaceships these companies have landed in the very place where the levels of poverty and unemployment demonstrate that people are actually worse off than before the new industries arrived. Inequality is on the rise with labor income inequality a significant component of overall inequality in Mexico (Hanson 1999).

These paradoxes are brought about by neoliberalism and globalization. The unequal geography of the electronics industry and the poverty-stricken areas that surround its factories form a "dual space" which gives meaning to the term "glocal." Only 16.6 percent of the Mexican population uses computers, and of this only 53 percent is connected to the Internet (INEGI 2003). A large majority of Mexicans do not use computers and therefore do not have access to this new technology. Thus, the promise of Silicon Valley appears to be unevenly allocated. A report by Dedrick and Kraemer (1998) noted that even though Guadalajara is growing as a computer-manufacturing center, it can scarcely be considered another Silicon Valley. Rather, it is becoming a satellite Silicon Valley, a position that fits very well into the uneven geographic development of globalization.

The satellite model is also more in line with the growth of urban dualization in Guadalajara. That "Silicon Valley" is part of a public relations strategy rather than a real place becomes clear when we see that none of the businesses is locally owned. Moreover, the connection between research and development is very weak. The only electronic components manufactured are hard disks, harnesses and cables, and most of these products are exported because contacts with local manufacturers are few and far between. There are no links between local universities and the marketing of research or managers of local companies; nor do local investors invest in the "local" computer industry. Thus, the image of these companies as gigantic high-tech spaceships that land and establish themselves in contrasting spaces is not purely architectural or fixed; it represents a series of social and economic processes. Recently some of these businesses have been put up for sale, advertised in English. Some of the "spaceships" are empty. The money is flying away and the surrounding cityscape has not changed at all. They never were connected to the local physical or social space. These are spaces of disappropriation.

The Concept of Appropriation

Appropriation is a typical human action when people exert their right to the city and the street as a space of encounter (Lefebvre 1976). Appropriation, according to Chombart de Lauwe (1976), involves a whole series of psychological processes of creating, relaxing, acting, dreaming and learning according to one's desires and projects. Appropriation is communication and social relatedness in urban space; it is urban culture and living memory.

Appropriation is different from other practices like simple possession for it involves collective activity. Possession as property ownership does not necessarily imply appropriation in the sense I use it here, as possessed objects can remain external to us (Sansot 1976). I do not need to be the owner of an urban space to appropriate it. I appropriate it, but the city also appropriates me in a process that always operates in both directions. Appropriation has an affective dimension which turns this relation into identification. Appropriation is based on identification, whether or not reality is changed. So, the psychosocial processes in space appropriation are related to urban cultural practices, perceptions, representations, desires, aesthetics and feelings; they entail the social and personal imaginary, the dialectical relationships between the person and the urban space. Appropriation, arising from spontaneous practices, is part of the struggle for the right to the city. It involves at the same time cognitive, affective, symbolic and aesthetic experiences, as well as explicit situations of power linked to the mode of property ownership and exclusion and the emergent social practices which confront it in the dual city, characterized by space fragmentation and social inequality.

As Chombart de Lauwe (1976) has established, the psychosocial processes involved in appropriation encounter obstacles in the present world and cannot be adequately explained without taking into account the socioeconomic context of appropriation and the technological transformations in place. The speed of transformations in built urban space, intended only to achieve greater efficiency of production for a greater profit for the builders, does not fulfill the needs for space appropriation of the poorest and does not allow people to become attached to the places. This process of disappropriation generates a tightening of public space, with restrictions placed on people's mobility and their isolation in spaces alienated from the meaning of the city as home, of dwelling in urban space.

Urban Corners: Local Appropriation and Global Disappropriation

The urbanized landscape continues to provide evidence of the duality of local appropriation and global disappropriation. Street corners/sidewalks, malls and street markets in Guadalajara highlight these contrasts. These sites, and the everyday behavior associated with them, reveal the coupling of globalized/controlled and localized/loosened in both spatial layouts and activity patterns.

Corners are a good example. The essential characteristic of a city is the way streets intersect to form crossroads and corners (Solá-Morales 2004). In that sense, any urban form is a multiplication of corners. But, when the contemporary city becomes a field of flows, what disappears are the corners as places of the social and of the local urban culture.

Traditionally corners have been places of spontaneous encounter, sites of the construction of neighborhood identities, as described in the well-known *Street Corner Society* (Whyte 1943), but they are also places of superimposition and conflict. The corner has never been the same since the irruption of the car into urban space. Cars have led not only to changes in the perception and use of the corner but also to transformations of metropolitan space. As a consequence, pedestrian mobility has been modified at urban corners (Cohen 2004). The ideal corner can be a space of encounter and mingling, of resistance to fixed images and routines when appropriated by urban users, but corners are dead or empty spaces when they are not used.

According to Sennett (2004), certain forms of organizing space, such as the grid, proved to be empty containers, socially and politically speaking. In 1573, when Philip II of Spain decreed the grid plan for governing the hostile territories of the New World, so that towns could spread in a symmetrical manner, it was a clear principle of exerting power over rationalized space that turned the lively encounters of corners into lethargic repetitions. After the seventeenth century, the grid suited the sale of regular units of land under urban capitalism. The last thing capitalists wanted was a space that was ambiguous, potent with surprise. And if we look at present urban peripheries, contemporary cities have created a kind of parallel universe with no corners; this is the new "Flatland" or "Nocornersland" (Zardini 2004).

In Guadalajara, a different but related phenomenon has occurred in recent years, combining several factors: cars, global capitalist companies freed from rules, changes in the use of space in traditional neighborhood houses, and corners transformed into parking space for cars in front of small supermarkets, many of which are open 24 hours a day. An increasing number of Guadalajara's street corners have fallen victim to intense competition between convenience store chains such as Oxxo (the property of the Mexican multinational FEMSA, with 3,000 stores built in 90 Mexican cities since 1977) and 7-Eleven (the property of 7-Eleven Inc., the world's largest convenience retailing company, with 26,600 stores operated and franchised in 18 countries and 421 locations in Mexico since 1971). This competition has scarred the urban landscape of a number of neighborhoods planned only for housing. Paradoxically, there are regulations in place that prohibit changes in land use as well as changes in architectural style. These kinds of changes alter the socio-affective attachment of people to places and landscapes that are part of every individual's identity and culture. Place identity is part of both self-identity and urban identity (Proshansky 1978; Lalli 1988).

However, while Oxxo and 7-Eleven have apparently been allowed to build at will, owners of neighborhood restaurants and small businesses are often fined for violating regulations concerning land use and architectural style. This is the case of a traditional restaurant serving local food, the Fonda la Santa Cruz, created in 1947 on the ground floor of the house of the owner and his family, just beside the Church of La Santa Cruz in the neighborhood of Colonia Ladrón de Guevara. The restaurant is basically an unfinished terrace with an open kitchen, a bathroom, tables and seats. When the owner began to improve the terrace with a new tile roof (rather than an aluminum one) in order to protect the clients from the heat of the sun and with flower stands placed on the border of the sidewalk, inspectors from the Mayor`s office came to tell him he was doing something illegal and altering the architectural style of the area and that he would be fined.

Meanwhile, with the complete approval of the same office, on the opposite corner the multinational 7-Eleven was building a new standard convenience store, following the usual demolition of a neighborhood house. These stores not only sell the usual supermarket items in a smaller place at higher prices but also spirits and beer, prepared food and coffee. Thus they include the functions of at least four different small businesses. In addition, there is parking in front, requiring the adaptation and partial privatization of the sidewalk so that it is no longer mainly for pedestrians, in a city where pedestrians are in the majority. This is the standard design of this kind of store.

Most of the customers at the Fonda La Santa Cruz restaurant are pedestrians who live nearby and come with their families mainly at dinner time (a well-established cultural habit) and people who work in the area and come during the lunch hour. Just at the corner of the restaurant terrace is a taco stand, and the men who prepare the tacos are usually talking as they stand around it. At mid-day the place is full of people and even some street musicians come to play. This corner is a meeting point where people interact and where everybody knows the owner.

The owner of the restaurant continued working and the customers continued coming while a yellow plastic barrier remained wrapped around the "illegal" terrace area. But in the end, he had to stop the construction work and remove the flower stands, give in and give money to the inspectors. One of them, actually a customer, still comes to eat and to ask for more money.

5.1
7-Eleven on a sanitized corner of Manuel Acuña Street

5.2
Fonda (Tavern) La Santa Cruz, on a corner on Manuel Acuña Street

The restaurant offers plenty of variety and spontaneity: it is an open space, belonging to the neighborhood while the 7-Eleven is a predictable, sanitized and commodified, closed space that is alien to the neighborhood. It is part of the process of "McDonaldization" (Ritzer 2000), which involves 125 countries around the world and 175 junk food restaurants in Mexico alone and which is devastating the urban landscape. To give one very significant example, one of the main McDonald's in Guadalajara was built on the site of the first residence of the Jalisco state governors. This intrusion into the vernacular architecture of Guadalajara on one of its most representative avenues (Vallarta) not only fragments local space but literally buries urban memory.

Nonetheless, many people remain loyal to the small businesses in their neighborhoods and continue going there not only to buy or eat but also to meet and talk. Social routines of interaction, communication and exchange of information and local stories are part of their urban culture and social identity. As de Certeau (1999) concluded, the pure consumer relation is not enough because it is too short. These are socially appropriated spaces, integrated into the neighborhood despite their provisional architecture. The convenience stores and supermarket chains may be well designed but they fragment the local space.

On another corner, we have a similar situation. Across the street from the church El Santuario, in a popular old neighborhood with the same name close to downtown, is a street food stand. On the corner diagonally opposite is an Oxxo store. On the fourth corner is a sugarcane stand where you can see the cane sticks piled up and the owners (mostly old men working in the area since they were young) always cutting cane in pieces for selling or making juice. Here the street restaurant, which is mainly open in the mornings, is surrounded by people and the available seats take up 40 percent of the street. They are not supposed to be there, but this is part of the way you eat in these places. Nobody cares about the passing cars, and the drivers usually respect the customers on the street and sometimes even stop in front, making the space for parking even larger and also serving as a protective barrier.

On the nearby corner of Zaragoza and Herrera y Cairo Streets, customers of a very popular taco stand take up half of the street at 9a.m. for breakfast, sometimes surrounded by cars.

Close to this taco stand, at the corner of González Ortega and Florencio Atillón streets, is another variation of eating on the street in the morning. Here the food is prepared inside a house but is served out front—on the sidewalk and in part of the parking space of the street. The owner puts a long table on the outside edge of the sidewalk: the bench is in the street and the whole eating space is covered by a sheet of plastic. When a car stops at that corner waiting for the green light, the driver can see and smell the food and listen to customers talking with the owner's family. It is easy for the driver to join them.

We can see another variation on this theme in the park in front of the Viejo Hospital Civil. Every morning a driver in a pick-up truck stops in front of one of the parking meters and in no more than 15 minutes is able to install a street restaurant

5.3
Breakfast in the street in front of El Santuario Church

5.4
Food stand set up at a metered parking space on González Ortega Street

with the help of his family. He puts one advertisement on the grass beside the sidewalk and another in front of the truck. Tables and chairs are placed on the sidewalk and shaded by a plastic sheet stretched from the truck to poles stuck in the grass. Part of the sidewalk between them is covered by this sheet of plastic. Then the people come to eat and the place serves as a loose space.

What I have described to this point are several variations of the appropriation of space for food venues: a restaurant on the first floor of a house turned into a corner terrace; a street corner turned into a street restaurant; a street corner house using the sidewalk in front for serving food in the space of a parking meter; a taco stand on a street corner; and a pick-up truck turned into a restaurant using the parking space, the sidewalk and one corner of the grass in a park. None of these activities is supposed to be there; in fact, they are just temporary. The people who pursue them appropriate the spaces in creative ways; with the support of their customers they negotiate the urban validity of the sites, turning them into loose spaces. People eat in these places sit or wander around—typical behavior at the taco stands—mingling with others. They create a real place out of the sidewalk, the streets close to the stands, the tables or whatever is available. For a moment they become partners, interacting with others like neighbors, which means neither anonymously nor intimately, according to de Certeau's short definition (1999). The only well-known names for such sites, the ones that give identity to the places, are the names of the former owners, which in most cases are not written down.

These kinds of space go beyond the European café as a meeting place; they operate like temporary neighborhoods that appear only in the mornings or at night

5.5
A hot food stand set up on a sidewalk next to the owner's pick-up truck, between a park and the Hospital Civil across the street

when people have breakfast or dinner—but not just to eat. They function as collective gathering points. As Benjamin argued, "the streets are the dwelling place of the collective" (1999: 879). This is what happens when people gather around these places: they are dwelling in the city, because the city is exactly that—the people in the streets (Borja 2003). And what is the street? The place of encounter, answers Lefebvre (1976).

As a site of dwelling, the city street can also be a place to hang laundry on the line. On the corner of Garibaldi and Mariano Bárcenas the sidewalk is used as a yard. The woman who does this lives in a room inside an old house there and has no other space for drying clothes outdoors. She does not do it all day but only between 9a.m. and 12p.m. when the sun is perfect in that corner. At first she sat on the entrance stairs reading a magazine, but she noticed that people do not mind the washing when passing by; they just walk around the line. Some even smile, and if they are in groups they make funny remarks, but nobody is disturbed by the washing hanging out on the sidewalk. They seem to understand the woman's practice. It looks like a spontaneous artistic installation or something funny in the way of the pedestrians and the drivers, but they definitely do not consider it an obstacle.

Walking in the Malls

The best illustration of the "dual city" is the replacement of public spaces with enormous shopping malls that, like transnational hypermarkets, are gradually destroying local small and medium-size businesses. At the same time, the new shopping malls are changing the urban landscape and partially expropriating it by privatizing it. An aesthetics of fear is created through explicit paramilitary surveillance which guarantees commercial "order" and defines "proper" behaviors and "suitable" people (Zukin 1995). The popular concept "non-place" can be applied to these types of spaces (Augé 1995). This approach understands a "place" to be a space with identity, history and relationships, and the opposite a "non-place."

Postmodernity, which Augé calls "super-modernity" (in order to place the current moment in time), is largely responsible for producing these non-places. These are not anthropological places (people's appropriated spaces) but exclude places that possess memory. Public space can be reconfigured—in the mall, for instance—to push civic consciousness aside and repress civic memory. Along these lines, our era's most important kind of public space is shopping malls (Zukin 1995). They serve as meeting places, but the fact that they are within the confines of private property throws doubt on whether all kinds of publics will have access to them and under what conditions. In the United States, legal proceedings have led to some courts recognizing the public nature of malls (Reed 2000). For such reasons, Zukin argues that the ultimate challenge is for shopping malls to become symbolic landscapes of public power. Far more public appropriation and subjective legitimization are required to make them into public spaces. As described in the case of Guadalajara, the automobile-centered urban model has been imposed in almost all of Latin America, giving the space of the street almost exclusively to cars. In the United States, activities that once took place in outdoor public space have been shut inside large, privately owned shopping malls with extensive security. Americans spend a good part of their leisure time in shopping malls; in the mid-1980s adolescents spent more time there than anywhere except home and school (Rifkin 2000).

In Guadalajara, once known as the City of Plazas, more and more and bigger and bigger shopping malls are being built. At present, there are nearly one hundred malls. In fact, the number and variety of its shopping malls are among the greatest in any Mexican city. Taking observations made in Guadalajara's most fashionable shopping mall, La Gran Plaza as a starting point, we can focus on the processes by which people appropriate space in malls. In one of the most frequented spaces in the mall, the food court next to the 16-screen cinema and across from the escalators, there was an elderly man who would sit every day for hours, without eating anything. His behavior was similar to the way someone might sit in a park to watch people pass by. The man yielded his space and did not mind the intrusion of others. On the contrary, he readily began chatting with neighboring strangers. The old man said he came there every day and sat in the same place because it was safe and very pleasant. He had everything he needed right there and could watch everything around him. Many people came to eat, others went down the escalators, young couples and pretty girls would come by on their way to the movies. He could spend the entire afternoon there, and because the mall provided shelter he would not get wet when it rained, as it did the day he was interviewed. It was always nice inside, and when it got dark all the lights came on and everything looked very pretty. He liked the dome in the ceiling, and concluded, "In fact, I don't even realize how late it's getting, and when I finally think of it, it's gotten really late." However, what he liked most was getting to see people and, when possible, talking with someone. He used to go to a park, but it became unsafe because people did not go there any more, and it was dirty and not maintained. At night it was dark and became very unsafe (Olivera 2001).

This example is a very clear case of how a tight space can become loose through personal experience and use. It tells us a lot about the process of appropriation and the emergence of loose spaces in spite of the control, rules and surveillance of these privatized sites. Moreover, the old man comes from a tradition of a communal public space and made the transition to a private, commercial space. The shopping mall was part of his trajectory of public space use which fits his habit of going to the park. He legitimized the mall as a public space through his use of it, a true appropriation of a supposed non-place.

It is clear that as shopping malls become more prevalent, the activities that previously took place in public plazas tend more and more to be contained within the enclosed spaces of shopping malls. These activities become commodified, given that a shopping mall is designed for public encounters yet inserted into the world of commerce. Even though their promenades, benches and trees give shopping malls the appearance of public space (they are even called plazas), they are not public spaces. But what is different in the appropriation behavior of the elderly man is that he uses the shopping mall as a substitute public space. His activities are not obstructed by commerce but rather dictated by a desire to continue his need for public contact. Kowinski (1985) argues that the shopping mall is a well-designed psychological selling machine and a televisual delivery system because it uses spectacle combined with performance as a hook to maximize sales. But the elderly man is not there to buy anything; he is just spending time engaged in the social act of watching. And he is not the only one. Most youngsters are there for hours, just strolling.

As Gehl (1987) suggests, when we observe how people behave in public spaces, we see that they adapt the space and change its functions so they can enjoy what is one of the most attractive attributes of urban life: to see, hear and meet other people in public spaces such as the street. Other people are the true spectacle that we come to enjoy. In this way, we appropriate non-places as replacements for places, as we have seen in the case of the elderly man. The premise of the enclosed shopping mall—dating from the first mall, Northland, created by Victor Gruen in 1954 near Detroit—is to create a climate-controlled environment with air conditioning and escalators, with scarcely any clocks—an artificial cultural environment that allows us to forget about the outside world and spend a number of hours without realizing how much time has gone by (Rifkin 2000). The experience of the elderly man attests to that sense of no-time when he said he did not even realize when it was getting very late. He also said he felt safe, in contrast to the park where he used to go, now poorly maintained and unsafe.

Public spaces are increasingly privatized worldwide, adopting the standards of maintenance of the private shopping mall as well as its other characteristics: security guards, controlled entrances and the privatization of services. Everything comes under the premise of offering security and quality. This can be described as "spontaneous malling," as Crawford (1992) calls the process of transforming urban spaces into malls. It seems as if malls make the world safe for a life of strolling (Baumann 1996). This is paradoxically true in third world cities, as we have seen. According to Abaza (2001), in third world cities, something which is normal in many places, like strolling in the open air, can become difficult with the growth of urban insecurity, the increasing number of cars and traffic jams, the heat and the shortage of parks, trees, and, we can add, of wide pedestrian sidewalks and safe public places.

Abaza remarks that in the Middle East and Southeast Asia, malls have different functions from the first world. A hybridization of tastes and different ways of spending leisure time are turning the malls into a new type of public space. For youth, young women, artists and the new professionals, malls provide alternatives. The coffee houses within malls have become a new space for social interaction that could also be considered a public space. Despite well-founded criticisms against consumerism, the use of these spaces might be a generational protest against their parents' conservatism. Strolling in clean, modern and air-conditioned spaces provides a sense of relief from the cities with their growing poverty, pollution and traffic jams.

But Abaza also recognizes how, in the face of the juxtaposition of these two worlds, the capitalist class is fast removing the popular quarters close to the malls and preventing the unwanted poor from strolling in them. Security measures, as everywhere else, are extremely tight and taking pictures is forbidden. Abaza concludes that:

> the mall is the place where the crowds are formed. It is the place of entertainment which replaces gardens and public spaces, which are scarce in Cairo. One might even speak of their democratization effects, through the accessibility of the space to all classes, despite the abrupt elimination of popular quarters and the economy of survival exemplified in the informal sector.
>
> (2001: 118)

Despite the security measures and the consumerist definition of malls everywhere, it is possible to create loose spaces out of what have been called non-places.

Buying in the *Tianguis*

The aesthetics of fear (Zukin 1995) and the discourse of urban fear (Low 2001) have increased the commercial popularity of malls and gated communities that privatize and fragment urban space causing the loss of urban identity and the deterioration of non-privatized public space. In a contradictory way, malls and gated communities create greater insecurity on a global scale. The fear of others and the use of aesthetics to exclude unwanted visitors have led to codes for inclusion and exclusion and a greater segregation of urban space.

In contrast, however, the street-market (*tianguis*) culture is thriving throughout Guadalajara. It is a culture of close contact, spontaneous talk and spatial disorder, like what we find in enclosed public markets; fear of difference vanishes in a sort of collective alternative consumerism. The *tianguis* are authorized (though informal) street markets whose origins date to pre-Hispanic times. They are set up on certain days of the week in various parts of town. They offer an economical and very popular alternative to supermarkets and hypermarkets by selling fresh produce, traditionally prepared homemade foods, and varied and fashionable clothing and shoes—all made by small producers. These markets also feature many kinds of household products from many different sources: imitation luxury goods; pirated CDs, cassettes and videos at very low prices; all brands of contraband appliances; computer programs which are not sold in large stores; and merchandise that appropriates designs and products from the global marketplace, such as copies of products seen in magazines. The *tianguis* thus produce "translations" that both outwit globalization and use it to create new local hybrids. The contradictory logic between globalization and localization shows the integration of nearly all metropolitan areas into global capitalism.

5.6
Buying in the *tianguis* (street market)

Several days each week these street markets transform different local streets into links with global trends and goods. They offer the possibility of buying what the prices of malls deny to many people as contraband goods or as imitations—you can choose the trademark you like from the trendy clothing produced in family workshops. Sometimes the imitations are so good that even multinationals such as Levi Strauss have a problem telling their jeans apart, and they spend millions advertising against the illegal competition. Youngsters wearing jeans stroll for hours in the malls and then go to buy in the *tianguis*. Sometimes, the authorities confiscate some of these goods, but they soon re-appear. The rule is to negotiate a bribe with the authorities and then go back to work.

Gaps between rich and poor are gradually increasing, while at the same time cultures are beginning to grow together. In this sense, changes that derive from globalization, such as flows of images, information, goods and people, lead throughout the world to a pluralization of culture in which culture moves beyond place and physical presence. This process gives rise to the unexpected creation of imaginary communities whose existence is localized. Moreover, that existence is linked more strongly to processes of appropriation than to processes of cultural dependence: audiences are not passive. These processes are the same everywhere, but the form in which the visual experience is appropriated and "translated" varies locally. The changing spaces for identity are related to the fact that meanings occur and are produced in diverse locations. Urban culture is linked to economic globalization and localized social inequality.

When the *tianguis* becomes an alternative praxis, harassment against merchants and other problems increase. After the *tianguis cultural*, a street market managed for and by young people, first appeared in 1995, taking place every Saturday, successive city governments tried to close it. The location was the Jardín Rolón, beside the church El Carmen and in front of the former Convent El Carmen, a cultural site owned by the local government. The success of the initiative for exchanging goods youth make themselves and for holding experimental cultural events raised moralistic objections from the priest and parishioners. Officials also questioned the various free cultural activities, mainly rock music concerts, for being alien to the commercial license and character of the market. When the *tianguis cultural* community protested in front of the government buildings, the authorities negotiated a relocation of the market (to the Plaza Juarez in front of the Park Agua Azul) along with tighter controls. The government used the case to gain support from young people, promising to change the policies towards them. The approach recognizes this alternative street market as part of the city's life and accepts the diverse uses of public space instead of pursuing futile attempts at harassment. The *tianguis* serves the cultural needs of young people with very few alternatives. It highlights both the success of young people's resistance practices and the government's commitment to develop an alternative space of exchange and culture for young people.

Conclusion

In urban places where street corners are still alive, the appropriation of space operates as a confrontation with the multinational convenience store chains. We see the traditional, parochial use of the street and sidewalk and daily appropriation of the corners by local food stands and restaurants. The corners are the locus of urban cultural meanings and public gatherings. In Guadalajara and in other third world cities, malls are turned unexpectedly into substitute public spaces for social interaction, strolling, encounters, watching others, much like a park, plaza or any other public place. Malls are also places for learning about novelties and fashionable goods and clothing, but people do not necessarily consume there. Instead they go to street markets where imitations or contraband goods are cheaper. These goods are sold within a completely different space, a space of closeness and social relatedness that goes beyond purely consumer relations. These are appropriated spaces.

References

Abaza, M. (2001) "Shopping Malls, Consumer Culture and the Reshaping of Public Space in Egypt," *Theory, Culture & Society*, 18: 97–122.

Augé, M. (1995) *Los "No Lugares": Espacios del Anonimato. Una Antropología de la Sobremodernidad*, Barcelona: Paidos.

Baumann, Z. (1996) "From Pilgrim to Tourist," in S. Hall and P. Du Gay (eds) *Questions of Cultural Identity*, London: Sage.

Borja, J. (2003) *La Ciudad Conquistada*, Madrid: Alianza.

Borja, J. and Castells, M. (1996) *Local and Global*, London: Earthscan.

Cabrales, F. (2005) "Urbanismo Defensivo y Ofensivo," *PISO*, 8: 126–133.

Chombart de Lauwe, P. (1976) "Appropriation of Space and Social Change," in P. Korosec (ed.) *Appropriation of Space: Proceedings of the 3rd Conference of the International Architectural Psychology Society*, Louvain la Neuve, Belgium: Coopérative Universitaire de l'Université de Louvain-La-Neuve.

Cohen, J. L. (2004) "Corner Adventures: Some Figures of the Cuneiform Space," in M. Solá-Morales (ed.) *Cities, Corners*, Barcelona: Forum Barcelona/Lunwerg Editores.

Crawford, M. (1992) "The World in a Shopping Mall," in M. Sorkin (ed.) *Variations on a Theme Park*, New York: Hill and Wang.

de Certeau, M. (1999) *La Invención de lo Cotidiano 2. Habitar, Cocinar*, México: Universidad Iberoamericana.

Dedrick, J. (1998) *National IT Policy Mexico Computer Report*, University of California at Irvine: Center for Research on Information Technology and Organizations (CRITO). Available: http://www.crito.edu (accessed July 20, 2004).

Gehl, J. (1987) *Life Between Buildings: Using Public Space*, New York: Van Nostrand Reinhold.

Hannerz, U. (1992) *Cultural Complexity*, New York: Columbia University Press.

Hanson, G. (1999) "Trade Liberalization and Wage Inequality in Mexico," *Industrial and Labor Relations Review*, 52: 271–288.

Harvey, D. (1996) "Globalization in Question," *Rethinking Marxism*, 8: 1–17.

INEGI (2003) National Institute of Statistics, Geography and Informatics. Available: http:// www.inegi.gob.mx (accessed November 19, 2004).

Kowinski, W. (1985) *The Malling of America*, New York: William Morrow.

Lalli, M. (1988) "Urban Identity," in D. Canter (ed.) *Environmental Social Psychology*, Dordrecht, The Netherlands: Kluwer Academic Publishers.

Lash, S. and Urry, J. (1994) *Economies of Signs and Space*, London: Sage.

Lefebvre, H. (1976) *La Revoluciòn Urbana*, Madrid: Alianza.

Low, S. (2001) "The Edge and the Center: Gated Communities and the Discourse of Urban Fear," *American Anthropologist*, 103: 45–59.

Olivera, A. R. (2001) Apropiación de un espacio supuesto público. Unpublished class exercise for "Appropriation of Space" course, MA Program in Urbanism and Development. University of Guadalajara, Mexico.

Palacios, J.J. (2001) "Globalization and E-Commerce: Growth and Impacts in Mexico," Project Globalization of E-Commerce of the Center for Research on Information Technology and Organizations (CRITO) at the University of California at Irvine. Available: http:// www.crito.edu (accessed July 20, 2004).

Proshansky, H. (1978) "The City and Self Identity," *Environment and Behavior*, 10: 149–169.

Reed, T. (2000) "New Public Spaces in America," available: http://www.zerohour.net (accessed May 1, 2004).

Rifkin, J. (2000) *La Era del Acceso: La Revolución de la Nueva Economia*, Barcelona: Paidós.

Ritzer, G. (2000) *The McDonaldization of Society: An Investigation into the Changing Character of Contemporary Social Life*, Thousand Oaks, CA: Pine Forge Press.

Sansot, P. (1976) "Notes on the Concept of Appropriation," in P. Korosec (ed.) *Appropriation of Space: Proceedings of the 3rd Conference of the International Architectural Psychology Society*, Louvain la Neuve, Belgium: Coopérative Universitaire de l'Université de Louvain-La-Neuve.

Sennett, R. (2004) "Corners: Resistance and Surprise," in M. Solá-Morales (ed.) *Cities, Corners*, Barcelona: Forum Barcelona/Lunwerg Editores.

Solá-Morales, M. (2004) "Cities, Corners," in M. Solá-Morales (ed.) *Cities, Corners*, Barcelona: Forum Barcelona/Lunwerg Editores.

Whyte, W. F. (1943) *Street Corner Society*, Chicago: The University of Chicago Press.

Zardini, M. (2004) "Corners of the Periphery, Where Are You?" in M. Solá-Morales (ed.) *Cities, Corners*, Barcelona: Forum Barcelona/Lunwerg Editores.

Zukin, S. (1995) *The Cultures of Cities*, New York: Blackwell.

Chapter 6

Urban Slippage

Smooth and Striated Streetscapes in Bangkok

Kim Dovey and Kasama Polakit

The typical inner city neighborhood of Bangkok is dense, diverse and subject to continuous pressure for change arising from traffic, modernization, commerce, tourism and migration. One of the key characteristics is instability: the identity of the place can be defined by its slippages, by the fluidity of forms, practices and meanings. A variety of proprietors, residents, hawkers and others use and appropriate public space for a broad range of functions, desires and practices. The use and meaning of public space are subject to both local and global flows of time and space with shifting meanings of secular/sacred, private/public and legal/illegal. This looseness is linked to a high population density and intense demand for the use of space but also to negotiable forms of governance and urban planning. Much of urban Bangkok has a multiplicitous urban character, held "in place" by the inertia of a robust urban morphology and a certain strictness of cultural coding.

Our aim here is to adopt the conceptual opposition of smooth and striated space from the work of Deleuze and Guattari as a framework for understanding the use and meaning of urban space in Ban Panthom, an old inner-city neighborhood of Bangkok. Our point is more practical than theoretical: such concepts are tools for re-thinking urban space, for prizing open the phenomenon of loose space. Our hope is that they may be useful for understanding complex and labyrinthine urban districts such as Ban Panthom that do not submit easily to the gaze of urban analysis. The conception of "smoothness" focuses attention on the "slippages" and movements of use and meaning, on the zones between categories and on the relationship between rhizomatic practices of everyday life and hierarchical systems of spatial control.

One can construe the looseness of public space in Ban Panthom as a conjunction of loose forms (or loose parts), loose practices (behaviors, functions) and loose meanings. Looseness of form is primarily linked to the loose parts which move around this neighborhood with a high level of flexibility—food stalls, hawker trolleys, chairs, tables, laundry, retail goods and vehicles. Looseness of function refers to the manner in which the same space is used for a multiplicity of functions either at the same time or different times. One function may slip into another or be camouflaged within it. The idea of loose meanings refers to instabilities of symbolic connotation and identity often based on ambiguous cultural codes and multiple naming. These loose forms, practices and meanings are inextricably linked in urban space as buildings and spatial territories slip between categories and one form, function or meaning folds into another.

Cultural Context

One of the traps in a study such as this is the tendency to see Bangkok through the lens of Western theory as an example of a more general order of "Asian" cities or streetscapes. Yet such Western theory has long been engaged in deconstructing its own limits. The "Asian" city is one of the products of what Said (1978) calls "Orientalism," a discourse that orients and stabilizes the identity of the West against the "Other" of the "Orient." Edensor (1998) bravely enters into this West/Other dichotomy with his description of the "Indian street" that he contrasts with the increasingly regulated, desensitized and over-determined "Western street." He celebrates the Indian street as a tangle of spatial forms and practices, smells, values and representations situated in opposition to the Western street in the context of theories of the *flâneur*, Foucault's (1997) heterotopic spaces and de Certeau's (1993) resistant walker. But to what extent is such "disorder" a mythic construction of the Western gaze, and what is the value of Western theory to its interpretation? While Indian and Thai streetscapes may be no more alike than those of North America and Australia, if there is a thread that unites many of the poorer streets of what Seabrook (1996) calls the "cities of the South," it is the relative weakness of the state in controlling a vibrant (if at times desperately poor) local economy. One consequence is slippage or looseness.

These slippages are accentuated in the cultural context of Thailand. While we have no desire to reduce this context to any kind of essentialism, the meanings of its urban places and the various spatial practices within them need to be considered in light of local nuances of culture, nationalism, religion and authority (Askew 1994). Thai social structure is strongly ordered by hierarchical oppositions of older/younger, parent/child, and higher/lower social status. Principles of deference permeate social practice at every level from the family to the nation (Morell and Chai-anan 1981). At the top of the hierarchy is a triangular formation of nation/religion/monarch. The King is "father" of the nation and Buddhism is the national religion and the source of moral order and merit. The authority of the state and the military has long been based on the ability to harness governance to this legitimating triumvirate (Reynolds 1991).

The authoritarianism of this hierarchy is, however, strongly mediated by a Buddhist belief in community, justice and the sanctity of life (Jackson 1991). The social hierarchy is geared to a conceptual opposition of order versus confusion (Morell and Chai-anan 1981). Confusion (*woon wai*) is a state of nuisance, instability or anarchy that upsets the social order. The high value placed on a stable social order links to a belief that only rigid and authoritarian forms of governance can maintain stability (Hindley 1976; Dhiravegin 1992). One might expect such a social structure to produce a highly ordered and rigidly controlled urban morphology. Yet in many ways it is the opposite: urban regulations are widely transgressed and the Thai streetscape can be very confusing, especially from a Western viewpoint.

Thailand has generally been very open to Western ideas and technologies (Reynolds 1998) and Thai culture is characterized by a remarkable capacity to absorb new ideas, beliefs, names and meanings without displacing existing ones. Through layering and juxtaposition, one can have both the traditional and the modern, Thai and Western, both the rule and its transgression (Wilson 1962). There is a great deal of slippage in spatial discourse and places often have several names which persist in common usage. Such different names can service different interests with different meanings that are often left unclear (O'Connor 1990). In the Thai context, oblique communication is often more effective than direct language; conflicts and contradictions are often avoided rather than resolved. New ideas, forms and spatial practices tend to form layers and juxtapositions rather than displacements. The social order and the urban order are at the same time both strongly hierarchically controlled and highly fluid.

Smooth and Striated Space

The tension between spatial practices and codes of control will be explored through the theoretical lens of Deleuze and Guattari's (1987) distinction between "smooth" and "striated" space. The term "striated" captures the etymological links to the Latin: *stringere* "to draw tight," linked to "strict" and "stringent." This is contrasted with the "smooth," which is not to be read as homogeneous but rather as without boundaries or joints. Smoothness implies a slipperiness and movement where one slides seamlessly from one site (place, meaning, image) to another. Deleuze and Guattari tease out this distinction through a number of further conceptual oppositions. In ontological terms, the opposition between the striated and the smooth is linked to that between "being" and "becoming." Striated space is where identity has become stabilized, as opposed to the smooth space of becoming. Striated space is structured like a tree, hierarchically organized and deeply rooted with a vertical stem. The smooth is identified with rhizomatic modes of practice—migrating horizontally within the interstices of a larger order. Such rhizomatic structures are contrasted with the tree-like structures of hierarchical control. Striated space is identified with sedentary dwelling practices and territorial roots while the smooth is identified with nomadic movement across surfaces. Smooth space is the space of the refugee and the migrant, a field of vectors (social, economic, historic, political, cultural, aesthetic and environmental) upon which we ride or slide, like surfing on the crest of turbulence. The politics of striated space is based on hierarchical social control, with identity and authority clearly demarcated. This contrasts with smooth spaces of resistance where power is practiced through camouflage and the blurring of identity and authority.

The smooth and the striated are not types of space or place so much as tools for thought; every real place is a mixture of the two in a reciprocal relation where they are constantly "enfolded" into each other (Deleuze and Guattari 1987: 486). "Folding" is a liminal condition associated with "becoming." A labyrinth is a multiplicity of spatial folds where the twists and turns of lanes and alleys disorient its subjects, producing a sense of both desire and danger (Deleuze 1993). The effect of the maze is to amaze. The folds of the labyrinth are its labia where a dominant order folds into its other as one loses the controlling gaze over spatial order. The fold is not a crease or a boundary, rather, it involves a focus away from things, elements or points of stability and onto the movements and foldings between them. This focus on the "between" is also a way to rethink binary and dialectic oppositions as an enfolding of each other. For our purposes here this entails the enfolding of public/private, sacred/secular, temporary/permanent and legal/illegal. From this perspective there is a focus on flows rather than points of stability and particularly on "flows of desire." Space is not a stable framework within which things or subjects exist but is constructed through flows of desire between them. Deleuzian thinking suggests that desire is the immanent productive force of life itself without which there is no city.

This attempt to re-think the city in terms of rhizomatic networks shows significant links to the urban design theories of Jacobs (1965) and Alexander (1965), who both opposed modernist planning ideologies which sought to stamp a rational, hierarchical order onto the city. Their approaches, while different, are united in the celebration of the diverse flows of urban life and in a quest to understand underlying principles of urban vitality, perhaps best encapsulated in Alexander's (1965) dictum: "A city is not a tree." His insight was to show how the vitality of urban life can be killed by rigid, hierarchical, tree-like thinking where the synergies of urban life are eradicated. Jacobs (1965) found the conditions for urban diversity in the mixing of functional zones, in the synergies between functions which sustain economic vitality and the vitality of public street life. These conditions are also found in the permeable structure of urban spatial networks, in a relatively small grain-size of urban fabric, and in the relatively high urban densities necessary to sustain dense pedestrian networks and pools of use. The work on linking urban spatial structure to social structure and urban economics has been taken further in Hillier and Hanson's (1984) work on "spatial syntax analysis" and urban "movement economies" (Hillier 1996), with a focus on urban spatial structure and the importance of the relative "depth" in mediating social relations between residents and between residents and visitors. The depth of urban space in this sense relates to the continuum between public and private space—deeper urban spaces are those that are located farther from, or are less visible from, the public gaze of the busier streets.

Urban Morphology

Ban Panthom is an old, inner city neighborhood of about 17 hectares, a short walk north of the tourist district of Khao San Road in Banglamphu and ten minutes east of the Chao Phraya River. It is bounded by an elevated freeway on the northeast and the traffic artery of Samsen Road on the northwest, with a derelict canal and minor street on the southwest and southeast respectively (Fig. 6.1). The area is primarily residential at a density of about 100 dwelling units per hectare; however densities are difficult to measure since official figures are quite inaccurate and there is a significant "floating population" who officially live elsewhere. The area is well served by public transport with many bus lines passing nearby. Like all of Bangkok, this was once a water-based settlement with a dense network of canals (*khlongs*), nearly all of which are now replaced by streets. While the site remains bordered by one of the city's largest surviving *khlongs* (Khlong Banglamphu), the last water taxi operated there in 1996, and while it is still used a little for fishing and swimming, it is heavily polluted.

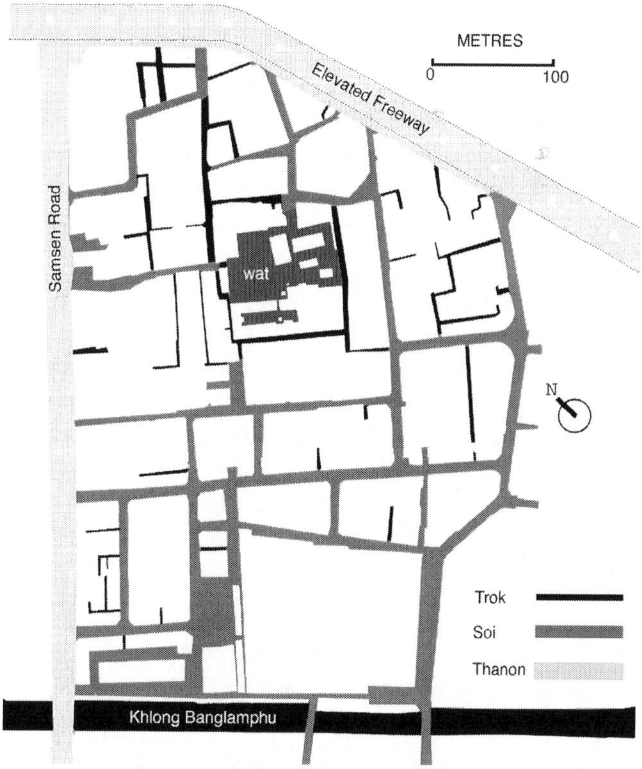

6.1
Ban Panthom: urban morphology and street hierarchy

The district centers on the temple and school compound of Wat Mai. In the southwest of the district are the remains of one of the city's major marketplaces which have long attracted entertainment functions and transgressive activities such as prostitution and drug use. Ban Panthom has been subject to major disruptions and changes during the twentieth century—a series of fires, subdivisions, filling of canals, road widening, new construction, migration (from northeast Thailand), new factories (including a large water treatment plant), growing tourism, removal of the marketplace and persistent attempts by authorities to eradicate illegal activities.

The street and pedestrian network of Ban Panthom can be divided into a street hierarchy of *thanon* (main street), *soi* (side street) and *trok* (pedestrian street or lane). The neighborhood is bordered by a major *thanon* to the southeast, and is penetrated by a network of *sois* and *troks* before opening into the *wat* compound at the center with a range of temples, religious buildings, a school and monks' quarters (Fig. 6.1). The *soi* is defined by being secondary to a main street, deeper into the neighborhood while still carrying vehicular traffic (Fig. 6.2). *Sois* often have no sidewalks; indeed many of them have been formed through an enforced widening of the narrower *trok* by removing the front section of houses. The definition of a *trok* is linked to the width of pathway (extending from half a meter to 3 meters wide) and to the exclusion of cars (Fig. 6.3). The word *trok* spans the English terms lane, alley and walkway except that the *trok* is generally lined with buildings and main entrances. It is not a "back," except in the sense of being internal to the block structure. The absence of cars and the capacity for a richer street life best characterize the *trok*. *Troks* are widely used for children's play, watching television and a broad range of economic and social activities. A number of *troks* have become *sois* as they have been widened for cars and appropriated for parking, retail and commercial functions. Those in the community over about 40 years of age refer to a number of streets with car parking and traffic as *troks*, after their former names, character and use. Community members over about 60 years of age tend to refer to all of the streets in the area as *troks*.

The public circulation network is also identified by places known as *paksoi* and *paktrok*—the entry points to the *soi* or *trok*—node points with a concentration of commercial and social life (Fig. 6.4). At lower levels of this street hierarchy, access and ownership become ambiguous. The smaller *troks* are often difficult to pass through due to narrowness or blockage by domestic appropriation. Some *paktrok* locations function as control points for the community within: strangers are asked their business and who they are looking for. The boundary between public and private thus becomes ambiguous in terms of both ownership and access.

Wat Mai is a temple compound of about a hectare incorporating temples, monks' quarters, cremation hall, school, community facilities and open space. The compound is enclosed within a 3m-high fence, with two entries for cars and two for pedestrians. *Wats* in Thailand are divided hierarchically into "royal" and "common" types; Wat Mai is a common *wat*. Much of the surrounding residential land is owned by the *wat* and inhabited by poorer residents; it is regarded by many locals as a slum.

6.2
Typical *soi* in Ban Panthom

6.3
Typical *trok* in Ban Panthom

The built form of Ban Panthom comprises a very broad range of building types, including the traditional temple architecture of the *wat* compound, two-storey detached teak houses, modern apartments and hotels, shop-houses in various styles, factories and modern detached houses behind high walls. There is also a good deal of makeshift housing in concrete, timber, corrugated steel and plastic. The row-house type, 4m wide and two to five storeys high, dominates the study area, particularly along the main roads and *sois*. The housing in smaller *troks* is less formal and more makeshift. The functional mix includes residential, office, retail, industrial, educational, religious and entertainment uses with a predominance of residential on the interior of the neighborhood. However, it is impossible to map functions fully: first, because activities are often mixed on the same site, especially a mix of residential, retail, industry and services; and second because there is considerable blurring between functions within the same space.

Public/Private

The boundary between private and public space is subject to continuous negotiation, particularly with regard to the ways in which private activities spill onto edges of the *sois* and *troks* (Figs 6.2, 6.3). Local, unwritten rules play a key part in the control and use of public space, increasingly so as one moves deeper into the *soi* and *trok* network. Most *sois* do not have defined sidewalks, yet in the section near the main streets the pavement is marked with yellow stripes to indicate the extent to which shops are permitted to appropriate the space, ensuring enough room for vehicles and pedestrians. As one moves deeper into the neighborhood, however, these striations are transgressed or disappear altogether and the boundary is managed in a fluid and local manner based on a shared understanding that the traffic—both pedestrian and vehicular—must continue to flow (Fig. 6.2). The zone of ambiguous space on the *sois* is generally up to 2m wide and is used for domestic and retail activities as well as car parking. There is a tacit, but loose, agreement that adjacent residents or proprietors control this space in front of buildings. Domestic activities include washing and drying clothes, gardening, dish washing, cooking, conversing and watching television. Retail activities include dining, product display and car repair workshops. When traffic eases, the streets are used for ball games and exercise.

Car parking on busy Samsen Road (on the northwest edge of the site) is regulated by police, yet within the Ban Panthom neighborhood it becomes subject to a set of local rules, framed in turn by the prospect that if traffic were blocked, then the authorities would act. Property owners have a tacit right to park in front of their buildings; however, this is not a legal right and there are no car parking spaces marked. Control over such parking is generally enforced by the use of territorial markers such as small screens and steel frames (often doubling as clothes driers) when the household car is not there. This system is enforced locally rather than officially; cars parked in violation of territorial rules are sometimes scratched. Beyond the semi-private zones in front of dwellings, people may park anywhere that does not block

6.4
***Paksoi* intersection**

traffic. This rule has the tendency to turn the larger intersections into small parking lots (Fig. 6.4). Those wishing to park often compete for this space with mobile street vendors. Some intersections are almost entirely appropriated by cars under repair from nearby workshops. Car parking on intersections often competes, on a first-come-first-served basis, with a busy breakfast market in food stalls and hawkers. The available social space of the neighborhood is clearly reduced by this fluid market in street parking.

One can construe the loose parts of this urban ecology as a continuum, from the almost continuously moving hawker trolleys to stalls that have become almost permanent. Itinerant street vendors range from those carrying goods, pushing carts and riding tricycles to those driving mini pick-up trucks very slowly. They move along the *sois* and *troks* but also gather to wait at the *paktrok* and *paksoi* intersections. Some of the mobile trolleys are set up in regular locations as temporary stalls for various periods of the day and night. This set-up may include a seat and umbrella for the vendor and even seats and tables for customers. Stands or trolleys are often wheeled or trucked into specific sites on a regular schedule. In some cases they remain permanently and even become extensions to the architecture over time (Fig. 6.4). In these ways, loose parts gradually become almost permanent yet camouflaged among the mobile stalls and trolleys.

On a larger scale this blurring between architecture and furniture becomes a blurring between renovations and new buildings. In a bid to create space for public sidewalks, building regulations require new construction to be set back 2m from the property line. The effect has been to stimulate an elaborate camouflage whereby buildings are "renovated" until they are completely replaced without setback. On one large site encompassing ten row-houses and a hotel, all of the façades were replaced with a single façade and no setback. Then all the buildings were demolished and replaced with a factory. This enabled the process to be defined as a "renovation."

Day/Night

The many appropriations of public space reach a sophisticated level on some sidewalks which different restaurants appropriate on a rhythmic cycle. One piece of sidewalk in front of a corner shop-house is the site for three different enterprises. In the morning from 6 to 9a.m. the shop-house is closed but the sidewalk is a breakfast stall selling fast food (coffee and pastry). From 10a.m. to 4p.m. the breakfast stall is replaced by another food stall and the shop opens to sell beverages and snacks. From 5 to 10p.m. it is replaced by an evening restaurant while the shop remains open for drinks. The operators/owners of the sidewalk stalls pay the proprietor for space, water and electricity as well as a "fee" to local government officers, part of which disappears as graft. Thus the income from customers flows in six different directions between the adjacent proprietor, three restaurants, the local authority and its officers.

Samsen Road, the major artery lining the northwestern edge of the neighborhood, shows dramatic daily transformations of use. During the day the 2.5m-wide strip of sidewalk is lined with shops about every 4 meters (Fig. 6.5). The traffic is heavy and noisy, making sidewalk conversation difficult during the day. The produce from some shops is displayed on the adjacent sidewalk and an occasional stall may be set up, but itinerant vendors are not permitted. After 6p.m. this spatial regime changes as shops close their roller doors and mobile restaurant stalls are wheeled out from storage in the *trok* network. By 7p.m. Samsen Road has become a busy strip of evening restaurants that are nearly all independent of the shops which line the footpath (Fig. 6.6). The spatial pattern is a series of fold-up tables and chairs against the shop-fronts, food stalls occupying the outer edge of the footpath, and a narrow walkway running in between. Due to the narrowness of the sidewalk, vendors use the gutter for serving space, food preparation and washing-up. As the evening traffic eases on Samsen Road, cars are permitted to park there and these "kitchens" compete with cars which then park further into the street.

This evening dining strip is technically illegal and is sustained by regular "fines" vendors pay to local authorities. Some of this payment is creamed off as graft and the remainder operates as a form of "rent." Despite its illegality, this is a sustainable system where the "fines" are matched to the food market, the vendors' profits and the regulators' salaries. The "fine" is also a "fee" in the sense that it is calibrated to ensure that the flow of money continues. This slippage between a "fine,"

6.5 and 6.6
Day and night on Samsen Road

a "bribe" and a "fee" keeps the fluid urban order under loose control. A stricter and fairer regime would legitimate the practice, establish a licensing fee and eliminate the graft. However, such a regime could eliminate the incentive for enforcement as it would establish a much more stable spatial order with markings on the pavement and higher prices.

Beyond the edges of the sidewalk, the local jurisdiction ends and the appropriation of the roadway becomes a matter for the police. Yet police control over parking diminishes, along with the traffic, after 6p.m., when parked cars begin to appropriate the traffic lanes. While the gutter and traffic lanes establish very clearly marked boundaries between both jurisdictions and functions, as the night wears on, these striations dissolve. Shop owners also have tacit rights over the use of the sidewalk and many of the evening vendors also pay them for rent and electricity. Other shop owners have lined the sidewalk edge with large, immoveable potted plants that screen the traffic and prevent food vendors from using the sidewalk during the evening.

Legal/Illegal

With its history as one of Bangkok's major market and entertainment districts, Ban Panthom has long been the site of a range of illicit activities, such as prostitution, gambling and drug use, which have proven difficult to eradicate. The sex industry in Ban Panthom was traditionally geared to the working classes, with the more recent influence from tourism. The industry developed through a series of motels which have long operated as camouflage for prostitution: single men who register are asked if they want a woman. These are primarily modern buildings of about five stories occupying large sites, surrounded by walls which offer high levels of privacy. They were originally designed as "curtain motels" where a curtain is drawn around the parking space adjacent to the room to secure complete privacy. The name "hotel," their use for regular accommodation and as love hotels with rooms available by the hour provide additional camouflage.

Since the proliferation of AIDS in the 1980s, attempts have been made to close down the prostitution industry; the greatest effect in this neighborhood has been the transformation of a number of hotels into apartments. Single rooms without kitchens, these apartments fill a need for cheap accommodation (often rented by students) and they stimulate the local market in cheap street food. The sex trade continues in the hotels along a major *soi* that extends east from Samsen Road south of the *wat*. This *soi* has a distinctly different character to the rest of the district and forms a semantic barrier between the north and south of the neighborhood; many locals are fearful of the area and distrustful of its inhabitants. Some restaurants on Samsen Road are geared to the sex trade through a certain slippage in the services of the waitress. Tourism has had a major impact on the sex trade in recent years; most of the hotel signs are now in English and the car-park curtains have largely disappeared.

While the sex trade extends from Samsen Road into the Ban Panthom neighborhood, other illegal activities tend to take place in the *troks* located at the greatest depth from the busy *sois* and *thanon*. The deepest public spaces in Ban Panthom are found in the *troks* immediately to the south of the *wat* compound, contiguous with it yet without direct access. Most of the illegal activities in Ban Panthom occur here and groups of children playing at the outskirts often operate as lookouts for the gambling that happens here. The only group of homeless people in the neighborhood is also based here, sleeping in semi-permanent beds beside the *trok*. While their place is scarcely secure, this is their home; their occupation is making garlands and they are accepted in the community. Indeed, many of these homeless people once lived on a canal running along the eastern edge of the *wat* before it was filled in 1989 to create what has become a rather derelict *soi*. On this *soi*, close to the deepest intersection, a small corner has been screened off with a curtain and a makeshift public urinal has been installed. This deepest *trok* network is easy to bypass and is often avoided by other members of the community. An interesting dimension of this deepest space of the Ban Panthom area is that it is unclear just whose police jurisdiction it lies within. Those running the gambling pay graft to each of the police authorities, and the ambiguity enables both authorities to act as if the problem belongs to the other. Transgressive activities slip through smooth urban spaces between jurisdictions.

Sacred/Secular

The central compound of Wat Mai establishes a conceptual opposition between the notionally sacred center of the *wat* compound and the notionally secular space of the surrounding streets (Fig. 6.7). While the compound has gates to control vehicular access, it is permanently accessible to pedestrians. The grounds within comprise the largest open space in the neighborhood and are generally packed with car parking which at times largely blocks the entry to the sacred space within the buildings. The

6.7
Main entry to *wat* compound

open space is used by neighborhood children when the parking eases, and it is cleared for festive occasions. The *wat* is surrounded by the poorest parts of the neighborhood, often makeshift housing on land owned by the *wat* where the poor have long taken sanctuary under Buddhist benevolence. Until relatively recently the *wat* was also surrounded by brothels, which made royal patronage difficult because the royal family could not visit. As a result, several former hotels/brothels at the entrance to the *wat* have been converted into apartments. The main entry *soi* has been transformed with an entry gateway on the main road; parking has been regulated along much of this *soi* which is lined with large potted plants.

The slippage between sacred and secular space extends throughout the street network. In the early morning the streets have a semi-religious character as monks in saffron robes walk through the network of streets where they accept food offered by residents, an exchange known as "merit-making" with benefits to both monks and residents. The streets are subject to dramatic shifts of meaning and behavior at particular annual festivals. During the celebration of the Chao Phor Nu shrine in September, the car park of an entertainment complex becomes a sacred space and the entire *soi* network of Ban Panthom becomes a dragon pathway as parades move through the *sois*, past temporary altars set up in front of shop-houses.

Several smaller sacred sites are located throughout the neighborhood, mostly comprising sacred trees festooned with fabric, garlands and small shrines. The locations of these range from the smallest *troks* to the most public spaces. These sacred sites also have spin-offs for other activities. A sacred phallic image with its associated tree and shrines partially blocks the footpath on busy Wusut Kasat Road.

6.8
Sidewalk shrine with car workshop

The adjacent proprietors, a restaurant and car repair shop, have taken the opportunity provided by this sacred blockage to extend it for secular uses, and much of the street is blocked by cars under repair (Fig. 6.8).

Class and Ethnicity

One of the ways in which residents see Ban Panthom is through a lens of social status—a mix of wealth, social class and ethnicity. The poorest residents are homeless and occupy the deepest levels of neighborhood space in a ring that encircles the *wat* compound. However, not all of the housing in this zone is low income. Indeed, most of the wealthiest housing is located in a zone to the southeast of the *wat* that overlaps the poorer areas. In Thailand, ethnic differences are perceived to occur along two axes. The first is between different kinds of Thai nationals: Thais of Chinese and Indian descent as well as Isaan (northeast Thailand) migrants are all conceived in varying degrees as "other" to mainstream Thai culture. These identities are loosely linked to districts within Ban Panthom: the wealthier Chinese are largely identified with the southern district and the Muslim Indian population is identified, largely as landowners, with the southwestern corner near the former marketplace. The people from Isaan are identified with the poorer areas surrounding the *wat* and are often referred to as "migrants." There is also a considerable population of students who are not identified with particular groups. The second axis is an opposition of all Thai nationals to foreigners. In Ban Panthom the foreign influence is considerable as tourist activity spills over from the nearby Kao San Road area, as the sex trade becomes more global and as cheap guesthouses open for backpackers.

Slippages, Resistances, Flows

Ban Panthom is a highly complex urban landscape that is easy to characterize as chaotic, but at the same time it is a highly structured neighborhood offering a stable experience of home and community to most of its inhabitants. Its labyrinthine spatial structure embodies its resilience and resistance to urban change. The district is subject to the flows of tourists but does not have a sufficient level of symbolic capital to be transformed by them. It is subject to considerable vehicular traffic and would certainly be safer and more inhabitable if it were more protected from traffic.

Our theoretical lens here has been the distinction that Deleuze and Guattari make between smooth and striated space. We have translated the idea of smoothness into various forms of slippage or looseness—loose parts, loose practices and loose meanings. In many ways the character, the social and formal identity, of the place is defined by these slippages: by a slipping between categories, by the movements through which one thing, practice or meaning becomes another. Functions slip from house to shop to factory, from hotel to brothel, from sidewalk to restaurant to shrine to car park, from laundry to café to gambling house. Hawker trolleys become building renovations and renovations become demolitions. Boundaries between districts, practices, meanings and social classes are blurred. Meanings slip from sacred to profane, from public to private. Exchanges of money slip from a fine to a license to a bribe; *troks* become *sois* as domestic reproduction slips into market production and local becomes global.

These forms of smoothness, looseness or becoming are not all of a kind. One can construe the looseness of urban space as different kinds of juxtapositions between loose parts, loose practices and loose meanings. Some slippages may be characterized as unstable boundaries as in the limits to parking and between police jurisdictions. In other cases two or more forms, actions or meanings may combine to form a hybrid: the house that is also a shop; the television in the *trok*. Hybrid spaces may operate asymmetrically where one serves as camouflage for the other: the fine/bribe and hotel/brothel are of this order. Differences of form, practice and meaning may be serial where one becomes another over time, as the renovation becomes a new factory.

Despite the focus on slippages, our point is not to suggest that this is primarily smooth space. Smooth and striated are not separate kinds of space but are constantly turned into each other, to varying degrees and in different ways. As Deleuze and Guattari put it: "Nothing is ever done with: smooth space allows itself to be striated, and striated space reimparts a smooth space . . . all progress is made by and in striated space, but all becoming occurs in smooth space" (1987: 486).

One can understand the character of Ban Panthom as a continuously negotiated tension between smooth and striated. Not all urban space is equally smooth: one theme here is that the forms of striation become weaker, and urban space becomes smoother, as one moves deeper into the neighborhood. The urban street network is apparently hierarchical, with its structure of *thanon*, *soi* and *trok*, yet the lower levels of this hierarchy are increasingly rhizomatic rather than tree-like. Control by the state does not saturate the city and such control weakens with increasing depth from the major streets. It is interesting to compare this with the Foucauldian model of the Panopticon as a disciplinary technology that spatializes the power of the state by generating maximum visibility deep into a socio-spatial structure while eliminating social contact between subjects (Foucault 1980). In many ways Ban Panthom does the opposite; it structures a deeper realm of relatively free circulation (for locals) and high levels of social capital; this deeper zone of public space becomes relatively invisible and protected from state control.

Tensions between globalization and local tradition are played out along this opposition of shallow (main streets) and deep (*wat*, *soi* and *trok*). The main street, with its global franchise stores, takes the Western name of "road" while the *sois* and *troks* are more locally and ambiguously defined. Both the *wat* compound with its traditional architecture and the everyday life of the *troks* are strongly identified with local Thai urbanism along with Buddhist values of benevolence and justice. And this deep/shallow spatial opposition is also economic: the rhizomatic practices in the deeper spaces—the migrating hawkers and residents, children playing, homeless people and illicit activities—are strongly linked, for better and worse, to the livelihoods of the poor.

In Ban Panthom, the fixed striations of urban morphology, particularly the street hierarchy, are linked to many of the slippages, some of which in turn enable resistance to the erosion of that morphology. The striated morphology of the *trok* network clearly plays a key role in both enabling slippage and resisting change and thus confounds any simple opposition between smooth and striated space. The striations of urban space serve to protect the local community and its various transgressive practices. As one moves deeper into the neighborhood, it becomes less urban with less traffic, fewer random encounters and greater private appropriation of public space. The higher levels of social capital serve to demarcate and protect the deeper zone of urban space almost as a housing enclave would. Yet Ban Panthom is not an ideal neighborhood, and in this it contrasts markedly with the new gated housing developments that proliferate on the outskirts of Bangkok—local variations on the global production of instant place identity which are enclosed both literally and symbolically. While the highest levels of social capital in Ban Panthom are located in the deeper *troks*, with their makeshift housing and poorer residents, they also have the lowest levels of symbolic capital.

Finally, one can see Ban Panthom as a complex confluence of flows. Flows of people, vehicles, trolleys and furniture are linked in turn to flows of goods, services and money. These flows are based in flows of desire that become spatial practices as desires for food, services and goods lead to a movement economy of stalls, hawkers and pedestrians. Spiritual desires are evident in the *wat* and other sacred sites and in the parades of monks and festivities. Desires for sex and the necessary privacy it entails are evident in both the built form and semiotics of the hotel strip; these are linked in turn to flows of customers and money and then to the flows of sex workers from rural areas, to which the money flows in return. Desires to consume the ambience of the place and its food are increasingly evident in the flows of tourists. Desires of car owners and traffic engineers are evident in the push to turn *troks* into *sois*, countered by the desires of residents to protect the social space of the *troks*. The desire of authorities to create and maintain a higher degree of urban order is evident in regulations concerning parking and construction. These desires in turn intersect with, and are often countered by, the desires of residents to survive, to make a life and to make a profit.

There is a sense in which all cities are slippery to varying degrees, an insight that owes much to a range of urban theorists from Benjamin (1978) through Jacobs and Alexander to Sennett (1996) and others. One way of construing a city like Bangkok is to see it within a duality of both the Orientalism of East/West (Said 1978) and the economic divide construed as North/South (Seabrook 1996). While there are inherent problems with casting a Western gaze upon the Eastern city, we hope to have shown that it is possible to use some Western theory as a lens for examining Eastern urbanism without essentializing. The global economic divide also poses a fundamental challenge for urban design theories. How is the looseness of space outlined here geared to poverty? In Benjamin's famous account of a city from a different "south"—Naples of the early twentieth century—he exalted a property he termed "porosity" where:

> The stamp of the definitive is avoided. No situation appears intended forever, no figure asserts its "thus and not otherwise" . . . one can scarcely discern where building is still in progress and where dilapidation has already set in. For nothing is concluded. Porosity results . . . above all from the passion for improvisation . . . Even the most wretched pauper is sovereign in the dim dual awareness of participating, in all his destitution, in . . . Neapolitan streetlife.
>
> (Benjamin 1978: 166–168)

The property of porosity that Benjamin exalts has a lot in common with the smoothness and slippage outlined above. Slippage co-exists with poverty because it enables those without a place in the larger order to make a place in the interstices and cracks within it. There is a great deal at stake in our understanding of urban districts such as Ban Panthom and of mega-cities like Bangkok. It is easy to see Ban Panthom, like much of Bangkok and other cities of Southeast Asia, as a problem that needs to be "fixed." Yet this often paternalistic desire to fix it, whether it flows from the global expert or the local planner, may run counter to the way the place operates for, and is experienced by, its inhabitants. Urban place identity and practices of everyday public life are not easily tied down, and understanding them requires a loosening up of our thinking. While there is no easy way to overcome the problems of Orientalism or of poverty, perhaps it is possible to analyze and understand such South-Eastern urbanism without essentialism or despair.

Acknowledgments

Fieldwork for this study was conducted in 2001–2003, initially as part of PhD studies by Kasama Polakit. Primary methods were semi-structured interviews with residents, morphological mapping and street life observation. See: K. Polakit, "Bangkok Street Life: Transformations of Place in Three Communities," PhD dissertation, University of Melbourne, 2004.

References

Alexander, C. (1965) "A City Is Not a Tree," *Architectural Forum*, 122, April/May; reprinted in R. LeGates and F. Stout (eds) *The City Reader*, London: Routledge, 1996.

Askew, M. (1994) "Bangkok: Transformation of the Thai City," in M. Askew and W. Logan (eds) *Cultural Identity and Urban Change in Southeast Asia*, Melbourne: Deakin University Press.

Benjamin, W. (1978) *Reflections*, New York: Harcourt, Brace, Jovanovich.

de Certeau, M. (1993) "Walking in the City," in S. During (ed.) *The Cultural Studies Reader*, London: Routledge.

Deleuze, G. (1993) *The Fold*, Minneapolis: University of Minnesota Press.

Deleuze, G. and Guattari, F. (1987) *A Thousand Plateaus: Capitalism and Schizophrenia*, Minneapolis: University of Minnesota Press.

Dhiravegin, L. (1992) *Demi Democracy*, Singapore: Times Academic Press.

Edensor, T. (1998) "The Culture of the Indian Street," in N. Fyfe (ed.) *Images of the Street*, London: Routledge.

Foucault, M. (1980) *Power/Knowledge*, ed. C. Gordon, New York: Pantheon.

Foucault, M. (1997) "Of Other Spaces," in N. Leach (ed.) *Re-thinking Architecture*, London: Routledge.

Hillier, B. (1996) *Space Is the Machine*, Cambridge: Cambridge University Press.

Hillier, B. and Hanson, J. (1984) *The Social Logic of Space*, Cambridge: Cambridge University Press.

Hindley, D. (1976) "Thailand: The Politics of Passivity," in C. Neher (ed.) *Modern Thai Politics*, Cambridge, MA: Schenkman.

Jackson, P. (1991) "Thai-Buddhist Identity," in C. Reynolds (ed.) *National Identity and its Defenders*, Melbourne: Monash Papers on Southeast Asia, 25: 191–232.

Jacobs, J. (1965) *The Death and Life of Great American Cities*, Harmondsworth: Penguin.

Morell, D. and Chai-anan, S. (1981) *Political Conflict in Thailand*, Cambridge, MA: Oelgeschlager, Gunn & Hain.

O'Connor, R. (1990) "Place, Power and Discourse in the Thai Image of Bangkok," *Journal of the Siam Society*, 78: 62–82.

Reynolds, C. (1991) "Introduction," in C. Reynolds (ed.) *National Identity and its Defenders*, Melbourne: Monash Papers on Southeast Asia, 25: 1–40.

Reynolds, C. (1998) "Globalization and Cultural Nationalism in Modern Thailand," in J. Kahn (ed.) *Southeast Asian Identities*, Singapore: Institute of SEA Studies.

Said, E. (1978) *Orientalism*, London: Routledge.

Seabrook, J. (1996) *In the Cities of the South*, London: Verso.

Sennett, R. (1996) *Flesh and Stone*, London: Faber & Faber.

Wilson, D. (1962) *Politics in Thailand*, Ithaca, NY: Cornell University Press.

Chapter 7

Transforming Public Space into Sites of Mourning and Free Expression

Karen A. Franck and Lynn Paxson

Many peoples of the world follow an age-old tradition of leaving offerings in outdoor public places to express spiritual feelings. Often sites are designed or officially designated for this purpose, such as in cemeteries, outside churches and temples or in shrines and niches, but in other cases people choose their own locations. Offerings run the gamut from simple ties and ribbons, candles, food and flowers to personal possessions and elaborate constructions. The Native American practice of leaving offerings in the landscape is as old as oral history (Paxson 2006).

Recently, this tradition of using public space to express private sentiment has grown, becoming a nearly universal means of expressing feelings of loss and mourning following sudden, tragic events that result in unanticipated death. Expressions of personal grief, once largely confined to cemeteries and private homes, now appear in highly visible, public locations where they accompany expressed opinions on related social and political issues. Through the creation of richly embellished displays, people transform what had been mundane locations into places that invite physical and emotional engagement, encourage the expression of emotions and opinions and offer a platform for demonstrating individuality, difference and conflict. The memorials people create on their own initiative reveal the potential looseness of public space.

Spontaneous Memorials

The most frequent and widespread examples of spontaneous memorialization appear by the roadside where a cross with flowers, placed by family or friends, marks the site of a traffic fatality (Fig. 7.1). Studies have documented such roadside memorials in: Mexico (Henzel 1989); Australia (Hartig and Dunn 1998; Clark and Cheshire 2004); Texas (Reid and Reid 2001; Clark and Cheshire 2004); Oklahoma (Reid and Reid 2001); and other western and southwestern states in the US (Collins and Rhine 2003). Similar markings, by the road, have been noted in Greece and the UK, where Monger (1997) uncovered references to the practice dating back to 1896. It is very common now to see such roadside shrines throughout the US, particularly in New Mexico and nearby states with Hispanic populations, where the tradition dates back at least 200 years (Collins and Rhine 2003), possibly following the precedent of the Mexican and Spanish *descansos* ("resting places") where a cross marked the resting place for those who carried a coffin from the village church to the cemetery (Anaza *et al.* 1995).

Today in New York and other US cities, immediately after a murder or an accidental death, a collection of flowers, candles and other items often appears on sidewalks or adjacent to building entries where the death occurred, left by those who knew the victim as well as by strangers. Similar displays, but on a much larger scale and attracting significant public attention, have emerged in cities in many parts of the world immediately following the sudden deaths of well-known public figures, the killings of students and terrorist attacks. Drawing upon existing research and the authors' own observations in New York City after September 11, this chapter focuses primarily on spontaneous memorializing that followed four events: (1) the assassination of Yitzhak Rabin in Tel Aviv in 1995; (2) the bombing of the Murrah Federal Office Building in Oklahoma City in 1995; (3) the killings at Columbine High School in Littleton, Colorado in 1999; and (4) the attack on the World Trade Center in New York City in 2001.

In all these cases, without official sanction or coordinated planning, citizens transformed public spaces into sites of mourning. The introduction to the exhibit "Missing: Streetscape in a City in Mourning" at the New York Historical Society in October 2001 captured this phenomenon very well:

> They neither asked permission from our city officials nor waited for religious or civil authority to say how we should respond. New Yorkers showed an amazing instinct and ability to use public space all over the city to gather and to express themselves and to give an opportunity to others to do the same.

It is both the immediacy of the memorial's creation and the absence of official organization that have led researchers to use the terms "spontaneous memorials" (Haney *et al.* 1997; Senie 1999), "spontaneous commemoration" (Engler 1999; Haskins and DeRose 2003) and "spontaneous shrines" (Jorgensen-Earp and Lanzilotti 1998; Grider 2001; Santino 2004).

MOM
PAULINE
ROHRS

Location

Spontaneous memorials usually appear immediately after the tragic event at, or as close as possible to, the very site where the death(s) occurred. Perhaps the sites of these public deaths "take on the sense of the holy" (Jorgensen-Earp and Lanzilotti 1998: 159) or a "sacred quality" (Haney *et al.* 1997). Immediately after the assassination of Prime Minister Yitzhak Rabin, following an evening peace rally at the Malchei Israel Square in Tel Aviv, people brought special stones to build a traditional *gal'ed*, or cairn, at the exact location of the shooting (Azaryahu 1996). Memorials also appear at other sites associated with the victims or the event. After the death of Princess Diana, which took place in Paris, memorials appeared: in Paris at the crash site and the hospital where she was taken; in London at Kensington Palace, Buckingham Palace and St James's Palace; at her family home in Althorp; and at British embassies and consulates in other countries (Jorgensen-Earp and Lanzilotti 1998).

In Oklahoma City, rescuers and others with access to the ruin of the Murrah building left messages on a cement slab right in the rubble (Linenthal 2001). People created the main memorial at the location closest to the site of the former building which remained accessible to the public: namely, a chain link fence erected to keep people out of what was first a crime scene and then a hazardous site. This came to be known as the "Memory Fence." The memorial for the Columbine killings was constructed across the street from the school, in Clement Park, as close as people as could get to the school itself. In the nearby high school parking lots, students also piled flowers and poems, photos and teddy bears on the cars and trucks of their murdered fellow students (Doss 2002).

Immediately after the terrorist attack in New York on September 11, 2001, citizens adopted all kinds of public spaces to express their feelings. Empty walls in public places, particularly in subways, train stations and bus stations, became covered with notes, photographs and drawings; a great many available vertical surfaces, including lamp posts, were affixed with the poignant "missing notices," displaying the name, photograph and physical description of persons lost in the disaster. Walls next to St. Vincent's Hospital and Bellevue Hospital became collages of poems, prayers and missing person notices. On the walls of fire stations throughout the city firefighters mounted the cards and notes the station had received, arranging bouquets of flowers on the sidewalk. At first, Manhattan below 14th Street was closed to non-residents and, partly for that reason, Union Square at 14th and Broadway became one of the most richly embellished and heavily visited memorial sites. When access below 14th Street resumed, Washington Square became the site of shrines (Fig. 7.2), and in October 2001, after Broadway in Lower Manhattan was reopened, the wrought iron fence at St Paul's Chapel, two blocks from the World Trade Center, fulfilled a similar purpose, as it became the location closest to the World Trade Center ruin that was open to the public.

7.1
Roadside memorial, Highway 30, Iowa

7.2
Construction fence, Washington Square Arch, New York City, September 2001

Appropriation

Through the placement of just one item and then gradual accumulation, what had been an ordinary public space becomes a memorial; what had been an anonymous and undifferentiated field becomes particularized and intimate. Widely divergent kinds of items and messages appear, often mixed together: crosses next to teddy bears; a poem about love and forgiveness next to a flag; a photograph of a loved one next to a t-shirt with an angry message on it. The mixture of disparate items "disavows the traditional separation of sacred and profane" (Haney *et al.* 1997: 164). What is left is often very personal (a victim's photograph, a letter or a poem) and may express strong emotions. Many contributors, but not all, leave their names and place of residence. In leaving messages at Malchei Israel Square and on the walls of City Hall, visitors often added their names, affiliations and where they came from. In New York after September 11, notes and drawings were sometimes signed. Often a family, school class or other group would indicate who they were and where they were from ("United we stand. The Brisben Family, South Carolina").

The vertical surfaces of walls, fences and lamp posts allow people to mount items so as to be easily seen and read, much like a display in a museum. At the Malchei Israel Square, after Rabin's assassination, people taped and pasted, wrote and spray-painted messages on all surfaces within the square, walls, railings, benches and even the Holocaust Memorial (Engler 1999). In New York City after September 11 drawings and writings attached to surfaces were far more common than graffiti, although the base of the statue of George Washington at Union Square was covered with the word "love" along with "no war" and "give peace a chance."

If the surface is a fence, items can be tied to or hooked on it. In Oklahoma City the surface area of the fence was very limited. Many of the text offerings were rolled up and inserted into the fence openings (Linenthal 2001). In New York, chain link fences around construction sites, such as one around the arch at Washington Square, took on a similar role. The wrought-iron fence at St Paul's Chapel on Broadway became another "memory fence," with the adjacent pavement offering a place for people to place candles and flowers, to stand and to move along in a linear fashion. Empty horizontal surfaces like ledges, tops of walls, and the tops of cement barriers offered locations for candles and other objects.

The first step seems to be the placing of objects but just as quickly the sites become places of pilgrimage, gathering, vigils and other rituals. Hours after the assassination of Yitzhak Rabin, thousands gathered at night in the open space of Malchei Israel Square (Azaryahu 1996). Over the subsequent weeks and months, large groups, mainly young people, stood in circles among the candles and flowers, reciting poems and singing peace songs (Engler 1999). One week after the assassination, on the day that concluded the customary Jewish mourning period, a memorial rally was held and the square was officially renamed after the slain leader. During the following year new political organizations started using the square as a site for activities supporting the peace process and protesting violence, with debates and petitions and distribution of materials (Fig. 7.3).

In Oklahoma City, the linear space along the fence enclosing the site of the bombing became a place to view the bombing site, a site of pilgrimage, drawing visiting political figures and thousands of tourists, and a place for rituals. Local church congregations held ceremonies at the fence (Doss 2002). For some survivors and family members "the fence has become a place to talk with the dead. Some people held birthday gatherings for deceased love ones at the fence" (Linenthal 1998: 3). Readings of the Bible, candlelight vigils and worship services were held at the shrine in Clement Park and memorial services were held in the park on the 2000 and 2001 anniversaries of the shootings (Doss 2002).

After September 11, Union Square was the site of candlelight vigils, prayer groups, singing and playing instruments. Informal rituals in New York frequently involved writing and drawing. Often large sheets of paper or white canvas and pens and markers were available. The wide open, hard pavement at Union Square allowed an NYU student to spread out large sheets of paper on the ground on the very afternoon of September 11. Sheets of canvas could also be hung on fences; as they filled up, volunteers provided new ones. Visitors to St Paul's Chapel filled 700 sheets of canvas that hung from the fence.

Spontaneous memorials attract commercial activities as well. In Oklahoma some people left poems with addresses for readers to obtain copies; others attempted to sell commemorative items (Linenthal 2001). During the two-week period of the memorial at Columbine, vendors sold sodas and hotdogs and local merchants advertised as they expressed their sympathy on large banners and signs visible from the street (Doss 2002). In New York immediately after September 11 vendors were

אותך, חבר
אמרת שהשלום זה בשביל
הילדים
PEACE
ליצחק רבין
שלום, חבר.
יצחק רבין
חבר, אתה זוכר?

selling photographs of the Twin Towers, intact and on fire, and t-shirts with images of the towers, the US flag and slogans. Subsequently vendors sold packets of pictures as well as small glass replicas of the towers. At Union Square some people clearly felt such commercial activity was inappropriate at a site of mourning and told vendors to move away.

Dynamic and Temporary

Spontaneous memorials begin with an empty space that is open to appropriation—that is, publicly owned and has sufficient space and physical qualities to allow for occupation and intervention—but, just as significantly, has not been officially designated for this use. What then happens is open-ended: the memorial's appearance is not regulated nor can its development be predicted. Unlike many cemeteries, there are no rules regarding what may be left and very little, if any, official control is exerted. A memorial's appearance changes over time as more objects are left, as messages fill up a sheet of canvas, as a full sheet is replaced with a clean one, as burned-out candles and withered flowers are removed, or as people re-arrange the collection of items.

Spontaneous memorials are temporary. Both their sudden appearance and subsequent disappearance interrupt the everyday routine of urban life, just as their physicality interrupts everyday space (Haskins and DeRose 2003). Their duration is largely determined by authorities who often base their decisions on the apparent "messiness" of the accumulation of items and their decay. Unlike traditional cultures such as those of Native Americans and Buddhists, mainstream cultures in the US and Israel have no tradition of allowing material offerings to decay over time. Therefore, many see the dead flowers, burned-out candles and rain-drenched, smeared sheets of paper as messy and possibly a sign of disrespect. The solution is to remove them and in some cases to preserve them for later formal display.

One month after Rabin's assassination, the city government cleaned up the pools of wax and removed offerings from the pavement. They attempted to remove the graffiti, but as they did so new messages appeared on the freshly painted walls (Engler 1999). The night before the dedication of the permanent memorial, authorities removed the *gal'ed*, indicating that it would be saved and exhibited in some future museum dedicated to Rabin (Engler 1999). Two books were published about the graffiti at the site; large photos of the early graffiti, which appeared in an art exhibit, were later added to one wall of the site as a permanent exhibition.

7.3
Graffiti on poster composed of children's drawings, Rabin Square, Tel Aviv, 1996. On poster: "You said peace was for the children." Some graffiti: "The blame is on us."

From the beginning, items left in Oklahoma City were regularly collected. As of 2001, 26,768 artifacts had been cleaned and catalogued (Linenthal 2001). As at other sites, the collecting seemed driven by two concerns: that the fence was getting too full and messy and that the erosion and weathering of items were disrespectful. Respect is thus shown through preservation. The Colorado Historical Society collected and preserved many of the items from Clement Park (Doss 2002).

Similarly, at Union Square in New York, a threat of heavy rainstorms on September 21 was enough for the Parks Department to clear the area of spontaneous memorials. However, various organizations including the Museum of the City of New York and the New York Fire Museum collected the durable items from many locations in New York to be preserved (Gardner and Henry 2002). St Paul's Chapel collected and preserved 230 boxes of artifacts from its fence.

Participating, Physically and Emotionally

Spontaneous memorials invite and encourage a high level of participation, both physical and emotional. Most of the items are small and they are often densely clustered. To see, to read, and especially to contribute to the memorial, one must come up close, enter into the space of the memorial and possibly touch it. A viewer might have to bend over or crouch down to see what has been left below eye level or stretch to see what is above. Reading letters and poems, viewing drawings take time and require concentration, as does composing one's own message. To view an entire display on a vertical surface, people move along it, negotiating the timing of their change in position with the movement of others. Other senses are also engaged: one may smell candles, incense, flowers; one may hear the quiet murmuring of conversation or possibly music or praying. In all these ways, even as a spectator only, spontaneous memorials engage senses beyond just the visual and invite movements, gestures and changes of position that are uncommon in everyday public life.

Those who start the memorial and those who subsequently contribute or participate in vigils or other rituals are actively creating a public space through their actions and demeanor. The range of movements and postures they adopt is broad. Writing and drawing might require stretching or bending over or even sitting on the pavement. Gathering in a circle, making origami cranes out of paper, praying, singing or playing music and reading the names of victims involve other kinds of movement and sensory experiences. People who are strangers to each other may speak, join hands, console one another and even hug or cry in each other's arms.

Engagement with the memorial is emotional as well. The impartial and rational urban citizen, walking quickly to catch a train or cross the street before the light changes, may now stop and feel moved. Emotions are strongly expressed in the contributions made to the memorial and strongly felt by its viewers, often visibly so. Spontaneous memorials transform the routine actions and demeanor of citizens: with clear expressions of grief and sorrow, through objects, actions, and demeanor citizens drop the emotionally neutral, impartial stance that, as Iris Marion Young has argued (1990c), is so common (and expected) in contemporary public life. And, albeit for a brief period, movement, gesture and bodily expressions of emotion are not denigrated or equated with a lack of objectivity and reason, as is commonly the case in other public discussions and debates (Young 1997).

7.4
Statue of George Washington, Union Square, New York City, September 2001

Designing and Curating

Members of the public design spontaneous memorials themselves through the items they contribute (and sometimes fabricate) and the ways they place them in the landscape. Often the placements are quite inventive as people make creative use of physical elements the sites have to offer. After September 11 the openings of drain pipes, awaiting use in construction, became the perfect place for single candles; lamp posts were good for wrapping the US flag and being the focus point of a radiating collection of candles and artifacts. A peace flag was placed in the hand of George Washington astride his horse and a US flag was hung below the horse (Fig. 7.4).

As dense collections of items that vary greatly in shape, size, color and texture, the memorials have an eclectic jumble-like appearance, but they are not chaotic. Often they are arranged with a sense of organization and appropriateness. Santino (2004) calls them "folk assemblages"; Grider (2001) describes them as "unmediated folk art assemblages." She notes the deliberateness of contributors, observing that in several memorials adjacent to walls and fences bouquets of flowers "flow like waves, breaking upon the vertical barrier. People place their floral and other offerings carefully to maintain this layered, wavy effect." Items also may be arranged symbolically or to form a message: candles to form the Star of David or the peace symbol or words at Rabin Square (Engler 1999).

At some sites, every effort is made to avoid any overlapping of writings and drawings; this was notable in New York after September 11. In other cases, particularly at Rabin Square, messages are pasted or written on top of each other, creating an intentional layering and collaging of texts. In an age of consumerism and commercialism, of the slick, the standard and the homogenized, this proliferation of the hand-made and hands-on, however crudely or elegantly crafted, stands out. The density, mixture and handmade nature of spontaneous memorials distinguishes them from the more controlled, sanitized and commercialized spaces of the city (Haskins and DeRose 2003) and from the more austere and abstract qualities of most official memorials. In comparison to these spaces, spontaneous memorials appear "messy" or "makeshift" to some (Fig. 7.5).

Some citizens may act as "curators," taking responsibility for removing dead flowers and burned-out candles, for arranging and re-arranging items and for

7.5
Viewing fence, World Trade Center site, New York City, September 11, 2003

providing new sheets of paper or canvas. Relatives and friends of those who died may take this role, overseeing and maintaining mementoes they have left in certain sections of the memorial, as in Oklahoma City (Doss 2002). Citizens may engage in some censuring and editing: one contributor to a September 11 memorial, with the assent of others present, removed an obscene statement about Osama bin Laden; a father of one of the victims at Columbine removed the two crosses built to remember the students responsible for the killings (ibid.). As flowers die and candles burn down, the authorities may remove decaying items and collect durable artifacts for preservation, as they did in Oklahoma City (Linenthal 2001). During the Easter season just prior to the first anniversary of the bombing, the Government Services Administration removed large wooden crosses that had been placed near the lone tree that survived the bombing (Linenthal 2001). This action seemed to stimulate an increased number of smaller crosses placed on the fence itself.

Creating Meaning

The creation of elaborate and highly visible spontaneous memorials has rapidly become a social convention. The media disseminates countless images of them worldwide, and this is perhaps why people in different cities and different cultures now undertake similar actions and leave similar kinds of items—flowers, candles, photographs, cards, notes, other writings and drawings. Since the nineteenth century, fresh cut flowers have been used to express grief and commemoration; they now appear to be the most common item at spontaneous memorials. Journalists called the overwhelming number of bouquets left in commemoration of Princess Diana, usually still wrapped in plastic, the "flower revolution": between 10,000 and 15,000 tons of flowers were removed from various royal sites (Greenhalgh 1999).

Other kinds of items are particular to certain memorials and the events and victims they honor. Two things seemed particularly characteristic of the memorializing of Yitzhak Rabin at Malchei Israel Square; first, the proliferation of writings, both on paper and directly onto built surfaces, in a culture that places great importance on the written word (Engler 1999) and, second, the presence of several symbols of nation (Israel), religion (Judaism) and peace (universal). These included an oil drum once used for target practice at a site symbolic of Israel's War of Independence, the tablets of the commandments with only the fifth commandment shown ("thou shall not kill") and photographs and candles arranged to form the Star of David and the Menorah (Engler 1999) (Fig. 7.6).

In recognition of the children killed at the on-site day care center in Oklahoma City, teddy bears and representations of angels figured significantly among the offerings; sometimes angel wings were attached to the stuffed animals. Notes indicated that the children killed were now angels or with angels. The animals, balloons, dolls, clothes and toys may have been gifts to the children themselves; cards and notes were often addressed directly to them (Jorgensen-Earp and Lanzilotti 1998).

7.6
***Gal'ed*, oil drum pierced with bullet holes (once used for target practice at a site symbolic of Israel's War of Independence), Israeli flag, and temporary shelter for Jewish holiday of Succoth, Rabin Square, Tel Aviv, October 1996**

Visitors to the fence left hundreds of crosses, ranging from sticks tied together to plastic or wooden ones to those handmade knitted, crocheted and cross-stitched (Linenthal 2001). The fashioning of crosses from twigs and other scraps became one of the particular traditions of that site (Jorgensen-Earp and Lanzilotti 1998). Religious items also included many Christian scriptural citations, printed prayers, religious medallions and evangelical leaflets (Linenthal 2001) and hundreds of bracelets inscribed with "What Would Jesus Do?" (Doss 2002). Overall, text offerings were very important. People wrote on all kinds of materials—from their own clothing to programs, flyers and scraps of paper and cardboard, which indicated that while many of the offerings were planned in advance, others were created on the spot.

At Columbine, along with the common offerings, people left objects characteristic of high school students including athletic equipment, class photos, school jerseys and letter sweaters (Doss 2002) as well as teddy bears and stuffed animals. Some have interpreted the stuffed animals left at memorial sites, particularly in memory of children or teenagers killed, as connecting the separation of children from parents at bedtime to this ultimate separation at death or as representing the desire to comfort someone left alone in the dark (Fast 2003). As in Oklahoma City, Christian religious symbols and writings figured prominently (Doss 2002).

At New York shrines after September 11, Christian symbols and statements, in drawings, writings and artifacts were joined by items reflecting other religions and by a great mixture of other kinds of items, especially ones expressing strong patriotic sentiment; religious sentiments did not dominate. Indeed, at Union Square, flowers, US flags, candles, and calls for peace and love seemed to be the dominant themes. Strings of 1000 hand-made origami paper cranes, a Japanese tradition that has come to symbolize peace, graced several September 11 memorials as did large sheets of paper covered with children's handprints in paint. T-shirts with hand-written messages on them appeared at memorials, including ones from the New York City Fire and Police Departments and from departments in other cities. Many people made drawings featuring the World Trade Center Towers, often with a religious theme, such as an angel carrying the two towers aloft or Christ bearing them on his shoulders. Objects left for one purpose prior to the towers' collapse took on a different meaning afterwards. Firefighters changing into their gear to go into the World Trade Center, before the towers fell, hung their civilian boots from the spikes of the fence at St Paul's. The boots that were left, unclaimed, belonging to those who died became part of the memorial at the fence. Perhaps what was most characteristic were the sheets of paper, with pictures and written descriptions of the "missing," often left intact long after all hope was lost, with hand-written notes of sorrow added by friends and strangers.

The meaning of the site and the kinds of items left and ritual activities pursued seem to differ between those who lost friends or relatives and those who did not. For the former the location of the event becomes a place to talk directly to loved ones who died, to leave gifts, belongings and cards addressed to them personally and to celebrate their birthdays and anniversaries. After a game, the baseball team of a coach who was killed in the Murrah building bombing would come to the fence and leave a ball in his memory (Linenthal 2001). Survivors and rescue workers may also feel a different kind of connection to the site. In Oklahoma City, rescue workers wrote messages describing what the event meant to them and sometimes left gloves, hard hats, shirts or team patches (Linenthal 2001).

Interpreting, Contesting

Through the kinds of offerings they leave, often without resorting to words, individuals are representing, physically, their own responses to the event—flowers in grief and commemoration, flags for patriotism, paper cranes for peace, religious symbols for redemption and salvation. Each contribution can be seen as a kind of small narrative. Often the response, however, is made through text, text that voices opinions and interpretations of both the event and the social or cultural issues that surround it, which may help to explain it or provide lessons for the future. Unlike cemeteries or official memorials, commemoration of the deceased occurs alongside commentary on broader issues (Haney *et al.* 1997; Doss 2002; Santino 2004), with contributors often urging others to adopt a particular understanding of the event (Jorgensen-Earp and Lanzilotti 1998). In memorials to Princess Diana, people left cards and notes with references to the press's role in her death through their relentless pursuit of photographs (ibid.). In notes, prayer cards and leaflets, many visitors to the Memory

Fence in Oklahoma City indicated their belief that the bombing was a warning to those who do not believe in Christ or whose beliefs have lapsed (Linenthal 1998). Serving as a "public forum" the fence became the site for messages about non-violence and abortions and statements about conspiracies related to the bombing (ibid.).

Malchei Israel Square, already the site of peace rallies before Rabin's assassination, became even more of a platform for expressing political opinions and the desire for peace, hosting meetings, debates and forming new political alliances (Engler 1999). Even after the official Rabin memorial was completed, visitors continued to add their messages to the walls of the adjacent City Hall. When the walls were painted over, new messages protested the move: "The walls, witnesses of the murder, cannot and will not be silenced" (ibid.: 9). The texts "were deliberate acts of public participation and communication; they offered a way for people to . . . take a stand, to fuel the democratic process that became threatened" (ibid.: 9).

In New York, contributors to spontaneous memorials expressed strong sentiments about freedom, democracy and the resilience of New York and the US. People also expressed strong and often opposing opinions on what the next step should be. No single group dominated the memorial spaces with a single point of view. Instead, the memorials were places of dialogue and debate. In the proliferation of written texts, people expressed feelings of resolve and confusion: "Go ahead, destroy our towers. Ruin our city but I dare you to try to kill our hope." "God's first rule is don't kill people, then why do people kill in the name of God?" Calls for revenge and war appeared side by side with calls for peace and forgiveness. On a canvas sheet: "Let's not magnify this terrible tragedy 100 fold by going to war" appeared next to "Kill Osama" and "Wake up America. We must fight back" and, in Spanish, "Peace and humanity." Onto a note "Our grief is not a cry for war!" was pasted a sticker "Zero tolerance for terrorism." A typed question, "How do we want to build?" received the handwritten response "Don't build on a grave." The dialogues were respectful; responses were made without covering or desecrating the previous message.

Differences can become combative and physically confrontational. An evangelical carpenter from Illinois brought 15 wooden crosses to Clement Park in Littleton, one for each of the students killed. This included the two students responsible for the shooting, and these two crosses were subsequently marked with vengeful graffiti. A fight broke out between friends of the victims and friends of the murderers who had brought flowers. Later, the stepfather of one of the victims tore down the two offending crosses (Doss 2002; Fast 2003).

At spontaneous memorials people can express opinions without preparation, sophisticated language or technology, formal presentation or critical argument. The location of these statements at sites of mourning, which deserve attention and respect, give the expressed opinions and positions a degree of effectiveness they might not have in other locations (Haney *et al.* 1997). Individuals and groups who are otherwise silent have a chance to "speak" and to draw upon many ways of doing so. Being able to employ figurative styles of expression, to use symbols, artifacts and drawings as well as written language, invites a wide variety of people to participate, particularly those who are more comfortable with these modes than with calm, controlled writing. It is precisely this wider range of speech styles that Iris Marion Young (1997) recommends for a "communicative democracy" and that Nancy Fraser (1997) endorses for free expression in the public sphere.

Official Memorials

Citizens create spontaneous memorials themselves, immediately and without direction from officials or designers. Official memorials result from lengthy contested deliberations among a variety of officials and design experts, sometimes with the participation of relatives of those who were killed. A review of recent official memorials that followed spontaneous ones suggests important differences between official and vernacular forms of memorializing and tensions between them (Jorgensen-Earp and Lanzilotti 1998). It is possible, however, for the official and the vernacular to work in tandem, for official memorials to be open to appropriation and the expression of difference.

Managing memory

Despite early and numerous suggestions from the public for a memorial that would encourage debate, similar to London's Speaker's Corner, city officials in Tel Aviv sought a memorial to Yitzhak Rabin that would express national unity. The final design, by Claude Grundman-Brigtmann, consists of squares of rough basalt which lie jumbled on the ground as if shaken by some violent force. The stones are enclosed by a steel edge and the entire area is surrounded by a low chain. People still place flowers and candles next to and immediately inside the chain. On one section of the wall of City Hall, graffiti and messages from the spontaneous memorialization activities have been preserved, under glass, and another section is set aside for ongoing graffiti writing, but people also continue to add their writings to other locations without official sanction. Tourists and others visit, to read the texts and to add their own (Engler 1999). While neither the design of the memorial or official policy sanctions this form of appropriation, the "graffiti" tradition established early on continues, pursued by a determined public.

The winning design for the Oklahoma City National Memorial, by Hans and Torrey Butzer, is A Field of Empty Chairs: each victim is represented by a stone and bronze chair, with smaller chairs for the children and larger ones for the adults. This grassy area is enclosed by a low chain despite the designers' repeated pleas that the chain be removed (Robinson 2005). On anniversaries of the bombing and other occasions such as Memorial Day, family members gather at the chairs of their relatives and leave offerings. On the boundary of the memorial site, at the request of families after the memorial had been designed, the designers added a section of chain link fence where visitors continue to leave items.

Until the World Trade Center Memorial is built, the sidewalk bordering the site on Church Street serves as an interim official memorial. After the removal of the ruins of the World Trade Center Towers was completed in 2002, the Port Authority of New York and New Jersey widened the sidewalk and erected a metal fence on which it placed plaques giving a history of the World Trade Center and listing the names of those who were killed. Since then the Port Authority has posted several kinds of signs. One very large one authoritatively lists the actions that are "PROHIBITED for this location" including:

> Distribution of printed material within 24 feet of the viewing fence and in other prohibited areas, Distribution or sale of merchandise, Coordinated continuous expressive activity as part of a group of 25 or more persons in the absence of a permit issued by the Port Authority of New York and New Jersey, Attaching any items to walls, posts, or fences, Littering or abandoning property.

Other, smaller signs state more gently: "Please understand all articles left behind must be removed" and "Please do not write anywhere on the viewing fence." Street vendors who sell postcards, photographs and other memorabilia mostly remain on the opposite side of the street. Small handwritten graffiti messages, written in pencil and magic marker, do appear on the larger posts composing the fence; many include the phrase "God Bless America." These are regularly removed. On the anniversary of September 11, the Church Street sidewalk is a major gathering space and a site of rituals such as the reading of victims' names, and many people attach photographs, flowers, notes and signs to the viewing fence.

These official memorials seem to share a common aesthetic: austere and serene, cool and empty, abstract. There are none of the handmade qualities or the density of sensations of spontaneous memorials. There is no evidence within most official memorials of difference, dialogue or diversity. Quite the contrary, the overriding objective seems to be unity, homogeneity and order, a sense of peace and harmony to be achieved both through architectural design and management policies. If memorial officials do accommodate contributions from the public, that happens outside the immediate precinct of the memorial itself. In all these ways, official memorials "manage" public memory (Doss 2002).

The difference between vernacular and official ways of memorializing correspond to Abramson's distinction between memory and history: "Memory privileges the private and the emotional, the subjective and the bodily. Against history's rationality, the reveries of memory rebel. Against history's officialism, memory recalls hidden pasts, the lived and the local, the ordinary and the everyday" (1999: 78). One might add that while memory is fragmented, contradictory, contested and messy, history is unified, organized and neat. These sets of distinctions correspond to two opposing views of the ideal public sphere: one that prizes unity and homogeneity, achievable only by the assimilation or exclusion of those who are different and another that prizes difference and heterogeneity precisely because these conditions encourage the participation of groups who are different and allow them to maintain those differences (Young 1990a, 1990b).

The official and the vernacular, together

Even before its dedication in 1982 visitors began to leave notes, letters and a tremendously wide variety of objects at the Vietnam Veterans Memorial designed by Maya Lin in Washington, DC (Allen 1995). From the beginning, one maintenance man took the initiative to collect and store what had been left, initially assuming people would return to claim their possessions. They did not, and eventually the US National Park Service decided to treat the wall as an "historical site" so that items left, excluding plant material and flags that have not been personalized, could be treated as an ongoing historical collection. The NPS's policy of collecting, preserving and exhibiting offerings left at the wall may well have encouraged this form of public mourning, helping to stimulate the wide-spread emergence of spontaneous memorials in other locations.

As of 2004, 70,000 items had been preserved and catalogued, forming a collection that serves as a resource for research and public exhibitions (Felton 2004). Many of the letters and notes are direct communications to soldiers and officers who died, some quite short "I'll see you later Sarge" or "Here is the dollar I owe you." Most are anonymous. More recently letters, birthday cards and even graduation diplomas have been left by veterans' children and grandchildren: "Dad, this diploma is for you." More than 1000 photographs have been left. Some items, including edible ones, have particular meanings for veterans: packs of M&M candies that soldiers commonly gave to children in Vietnam, cans of beer, packs of cigarettes, parts of uniforms, and dog tags. As visitors have learned that the offerings are collected, larger and more elaborate items and installations have been left—a motorcycle, a trumpet, a French rifle captured during the war, a tree of lollypops, an assemblage of 200 dog tags, a helmet, a flag and a service ribbon, a backpack with rocks and the note "I finally laid my burden down."

Some veterans visit the memorial only at night when no one else is there. Other visitors come on an anniversary—the day a veteran returned to the US, a wedding anniversary (two glasses, a bottle of champagne and the message "This would have been our 20th anniversary")—or Veterans Day or Memorial Day. The wall also serves as a platform for publicly airing differences on a variety of issues—the Gulf War, the Iraq War, abortion rights. In protest of President Reagan's policies in South America, Lt. Liteky left his Medal of Honor at the wall (Felton 2004).

It is remarkable how much this official memorial evokes the same kinds of movements and gestures that are common at spontaneous memorials. People come up close to read text; they touch it, make their own contributions and study the contributions of others. Visitors appropriate the Vietnam Veterans Memorial for unanticipated uses, making it a site of pilgrimage and ritual and a platform for expressing opinions. Here the official and the vernacular come together, every day (Fig. 7.7).

7.7
Vietnam Veterans Memorial, Washington DC, 1980s

Freedom to Mourn and Freedom to Debate?

Through their offerings at spontaneous memorials citizens express feelings of loss, sorrow and condolence as well as their own, quite varied interpretations of a violent event, interpretations that may be quite personal, idiosyncratic and even obscure. Those who might not otherwise "speak" in a public forum, including children, women and minorities, do so. With their individual contributions, people speak directly and strongly to their fellow citizens. They may address social issues broader than the event itself, searching for explanations, lessons, consequences, sometimes sparking debate. The variety of the offerings and the contrasts and contradictions among opinions expressed all suggest difference and diversity, a far cry from what occurs at most official memorials. For the most part official memorials project a single, officially determined meaning and restrict (or forbid) opportunities for individuals to express their feelings and opinions in order to maintain a formal, unified, harmonious and calm appearance. They are quiet, muted in color and texture, clearly professionally designed and crafted, inspiring, at best, contemplation but not participation.

Some who observed the energy and liveliness of spontaneous memorials at Rabin Square in Tel Aviv and in New York after September 11 favor official memorials that are open to individual expression, difference and debate. Engler envisions uncensored graffiti walls, additional structures for writing on and podiums, steps and paved areas to support speaking and debating: "The city government . . . should reap the opportunity to use the emotional energies to reinforce democracy and civic life" (1999: 11). Similarly, Haskins and DeRose comment: "the noisy democracy of ephemeral street commemorations suggests that the model for a memorial to 9/11 should be a place that guarantees the rights to express, disagree, assemble, claim and collectively own" (2003: 383). As it turns out, this recommendation runs completely counter to the management of the viewing fence at the World Trade Center site and plans for the official memorial and adjacent cultural buildings.

While spontaneous memorials can accommodate both mourning for the deceased and discussion of social issues without showing disrespect, (Fig. 7.8) many people seem to believe that official memorials cannot. This perspective is apparent in the opposition of victims' groups, families, police and firefighters' unions and others to the very creation of the International Freedom Center which was originally planned for the World Trade Center site, immediately adjacent to the memorial. These groups

7.8
Steps, Union Square, New York City, September 2001

strongly opposed the center precisely because it would have addressed issues beyond the September 11 attack: that is, historic and contemporary struggles for freedom. One concern was that exhibits at the IFC would contain implied or explicit criticisms of the US, hence threatening the sanctity of the site and undermining the unity that so many official memorials seek to embody (Dunlap 2005a). Some called for greater restrictions, demanding that the only events that should be addressed were those that occurred on September 11 itself. The website for the organization "Take Back the Memorial," which fueled these demands, stated there must be no facilities "that house controversial debate, dialogue, artistic impressions or exhibits referring to extraneous historical events" (Editorial 2005).

Under intense pressure, New York State Governor Pataki, who had originally fully endorsed the existence and location of the Freedom Center, barred it from its site, saying "Freedom should unify us. This Center has not" (Dunlap 2005b).The imperative underlying the opposition to the International Freedom Center privileges unity over difference, equates the appearance of harmony with homogeneity, and sees any debate or even social commentary as a sign of disrespect to the dead and a lack of patriotism. This imperative assumes an ideal of the public as singular and homogeneous. Such an ideal is only achievable, however, when all those persons and issues deemed different are excluded (Young 1990c) which is exactly what the removal of the Freedom Center did.

It is precisely in this regard that spontaneous memorials epitomize some of the very best aspects of public space: they are inclusive; often differences are allowed and respected; the positing of opposing views is possible. A great variety of individuals speak in their own voices, in a variety of ways without mediation, and some contest the views of others. Emotionally charged disagreements and outright conflicts may occur as well, further encouraging participation by different groups (Fraser 1997). Spontaneous memorials, although they are fleeting, are vital spaces for a participatory and inclusive democracy.

References

Abramson, D. (1999) "Make History, Not Memory," *Harvard Design Magazine*, Fall: 78–83.

Allen, T. B. (1995) *Offerings at the Wall: Artifacts from the Vietnam Veterans Memorial Collection*, Atlanta, GA: Turner Publishing.

Anaza, R., Chavez, D. and Arellano, J. E. (1995) *Descansos: An Interrupted Journey*, Albuquerque, NM: El Norte Publications.

Azaryahu, M. (1996) "The Spontaneous Formation of Memorial Space: The Case of Kikar Rabin, Tel Aviv," *Area*, 29: 501–513.

Clark, J. and Cheshire, A. (2004) "RIP by the Roadside: A Comparative Study of Roadside Memorials in New South Wales, Australia, and Texas, United States," *Omega*, 48: 203–222.

Collins, C. O. and Rhine, C. D. (2003) "Roadside Memorials," *Omega*, 47: 221–243.

Doss, E. (2002) "Death, Art and Memory in the Public Sphere: The Visual and Material Culture of Grief in Contemporary America," *Mortality*, 7: 63–82.

Dunlap, D. (2005a) "Blurred Line for the Ground Zero Museum," *New York Times*, September 23: B9.

Dunlap, D. (2005b) "Governor Bars Freedom Center at Ground Zero," *New York Times*, September 29: A1, B8.

Editorial (2005) "A Sense of Proportion at Ground Zero," *New York Times*, July 29:A22.

Engler, E. (1999) "A Living Memorial: Commemorating Yitzhak Rabin at the Tel Aviv Square," *Places*, 12: 4–11.

Fast, J. D. (2003) "After Columbine: How People Mourn Sudden Death," *Social Work*, 48: 484–491.

Felton, D. (2004) Authors' interview with Curator, Vietnam Veterans' Memorial Collection, Lanham, MD, National Park Service, September 23.

Fraser, N. (1997) "Rethinking the Public Sphere," in N. Fraser (ed.) *Justice Interruptus*, New York: Routledge.

Gardner, J. B. and Henry, S. M. (2002) "September 11 and the Mourning After: Reflections on Collecting and Interpreting the History of Tragedy," *The Public Historian*, 24: 37–52.

Greenhalgh, S. (1999) "Our Lady of Flowers: The Ambiguous Politics of Diana's Floral Revolution," in A. Kear and D. L. Steinberg (eds) *Mourning Diana*, London: Routledge.

Grider, G. (2001) "Spontaneous Shrines: A Modern Response to Tragedy and Disaster," New Directions in Folklore, October 5, online. Available: http://www.temple.edu/isllc/newfolk/journal.html (accessed March 7, 2005).

Haney, C. A., Leimer, C. and Lowery, J. (1997) "Spontaneous Memorialization: Violent Death and Emerging Mourning Ritual," *Omega*, 35: 159–171.

Hartig, K. V. and Dunn, K. M. (1998) "Roadside Memorials: Interpreting New Deathscapes in Newcastle, New South Wales," *Australian Geographical Studies*, 36: 5–20.

Haskins, E. V. and DeRose, J. P. (2003) "Memory, Visibility and Public Space: Reflections on Commemoration(s) of 9/11," *Space and Culture: International Journal of Social Spaces*, 6: 377–394.

Henzel, C. (1989) "Cruces in the Roadside Landscape of Northeastern Mexico," *Journal of Cultural Geography*, 11: 93–106.

Jorgensen-Earp, C. R. and Lanzilotti, L. A. (1998) "Public Memory and Private Grief: The Construction of Shrines at the Sites of Public Tragedy," *Quarterly Journal of Speech*, 84: 150–170.

Linenthal, E. T. (1998) "Memory, Memorial, and the Oklahoma City Bombing," *The Chronicle of Higher Education*, November 6, *Opinion and Arts*: B4.

Linenthal, E. T. (2001) *The Unfinished Bombing: Oklahoma City in American Memory*, New York: Oxford University Press.

Monger, G. (1997) "Modern Wayside Shrines," *Folklore*, 108: 113–114.

Paxson, L. (2006) "Towards a Theory of Contestation in Public Space," PhD diss. New York: City University of New York.

Reid, J. K. and Reid, C. L. (2001) "A Cross Marks the Spot: A Study of Roadside Death Memorials in Texas and Oklahoma," *Death Studies*, 35: 341–356.

Robinson, C. (2005) "Event and the Creation of Sacred Space in Oklahoma City," unpublished paper, Berkeley, CA: College of Environmental Design.

Santino, J. (2004) "Performative Commemoratives, the Personal and the Public: Spontaneous Shrines, Emergent Ritual and the Field of Folklore," *Journal of American Folklore*, 117: 363–372.

Senie, H. F. (1999) "Mourning in Protest: Spontaneous Memorials and the Sacralization of Public Space," *Harvard Design Magazine*, Fall: 23–27.

Senie, H. F. (2003) "A Difference in Kind: Spontaneous Memorials after 9/11," Sculpture: Web Special online version. Available: http://www.sculpture.org/documents/scmag03/jul_aug03/webspecial/senie (accessed April 2, 2005).

Young, I. M. (1990a) "City Life and Difference," in I. M. Young (ed.) *Justice and the Politics of Difference*, Princeton, NJ: Princeton University Press.

Young, I. M. (1990b) "Social Movements and the Politics of Difference," in I. M. Young (ed.) *Justice and the Politics of Difference*, Princeton, NJ: Princeton University Press.

Young, I. M. (1990c) "The Ideal of Impartiality and the Civic Public," in I. M. Young (ed.) *Justice and the Politics of Difference*, Princeton, NJ: Princeton University Press.

Young, I. M. (1997) "Communication and the Other: Beyond Deliberative Democracy," in I. M. Young (ed.) *Intersecting Voices: Dilemmas of Gender, Political Philosophy and Policy*, Princeton, NJ: Princeton University Press.

Chapter 8

Central Park, the Aesthetics of Order and the Appearance of Looseness

Julia Nevárez

An aesthetics of order operates in many public spaces through the enforcement of high standards of maintenance, surveillance and beautification. The possibilities for difference that public space affords seem to pose threats and thus in many instances are contained, pre-empted or disciplined. Even though this order is not absolute, it does regulate use and behavior. The aesthetics of order, a concept I have developed based on observations in Central Park and public spaces in other countries, identifies the structural components that lead to public spaces being perceived as safe.

The aesthetics of order is not foolproof; there can be looseness in our uses and expectations of public spaces. However, any attempt at generating a loose component in park use tends to be immediately detected and disciplined. Unexpected looseness, those aspects of the experience of place that are spontaneous and different from the "normality" of everyday life—loose parts, incidents, events and people—are constantly monitored and quickly controlled or assimilated into the planning and programming of public space by the organizations and institutions that manage them. This is an active and reactive process, one that foresees and manages change to fit the prescriptive indications of what is acceptable in public space and also to absorb tolerable difference, transforming it into normative expectations of public use. Despite the pervasive regulating strategies of the aesthetics of order, public space still offers possibilities for the strange, unfamiliar and unexpected, making public spaces sites of complex and contradictory experiences.

The aesthetics of order presents the façade of function, order and safety while simultaneously identifying and adapting (in a regulatory manner) possible instances of unanticipated dissent. What could constitute looseness is then

8.1
Boathouse, Central Park

ambiguous, but the response the aesthetics of order implements is to manage, define and prevent further conflict. This poses a dilemma with both positive and negative aspects. While providing an ideology of improvement, the aesthetics of order relinquishes the possibility of difference and dissent by regulating it with anticipation. Regulating difference and dissent stops loose use and becomes incorporated into yet another component of the experience of how order should look.

In their attempt to position themselves competitively within the global economy, cities seek to attract the skilled professional class as residents and tourists. In order to accomplish this, public spaces, as a main component of urban living, undergo transformations to meet standards for beautification, maintenance and surveillance that have been raised to satisfy the class-based expectations of these two groups. What people tend to expect of public space increasingly requires the funding of private individuals and organizations. The strategies implemented by an aesthetics of order are not only followed in Central Park, nor are they unique to a global city like New York City (Sassen 1991). These are global strategies employed in many parks in different countries and are tied to concerns about terrorism where safety in public space is threatened. Privatization and terrorism have accentuated the linkage of beautification and maintenance to surveillance or the perception of it. For a beautiful and well-maintained place offers indications that surveillance tactics are in effect, conveying the message that the space is safe. The ideological use of the aesthetics of order benefits authorities, organizations and institutions seeking to portray an air of safety, which directly influences the city's image.

How Aesthetics Are Made Orderly

The aesthetics of order guides the planned appearance of contemporary public space. Surveillance is achieved with the presence of police, parks and/or security guards—strategies that provide a "veil" of safety in public spaces. The maintenance component includes the cleanliness and manicure of landscapes to a level where they look and are appropriately cared for. Beautification translates into the landscaping of public spaces (especially parks), the display of visually attractive flowers, bushes and grass as well as the use of the natural topography in the landscape's design.

Beauty is a social construction that is historic and class-specific. What is considered beautiful by specific groups at particular moments in time might not be considered so by others. The notion of beauty operating in Central Park currently has its origin in the English pleasure gardens; Frederick Law Olmsted's vision assumed leisure as a quality of life issue used by the elite to educate the masses. The elite—the non-productive leisure class—establishes the standards of taste and beauty that other classes adopt (Veblen 1994). Since 1980, the Central Park Conservancy has developed and protected Olmsted's ideas through the restoration of landscapes, completed with private funds, to satisfy the taste and manners of the new elite: the professional middle class that works and lives in the city and the tourists for whom New York City is a preferred destination. The aesthetics of order caters to the sense of safety and the standards of beauty of the class that the park and the city's urban development initiatives seek to attract.

Increasing enforcement of park rules is exemplified by curfews (residents in neighboring areas receive fines for walking their dogs in the park after 10p.m.), posting of cycling rules (warnings about the enforcement of rules with fines), presence of police cars and mounted police not only at special events but also stationed at specific places in the park and in movement around Central Park. Signage with safety tips and rules seeks to alert people to their behaviors in the park. Many of the rules and regulations involve issues of access to the park as well as activities considered to be harmful to the park's landscapes or to other users. Rules and regulations cover such matters as the use of illegal substances and alcohol, disorderly behavior such as gambling, fighting or assault as well as the use of firearms and weapons, failure to control animals, sexual activity, unlawful exposure, camping, solicitation and commercial activities. Some rules forbid acts that endanger the safety of others or that alarm or seriously annoy other people. Regulated uses involve permits for demonstrations, unlawful posting of signs, and unauthorized commercial cinematic productions among many others. Many of the maintenance rules in Central Park are similar to those in other parks in the city, regulations developed by the Department of Parks and Recreation. Other rules and regulations prohibit loitering, placing garbage on containers, littering, spitting, non-hygienic use of the fountains, pools and water, unlawful fires and destruction or abuse of trees, plants, flowers, shrubs, grass or animals.

I would argue that spectacle mediates the experience of the park, not directly as a good to be consumed but as an iconic space that displays a form of leisure seductive to the professional class and to tourists. The aesthetics of order portends to homogenize by producing class-based aesthetics and types of leisure. The spectacle that the aesthetics of order creates reduces users to passive spectators. Despite the fact that the spectacle of consumption in Central Park is that of a representation and that Central Park does accommodate active recreation, the aesthetics of order distances users by protecting landscapes, implementing rules and managing behaviors within a specific vision of what the park should represent for the city.

Looseness can be considered a form of alternative meanings and uses possible in a specific setting. In Central Park, however, looseness seems to be embedded within the frame of a subtle implementation of rules and regulations. The apparent looseness that seems to envelop experience is a façade for what could be experienced as the claustrophobic effects of the aesthetics of order. Beautification, maintenance and surveillance of the park—within the context of passive recreation which the park was designed to create—play a key role in taming the possible conflict a looser use could trigger.

Based on observations of Central Park conducted over a period of two years, the discussion of the park in this chapter proceeds through three layers: (1) the design of Central Park and the ideological notions of beauty and natural landscape that shaped the design; (2) privatization of public space and the preservation and restoration pursued by the Central Park Conservancy; and (3) loose situations that occur in the park and the way they are mediated by flexible and adaptive mechanisms of the aesthetics of order.

Historic Central Park and the Power of Scenery: Elites and Leisure

Frederick Law Olmsted and Calvert Vaux won the design competition for Central Park, and the park's construction began in 1876. To a large extent, the design involved an aesthetics that conveyed a specific message that, while populist at the time, can also be considered exclusive, alienating and elitist. Central Park emerged from the notion of pleasure grounds. From the 1850s to the early 1900s, parks were considered spaces where one could escape the limitations of urban living: an escape to the countryside within the city (Rosenzweig and Blackmar 1992). Parks as "pleasure grounds" were designed to offer the city dweller fresh air, lakes, sunshine and meadows (Cranz 1982). The idea of pleasure grounds was an outgrowth of the garden cemetery, a popular trend during the end of 1830s (Boyer 1978).

During the progressive era the notion of managed and administered parks emerged. Progressives' notion of park design and programming functioned as a social control mechanism. The design of parks explicitly expressed symbols of control, power and the social values shared by planners and administrators in the kinds of activities offered there to be used as an assimilating mechanism for poor immigrants. At the beginning of the twentieth century, reformers in New York considered that parks should also accommodate recreational activities (Cranz 1982). The reformers' vision eases the rules for park use and definition by including active recreation. The restorative qualities of pleasure grounds were kept when these were transformed into reform parks for organized activities. The restorative function of the park was masked by the permissive assumption that has generally characterized parks as neutral grounds whose boundaries are set outside the spheres of social and economic class issues (Rosenzweig and Blackmar 1992).

Olmsted's and Vaux's design for Central Park was based on an ideal of visual enjoyment of the scenery as a form of recreation. The combination of beauty and nature produced the picturesque style, a representation of an idyllic landscape. It required rich and varied plantings that created "complexity of light and shadow near the eye in contrast to the open spaces and delicate, indefinite boundaries of the pastoral style" (Beveridge and Schuyler 1983: 18). Range and openness became key components of the park's landscape.

Olmsted designed the park anticipating the massive urban growth the city would undergo, providing for access to the experience of the countryside in the middle of the city. The sensibilities embedded in the design of Central Park are based on an English park tradition and the concept of bringing the experience of the countryside to the city, "the visitor to Central Park, Olmsted believed, could escape the harsh sights and sounds of the city and find serenity in a created rural experience" (Hall 1995: 209).

8.2
Bridge on lake, Central Park

8.3
Path, Central Park

People's use of the park was directed by the trajectory of paths, a subtle indication of where to go that did not require a conscious, decision-making effort on the part of the park user. Direction was suggested. The aesthetics the design produced sought to integrate most people into the enjoyment of a placid and serene atmosphere in a subtle way.

Olmsted designed parks that portrayed the worldview of an elite with a particular sense of time and leisure. The spaces created for this purpose recreated the kind of leisure activities suited for the sensibility of the elite: they sipped tea; they strolled; they called upon each other (Goodman 1979). "Elite New Yorkers established an unwritten set of social rules for park use: who should use the park, for what purpose, and what time" (Rosenzweig and Blackmar 1992: 215). Over the course of 1806, four million New Yorkers arrived in carriages and on horseback; another three million or so came on foot. These were families of independent artisans, young professionals and shopkeepers, visiting the park to skate, stroll, listen to music and have picnics, promenade on the mall and visit the zoo, among other activities (ibid.). The leisure class of conspicuous consumption set the stage for the way the park was to be used, enjoyed and experienced. They paraded, rode carriages and participated in cultural events where the form of leisure was characteristic of the non-productive class, the class that showed no need for manual labor to sustain their lives. Olmsted himself belonged to this class and believed in notions of the ideal citizen who was "nonetheless accorded full citizenship only to men like himself—white, upper class, affluent, privileged—but, in keeping with his age, insisted that much in the way of social responsibility was required from those so blessed" (Hall 1995: 133). However, due to the distance from their residences to the park, long hours of work and large families, the working class made less use of the park than its designers intended.

Olmsted and Vaux conceived of a park as voyeuristic rather than vibrant and participatory. Their ideals were anchored in a class *habitus* (Bourdieu 1977): a rhythm of cultural practices in a place of leisure where quiet, subtly-designed landscapes served to emphasize passive recreation. The intention was to re-create an atmosphere of leisure and security rather than efficiency and commerce (Beveridge and Schuyler 1983), addressing the sensibilities of a privileged class (Cavallo 1981) while also educating other classes into the elite's sense of leisure (Beveridge and Schuyler 1983). This was a strongly democratic attitude, although liberal and condescending.

Contemporary Central Park: The Central Park Conservancy

The Central Park Conservancy plays an extremely important role in the implementation of the aesthetics of order in Central Park. The sensibility of an elite's aesthetics is brought to contemporary times mostly through privatization. The simultaneous processes of the aesthetics of order and the privatization of public space are strongly linked: for the privatization of public spaces involves directing funds, not available from the public sector, to improve maintenance, surveillance and landscaping.

After its founding in 1980, the Central Park Conservancy focused on the improvement of deteriorated landscapes, based on the Greenswald plan (the original park design). The effort started with a restoration and management draft for the park, later transformed into a master plan that included capital projects to restore the park's landscapes (Barlow 1987), projects completed by the late 1990s. Currently the focus is on the maintenance of these landscapes.

The Central Park Conservancy works in partnership with the New York City Department of Parks and Recreation and manages Central Park. Its budget has grown significantly allowing the Conservancy to provide for maintenance and operations comfortably as well as to fund a number of substantial capital projects. Fundraising by the Central Park Conservancy has been extremely successful, mainly targeting private donors including individuals, organizations, institutions and corporations. This work has been led mostly by affluent women who were concerned and had the time to develop funding for the park, exemplifying what Veblen described as "the portion of the leisure class that has been consistently exempt from work and from pecuniary cares for a generation or more is now large enough to form and sustain an opinion in matters of taste" (1994: 83). The Conservancy has implemented a standard of taste specific to the class of its fundraisers, shared by tourists and users who increasingly come from the professional middle class (who can afford to live in the increasingly upscale neighborhoods of Manhattan).

The Conservancy's budget has exceeded that of the Department of Parks and Recreation, which by economic standards makes it very successful. Contributions have helped improve the physical structure of the park, maintenance and operations and also provide public programs to park users and visitors (Nevárez 1999). According to the Central Park Conservancy's official website, the Central Park Conservancy manages 20 to 25 million visitors per year and covers 85 percent of the US$20 million budget for operations and maintenance. The Conservancy also supports the income of four out of five employees who

> aerate and seed lawns; rake leaves; prune and fertilize trees; plant shrubs and flowers; maintain ball fields and playgrounds; remove graffiti; conserve monuments, bridges, and buildings; care for water bodies and woodlands, control erosion, maintain drainage system and protect[s] over 150 acres of lakes, streams from pollution, siltation and algae.
>
> (Central Park Conservancy 2005)

The kind of work developed by the Central Park Conservancy supports a variety of activities and rhythms of use as well as various types, groups and classes of users. The improved safety, especially when compared to the derelict conditions of the park in the 1970s and 1980s, has resulted in increased use of the park. The increase in solitary visitors to Central Park since 1982 has been attributed to perceptions of the park as safer and to an increase in active uses such as biking and skating (Kornblum *et al.* 1996). Even though Central Park's landscapes have been significantly improved, the example that the Central Park Conservancy sets does not necessarily apply to other, less affluent neighborhoods. At the same time, the privatization of public space and the higher standards reached tend to make high levels of maintenance, surveillance and beautification expected conditions in public spaces.

By relying on the private sector and private individuals to provide for the maintenance, surveillance and beautification efforts in Central Park, a specific notion of how the park should look is produced. The Central Park Conservancy works as purveyors and representatives of Olmsted's vision framed within the ideological tool of historic preservation. The power of the aesthetics of order in Central Park relies on the Central Park Conservancy's staff's interpretation of Olmsted's design while making adjustments to contemporary ideas of what the park should offer to its visitors. By developing and safeguarding a landscape that represents a sophisticated taste and knowledge about aesthetics, the Central Park Conservancy—landscape architects and other staff—implements the aesthetics of order. Therefore the aesthetics of order in Central Park will tend to be more representative of the aesthetics of the class it seeks to attract and less so of a different aesthetics or possibilities for public park use and functioning other than those of the class it seeks to attract.

Central Park signifies a standard of living that corresponds to a marker of taste and distinction (Bourdieu 1984). The form of management, mediated by discourses of historic preservation (protecting Olmsted's legacy), does not rely only on explicitly stated rules but also on more subtle indications such as, for instance, soft borders that limit use and the planting of trees, shrubs and flowers in specific areas. In general, the landscaping of the park signals where use is permitted or forbidden. This subtle implementation works well with the expectations and use of the park by a constituency with sophisticated taste.

The ideologies of restoration of landscapes and capital projects are selective of what is considered an acceptable use. The way these accommodate, or do not accommodate, different uses does not seem to flow effortlessly or without problems. Conflicts and dilemmas have emerged; denying permits for political demonstrations has caused conflict. But mostly the Department of Parks and Recreation and the Office of the Mayor handle requests for such events. The organizational hierarchy directs conflicts in such a way that the city government handles political issues, placing these concerns outside the circle of responsibilities for the Conservancy. The Conservancy only handles maintenance and operations. However, the arguments used to deny permits are based on issues involving the protection of the landscape. Use of the North Lawn and Great Lawn for political demonstrations has been denied using the argument that large numbers of people damage the lawn. The falseness of this argument is demonstrated by the fact that for events such as concerts and movies, those same spaces have been used by large numbers of people. Private uses of the park are allowed mostly for fundraising efforts sponsored by the Conservancy. They include upscale private events for donors (where fees are paid to the Conservancy) in Central Park landscapes such as the Conservatory Garden.

The privatization of public space is one, if not the most relevant, effect of the changing patterns of the global economy. At the structural level of the political economy and the production of space (Lefebvre 1991), privatization results in an aesthetics of order generated by private institutions who take over the responsibilities once fulfilled by the government. This practice regulates and controls public spaces according to the needs of capital in urban areas. Privatization has, to a large extent, afforded the higher standards characteristic of the aesthetics of order. The reception of the changes to public space is favorable; these changes fit smoothly into official discourses on safety. In that sense, the aesthetics of order are ideological.

Loose or Not: Contrasting Aesthetics and Accommodated Serendipity

We do not tend to consider Central Park a rigidly defined environment. In the literature, attention has been given mostly to malls and other spaces that have been privatized (Crawford 1992; Sorkin 1992; Dovey 1999) and control and order have been studied in those locations. In shopping malls and theme parks there seem to be more clear-cut expectations and forthright implementation of control and order. The aesthetics of order in Central Park functions in more subtle ways. It has been able to diffuse some alternative uses and to assimilate others; that is one of its strengths. Both looseness and order are present in the contrasting aesthetics and the subtle effects of the park's design. What could be considered loose emerges in journeys through the park, in the contrasting aesthetics and the design of the park that accommodate diverse experiences and in its spatial and temporal rhythms (Lefebvre 2004).

The role of beauty in Central Park is pivotal. The image of the landscape is an intentionally designed aesthetic. Central Park has the appearance of a natural and in some areas wild landscape that appears uncontrolled, but is in fact highly designed. The meaning of that aesthetics is embedded in the restorative experience it offers in contrast to the rest of the busy, concrete packed city. The landscapes in Central Park offer a sublime and awe-inspiring beauty and views striking in their simplicity. These landscapes are portrayed in an almost innocent way, inconspicuous and socially constructed as natural. The way in which beauty and order anchor the experience of Central Park is less prone to controversy because it is hidden under the ideology of pastoralism and passive recreation. Even though it accommodates active recreation, Central Park's landscapes were designed with an idea of leisure that emphasized passive recreation. The strength and convincing ideology of pastoral landscapes and passive recreation are distinct, as assigned to Central Park, and different, for instance, from the "edgy" aesthetics and "hip" atmosphere and history of Tompkins Square Park on the Lower East Side (Lees 2000).

The park's design and its juxtaposed spaces provide opportunities for fleeting events (the passing of clouds seen in the openness of the landscape) as well as the subtle (framing a beautiful view with the canopy of trees) and the vast (comprehending the vastness of the landscape through the extended views). Familiarity also offers comfort while cycling on the smooth surfaces of the paths that envelop the park, its "ribbons of asphalt" (Carter 2002).

Cycling around the peripheral road in Central Park tells one story of the aesthetics of order from an experiential perspective, a narrative that includes many elements and many possible interpretations (de Certeau 1985). Destinations on my loop, such as the Great Lawn, the Sheep Meadow or Summerstage, are specific places to be visited, but the trajectory to arrive at those places and what one encounters are part of what the park offers most of its visitors. The way the paths and drives are designed helps one traverse the park smoothly without a complicated decision-making process while also offering opportunities for discovery.

This managed trajectory through the park exposes one to the mystery and beauty of landscapes such as at the north end of the park where large rocks border the drive and a "wild" landscape with tall trees provides the foliage of a forest. Empty of people most of the time, the trees and rocks create a dark, shadowy atmosphere. One may encounter wildlife—raccoons, squirrels, falcons and other birds. A kitten that escaped an apartment across Central Park West and ended up in Central Park attracted the attention of passers-by when the authorities were trying to find ways to rescue it. This vignette offers an idyllic representation of the park, where the aesthetics of order functions to provide a safe, beautiful and tamed natural environment.

Central Park provides elements of excitement (running events and musical performances), mystery (people visiting the park who differ in demeanor and clothing), and adventure (attending a large crowd event, such as the Philharmonic Orchestra Concert or Christo's installation *The Gates* or showing secluded places to visitors). These experiences also form an urban wisdom of knowing the city at levels other than just the cartographic; the city allows and even promotes a certain level of introspection since many the experiences of the park also happen in the city. A sense of awe sometimes accompanies the discovery of people and places in the city, including Central Park.

The self-proclaimed "street philosopher" artist De La Vega leaves his mark on the ground in many areas of the city, including chalk drawings in Central Park. One of these drawings is a large fish jumping into a smaller bowl showing what I would like to call the absurdity of unrelenting ambition. An example of ephemeral art, the rainwater washes the drawing away.

While I rest from riding the bicycle on the park's loop on a small lawn behind the Metropolitan Museum, I see a man picking up crab apples as he might on a farm. There many birds and insects eat while people sun tan and pedestrians, cyclists and in-line skaters make their way. Near the Literary Walk, on the mall and at the Bethesda Terrace, people dance the tango. Summerstage, the Philharmonic and the New York Opera provide music events for different tastes. Many of those I have visited while riding my bicycle either as destination or as accidental encounters. Even when incorporating traditionally considered upper-class tastes such as the classical music concerts, those are now part of the repertoire of the ethnically diverse new professional middle class. Other musical events convey the sense that playing at, for instance, Summerstage is a unique opportunity, a privilege.

Some places in the park are less tightly designed and managed than others. While places such as the Great Lawn are well manicured, the landscapes at the north end of the park have a more rugged and wild appearance, equally designed, but there is a difference in the kind of maintenance and attention to landscaping. Rather than a continuous experience of traversing the park, experience here is composed of discrete moments.

The aesthetics of order allows this variety within the tamed landscapes of the park where conditions of safety and surveillance prevail, responsible for the park's familiar and comfortable aura. The order that permeates these events allows the events to be safe but contained within the very specific boundaries of the site and the time allocated. Police officers are parked in areas that are hidden and out of the way such as the Lasker Rink at the North End of Central Park. From what I have witnessed while cycling it is not difficult to find a police officer, a park guard or a maintenance worker in the park. Shakespeare in the Park (the summer plays presented at the Delacorte Theater), even if free and open to the public, is heavily monitored by the Central Park Conservancy staff who implement myriad rules regarding the distribution of the tickets.

8.4
Cycling in Central Park

The aesthetics of order is more evident during major events than during more everyday life moments. During concerts, the New York City Marathon, parades on 5th Avenue that spill into the park, control spreads through the whole park including areas which usually have less surveillance. When major events take place, boundaries are more rigidly marked. Fences are placed around otherwise accessible landscapes; more police and maintenance crew are deployed; and trash receptacles are strategically located in the park. Moreover, at a major event the park is on display and its image seems to be used as an example of the successful functioning of the aesthetics of order, of what is and what is not to be tolerated and allowed. The park's idyllic stature as an iconic place for peace and tranquility is reinforced. Large events transform Central Park from "my own backyard" for the nearby residents to a large spectacle for the consumption of the experience the city can offer.

Disciplining Looseness: Aesthetics of Order in Pre-emptive Mode

The strategies employed by an aesthetics of order are seductive in that they are perceived as improvements, as positive interventions in public space. It is hard to argue against beauty, cleanliness and safety. There are situations, however, that do not fit within what is expected, which the aesthetics of order seeks to identify and control: disruptions or looseness in the uses of the park. One such situation happened to me in the park immediately before the Republican National Convention in New York City in August 2004.

I left my bicycle unattended for a short moment while I bought water at a nearby cart. Immediately an undercover car and a police car stopped near the bicycle. I told them from afar that it was my bike. The undercover car left. The African-American policeman in the car gave me a flyer with safety tips and mentioned that I should not leave property unattended. I replied that I just went to buy water and that I had asked the people nearby to look after the bike. He said that anyone could steal my bike in a second. He and a Latino policewoman talked among themselves and she grabbed a piece of paper and a pen. I became defensive, thinking they might give me a ticket. Leaving the bicycle unattended did not deserve such a strong reaction, I thought. The policewoman stepped out; in her sweetest voice she told me that they were asking the names of the people they were giving flyers to, in case anything happened to the bicycle. I told her that I did not feel comfortable giving my name. She was a bit startled but she could not force me to give my name. Then she wrote on the piece of paper: "female" and asked me if I was white or Hispanic. I said "Hispanic," which she wrote down and then left. I was forced to consider how what I had done could qualify as being outside the expected order.

From the perspective of the police, leaving the bicycle unattended generated a loose situation outside the boundaries of control usually in place in Central Park. The aesthetics of order were disrupted and the behavior was disciplined under the guise of protection. Leaving the bicycle unattended generated, in the eyes of the police, a possibility, a gesture that could invite disruption.

A second situation occurred just after many participants in a Critical Mass event were accused of not having a permit to gather as a group in the city during the Republican Convention. Park guards distributed new rules and regulations to be applied to cyclists. In what seemed like a reaction to Critical Mass in the city, individual cyclists were stopped along the park loop and handed a small bright green piece of paper where the following rules were listed:

> All bicyclists are subject to the rights and duties of vehicle operators. No more than one (1) earphone, No bike riding on foot paths, drive bicycle at reasonable speed, do not create risk of physical injury, (bicycle will be seized as evidence). You must stop at red lights and yield to pedestrians in crosswalks, bike routes in the park are one-way (counter-clockwise), bike must have warning device (bell, etc.).

This kind of measure implemented through new rules and regulations fits well within the workings of the park's design and programming. The program is already in place to accommodate changes that enable the aesthetics of order to apply standards of behavior. There is increasing surveillance that identifies those loose moments where people act in ways not accepted by the standards developed through the aesthetics of order.

Issues of democratic practice and the uses of public space were evident in the debate about the use of Central Park for a demonstration—denied by the city—against the Republican Convention. Even though the demonstration did not take place in Central Park as originally planned, after marching around Madison Square Garden marchers did go to the Great Lawn in Central Park. The organizing group described Central Park in the following way:

> Central Park is New York City's town commons, a traditional public forum that belongs to all the people of this city. What came to light in our court case, however, is that the City of New York and Central Park Conservancy have made a secret, private deal to withdraw the park from public use.
> (United for Peace 2004)

8.5
Sheep Meadow, Central Park

8.6
Billionaires for Bush, "Leave No Billionaire Behind," Sheep Meadow, Central Park

Conclusion: Achieving a Critical Distance

The subtle ways in which the aesthetics of order functions make Central Park a successful screen for the display of order in public space. There is lack of citizen impact on how beauty, maintenance and surveillance are defined without being filtered through the privatized initiative of the Central Park Conservancy. The aesthetics of non-inclusive corporate power through privatization generates a contrived public space. Moreover, the class of users the park seeks to attract is not a threatening element to the aesthetics of order; to the contrary, it represents the new professional class interests.

Debord's *The Society of the Spectacle* (1967) is convincing in articulating the tendency of a consumer society to produce spectacle as a way of experiencing reality, relegating citizens to a passive role with limited opportunities to creatively alter these conditions. Surrounded by displays such as television, cinema, computers and mobile phone screens, Central Park also has become a screen *par excellence*. The aesthetics of order is present not only in the way landscapes are designed to look but to a certain extent in how that design dictates use and the quality of that experience. The maintenance, beautification and surveillance of a public space such as Central Park delimit the uses and meanings of the park. There is an ease with which the aesthetics of order anticipates and assimilates disruption and the possible loose components encountered in trajectories through the park. The aesthetics of order enforces a subtle but pervasive power through the appearance of the natural landscape that could remain unquestioned and unchecked.

Trajectories through the park are a way of discovering possibilities for different interpretations, negotiated at the margin of what is scripted in the design of the space. Through the journeys in the park, a critical distance can make one aware of the constraints and limitations under which the park functions. Even if individually based, interpreting the experience of the journeys through the park allows loose moments to be recognized, revealing the ways the aesthetics of order is implemented. Signing a petition to keep cars outside the park drive could be an example of loose behavior, an unexpected encounter with a situation not planned by the park's management. So could riding a bicycle in an area with less surveillance (intentionally avoiding contact with police presence) or as part of a Critical Mass event (where cyclists form a group that blocks traffic). At another time, the same behavior of riding the bicycle in a group (sponsored by an official organization) could be considered part of the official use of the park or the orderly use of the park as planned and designed.

Beauty, cleanliness and surveillance are conditions difficult to argue against. However, the ways they limit use and reduce participation to that of a passive spectator form a trend that deserves serious consideration. The possibility of looseness is mostly obtained through the trajectories and rhythms of use in the park that allow for a critical distancing that, even if framed within the role of the spectator, offer possibilities for an informed reading of how the landscape functions. This critical distancing offers opportunities to question the functioning of the aesthetics of order and to determine the degree of looseness of trajectories rather than to adhere to absolute notions of the aesthetics of order.

References

Barlow, E. (1987) *Restoring Central Park*, Cambridge, MA: MIT Press.

Beveridge, C. E. and Schuyler, D. (eds) (1983) *Creating Central Park: 1857–1861 (The Papers of Frederick Law Olmsted)*, Baltimore, MD: The Johns Hopkins University Press.

Bourdieu, P. (1977) *Outline of a Theory of Practice*, Cambridge: Cambridge University Press.

Bourdieu, P. (1984) *Distinction: A Social Critique of the Judgment of Taste*, Cambridge, MA: Harvard University Press.

Boyer, P. (1978) *Urban Masses and Moral Order in America: 1820–1920*, Cambridge, MA: Harvard University Press.

Carter, P. (2002) *Repressed Spaces: The Poetics of Agoraphobia*, London: Reaktion Books.

Cavallo, D. (1981) *Muscles and Morals: Organized Playgrounds and Urban Reform, 1880–1920*, Philadelphia, PA: University of Pennsylvania Press.

The Central Park Conservancy (2005) available :<http://www.centralparknyc.org> (accessed April 10, 2005). United for Peace (2004). E-mail (August 24, 2004).

Cranz, G. (1982) *The Politics of Park Design: A History of Urban Parks in America*, Cambridge, MA: MIT Press.

Crawford, M. (1992) "The World in a Shopping Mall," in M. Sorkin (ed.) *Variations on a Theme Park: The New American City and the End of Public Space*, New York: Noonday Press.

Debord, G. (1967). *La Société du Spectacle*, Paris: Editions Gallimard.

de Certeau, M. (1985) "Practices of Space," in M. Blonsky (ed.) *Signs*, Baltimore, MD: The Johns Hopkins University Press.

Dovey, K. (1999) *Framing Places: Mediating Power in the Built Form*, London: Routledge.

Goodman, G. (1979) *Choosing Sides: Playground and Street Life on the Lower East Side*, New York: Schocken Books.

Hall, L. (1995) *Olmsted's America: An Unpractical Man and His Vision of Civilization*, New York: Bulfinch Press.

Kornblum, W., Nevárez, J. and Meyersohn, R. (1996) *Central Park Market Survey, LWRD Initiative*, New York: The City University of New York Graduate School.

Lees, L. (2000) "A Reappraisal of Gentrification: Towards a 'Geography of Gentrification,'" *Progress in Human Geography*, 24: 389–408.

Lefebvre, H. (1991) *The Production of Space*, Oxford: Blackwell.

Lefebvre, H. (2004) *Rhythmanalysis: Space, Time and Everyday Life*, London: Continuum.

Nevárez, J. (1999) "Landscapes of Public Value: A Study of Public Space and Public Safety in a New York City Playground," PhD dissertation, Graduate Center of the City University of New York.

Rosenzweig, R. and Blackmar, E. (1992) *The Park and the People: A History of Central Park*, Ithaca, NY: Cornell University Press.

Sassen, S. (1991) *The Global City: New York, London and Tokyo*, Princeton, NJ: Princeton University Press.

Schuyler, D. (1986) *The New Urban Landscape: The Redefinition of City Form in Nineteenth Century America*, Baltimore, MD: The Johns Hopkins University Press.

Sorkin, M. (ed.) (1992) *Variations on a Theme Park: The New American City and the End of Public Space*, New York: Noonday Press.

Veblen, T. (1994) *The Theory of the Leisure Class*, New York: Dover Publications.

Part III

Resistance

In cities around the world, groups of people inhabit pockets of urban space that, in one way or another, are marginal to better-known, more visible sections of the city. The ways people inhabit them are forms of resistance against the dominant forces of urban re-development and assimilation into mainstream ways of living, working and relaxing. Submission to these forces would mean the loss of place, practices and identity.

The chapters in this section document such cases of resistance and, in addition, chronicle more overt, organized acts of opposition undertaken to improve conditions in these marginalized communities or to prevent their destruction. In Chapter 9, Stavros Stavrides recounts the history and current circumstances of a modernist housing development built in Athens in 1935 to house Greek refugees from Asia Minor, demonstrating how residents, from the beginning, resisted the social and spatial limitations imposed upon them. In Chapter 10, Peter Lang describes the multi-disciplinary research collective Stalker and its wide-ranging efforts to uncover and intervene in communities of the "other." In a former slaughterhouse in Rome this included Kurdish exiles, Somali immigrants and itinerant Gypsies. In his travels Gil Doron discovered a wide variety of marginalized groups: Palestinian villagers on the outskirts of Tel Aviv; homeless people in San Francisco; alternative communities in former military and industrial sites in Copenhagen and Los Angeles; and gay men in London parks.

Occupants of the various sites presented in this section are not only marginalized but also stigmatized for their ethnicity, their immigrant status or their lifestyles. Such stigmatizing makes it easy for dominant social groups to ignore the existence of these "others," to close down the places they frequent or inhabit, or to tear them down. Such initiatives are often undertaken in pursuit of so-called "community" needs or "the public good:" concepts that exclude those who do not conform to established norms. Efforts to resist these actions also challenge such definitions of community interest as being inequitable and unjust.

Marginality is not necessarily geographical; the sites in these chapters are often in or near the center of cities and exist in both the developed and developing worlds. In fact, marginality is not always the characteristic of a place but, as Doron recounts, the characteristic of a group of people or their practices taking place in a space shared with others. It is typically the people and the practices that are stigmatized. If those who are stigmatized make up a majority of the occupants of a space then, by association, the space is also stigmatized, a situation that is all too easily and frequently "remedied" by removing the occupants from the space and converting it to another, more limited use.

In the case studies in this part, groups of intellectuals, artists and architects come to the aid of those whose ways or places of living are under threat, collaborating with them in acts of resistance. In these efforts, boundaries between disciplines are crossed; standard approaches to research, reconciliation, protest and publicity are rejected in favor of more experimental, inclusive, individualistic and site-specific methods, adopting strategies from a variety of disciplines. Marginal sites and communities are discovered, sometimes unexpectedly, by means of planned journeys through areas uncharted and through chance encounters. Openness to serendipitous discoveries is combined with intention and rigor. Events, including artistic and architectural installations, exhibitions, rituals and festivals, are organized to improve current conditions or to resist the actions of authorities. While the given situations are serious ones, troubling to occupants and their advocates, the actions taken in response involve elements of play and joy. Typically it is the spaces under threat that serve as the sites for these events. Resistance is situated, responding to concrete physical conditions. Sometimes, as with the interventions in public squares in London by Transgressive Architecture, the installations are immediately removed by the municipality.

Many of the communities and groups profiled in this part were, at one point, largely invisible to the rest of the urban population and municipal authorities, invisible enough that the areas they occupy were, as Doron discovered, called "dead zones" on city maps in the planning department. These sites too are officially "invisible." Such a designation, a kind of official erasure of the place and anyone who might be there, treats the given area as "empty" and hence available for re-development with impunity. Overt acts of resistance recounted here were undertaken, in part, to make the communities and their plight visible to the public and to pressure authorities to acknowledge their existence and their rights to remain.

The social and spatial segregation from mainstream society that characterizes the cases in these chapters was not always freely chosen; often it was forced upon people, particularly upon immigrants and refugees. Several authors describe ways in which these forms of segregation have been breached, illustrating how social and spatial boundaries can be softened or, in Stavrides's terms, made "porous." In a variety of ways, over a period of many years, refugees housed in the Alexandras housing complex in Athens perforated the boundaries of their own seclusion, creating in-between spaces and shared experiences that strengthened their relationships to each other and to their surroundings beyond the walls of the complex. Stalker's interventions, described by Lang, foster refugee groups' interactions with each other and with the wider public. Stalker's *Transborderline* project both symbolizes and actualizes the crossing of boundaries, as does Transgressive Architecture's *Limits of Inclusiveness* project, presented by Doron in Chapter 11. In this part, thresholds—crossings of boundaries—are created in variety of ways; each is a form of resistance against forces of separation and segregation, each is a way of loosening social and spatial constraints without losing identity through assimilation or suppression. Each contributes to what Stavrides calls a city of thresholds that would support a public culture of co-existing, mutually aware and interdependent identities.

Chapter 9

Heterotopias and the Experience of Porous Urban Space

Stavros Stavrides

Instead of thinking of social identities as bounded regions, one can consider them interdependent and communicating areas. In an effort to describe urban space as a process rather than a series of physical entities, we can discover practices that oppose a dominant will to fix spatial meanings and uses. These practices mold space and create new spatial articulations since they tend to produce threshold spaces, those in-between areas that relate rather than separate. Urban porosity may be the result of such practices that perforate a secluding perimeter, providing us with an alternative model to the modern city of urban enclaves. A city of thresholds could thus concretize the spatiality of a public culture of mutually aware, interdependent and involved identities.

Urban experiences connected to a social housing complex in Athens are used as a case study in this chapter. The inhabitants of these buildings were stigmatized as "others," coming to Athens as refugees from Asia Minor. How were they able to perforate the borders of their seclusion? How could they invent spaces of negotiation, spaces that mediated between differing cultural traditions?

The concept of heterotopia can describe a collective experience of otherness, not as a stigmatizing spatial seclusion but rather as the practice of diffusing new forms of urban collective life. In search of potentially emancipating urban practices we may thus find heterotopic moments in the history of specific urban sites. Can we locate such moments? And can we describe them as thresholds, in social time as well as in social space, opening towards an alternative public culture?

Recognizing Urban Thresholds

The porous rocks of Naples offered Walter Benjamin an image for a city's public life. "As porous as this stone is the architecture. Building and action interpenetrate in the courtyards, arcades and stairways" (Benjamin 1985: 169). Porosity seems to describe, in this passage, the way in which urban space is performed in the process of being appropriated (Sennett 1995: 56). It is not that action is contained in space. Rather, a rich network of practices transforms every available space into a potential theater of expressive acts of encounter. A "passion for improvisation", as Benjamin describes this public behavior, penetrates and articulates urban space, loosening socially programmed correspondences between function and place. Porosity is thus an essential characteristic of space in Naples because life in the city is full of acts that overflow into each other. Defying any clear demarcation, spaces are separated and simultaneously connected by porous boundaries, through which everyday life takes form in mutually dependent public performances. Thus, "just as the living room reappears on the street, with chairs, hearth and altar, so, only much more loudly, the street migrates into the living room" (Benjamin 1985: 174). Porosity characterizes above all the relationship between private and public space, as well as the relationship between indoor and outdoor space.

For Benjamin, porosity is not limited to spatial experience. Urban life is not only located in spaces that communicate through passages ("pores"), but life is performed at a tempo that fails to completely separate acts or events. A temporal porosity is experienced while eating in the street, taking a nap in a shady corner or drinking a quick espresso standing in a Neapolitan café. It is as if acts are both separated and connected through temporal passages that create the precarious, fleeting experience of occasion. Everyday occasions thus seem to shift and rearrange rhythms and itineraries of use (de Certeau 1984: xix).

Porosity may therefore be considered an experience of habitation, which articulates urban life while it also loosens the borders that are erected to preserve a strict spatial and temporal social order. In our need to suppose a founding act for architecture, we usually imagine humans delimiting a territory by marking boundaries. In the rich complexity of city life, however, architecture becomes above all the art of creating passages. Simmel, the well-known dissector of early modern metropolitan experience, pointed out that "the human being is the bordering creature who has no border" (Simmel 1997: 69). For him, the bridge and the door become the archetypal artifacts that concretize an essentially human act, the act to separate and connect simultaneously. As the door presupposes a separation between inner and outer space only to transcend it, so does the bridge define the banks of a river as separated and not merely apart, in order to concretize the possibility of crossing. This interconnectedness of an act and a will of separation with an act and a will of connection can be taken to epitomize the double nature of a porous border: a borderline, transformed to a porous membrane, separates while connecting bordering areas (as well as bordering acts or events).

Acts of Regulating Passage

Thresholds both symbolize and concretize the socially meaningful act of connecting while separating and separating while connecting, the act that Simmel considered a characteristic human ability. Thresholds are constructions that are present mentally as well as materially. This is why thresholds not only ensure the act of passage, but also serve as representations of the act of passage (we say we are on the threshold of a new era). And these representations, as we know from anthropological research, are explicitly involved in crucial ritual acts (Van Gennep 1960).

We can include in the category of social artifacts that symbolically and literally regulate the act of passage all those spatial arrangements that perforate boundaries. We may also include all those areas marked by human crossings that attribute to space characteristics of passage. All these spatial artifacts that are either materialized in constructions that endure over time (gates, stairs, squares) or are temporarily created through use (as the route of a pilgrimage or a quest, or the ephemeral appropriation of a street for a feast or a demonstration) can be considered thresholds. Either created by stones or bodies in action, these arrangements exist to indicate the importance of the act of passing from one condition to another. Thresholds separate while connecting areas that are distinct but also interdependent. The social meaning of a crossing act is indeed to leave a condition that is familiar and to enter a condition that is essentially "other." By regulating passages, thresholds indicate a potential movement towards otherness.

Otherness is, after all, a relational term. Approaching otherness is therefore an act involving both spatial and temporal passages. This can give new meaning to Harvey's assessment: "The relations between 'self' and the 'other' from which a certain kind of cognition of social affairs emanates is always . . . a spatiotemporal construction" (1996: 264).

In contemporary metropolitan experiences, urban thresholds define the quality and meaning of spatial as well as social borderlines. In today's partitioned cities (Marcuse and Van Kampen 2002) thresholds are rapidly being replaced by check-points, control areas that regulate encounters and discriminate among users. Residential enclaves can define recognizable urban identities. The suburban areas of American cities, the shanty towns in Latin America or Asia, the gentrified residential areas of different European cities or the immigrant ghettoes all over the world all possess visible urban identities. Public space contained in these areas is eventually separated from the rest of the city, and its use is essentially restricted to the members of the corresponding community of residents. Gated neighborhoods and impenetrable *favelas* obviously take this separation to the limit. Urban identities are thus exhibited in spaces where a common feeling of belonging dominates every experience of being in public (Sennett 1993). Spatially and conceptually framed identities therefore correspond to the experience of a partitioned urban space where residential enclaves seem to be completely independent of their surrounding public space or are, rather, fantasized as being independent.

Walter Benjamin, seeking to redeem the emancipating potential of modernity, offered a way to reclaim the power that thresholds possess to mediate actions that open spatially (as well as socially) fixed identities and encourage chance encounters. Threshold awareness could provide opportunities to defy the dominating myths of progress that had re-enchanted modern urban experience. Such an awareness was characteristic of the *flâneur*, that ambiguous hero of modernity, who "stands on the threshold of the metropolis as of the middle class" (Benjamin 1999: 8).

Thresholds can perforate the unity of urban myths as well as the unity of history considered as the site of "homogeneous empty time" (Benjamin 1992: 252). Thresholds mark occasions, opportunities for change. Thresholds create or symbolically represent passages towards a possible future, already existing in the past. Recognizing such thresholds, the *flâneur*, and the inhabitant as *flâneur*, can appreciate the city as a locus of discontinuities, as a network of crossroads, turning points. In the unexpected connections realized by these thresholds, otherness emerges, not only as a threat but also as a promise.

Today's partitioned city is not, of course, the nineteenth-century metropolis. Threshold-awareness, however, may reveal encounters between differing social groups and also between different life courses. Literally or symbolically perforating the perimeters of enclaves might mean comparing and connecting separated others. Threshold experiences actualize the mutual recognition and interdependence of identities. The prospect of a "city of thresholds" might constitute an antithesis to the city of enclaves. In such a prospect, becoming aware of the power of thresholds to compare spatially performed identities is already a step towards a culture of mutual involvement and negotiation. Instead of facing otherness as clearly marked in space, one is encouraged to cross boundaries, invent in-between spaces of encounter and appreciate situated identities as open and developing.

Heterotopias

When we confront spatial experiences that tend to actualize in time and space this precarious prospect of a city of thresholds, we can speak of heterotopias—places where differences meet. With the notion of heterotopia, Michel Foucault described those "counter-arrangements," those spaces that are absolutely other compared to the normal spaces they "reflect," representing them, challenging them and overturning them (Foucault 1993: 422). Heterotopias are real places, existing in real societies and inhabited in ways that deviate from what these societies consider and impose as normal. This deviance may, however, be either constitutive of groups of people considered as other (people in prisons, in psychiatric clinics or rest houses) or characteristic of a temporary period of crisis (usually marking crucial transformations of social identities, as during young men's military service).

According to Foucault, "heterotopias always presuppose a system of opening and closing that isolates them and makes them penetrable at one and the same time" (ibid.: 425). These "other places," therefore, are being simultaneously connected to and separated from the places from which they differ. We could consider this characteristic of heterotopias an indication of their relational status. And we could name as thresholds those arrangements that regulate the relationship of heterotopias with their surrounding spaces of normality. Heterotopias can be taken to concretize paradigmatic experiences of otherness, defined by the porous and contested perimeter that separates normality from deviance. Because this perimeter is full of combining/separating thresholds, heterotopias are not simply places of the other, or the deviant as opposed to normal, but places in which otherness proliferates, spilling over into the neighboring areas of "sameness." Heterotopias thus mark an osmosis between situated identities and experiences that can effectively destroy those strict taxonomies that ensure social reproduction. Through their osmotic boundaries, heterotopias diffuse a virus of change.

"Heterotopias are linked for the most part to bits and pieces of time" (ibid.: 424). We could thus understand their status as historically ambiguous. It is at specific historical conjunctures that specific spatiotemporal experiences can be recognized as heterotopias. Heterotopias can become the places of an emerging new order that will turn the experience of otherness into a new rule of sameness (Hetherington 1997), or they can contain moments of rupture in social and spatial history.

Heterotopias may be reduced to the thresholds that connect them to the rest of social space–time. We can speak then of heterotopic moments, moments of encounter with socially recognizable otherness, that become possible because of acts of perforating normality's perimeter. Heterotopias assume a threshold character, being both present and absent in a different time, existing both as reality and potentiality.

In the diverse histories of urban porosity, heterotopias may occur during moments where otherness as a different form of habitation erupts as a counter-paradigm. This counter-paradigm, always ambiguous and sometimes still bearing the traces of the prevailing culture, may either become demonized (confronted by attempts to delimit and control it), or may become seductively meta-stable, insinuating itself into the rest of society.

What follows is a history of urban porosity that has marked a housing complex in Athens. Through instances of urban porosity, I will trace not only chronicles of past acts, but also possibilities for future ones. And in the exceptional periods where porosity seems to impose itself as a counter-paradigm, perhaps it will be possible to discern, in this fragmented history of specific urban experiences, heterotopic moments. It is during these periods that the Prosfygika area of Alexandras temporarily became the locus of a potentially "other" public culture.

A Collective Experience of Urban Porosity

The year 1922 marks a crucial turning point in modern Greek history. An increasingly dominant nationalist ideology, focused on "liberating" Greek people then living in Turkey, culminated in the disastrous expedition of the Greek Army into Asia Minor. The Entente Coalition (Russia, England and France) seems to have encouraged such an expedition after the Sèvres Treaty (1920), or at least did nothing to prevent it. The Turkish Army, part of the National Revolution headed by M. Kemal Atatürk against the Ottoman state, won this war, an outcome marked in Greek history as the "Asia Minor disaster." After the war, a treaty was signed specifying a large-scale population exchange to be supervised by the League of Nations (Svoronos 1972). Some 1,200,000 Greeks, mostly from cities on Turkey's Aegean coast, had to leave their homes and be transported to Greece, deprived of all their possessions. Turks from the Greek mainland, mainly peasants, had to follow the opposite route (Vlachos *et al.* 1978).

The state's policy in Greece was to keep almost half of the refugee population around major cities, so as to control them and to "integrate" them into the local economy. Those who were allowed to stay in Athens had to build their houses on empty public lots, mainly outside the city, using whatever building materials they could find and with almost no money. Shanty towns with no roads or public facilities erupted around Athens and Piraeus. Uprooted people tried to live in a country that appeared more hostile to them than they ever expected.

Of course, these settlements provided Greek industries and handicraft workshops with low wage labor. This is why many people considered the refugees a threat to their jobs, and to their well-being. Refugees were demonized as invaders who would destroy the city's public life. Forced to cross a threshold in a period when it separated rather than connected two neighboring countries, they were allowed neither to return nor to feel at home in their new destination. These people were actually not allowed to belong anywhere. And the Greek government aimed to ensure that poverty and discontent would not cross the borders of the shanty town: refugee settlements were spatially and socially formed as ghettoes.

The people coming to Athens from Asia Minor were mostly urban dwellers. They had a highly complex urban culture, so their life, even though almost completely destroyed, followed forms of sociality that were sometimes far richer than those of the surrounding neighborhoods. Refugees slowly re-established a public life based on community rhythms, making their small shops or houses into meeting places to accommodate a rich tradition of collective festivities, music and oriental cuisine. Their way of life invited other city people to share new experiences of urban companionship. Slowly the refugees converted the sanitary zone that was erected around them, those literal or symbolic walls of prejudice and status (Marcuse 1995: 249), into a porous membrane that allowed their culture to diffuse into the city. Instead of representing an unwillingly invading other that stood on the threshold separating two opposing neighboring countries (Turkey and Greece), the refugees thus came slowly to be recognized as people who dwell on a threshold that connects two cultures sharing many common values and habits. In spite of opposing nationalisms, cultural porosity was to emerge once again, rooted in a history of cultural exchanges among different peoples in the Balkans and Asia Minor. After all, this region was and is still a threshold connecting as well as separating "East" from "West."

The Alexandras Avenue Refugee Building Complex

After a long period of emergency, during which most of the funds of the Greek Refugee Rehabilitation Committee were used in rural rehabilitation, the responsibility for social housing development was shifted to the Technical Department of the Ministry of Welfare. Almost ten years after the Asia Minor exodus, a slum clearance project produced a series of model settlements (Vasileiou 1944; Vlachos *et al.* 1978).

The Alexandras building complex, built during the years 1934–35, was among them. The 1930s represents a crossroads in the urban history of Athens. In 1929, a new law which established floor ownership in apartment buildings opened the road to rapid commercialization of residential development. In the same period, however, some of the best examples of social housing were constructed in Athens, designed by Greek architects working with the Technical Department. Those buildings constituted an alternative model of housing, contrasting with the packed multi-storey buildings of private housing that were soon to engulf all Athenian neighborhoods.

The Alexandras complex is distinctive in its abundance of open space between the buildings. Although apartments were relatively small (most of them with two rooms, a kitchen and a small bathroom), all of them had ample sunshine and ventilation. Those buildings were among the first to concretize the new spirit of Modern architecture in its programmatic manifestos and works on social housing. In 1933, the International Conference on Modern Architecture (CIAM) culminated in the Charter of Athens, proclaiming the objectives of the Modern Movement. Quality mass housing was one of the major goals. It is not by chance then that when Greek architects were encouraged to participate in the design of refugee housing complexes, they employed concepts and models from the Bauhaus School to produce houses appropriate for the new standards of living. Not being the direct result of market laws which had completely reduced housing to a commodity, these buildings could have set an example to follow in the rapid urbanization of the post-war years.

When it was completed, the Alexandras building complex consisted of eight blocks totaling 228 apartments of two types. An effort to provide the essential household facilities in the minimum space reflects the Modern Movement's obsession with efficient minimum spatial standards. Uniformity and a rational layout were absolutely characteristic. Socially, the buildings were a place where the refugees were to be secluded. No care was taken for the remaining open space; no initiatives were established for the complexes to be incorporated into the city. These complexes were both physically and symbolically set apart from the city, surrounded as they were by amorphous public space easily read as a separating zone.

This separation was reinforced by the distinct and already stigmatized category of residents in the new complexes, which most Athenians considered places of otherness. A kind of deviation from "normal" urban life must have been attributed to such residential areas that appeared morphologically and functionally different to every other residential neighborhood in Athens. Although symbolically quite effective, separation was not based on a layout that tried to impose physical segregation.

Formless outdoor space was left to surround and contain the blocks. A loose space, with no defined uses, sometimes even without trees, characterized the Alexandras complex as well as most of the other refugee building complexes. Residents, who had to face a hostile and unfriendly environment, nonetheless appropriated the loose space through private and common activities that could not be contained in the buildings. A rich and evolving common life burst out of the buildings, transforming outdoor space into an ambiguous network of small courtyards, pavements, tree-shaded areas, improvised playgrounds and meeting places (Stavrides 2002b).

In direct contrast to the rational and function-oriented design of the buildings, outdoor space was not marked by absolute boundaries. Most of the basement flats were extended into small private courtyards, which were either circumscribed by low walls and fences or integrated into a recognizably communal outdoor space. In the latter case, private and public uses were not clearly demarcated. Visiting, small feasts and everyday encounters between neighbors wove the fabric of a diverse and porous urban environment. Terraces, where common laundry facilities were situated, became minuscule stages of an everyday theatricality where mostly women met. During the winter, staircases were transformed into noisy play areas absolutely integrated into the life of the buildings. The "passion of improvisation" that Benjamin found in prewar Naples came to characterize the activities of residents, who became highly inventive in inhabiting their standardized and minimum houses. Improvisation seemed to mark their ability to collectively appropriate threshold spaces, converting them into lived spaces. The staircase was not simply used to cross an in-between area. Rather, much of everyday life came to take place in the stairways, as well as in front of doorways, in the pavement areas and in the empty space between the kitchens of facing blocks which was constantly being crossed. Activating in-between areas as crucial public spaces meant creating urban sites without clear boundaries. A permeable membrane, a porous membrane, was thus imposed through everyday use.

This kind of urban osmosis was not unknown in Athenian neighborhoods. Empty lots and outdoor public spaces that were not designated as streets or squares served as informal centers of sociality. Children used them in their games, grown-ups in their walks, younger ones in their exciting journeys into adolescence. Outdoor loose space was, however, demonized in middle-class morality. The word for such places was *alana*, and the people who in middle-class imaginary are only worthy of wandering there are *alani*, a word that became synonymous with "vagabond." *Alana* was, however, a rich and porous urban space, always in the process of being transformed through use, especially in low-income neighborhoods.

Heterotopic moments

One of the most infamous prisons in Athens stood on one side of the building complex. The large multi-storey building was used to detain common criminals as well as political prisoners, until it was demolished in the mid-1960s. People living in the nearby buildings of the Alexandras complex remember how friends and relatives gathered outside the neighboring wall of the prison, communicating with the prisoners by shouting or receiving notes. People also remember how during the German occupation they used to look from their building terrace into the prison courtyard, trying to gather information about the detained patriots of the Resistance. They recite stories of young boys and girls daringly approaching the high walls to collect the messages the patriots used to throw from the windows, usually messages to announce that they were to be executed the next morning. And of course nobody will forget the image of a small black cloth hanging from a cell window to indicate that one of the cell's inhabitants had been executed that day (Papavasileiou 2003).

Through such collective experiences, the Prosfygika inhabitants formed a kind of hidden solidarity, participating in their own way in the Resistance. An impossible osmosis of the prison space with the outdoor areas of the complex was realized through acts that symbolically perforated the separating wall. A recognizable osmosis between different families in such a period of tacit solidarity and mutual help formed the basis of those qualitatively different social bonds that characterized the community during the years of the German occupation (1941–44). Due to the active involvement of the Alexandras complex residents, those buildings were part of the liberated Athens months before the retreating Germans abandoned the city.

One can imagine this period as punctuated by heterotopic moments. Solidarity seems to have transformed the already osmotic relations between private and public space into mutually recognized common uses of both private and public spaces. Many residents used to share their poor food supplies and families used to help each other in taking care of the children or cooking. Out of an extremely precarious situation, and due to the growing appeal of the Left Resistance movement, a communitarian culture that was distinctively urban manifested itself in the refugee neighborhood (Fig. 9.1).

In the years that followed, this culture was literally blown to pieces by British canons and airplanes as well as by Greek government troops in the incidents of December 1944. During the so-called "Battle of Athens," the Greek Popular Liberation Army (ELAS), the major anti-occupation resistance movement, was opposed to British policy in the area, which denied the popular will for post-war democracy and social justice. British politics resulted in a massacre on December 3, 1944, when a huge peaceful demonstration was attacked by royalist troops, sparking a long and devastating civil war (Svoronos 1972). Members of ELAS fought a decisive battle in defense of the Alexandras buildings that were attacked by the above-mentioned forces. Many men decided to side with the fighting guerillas while women and children took shelter in a nearby football stadium. As if to dramatically symbolize the osmotic space between the houses, holes were made in the inner walls of adjoining flats. Those passages enabled the defenders to move from one flat to another. The Battle of Athens was only a dramatic prelude to the civil war that followed. People living in the buildings in those days of December still remember the romantic young fighters who sought in vain to defend the dream of a just society (Tsougrani 2000).

9.1
Massive demonstration passing in front of the Prosfygika buildings, Alexandras Avenue, Athens (probably December 1944)

Resisting Decay

A 94-year-old inhabitant of Alexandras Prosfygika, who has spent years and years sitting by his window due to a serious disease of his knees recalls: "People used to walk differently in those years [during the 1940s and 1950s], they used to look at you differently, they used to say good morning" (Tzanavara 2000). Overlooking one of the streets between the buildings, which used to be a dirt road, this old man used his window during the years after the war as a "box in the theater of the world" (Benjamin 1999: 9) (Fig. 9.2).

This man could not experience urban porosity directly by inhabiting public space. He could, however, appreciate the characteristics of an osmotic public culture, feeling the way his window was integrated into a network of thresholds, as opposed to the screen character of windows in modern big cities. Recently, however, during the Athens 2004 Olympics, the lifeless building facing Alexandras Avenue was indeed used as a screen. An enormous image of Athens, with the Acropolis in a prominent position, was used to completely cover the building's façade. The image was obviously meant to hide the derelict building. The building's pores were temporarily effaced. How did things come to this?

Since the late 1960s, these buildings have been, from time to time, the focus of successive governments who promised a park in place of a degraded housing area. The pressure produced a precarious situation for the inhabitants who in most cases were hesitant to spend any more money for house maintenance. Communal porous places—terraces, staircases and pavements—started crumbling. The municipality of Athens did not maintain the vast surrounding open space, which could have been transformed into an urban green area. Instead this area became a large informal parking lot for people using the nearby hospital or watching a football game in the large football stadium facing the complex. This lot is also used every day by those

9.2
Balconies as boxes in the theater of the world; history is marked by the presence of a US Army vehicle just below (1943)

who work in the Supreme Court building (erected on the site of the former prison) and in the Athens Police Headquarters, located on the next block.

The shapeless *alana* that used to be here provided a space for informal uses and encounters. In this way it was a porous public place. By contrast, today's parking area, in its informal use, remains an inert urban space. People come and go with only the aim of finding a place to leave their cars, sometimes extremely frustrated, since this area is now very near the center of the city, crowded with multi-storey buildings. The space continues to be loose since it has neither an explicit design that organizes different uses nor does it have a defined role in the surrounding urban environment. The absence of defining urban boundaries and the absence of control are not enough, however, to create the condition of urban porosity. What can transform loose spaces into generators of urban porosity is the common will to inhabit public space and transform it through everyday negotiations of meaning that characterize a rich and multifarious public culture (Minca 2001).

Once again the inhabitants of the buildings are demonized as feared other. Otherness is identified with stigmatized urban poverty and marginalization, emphatically represented in the image of derelict and mostly deserted buildings. Most of the inhabitants had become owners of their apartments, having paid off state mortgages under very favorable terms. A lot of them, however, in fear of imminent compulsory expropriation, sold their apartments to a public development company. Others have either abandoned their houses or have rented them to contemporary immigrants and refugees or other low-income people. Some inhabitants though, descendants of the original Asia Minor refugees, remain, claiming their right for a better future in a place where the past was generous, no matter how hard. The area appears to be almost abandoned, symbolically as well as literally "out of order." In the heart of Athens, this building complex appears as a downgraded housing area that belongs to a collectively repressed past, more or less an obstacle to urban development and a stain on the city's image.

However, a new set of experiences of urban porosity has recently emerged, scattered among the devastated everyday life of the buildings, resulting from initiatives taken by those who resist the demolition of the complex. A residents' coalition, with a few determined and active members, has managed to combine its forces with architects and teachers from the School of Architecture at the National Technical University of Athens (NTUA). Volunteer and ecological organizations have contributed to this struggle that started in 2000. Through public appeals, demonstrations, exhibitions, happenings and discussions taking place in and around the buildings, the residents and activists from the Left and anti-authoritarian movement have shown that this housing area presents an anti-paradigm to Athens housing history (Vrychea 2003).

Participating in a course focusing on social housing, students of the NTUA School of Architecture showed, through various proposals, that a revival of the area can be achieved through regeneration plans that respect the history of the buildings and that learn from the informal uses of their inhabitants. In those student projects, the rich variety of extensions offers an architectural vocabulary that gives form to additional spaces for small apartments, encouraging at the same time an osmosis between collective and private uses (Figs 9.3, 9.4).

Celebrating the prospect of such a public culture, a two-day festival was organized in 2003. This same year, because of the 2004 Olympic Games programmed to take place in Athens, the government placed extreme pressure on the inhabitants. The Council for Modern Monuments took a controversial decision to support the government's main target. This decision proposed the preservation of only two out of eight buildings in the complex, considering them worth preserving as an example of a Modernist housing project. Sampling, of course, has nothing to do with the essentially paradigmatic nature of this building complex. Such a decision can preserve neither the porous condition of its urban space nor its potentially heterotopic character.

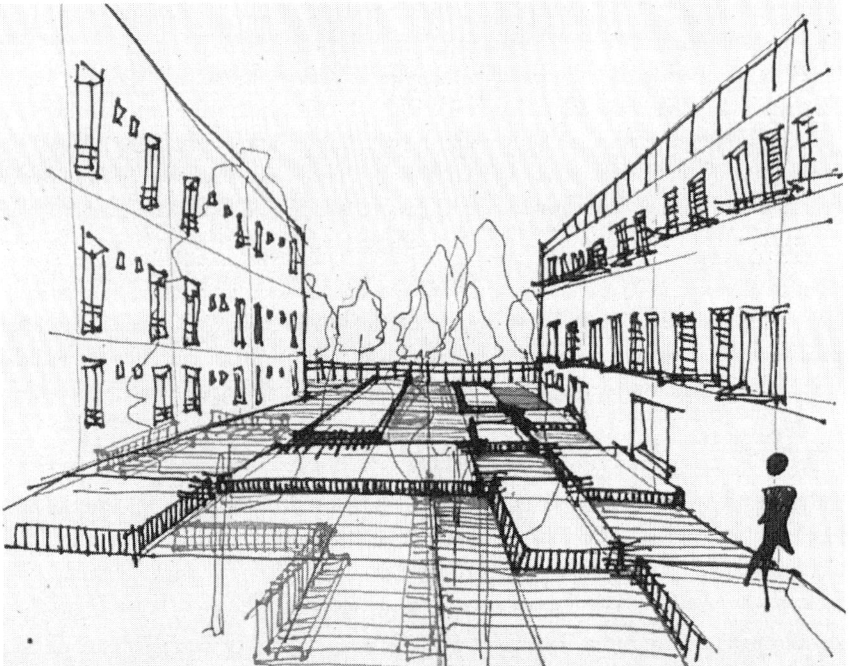

9.4
Redesigning outdoor in-between spaces
Source: Student project by Emiliano Zapatero

9.3
Life bursting out from the building; deviating from the order of the Modernist spatial vocabulary (2004)

9.5
Buildings transformed through ephemeral appropriation. "Say no to the effacement of a refugee neighborhood"

Through exemplary acts of re-inhabiting the two-day festival aimed to show a different concept of social housing that was once and can be again concretized in the Prosfygika of Alexandras. Different groups of young activists and students of architecture organized temporary squatting in empty apartments now belonging to the government-run Public Real Estate Company (KED). Exhibitions presenting the housing problems of Athens and a history of the refugee settlements and struggles were organized. Prototypical children's areas and environmental awareness exhibits were housed in appropriated empty flats. The prospect of an osmotic relationship between public and private uses was also explored by improvised constructions in outdoor space, obstructing parking uses and encouraging various acts of collective appropriation and companionship (Fig. 9.5). A small deserted coffee kiosk that used to be a neighborhood meeting point was reconstructed *ad hoc* and re-used. An improvised stage was constructed in one of the open spaces. Musicians as well as other performers had the opportunity to communicate with the residents and all those who use the area daily, unaware of its potentialities as a public urban space (Fig. 9.6). Many people, including numerous remaining inhabitants, had the opportunity to experience an essentially heterotopic organization of space. Just as this building complex can be interpreted as other, in comparison with modern Athens's housing areas, so can the festival be taken to illustrate another way of inhabiting housing.

9.6
In defense of the Prosfygika. Porous public space recreated during a feast organized to proclaim the will to resist government plans that vaguely refer to area development, including unspecified outdoor spaces (2003)

All these festive and paradigmatic acts attempted to regenerate a porous urban space. They tried to show that the history of the buildings has transformed them to potential sites of an osmotic public life. Staircases were to become again spaces of life and everyday improvised encounters. Windows were transformed into doors, establishing a direct communication between basement flats and the outdoor spaces. Balconies were used as temporary boxes overlooking theatrical sketches in the public space, balconies which at the same time are miniature stages of individuality that differentiate the uniform appearance of the façades.

The festival culminated in a large feast, which was enjoyed even by the patients of the neighboring hospital. An active group of doctors supported the idea of converting some of the empty flats into a free guest house for the patients' relatives who come from all over Greece to this public anti-cancer center.

This festival demonstrated that the preservation of this building complex cannot and must not take the form of a museum-like renovation of the buildings. What is worth preserving is not the memories attached to the buildings but the passages that can connect these memories with the present. What may appear as a period of history that has reached its end can instead be taken as a series of turning points in history that represented heterotopic opportunities.

Memories of Porosity

We can understand the history of these buildings as perforated by moments of heterotopic potentiality. Rather than a continuous chain of events culminating in the present, this history is more like a discontinuous and shifting flow influenced by critical turning points. We can understand those turning points as temporal thresholds, periods that seem to disconnect past and future only to establish new unpredicted links.

The very construction of this complex exhibits heterotopic qualities. The Modernist buildings appeared completely different from the surrounding urban environment. Otherness became apparent in their form (rational free-floating boxes), their layout and their indoor facilities. Much in alignment with Foucault's reasoning, this area can be considered a Modernist heterotopia. We can, however, also understand these buildings as concretizing a turning point, a threshold, in the housing history of Athens. Through the appropriation and transformation of the buildings by their refugee inhabitants, the area became embedded in the rich urban fabric of Athens, forming an osmotic relationship with the surrounding neighborhoods. The memories of a rich public life prevented the refugees from retreating into their long-hoped-for private shelters. But more than this, a surviving neighborhood culture in Athens gave them the opportunity to find ways to connect with a recognizable common past. *Alanas* are only one example of unplanned neighborhood spaces that supported an informal sociality. The long-term use of the surrounding outdoor area as *alana* has created a common cultural and literal ground for the refugees and their Athenian neighbors.

Residents had to acquire threshold awareness (Fig. 9.7). They had to understand that what separates or is aimed at separating can also be used to connect. This was true both spatially, as shown by their experience of converting outdoor space from a *cordon sanitaire* to an area of encounter, as well as temporally, as their common memories that separated them from the others were used as the basis of an osmotic relationship with an Athenian urban culture embedded in similar habits and values. Neighbors could thus discover common traditions, even though their history differed.

Memories of a rich urban porosity, stemming from experiences of mixed traditions co-existing in Asia Minor's cities, allowed residents to transform the standard indoor spaces and the unplanned outdoor areas into a network of communicating and differentiated places. Those reminiscences, however, were actualized over time in very different circumstances. Life conditions for residents changed dramatically more than once. Memory, collective as well as individual, was thus formed not by reminiscences of continuity but by recollections of discontinuity. This kind of memory recognizes the past as full of turning points, full of temporal thresholds. Residents witnessed the agonies of post-war Athens, the hopes for a better future shattered by the civil war and the nightmare of discrimination that characterized the crippled civil society that emerged from this war. Their houses certainly took part in an eventful history.

9.7
Life on the threshold; women posing in the places they have transformed into porous public spaces (1945)

A housing complex is not a monument built to represent a single glorious event. A housing complex absorbs history through its porous walls. Memories seek out traces; mostly, however, memories interpret and re-interpret traces. What the festival sought to establish is exactly this memory of turning points, this memory of fertile discontinuities in history. Refugees in the Alexandras complex, people on the threshold, have witnessed a history of threshold moments, both in the micro-history of their places as well as in the macro-history in which their places were directly involved. Monuments, on the contrary, are marks in a national narrative obsessed with continuity, marking the road from "glorious ancestors" to the present (Boyer 1994: 343).

This refugee housing is connected with ruptures in this homogenized narrative. The refugees interrupted national history and caused conflicts and collective hostility. Packed into their modern buildings they were both outside the city and outside the prevailing urban ethos. However, they managed to perforate the separating spatial and temporal membranes. The German occupation, the liberation of Athens and the civil war that followed were major ruptures in modern history that were mended by the dominant ideology of post-war discriminatory democracy. In the Prosfygika of Alexandras, the marks of these ruptures remain, indicating thresholds that might have led to an alternative future. Life could have evolved in a different direction, if the refugees had been allowed to develop their own distinct sociality in a Modernist environment transformed through use. A rich public and private life found ways to produce spatial experiences of differentiation, as well as communality, deflecting the homogenizing Modernist vocabulary. Those buildings could have become an experimental prototype for modern urban concepts in the city of Athens. Instead they were allowed to crumble, waiting to be wiped out by the Modernist market version of collective housing—the Athenian private development "boxes."

Houses accumulate memories, monuments separate them. Houses provide the material for a geology of historical time. Usually monuments preserve and freeze time so as to indicate periods which follow one another in an explicit and meaningful succession. Monuments mythologize events, arranging them in series that establish fixed collective identities. Houses can, in contrast, offer a palimpsest, the experience of ruptures, turning points, thresholds in personal as well as collective history.

Spatial experiences, such as those that punctuated the Prosfygika building complex with heterotopic moments, can challenge the order of historic time that is being constructed as "national history." A loosening of space expressed in urban porosity may actually loosen time. Instances of otherness, glimpses of radically other social experiences may emerge in those moments, in performances of a public culture based on the negotiation between differing identities. The refugees of Asia Minor were people who had to wait for a long time on the threshold, trapped between the world they were forced to leave and the one they were seeking. These people, perhaps more than anyone else, were in a position to understand how important it is for the city to include and not separate. Their ambiguous and discontinuous life in the refugee settlements can indeed indicate the possibilities of an osmotic urban experience. At the culmination of such osmotic experiences a city of thresholds may emerge, offering glimpses of an emancipating spatiality (Stavrides 2002a). A city of thresholds may be imagined as punctuated by heterotopic moments or periods. And it is in these moments that diversity and possibility in urban life can indeed emerge.

Acknowledgments

The author wishes to thank D. Eutaxiopoulos for his help in documenting the case of Prosfygika. This chapter would not have been written if it were not for the inspiring support of the late Professor A. Vrychea and the experience of working with fighting inhabitants, fighting, and with students of architecture, dreaming.

References

Benjamin, W. (1985) "Naples," in W. Benjamin (ed.) *One Way Street and Other Writings*, London: Verso.

Benjamin, W. (1992) "Theses on the Philosophy of History," in H. Arendt (ed.) *Illuminations*, London: Fontana.

Benjamin, W. (1999) *The Arcades Project*, Cambridge, MA: Belknap Press.

Boyer, C. (1994) *The City of Collective Memory*, Cambridge, MA: The MIT Press.

de Certeau, M. (1984) *The Practice of Everyday Life*, Berkeley, CA: University of California Press.

Foucault, M. (1993) "Of Other Spaces: Utopias and Heterotopias," in J. Ockman (ed.) *Architecture–Culture 1943–1968: A Document Anthology*, New York: Rizzoli.

Harvey, D. (1996) *Justice, Nature and the Geography of Difference*, Oxford: Blackwell.

Hetherington, K. (1997) *The Badlands of Modernity: Heterotopia and Social Ordering*, London: Routledge.

Marcuse, P. (1995) "Not Chaos, but Walls: Postmodernism and the Partitioned City," in S. Watson and K. Gibson (eds) *Postmodern Cities and Spaces*, Oxford: Blackwell.

Marcuse, P. and Van Kempen, R. (eds) (2002) *Of States and Cities: The Partitioning of Urban Space*, Oxford: Oxford University Press.

Minca, C. (2001) "Postmodern Temptations," in C. Minca (ed.) *Postmodern Geography: Theory and Praxis*, Oxford: Blackwell.

Papavasileiou, E. (2003) "A Personal Account and an Appeal," *Avgi* (Greek newspaper), November 2: 37.

Sennett, R. (1993) *The Fall of Public Man*, London: Faber and Faber.

Sennett, R. (1995) "Theory," *Harvard University Graduate School of Design News*, Summer: 54–56.

Simmel, G. (1997) "Bridge and Door," in N. Leach (ed.) *Rethinking Architecture*, London: Routledge.

Stavrides, S. (2002a) *From the City-Screen to the City-Stage*, Athens: Ellinika Grammata (in Greek).

Stavrides, S. (2002b) "Inhabitation and Otherness: Refugees and Immigrants in the City," in T. Koubis, Th. Moutsopoulos and R. Scoffier (eds) *Athens 2002 Absolute Realism*, catalogue for 8th International Exhibition of Architecture, Venice Biennale, Athens: Hellenic Ministry of Culture—Association of Greek Architects.

Svoronos, N. (1972) *Histoire de la Grèce Moderne*, Paris: Presses Universitaires de France.

Tsougrani, B. (2000) "When Memory Shoots Oblivion," *Rizospastis* (Greek newspaper), June 11: 18–19.

Tzanavara, H. (2000) "They Tear Down History," *Kyriakatiki* (Greek newspaper), March 25: 93.

Van Gennep, A. (1960) *The Rites of Passage*, London: Routledge and Kegan Paul.

Vasileiou, I. (1944) *Popular Housing*, Athens: publisher unknown (in Greek).

Vlachos, G., Yannitsaris, G. and Hadjicostas, E. (1978) "Housing the Asia Minor Refugees in Athens and Piraeus between 1920 and 1940," *Architecture in Greece*, 12: 117–124.

Vrychea A. (2003) "A Spurious Remodelling," *Avgi* (Greek newspaper) June 15: 24.

Chapter 10

Stalker *on* Location

Peter T. Lang

On October 5, 1995, a group of young architects and artists began a four-day tour on foot through Rome's expansive outskirts. The event concluded when the tour's participants, all school companions who lived and worked in the capital, succeeded in reaching their initial point of departure. While conducted well outside the city's densely settled urban fabric, the Walk about Rome never strayed beyond the official city limits. The explorers nonetheless traversed entirely unfamiliar and uncharted territories, entering in the process some of the most unusual environments to be found anywhere in Europe. Nestled within these natural folds within the city proper were hidden worlds inhabited by undocumented immigrants as well as pastures for grazing sheep; many areas were neglected and in a state of abandon.

The action, conceived to document Rome's local periphery and record experiences along the way, drew considerable attention from Italy's local and national media. The name that stuck with the group was almost an afterthought, when a news reporter who had seen the 1979 film *Stalker* by the master Russian director Andrei Tarkovsky suggested similarities between the film's enchanted "zone" and the areas traversed during the Walk about Rome.

The Stalker of the Tarkovsky film is a rogue explorer who guides two middle-aged men, a scientist and a writer, into the tightly cordoned "forbidden zone," a post-apocalyptic no-man's-land that serves as the film's principal setting and main subject. The trio's haphazard progress through this eerie landscape eventually leads them to mysterious ruins, the zone's inner sanctum. Tarkovsky orchestrated this epic tale of human redemption by releasing his characters into a world completely disconnected from contemporary civilization. His laconic narrative of a Virgilian passage through unfamiliar landscapes aptly foretold the Roman collective's explorations inside the capital's marginal spaces.

The Roman Stalker penetrated deep into the city's *terrain vague*. These areas are not merely voids on a city planner's map, but vast quasi-parks stretching around the Italian capital and extending like fingers into the city proper. These scruffy, marginalized areas are buffer zones that relieve the city's relentless expansion and urbanization. They host squatter settlements, provide sites for undocumented black market activities, and are used as parklands by people from outside the city.

The group's journey progressed through uncharted areas of the city: wide open fields with grazing sheep, dark ravines and gullies, estuaries where a boatman came to their aid, fenced-off areas guarded by snapping dogs, unfinished industrial structures inhabited by immigrants, lakes formed in abandoned quarries, unfinished highways, an out-of-service rail line and an abandoned subway tunnel. Each evening the group set up camp, and slept under the open sky. They brought still and video-cameras, musical instruments and flour, an ingredient reserved for marking their passage across the landscape (Fig. 10.1). From Lorenzo Romito's diary, dated October 9, 1995:

> This night, coming out of the tunnel, we put our feet back right where we started out four days ago at the inauguration of crossing actual territories. We got out of our journey imprecise descriptions. All we did was walk, be in places, cross them, and tie their destiny to ours. Every time we climbed over a wall or we went through a hole in a chain-link fence, we experienced apprehension, which made us more attentive to these unknown places, even if they are in our backyard. These existing terrains have been unveiled. We have the key to their access; we know where to return to listen to the voice, to sing the streets, to celebrate the locations, but also to conduct any others who might feel the need to discover.
>
> (Romito 1997: 140)

10.1
Walk about Rome, marking the concrete piles with flour

At times, the group grew to about two dozen traveling companions. Not everyone was related professionally, nor did they all share the same environmental concerns. Yet the mix of backgrounds and interests—participants included architects, artists, photographers and video artists, professional urbanists and an astrophysicist—sharpened the collective experience and brought added depth.

The Walk about Rome succeeded in breaking new ground because it introduced something thoroughly unexpected. Though the city had been meticulously scrutinized for centuries, suddenly there was another Rome emerging before the public, a Rome that had little to do with its souvenir ancient monuments and famous historic core. Yet it would soon become clear that this other Rome, the one few people had ever set eyes on, was a fascinating world unto itself, a poetically charged alternative realm where local customs and lifestyles departed radically from the city's mainstream society. The group that hopped over the fence initiated a contemporary quest to map these spaces and experiences, first-hand, discovering the vast landscapes on Rome's urban perimeter.

"Actual territories" constitute the built city's negative, the interstitial and the marginal, spaces abandoned or in the process of transformation. These are the removed *lieux de la mémoire*, the unconscious becoming of the urban systems, the spaces of confrontation and contamination between the organic and the inorganic, between nature and artifice. Here the metabolization of humanity's discarded scrap and nature's detritus produces a new horizon of unexplored territories, mutant and by default virgin, that are for Stalker "actual territories." The term "actual" indicates the process in which space comes into being. The "actual" is not what we are, but rather what we are becoming, that is to say the "other" that becomes other (Stalker 1995).

The Walk about Rome did not spring from nowhere, *sui generis.* Planning for the tour drew on previously shared experiences, culled from highly eclectic personal research and sharpened by years of opposition to prevailing educational practices. The individual members of Stalker succeeded in leapfrogging the many obstacles that had usually discouraged professional advancement in Italy. These were the unreformed, notoriously stilted university hierarchies, the paucity of paid work opportunities, and—perhaps most significantly—the poverty of contemporary architectural experimentation at that time.

Stalker's original breakthrough was the abandonment of traditional architectural language in order to transcend the discipline's narrow conceptual boundaries. The group culled their research from disciplines not usually associated with architectural practice. Some of their main influences came from the conceptual arts, postmodern philosophy, contemporary anthropology and astrophysics, especially drawing on recent advances in chaos theory. Stalker succeeded in binding these approaches together through a highly creative use of multimedia documentation, including the creative deployment of mapmaking, audio and video recording, photography and digital media. Taken together with the group's unwavering focus on non-conventional landscapes, this would help generate a new architecture, one that would set in motion the critical advancement of contextual urban research.

Tarkovsky's film is a cautionary tale, admonishing those who might threaten nature's tenuous balance: merely entering inside the prohibited zone introduced the risk of irreversibly altering its mystical presence. Could human exposure to this sequestered place fatally compromise these territories' special state of isolation? The Roman project bore witness to an environment of spectacular beauty and social seclusion that could have also been made an easy target for exploitation by the unscrupulous world outside. Revealing the spaces that were traversed during the walk became one of the more polemical aspects of the Walk about Rome. The consequences of sudden public exposure demanded critical reflection.

Shortly after the Walk about Rome, the collective established a non-profit association under the name of Stalker. They could already foresee themselves planning complex public events, gathering large audiences and capturing the attention of the local and national media. The notoriety generated by this one tour suggested that their method of urban research was accomplishing something unprecedented. They were unlike any other organization, official or unofficial.

Proto-Stalker

Five years before the walk, in 1990, a number of Stalker's future protagonists were involved in a several-months-long student protest that occupied the School of Architecture at La Sapienza in Rome. This action, which took place in the spring, was in response to a series of ministerial reforms that sought to privatize the state university system. The sprawling School of Architecture became the locus for a nation-wide university protest. The nucleus of students involved in the action took the name La Pantera, after a lone panther that had escaped from the city zoo the week before. The protest proved successful in halting the reforms. While the students' core concern was the scheduled privatization of the university program, their politicization seemed also to follow from recent events surrounding the collapse of the Berlin Wall and the renewal of broad debate on the political fate of Europe.

A re-evaluation of core educational values, at a time when the post modern architecture movement was beginning to fray at the seams, proved critical to building an unprecedented intergenerational consensus on the contemporary urban landscape. But the practical lessons learned over the period when the students occupied the university would prove to be just as significant. The Pantera movement succeeded over its brief lifespan not only in coalescing the practices of political organization and engagement, but also in developing a series of strategies to seize the moment, agitprop tactics designed to maintain public pressure. These tactics included art and theatrical events, physical interventions in the university grounds and collective assemblies that sought to counteract the stagnant educational system.

This set of protest skills came in handy in 1993 in relation to an overgrown area on the banks of the Tiber, downstream from Rome's historic center, opposite the Marconi industrial plant. For years this area had remained largely abandoned, though it was a popular hangout shared by young local drop-outs and undetectable homeless individuals. Many former Pantera student activists found themselves again joining ranks. They stumbled upon large piles of wooden rolling window blinds that had been illegally dumped in the area by workers installing newer plastic blinds in large apartment houses near the riverbanks. These provided a serendipitous opportunity to transform the wild thickets by the Tiber. The group improvised one of the first proto-Stalker actions, a carefully concerted, unofficial event to confront the area's longstanding negligence.

This action anticipated many of the tactics that would make up the repertoire of future Stalker projects. The principal action was re-using the hundreds of rolls of latticed wooden blinds as flat walking surfaces, creating a series of pathways through the underbrush. The operation, conducted over a three-day period, succeeded in transforming the banks below the urban residential neighborhood into a temporary riverside park. Entitled "Long live the river banks: For an environmental practice of waste," a series of micro-events was organized, including on-site artist installations, musical events and festivities, that together succeeded in animating the area. The operation drew an abundant public and plenty of press coverage. Write-ups described the event as giving renewed life to the area, "if only for the three days of the program" (Buonassisi 1993: VIII).

The event spotlighted the area's potential and served to convince Rome's municipality to make this site permanently accessible by converting it into a park. The success of this action proved that this process of multivalent territorial valorization worked. It provided ample evidence that this group of architecture students had a successful *modus operandi* for dealing with Rome's marginal urban strata. Their initial successes reflected the group's broad range of background interests. Some were well versed in Deleuzian philosophy. Others had taken to experimenting with the conceptual arts and video documentation. One member was an expert in fractal sciences. Almost all of them were extremely knowledgeable about Rome's history and its contemporary context. The assembling of a loose multi-disciplinary collective of architects and artists brought a particularly rich multi-dimensionality to the group's early territorially-based projects. But from early on, the group recognized that its greatest resource was precisely the indeterminacy of its collective identity:

> Stalker is not a group: it is an interrelated open system, which is growing and emerging through its actions and through all the individuals that operate with (for and among) Stalker. It is a collective subject that engages in actions and research to catalyze creative motions in time and space, to produce self-organized places, environments and situations.
>
> (Careri and Romito 2005: 227)

The group's critical social and environmental concerns were the catalyst for their subsequent political and conceptual actions. Throughout Stalker's early development, its young founders consistently focused on those urban places where powerful political and economic actors rarely considered investing time or money because of the limited opportunities for lucrative gains. Money was not easy to come by for Stalker either. For most of the first five years of the group's activities, hardly any funds existed to support the costs of the separate projects, let alone compensate members for their time. Many earned their living through outside employment or simply lived at home with their families and hunted around for temporary odd jobs.

Precedents, Homages and Methods

The Walk about Rome established the primary set of strategies that would constitute the group's *modus operandi*, instigating a new kind of practice for marginalized territories. The group's sensitivity towards these terrains and their mounting concerns for the populations found settling them came in part from the accumulation of on-site experiences and chance local encounters. But Stalker's highly critical form of field research was also inspired by a broad range of artistic and literary sources. These influences helped the group calibrate their research projects and contributed to the articulation of the Stalker Manifesto.

To interact with a place means understanding the dynamics that sustain it, including a sensitivity towards how such environments are entered and traversed. Stalker's passage across Rome's spaces of abandonment was inspired by European and North American avant-garde conceptual art culture of the late 1950s and early 1960s. The International Situationists (1957–72), like the Surrealists before them, set historic precedents that subverted basic perceptions of the European urban landscape. They excelled in opening up random ludic pathways through the modern city, "drifting" further and further into the generic urban fabric. Guy Debord, the group's lead pamphleteer, described the process as a *dérive*, an attitude towards the landscape that would open one's perception to its "psychogeographical effects" (Careri 2002).

For Lorenzo Romito, one of the founding members of Stalker, the wide-ranging success of the International Situationists' doctrine ultimately undermined its critical legacy. The *dérive* itself became a common cliché, merely another aesthetic mechanism to be manipulated in the name of Art. Especially problematic in relation to architecture and the city, the *dérive* has become an empty catch phrase for all that does not follow the city's rules (La Cecla 2000). The banalization of the Situationist movement alerted Stalker to the potential threat of a message's misappropriation, a lesson that the group would take seriously in its own dealings with the Italian and international media later on.

Italian cinema was more explicit in its embrace of the city's fundamental contradictions, especially with regard to the nation's rising post-war economic prosperity and the simple but impoverished world it was rapidly leaving behind. The sober Modernist backdrops that were increasingly present in the works of Vittorio de Sica, Michelangelo Antonioni and Pier Paolo Pasolini added disturbing new dimensions to the standard repertoire of quaint historic streets, packed baroque piazzas and idyllic country landscapes. These new backdrops were the unattractive and unadvertised terrains sprouting up outside major urban centers, environments ripe with land speculation and illegal settlements. Stalker paid homage to Pier Paolo Pasolini's brand of Italian *neo-realismo* in November of 1995 by marking one of the filmmaker's preferred haunts in the capital city, Via del Mandrione. The group painted this roadway, flanked by an ancient, roughly-hewn stone wall, in blue. By commemorating Pasolini, Stalker made a clear association with the filmmaker and his perception of this other, grittier Rome. Pasolini portrayed these peripheral worlds throughout his own work. In such films as *Mamma Roma* (1962), and *Hawks and Sparrows* (1966), he captured the violent transformations brought about by the capital's speculative post-war expansion. In particular, *Hawks and Sparrows*, filmed in the distant area towards Rome's Fiumicino airport, portrayed the hard-luck struggles of its local inhabitants as the capital mutated from shantytowns into modern housing blocks. Many such extraneous spaces scattered around the periphery of the capital became the focus for Stalker's first exploratory walks.

In a second homage, the group staged a re-enactment of *Asphalt Rundown*, a project by the American Robert Smithson created in 1969 during one of his visits to Rome. Smithson, one of the early leaders of the American land art movement and creator of the renowned *Spiral Jetty* on Salt Lake, Utah (1970), moved his art beyond the pristine galleries of the New York City scene. For Stalker, one of Smithson's most important contributions was his renowned essay "Tour of the Monuments of the Passaic, New Jersey" (1967). Smithson judged the disaffected American suburban landscape to be a new kind of artistic landmark. He sought not to romanticize but to recognize the importance of this formerly undervalued world of steam shovels, drainage pipes and smokestacks.

The art world proved rich in conceptual precedents. Further refinements to the group's approach came about through constant tinkering with a philosophy of the contemporary environment. Those members of Stalker who debated such issues were drawn to Deleuze and Guattari's rhizomatic construct of a heterogeneous universe. What slowly fell into place was a theory of environmental cognition drawing much of its substance from the opus *Mille Plateaux* (Deleuze and Guattari 1980). This treatise proved instrumental for understanding both the potential of a non-linear, non-hierarchical, multivalent approach to space and the societal transformations characterized as nomadism and deterritorialization. Other influences included Merleau-Ponty's aesthetic theory on reading cultural artifacts, Virilio's work on fluid spaces, Foucault's treatise on socio-spatial discipline and Vattimo's development of *pensiero debole* (weak theory). Aldo Innocenzi and Lorenzo Romito highlight Stalker's commitment to philosophical research, especially during its formative years. This is most evident in the nine points of reflection that constitute the group's 1996 Manifesto: "Entering the Territories; Crossing the Territories; Perceiving the Becoming; Fractal Organization; Continuity and Penetration of Actual Territories; Through the City; The Route as the Cognitive Map; The Abandonment; The Project." The astrophysicist Francesco Sylos Labini, a close colleague and fellow traveler, also assisted the group in understanding local territorial phenomena through the application of chaos theory.

Stalker's encounter with the anthropologist and architect Franco La Cecla proved unique in that he first influenced Stalker's research and then later wrote about their work. La Cecla recognized the ways in which consciousness of place fundamentally informs the human condition. He provided clues to understanding the play between environment and knowledge. The act of getting lost, according to La Cecla, elevates to the extreme both the tenuousness and the vitality of the relationship between individual identity and territory. It is also particularly clear when one looks at the most far-flung and dispersed societies, and the mechanisms which they invent for their own survival, that their relationships with place are accentuated and vital. The process of habitation outside the city centers contributes vibrant new layers of cultural production (La Cecla 2000). Stalker would prove this thesis.

Like Gordon Matta Clark's carving of buildings that went deep into the heart of the architectural artifact, Stalker goes beyond research to intervene in its subject, establishing dialectical exchanges that can recognize and reinforce conditions on the ground. At play are different but related logics that transcend singular professional stances and narrow analyses. Stalker acts to reconcile territorial conflicts precisely because the group represents a broad intellectual and activist base, drawing into its circle people with a wide variety of backgrounds, philosophies, artistic talents, media skills and urban smarts. The more eclectic the better. This approach is forged through an ever-expanding topography of actions that, just as importantly, move towards a wider scale of territorial engagement and social action.

This is, according to Stalker, "architecture" in the making: a process of engagement tailored to the "actual" context. Stalker gradually developed a new language of mapping, capturing knowledge that would have been lost to more standard methods of surveying. For Stalker the act of tracing creates an amplified path, in the process temporarily altering an existing environment yet teasing out its inherent complexities, celebrating its unique condition. The act of mapmaking itself becomes part of the critical initiative of surveying a territory. The construction of maps, such as the blue and gold archipelago sphere delineating the 1997 circuit around Rome, becomes instrumental to understanding the landscape's core characteristics. By manually tracing roadways, public hardscapes, trails and green spaces, inverting standard planning symbols or subverting long-held prejudices, Stalker's maps begin to reveal alternative territorial routes. The process of mapping also becomes more and more bound up with ancillary forms of documentation and creative actions, including the use of audio and video, photography and planned happenings. This approach suggests a performative architecture. It harmonizes together with the territory, its local community and the broader society.

Stalker operates in contexts where knowing how to communicate, using the appropriate multimedia is critical to the success of the project. There is no point in remaining loyal to traditional architectural and planning presentation styles. Stalker plies the internet, develops video broadcasts, creates local grass-roots networks, produces newspapers, journals or books. But there is a cautionary side to the use of the media since this relationship can cut both ways. Stalker prefers to take charge of the way it communicates itself, but the group has from time to time become a media target. The commercial media's usurping of Stalker's open working dynamic, resulting in several attempts to mix reportage with pseudo-reality television, risks confusing the boundaries between the real and the political, distorting Stalker's openly ludic intentions. This may end up as one of Stalker's biggest future challenges, to remain uncompromised in a world where the commercial media reifies every form of cultural production in the quest for ever greater audiences.

The members of Stalker have succeeded in developing a highly sophisticated critical process, geared to teasing out hidden contexts and social situations taking place within the non-conventional ex-urban landscapes surrounding major city centers. But by the end of the 1990s, the group had begun to tackle an even broader category of issues through its direct involvement with refugees, migrants and nomad communities who lived displaced lives, often far from their original homelands. These groups—Albanian workers, Somali entrepreneurs, Gypsy caravaners—whom Stalker frequently found living by simple means in the marginal zones that were Stalker's main focus, had been approached in the past, but were, out of respect, left to their own devices.

Stalker members started becoming more directly involved in these communities' living and social conditions. They sought a means of interacting with these marginalized communities that could not only deal with their basic survival needs but also could address their interrelations with society at large: a means of "humanizing" such communities *vis-à-vis* the general public, which tends to retreat into its xenophobic cocoon rather than reaching out to new social contexts. Stalker's work would take another significant step forward, one that has fundamentally shaped its present approach to marginal territories.

Campo Boario: The Ararat

The opportunity to broaden the social scope of the group's work presented itself in a pair of unexpected developments: the arrival in Rome in 1999 of a group of Kurdish exiles who were following their exiled political leader Ocalan as he moved from one country to another and the fortuitous availability of an inhabitable structure—the old veterinary offices located in the former Roman *mattatoio* (slaughterhouse), next to Monte Testaccio in the heart of the Campo Boario district.

To bring greater national attention to their plight, about a hundred Kurds created an improvised settlement called Cartonia, built entirely of recycled cardboard and other found materials, which they located in a park in sight of the Coliseum. In this cobbled-together village the Kurds set up a small restaurant, a tearoom, a barbershop and a store for provisions. When Ocalan was suddenly deported from Italy in 1999, local law enforcement officers pulled down the temporary encampment by the Coliseum. Stalker took quick action and offered the Kurdish community a fixed residence on the grounds of the Campo Boario, taking advantage of an invitation from the Biennale of Young Artists of Europe and the Mediterranean. The project "From Cartonia to Piazza Kurdistan" took the form of a student workshop, sponsored by the architecture section of INARCH, the Society of Roman Architects.

This initial phase brought students and refugees in close contact with each other and contributed to the re-creation of a barbershop and multi-ethnic tearoom as well as a reading room and dormitory. Bit by bit, Stalker renovated the ex-veterinary offices with the help of Azad, a Rome-based social assistance organization and the Villaggio Globale, a cooperative squatter group with its headquarters and social center in the same compound. The veterinary building was renamed the Ararat after the biblical mountain site recounted in the story of the universal flood.

Sharing the large courtyard area of the compound were: the coachmen and their horses serving the tourist trade, with their hay feeds and perimeter stalls; the Gypsy Kalderash community who habitually returned to the sprawling grounds of the ex-slaughterhouse and lived mainly in parked mobile homes (Fig. 10.2); a group of immigrant Somalis; a popular Palestinian restaurant; and a health club accessed from outside the perimeter. Inside the slaughterhouse compound, each of these groups had traditionally fended for themselves with little municipal presence. The mood in the area resembled an "open city," secluded from the rest of the capital and largely forgotten by the outside world.

Following the introduction of the Kurdish community into the Campo Boario, tensions began to rise among the diverse groups of occupants who saw their interests compromised or even threatened. Up until then these recalcitrant refugee populations had no overarching cooperative structure to settle disputes among themselves. Stalker assumed the role of intermediary and sought ways to develop greater trust between the groups and work towards a peaceful means of cohabitation. Stalker took on the role of artistic arbiter, seeking to overcome inter-ethnic conflicts through a series of communal happenings and conceptual installations performed *in situ* at the Campo Boario.

The group's members established a series of performance events, culminating in the Pranzo Boario (Boario Dinner) developed together with the Japanese artist Asako Iwama. A huge outdoor banquet was staged on November 14,

10.2
Mobile homes in Campo Boario, the former slaughterhouse, Rome

10.3
Pranzo Boario. The Campo Boario courtyard with tables arranged in a circle for the dinner featuring Japanese, Kurdish and Gypsy cuisines

1999, featuring Kurdish-Japanese-Gypsy cuisines, a historic event in its own right (Fig. 10.3). The broad circle of tables arranged in the middle of the courtyard succeeded in creating a common platform that opened a playful dialogue between the diverse ethnic communities. Adults and children from each of Campo Boario's neighborhoods came and took part in the meal, as did many Romans curious to experience the event.

Stalker organized additional events at the Campo Boario involving the local residents in a series of open-air actions, such as the construction of a garden, Orte Boario, part of an effort to reclaim the large central area in the compound from invasive nighttime parking, and an annual spring festival Newroz. The advantage of this approach to these untutored spaces became evident as the creative performances and collective projects succeeded in dissolving longstanding prejudices on both sides of the compound's walls. The events became important opportunities for overcoming popular stereotypes, providing new contexts for public exchange. This area of Testaccio mostly had a reputation for nighttime dance clubs, loud partying and other kinds of transgressive behavior. But inside the slaughterhouse a different atmosphere reigned, anti-commercial and openly multi-cultural. The compound was a retreat from the bustle of the capital.

Transborderline

In the same period Stalker sought to develop a range of corollary projects that could provoke debate concerning protracted immigrant issues, especially the closed frontiers and the preponderance of migrant communities settling all over the Italian peninsula and beyond, in the rest of Europe. The second-stage Stalker projects addressed some of the more tragic aspects of transmigration: the dangers of border passage and increasing public resistance to the growing presence of non-natives within local communities. The *Transborderline* project transcended the Campo Boario locale by initiating a series of traveling events that moved well beyond Rome. Subtitled "The Habitable Infrastructure to Support the Free Circulation of People," the aim was to contrast the threatening image of the barbed wire fence dividing national borders with an entirely soft version, mutable, penetrable and user friendly.

Transborderline is a proposal for a new kind of border that maintains the spiral shape but looses its thorns and widens into a ludic space, crossable and at the same time habitable. Prototype of a possible future public space born from the "unfolding" of borders, it creates an ideal place for exchange and diversity, an infrastructure that can be the structure and the conduit for free transit (Stalker 2000).

The project was first conceived over the spring of 2000, for the exhibition "La ville, le jardin, la mémoire," organized by the French Academy at the Villa Medici in Rome. The installation consisted of a large tubular spiral, wide enough for an average person to pass through inside or sit down. For the Villa Medici, the structure was sheathed in plastic, creating a translucent tunnel environment. From there it was moved the short distance to the Campo Boario, where it underwent a metamorphosis (Figs 10.4, 10.5). About a thousand soccer balls were handed out to the Kurdish, Gypsy and Somali communities living inside the compound. Each individual was asked to sign his or her name on a ball and record his or her place of origin. The balls, kicked around for a couple of days by the many children in the area, were later collected and packed off for the next part of the project, the *Global Game*.

The signature soccer balls, along with the tubular structure, were transported to Venice where the project was re-installed for the VII Biennale of Architecture. *Transborderline* functioned as a two-part mechanism, the spiral bringing attention to the issue of Europe's guarded frontiers, the soccer balls reminding the public of the very real lives of the refugees these borders were meant to keep out. Visitors were encouraged to play with the balls, to engage personally with the individuals' stories. Finally, in conjunction with the Manifesta 3 exhibition, *Transborderline* was repositioned one last time on the frontier border zone between Italy and Slovenia. The large tubular spiral was set down with great stealth, without any of the requisite permits, on a creek along the border and then abandoned there. None of the members of Stalker who installed the piece on the border were caught in the act, a curious demonstration of the casual arbitrariness of frontier justice.

Transborderline provided a lesson on how it is possible to work at different levels without losing sight of the human suffering and capacity for resistance that are universally shared conditions. *Transborderline* proved to be an effective model, setting the parameters for Stalker's next and much more ambitious project, *The Flying Carpet*, which came about between November 2000 and January 2001. This piece was a three-dimensional representation of the ceiling of the Palatine Chapel, the famous Arabic monument in Palermo, Sicily. An intricate hanging structure of rope and copper,

10.4
The installation of *Transborderline* at the Ararat, on the grounds of the Campo Boario

10.5
Children kicking footballs inside the *Transborderline* installation at the Ararat. Each of the balls has been signed by one of the local inhabitants, and describes their journey from their place of origin to Rome.

it was digitally generated on computer but hand-built by Kurdish craftsmen from the Ararat. The Kurds, along with a small number of other Campo Boario residents, were able to support themselves with the income from the art project. *The Flying Carpet* project also featured a sound installation that emanated unseen from the ceiling. The ropes approximated the delicate contouring of the original ceiling, yet at a scale and height that invited people to gather comfortably below, on carpets and pillows arranged by Stalker. *The Flying Carpet* was scheduled to travel from the Ararat in Rome to a series of cities including Sarajevo, Tunis and Tirana. Its tour has since been extended to many more Middle Eastern destinations, including Egypt, Jordan and Qatar. Sponsored by the Italian Foreign Office, the project remains one of the few Italian cultural programs to ever successfully tour the Islamic world. *The Flying Carpet* has brought together peoples, regions and nations in a celebration of diversity.

The extreme lightness of such projects and their playfully experimental qualities might appear to undercut Stalker's expressive critique of the general state of global society today. Yet this has hardly been the case. Quite to the contrary, the often playful approach to some of the more intractable urban contexts and communities found in Italy and elsewhere accentuates the role of creativity in bridging social and political divides. Given globalization's relative newness and its poorly understood impact on local contexts, it is precisely this kind of approach mingling disciplines and strategies that has the most immediate benefits. The ultimate goal is to identify, connect with and participate with these communities on the margins in ways that break down barriers and boundaries, in contrast to more unilateral forms of tutelage.

New Approaches for New Situations

Traditional urban and architectural practices, shaped in the industrial era, are ill-equipped to cope with the forces driving the contemporary sprawl of cities or with their increasingly heterogeneous societies and marginalized communities. For quite some time illegal and quasi-legal immigrant communities in abandoned warehouses and factories, sequestered on distant camp grounds and residing in inner city squats have been seen merely as disassociated elements in the daily affairs of the traditional city. But over the past 15 years it has become evident that population displacements in many major world cities and their informal patterns of settlement are re-shaping entire social and geographic relationships. The emerging settlements are global "crashlands" that host globally-connected but hyper-local outsider communities that are proving to be the true forces behind the new hybrid, heterogeneous city. The drivers of urban transformation today are these disaffected populations and their stimulating contributions to urban culture. New York, Moscow, Paris, Rome, Athens, Istanbul, Cairo and Hong Kong cease to be just national economic and political centers as they become hybridized global megalopolises. These sprawling cities have more in common with each other than with their surrounding hinterlands.

That most nations actively consider the steady waves of human migration to be illegal and therefore criminal does not mean that their movements can somehow be limited or easily reversed. Quite the contrary, the increasing hardening of national borders and restrictions on residence permits for foreigners serve only to enhance ignorance. These xenophobic over-reactions are entirely counterproductive to the long-term good. Rather than seek ways to guarantee the perseverance of a Fortress Europe or a Fortress America, more should be invested in understanding precisely what kinds of changes are actually taking place in order to share the many undervalued advantages. In contemporary society, according to Appadurai,

> What is new is that . . . both points of departure and points of arrival are in cultural flux, and thus the search for steady points of reference, as critical life choices are made, can be very difficult. It is in this atmosphere that the invention of tradition and of ethnicity, kinship and other identity markers can become slippery, as the search for certainties is regularly frustrated by the fluidities of transnational communication.
>
> (1996: 44)

This fluid society and the "ethnoscapes" that Appadurai describes are rapidly seeping across the globe. Territorial space has become unevenly porous, permitting entirely novel patterns of population dispersal and movement. Cultures jump from region to region, or country to country, while being forcibly repelled by others. Cities swell, centers disintegrate, communities rapidly reinvent their networks.

Those who should be most concerned with these issues, the cadre of urban professionals called on to intervene in city affairs, are ill-prepared to address these new contexts. Government agencies, professional practices and universities are confined to narrow disciplinary fields. They are unprepared to rally the kind of multi-disciplinary expertise required to address complex issues linked to political and economic exodus and ethnic national and immigrant networks, the myriad local settlement patterns or the long-term impact of these forces on domestic and public spaces. New multi-disciplinary, experimental forms of research and intervention, unfettered by traditional boundaries and practices, are needed.

In the past decade, in addition to the work of Stalker, a respectable body of research has been taking shape to meet this need: the large-scale documentary investigations into European, Asian and African cities presented in the anthology *Mutations* (Koolhaas *et al.* 2001); the urban research conducted by Koolhaas (The Harvard Project on the City, continuing in the Rotterdam-based offices of OMA and AMO); the "datascapes" introduced by the Dutch research group MVRDV, led by Winy Maas; the work compiled by the Ghent Urban Studies Team (GUST) in Belgium. In Israel, a group of architects and scholars led by Segal and Weizman (2005) have contributed a series of highly-controversial political studies on the control of territory. In Taiwan, Ti-Nan Chi created the international network Urban Flashes, focusing on short-term, micro-urban phenomena (Lang and Boyarsky 2003). In Greece, the group Paradigmata has pursued this line of urban/periphery research through a series of on-site workshops developing the Greek architecture pavilion for the 2004 Venice Biennale, where they focused on zones of conflict and areas of social and geographical indeterminacy (Paradigmata 2004). Istanbul's vast and rapidly expanding urban environment is also undergoing similar critical investigations. The city was the subject of the last two Istanbul Art Biennales, as well as numerous recent exhibitions and symposia, where groups like Platform and Oda Projesi and individual work such as Esra Akcan's dystopian research on Istanbul and Pelin Tan's sociologically-driven urban studies are changing the way the city is understood. In the United States, Kyong Park has dedicated several years to mapping Detroit (Park 2005). Michael Sorkin (2005) is a strong voice for this alternative territorial perspective from within New York's academia.

In Italy, a related approach to territorial research is being conducted on many fronts, spearheaded by groups like Multiplicity in Milan, Cliostraat in Turin, and Ma0, IAN+, Sciatto and Stalker/ON in Rome (the long-range research arm of Stalker developed to conduct transnational projects for the European community). These names have been associated with each other through works featured in important international art and architecture expositions such as the Venice Architecture Biennale and the Milan Triennial (Molinari 2005). In Germany, France and Spain, there are formidable movements that can make similar claims as well as in Central and South America.

While each group has developed working methods to observe and respond to various urban pressure points, Stalker has made its mark by developing strategies that go beyond documentary research, engaging the territorial subject both critically and creatively. In the past decade, Stalker has succeeded in recognizing the city's mostly hidden liminal spaces, making concerted efforts both to document and to interact within these uncertain contexts. Drawing upon a deep concern with both cultural production and geographical space, Stalker engages a "geo-cultural" vision that cuts between local and global spheres of influence, reaching out to those whose condition is extraneous, whose world is detached from their immediate social and territorial surroundings. Through its multi-disciplinary acts of engagement, through deployment of a series of experimental fieldwork, Stalker succeeds in establishing the grounds for reconciliation and exchange that dissolve boundaries and create bonds, that encourage exchanges and provide the means for self-determination. The architect Giancarlo De Carlo did not name but nonetheless seems to accurately describe Stalker's contribution to enlarging the contemporary field of architecture:

> Everywhere small groups of young people, even temporarily working together to tackle some specific problems, are paving new roads such as the identification with the laws and rhythms of nature, or the active redefinition of the territory as cause and effect of any spatial event; they aim at "reading" the city and the region, no longer as an analytical collection of data but as a physical and mental interpenetration of places to spy out real history and its probable evolutions. They see the "tentative design" as a sequence of hypotheses to be explored not to reach univocal solutions but to open possible ones whose meaning relies on the circumstances surrounding the problem
>
> (De Carlo 2004: 61).

To this generation of architects, artists, researchers and critics the city has grown more complex, more insidious and more unrecognizable than it was only some 17 years ago when the Berlin Wall came crumbling down. Historic city centers have become, "heterotopias of illusion" (Shane 2005: 259), another phenomenon that contributes to the destabilization of earlier architectural and urban canons. The city today is composed of a much larger quilt of outlying experiences which, as an ensemble, make up the complex working mechanics of today's megalopolises. It is these far-flung pieces that remain most unknown and least documented, yet these are the loose spaces that guarantee future generations of creativity and vitality. Stalker investigates and engages in the areas that have grown out of the miasma of international networks, migration corridors, the *terrain vague* and temporary places of refuge. These are the spaces of transformation, the "actual territories" that encumber the more traditional city fabric. These are the places that ultimately need the greatest attention.

References

Appadurai, A. (1996) *Modernity at Large: Cultural Dimensions of Globalization*, Minneapolis: University of Minnesota Press.

Buonassisi, A. (1993) "I Tre Giorni a Riva Marconi," *La Repubblica*, Rome, July 22 VIII.

Careri, F. (2002) *Walkscapes: Walking as an Aesthetic Practice*, Barcelona: Gustavo Gili.

Careri, F. and Romito, L. (2005) "Stalker and the Big Game of Campo Boario," in P. B. Jones, D. Petrescu and T. Till (eds) *Architecture and Participation*, London: Spon Press.

De Carlo, G. (2004) "The Memory of Architecture," *Domus*, 870 (reprinted in *Writings for Domus*, Milan: Domus, 2005: 61).

Deleuze, G. and Guattari, F. (1980) *Mille Plateaux*, Paris: Minuit.

GUST (eds) (2002) *Post Ex Sub Dis: Urban Fragmentations and Constructions*, Rotterdam: 010 Publishers.

Koolhaas, R., Boeri, S., Kwinter, S., Ulrich Obrist, H. and Tazi, N. (eds) (2001) *Mutations*, Barcelona: Actar.

La Cecla, F. (2000) *Perdersi: L'uomo Senza Ambiente*, Roma and Bari: Laterza.

Lang, P. (2005) "Over My Dead City," in K. Park (ed.) *Urban Ecology: Detroit and Beyond*, Hong Kong: Map Book Publishers.

Lang, P. and Boyarsky, N. (eds) (2003) *Urban Flashes Asia: New Architecture and Urbanism in Asia*, London: Wiley-Academy.

Molinari, L. (2005) "Italian Metamorph," *A+U* August: 8–16.

Multiplicity (eds) (2003) *USE: Uncertain States of Europe*, Milan: Skira.

Paradigmata (2004) (Urban Void, curators) *Catalogue for the Greek Pavilion*, Athens: Venice Biennale of Architecture.

Park, K. (ed.) (2005) *Urban Ecology: Detroit and Beyond*, Hong Kong: Map Book Publishers.

Romito, L. (1997) "Stalker," in P. Lang and T. Miller (eds) *Suburban Discipline*, New York: Princeton Architectural Press.

Segal, R. and Weizman, E. (2005) "A Civil Occupation," in M. Sorkin (ed.) *Against the Wall*, New York: The New Press.

Shane, D. G. (2005) *Recombinant Urbanism: Conceptual Modeling in Architecture, Urban Design, and City Theory*, London: John Wiley.

Sorkin, M. (ed.) (2005) *Against the Wall*, New York: The New Press.

Stalker (1995) "Manifesto," available: http://digilander.libero.it/stalkerlab/tarkowsky/manifesto/manifesting.htm

Stalker (2000) "Transborderline: Project statement, Manifesta 3 Ljubljana, Slovenia," available: http://digilander.libero.it/stalkerlab/tarkowsky/transbord/transborderlng.html.

Chapter 11

Dead Zones, Outdoor Rooms and the Architecture of Transgression

Gil M. Doron

A few years ago, while working as an architectural journalist in Tel-Aviv, campaigning against plans to build luxury housing along the shore of the city, I received an invitation to lunch from a fisherman, Aaron, in a place called the Dead Zone. "Striking name for a restaurant," I thought, but I could not recall any restaurant with that name. "Is it a new place?" I asked. "Sort of, but you won't find it in the Yellow Pages. The name of the place is written only on the city maps in the planning department." Then the fisherman whispered, "By the way, it is not a restaurant." So, I thought, a home-cooked meal sounds promising. But when I arrived, I saw that it was neither.

After paying Aaron a visit, I asked a planner in the planning department to show me the Dead Zone. He pointed to a white mark on the city map that covered Ha'Yarkon Estuary, on the boundary of downtown Tel Aviv. The white mark concealed the place where a few days ago I had eaten lunch in a charming hut, rebuilt from the ruins of a Palestinian fishing village, by a few of its descendants—Aaron, and his sons. The village was erased from the history of Palestine/Israel but its ghosts are still haunting this estuary as well the entire Middle East.

In other huts, a few squatters had been celebrating, and Aaron told me that in a few days they were going to be evicted. The sun was setting. On the opposite bank of the river, where it meets the sea, a few nudists were about to leave, and a few

11.1
South bank of the Ha'Yarkon River, Tel Aviv, after regeneration, and the north bank with fuel tanks of the nearby power station and remnants of the Palestinian village

kids were taking their place, preparing a bonfire. Further on, between the dilapidated industrial ruins of the Orient Fair, which attracted half a million visitors to Israel in the 1930s and was one the masterpieces of the international and constructivist style (Regve and Raz 1996), I saw a few cars. I crossed the river. In one car, there were a couple of teenagers, maybe having their first kiss; in another car old men and a young woman. I went down to the desolated riverbank again. Sixty years ago, there had been a Bedouin tribe here. In a few hours new nomads of consciousness, on Ecstasy and acid, would be dancing while the city slept. And while they danced, in the sunrise, Aaron would start his day again. And all of this was happening in a place happily detached from the city, but actually only 500 meters away, in a place marked "dead zone", its days numbered before the bulldozers arrived.

I said to the planner, as innocently as a journalist could, "But it is a white dot on a map that you have shown me. It is not a dead zone." "Ah," he mumbled, and ran away to finish some project.

Defying Definition

"Dead zone"—translated from a slang Hebrew term meaning an area that is derelict, abandoned and empty—is a synonym for other terms such as void, *terrain vague*, *tabula rasa* and no man's land.

Death, an hiatus *par excellence*, opens an infinite gap between subject and object; in this case between the zone and us. Indicating that the zone is one of death is to indicate that no communication, information or negotiation can exist between it and us. No bridging the gap is possible; hence the designated area can be considered only from a detached position—characterized by de Certeau as "the 110th floor of the World Trade Center" (1988: 91). The other terms indicate similar positions. The void can be examined only from outside; enter it and it is no longer a void. The no man's land can be surveyed only through binoculars. The *tabula rasa* can be imagined only on plans and maps. Nevertheless, as gap spaces they are all also endless openings. They are pure possibility; hence the utopian sentiment that is attached to them. This zone is so alluring that Tarkovsky's (1979) Stalker would sacrifice his life just to be able to be there.

Naming these areas dead zone, void, *tabula rasa* and no man's land makes them, by definition, intangible. This abstraction through naming is also reflected in planners' ostensibly impartial and detached methods of defining and quantifying such areas. Take, for example, the most mundane and procedural definition for derelict land made by the British National Land Use Database (NLUD): derelict land is "land so damaged by development that it is incapable of beneficial use without further treatment" (NLUD 2003: 14). However, the database, which is assumed to be accurate and objective, does not clarify what "beneficial use" is, leaving their definition exposed as subjective. And, indeed, the final report of the British Urban Task Force (Rogers *et al.* 1999) gave two very different figures for the amount of derelict land in the UK. The special Thames Television Report *Wasteland* used the NLUD's definition, and after an extensive survey, found that "a precise definition of dereliction is virtually impossible" (Naabarro *et al.* 1980). The report made clear that the NLUD definition was not sufficient since some of the sites categorized as derelict or vacant were actually being used informally and temporarily. Aesthetic judgment had to be used to discern what a derelict site was, but in the end the report concluded that defining a building or a site as derelict remains to some extent a matter for subjective judgment (ibid.).

Kevin Lynch perhaps cast the strongest doubts on the enterprise of defining wasteland and dereliction. In *Wasting Away* (1990), he observed that the term "waste" refers to things or places that were in use, or are potentially useful but are not currently in use. Similarly, the term "derelict" refers to land that has stopped generating capital. Ironically, much of the derelict land in American cities is put into this state for speculative reasons, so although the land might look derelict, it is in fact generating capital, in terms of future gain in its own value; thus it cannot be considered waste. This was also asserted in the British Land Use Database 2002 where more than half of the "vacant" and "derelict" land in England had planning permission but, mainly for speculative reasons, was left as it was (CABE 2003: 11). Lynch argues that even if land is not generating capital, if it does not require any expenditure, it cannot be considered wasteland since nothing is being wasted. "Thus," Lynch concluded, "a desert, or even an empty building or an unused machine, may only apparently be wasteful . . . but the labeling of something as waste must always ask: waste for whom?" (1990: 101–102).

Language is a Virus

The depiction of Ha'Yarkon Estuary as a dead zone by Tel Aviv's municipal planners was not accidental. The discourse of the dead zone, wasteland, and void is rooted in the Zionist myth of the foundation of Tel Aviv. The city, according to the dominant narrative, "grew out of the sand"; that is, from the desert or a void. In welcoming Lord Alfred Milner to Tel Aviv in 1922, the first mayor of the city, Meir Dizengoff, described it thus: "This whole little town, as far as the eye can discern straight streets and modern buildings, is Tel Aviv. Thirteen years ago not a single house existed in these parts, nothing but sand-dunes covered the region" (LeVine 2005: 285). However, aerial photographs from the First World War, maps, photographs and testimonies summarized in only a few studies show that Tel Aviv's area was originally dotted with about six Palestinian villages, the residents of which left or were evicted in 1948 (Palestine Remembered 2005; LeVine 2005). And the stretch of sand on which Ahuzat Bayit, the first neighborhood of Tel Aviv, was built had been periodically cultivated by a Bedouin tribe and was known as Karm al-Jabali or the Vine Grove of al Jabali (LeVine 2005).

Imagining a void where there was none was the grounds for implementing the Zionist dream in Tel Aviv and in Palestine as a whole. In *Imagining Zion*, Troen writes: "Like other European colonizers since the time of Columbus who imagined their extra-European land could be made to conform to the images and ideas of the lands of their birth, they set out to impose the familiar on the new" (2003: 89).

In the case of Tel Aviv and Ha'Yarkon Estuary, the new was imposed on the old: the garden city in contrast to old Jaffe and the surrounding villages, new development on the remnants of the Palestinian village and the International-style pavilions of the Orient Fair. By seeing the space as a void, the planners could imagine any program or design they chose since apparently there was neither any context they had to refer to nor any community they needed to consider. In the building of Tel Aviv in the early twentieth century, this distorted view of reality made the city an architectural laboratory where the latest architectural trends were implemented, disregarding the nearby existing city, Jaffe and surrounding villages (Troen 2003). This also explains how, in an international design competition in 1996, two completely different proposals won first prize while neither acknowledged the past or the present of the actual site (Doron 1995).

To perforate the planning map, which colored the area white, Aaron took his case to court with supportive coverage from *Ha'ir Weekly* and won. British Air Force aerial photographs from before 1948 clearly showed his and others' huts where the Palestinian fishing village was. However, other parts of the site have been gradually sanitized and redeveloped. Even though some of the unregulated activities have been endorsed, in particular commercial ones like clubbing, sanitization and segregation have erased former qualities of the site. The grand new plans for office and residential towers are still in the pipeline, and no doubt the unique character of the site, its exteriority to the regulated city, will be lost.

Portraying a place as a void in order to colonize or "regenerate" it is not unique to Tel Aviv or Palestine. This case, however, makes a clear connection between colonization on a global scale and regeneration as re-colonization on an urban scale. Such a connection was implied in *Colonizing the Void*, the catalogue for the Dutch Pavilion in 1996's Venice Biennale of Architecture. Han van Dijk wrote:

> As far as I am aware, no one has ever written a cultural history of the void. But it would coincide to a large extent with that of colonialism. Colonists were attracted by the "empty" spots still to be found a hundred year ago on globes and maps.

To an even greater extent in Tel Aviv, the colonized space "turned out to be less empty than the European adventurers thought and subsequently had to be cleared. The dream of the void to be occupied was so strong that reality was roughly altered to suit it" (van Dijk 1996: 34).

Global *Dérive* in the Dead Zones

Upon learning that the term "dead zone" and its equivalents are commonly used by architects and planners, I embarked on a global *dérive* to find these zones (Doron 2000a). The method of finding these places was similar to the Situationist *dérive*. As the research progressed, the spatial location and timing of these zones became easier to track, but as with Tarkovsky's *Stalker*, sometimes the only way to find them was by throwing a stone in a random direction and following it. It became clear that in each of the very diverse cities I visited, one could always find some areas or some time segments in which the conditions of the dead zone existed. These conditions transform cities at various scales and in various ways. Such transformations can be described according to the spatial qualities of zones, edges and overlapping spaces.

Zones

Christiania, the Free-Town, an 82-acre site west of downtown Copenhagen, had been a military base until it was abandoned in 1969. It straddles the former fortifications of the city and a lake and is enclosed by a 5m-high wall. In 1997, residents from the neighborhood around squatted in the base, seeking in it the green open spaces they lacked. This was followed by the establishment of a community of about 1,000 who, until recently, had their own local government, laws, urban planning system. Since its founding there have been several attempts to evict the squatters. These attempts failed mainly because the site's listed building status prevented any concrete development plans, but also partly due to the Danish government's recognition of Christiania as a social experiment in the early 1970s.

Since 2000, it has become the most popular tourist attraction in Denmark, with more than half a million visitors a year attracted by the semi-legal soft drug

11.2
A tenant next to New York's derelict elevated train line created a small garden. Currently the High Line, which can be considered as a linear dead zone that cuts through the city, is being redesigned into a linear park by Diller Scofidio and Renfro.

market, cheap restaurants, music venues, and the serene atmosphere created by the banning of cars. It stands in contrast to Copenhagen's sanitized and over-commercial downtown, celebrated by planners (Rogers and Power 2000). The rise of the center-right government in 2001 has changed attitudes toward the town and residents have had to accept dramatic reforms that in many ways have abolished the uniqueness of the place.

Another alternative colony, albeit less ideological and more the result of economic necessity, was established during the 1980s under the nose of the Los Angeles planning authorities. The zone where this artists' colony established itself, which in the past few years has become known as the Arts District, is a former industrial area between the Hollywood and Santa Monica Freeways and between

Alameda Street (Little Tokyo) and the L.A. River. As with Christiania, the area is a kind of enclave where the former uses have been abandoned and new ones, against the original plans, took their place.

With the decline of manufacturing in the 1970s, artists started to move into the area, even though until 1998 it was forbidden to live in the industrial buildings. After the city planners discovered that the area had effectively been transformed into a semi-residential neighborhood, they passed the Artists in Residence Ordinance, which allowed artists to live legally in any building. Since then the demand for studios and levels of rent have increased dramatically. However, the city planning authorities were not fully aware of the dramatic change until the early 1990s. Architect Jim Y. Tokunaga, from the Department of City Planning, admitted in an interview:

> We were absolutely blind to the transformation of the area from an ex-industrial zone to an artists' neighborhood. It was without permission, and they did not give it any publicity. Around 1993 we went to the area as part of the preparation for a new city plan for central L.A. We walked in the street and were surprised to see these phenomena. Actually, it struck us.

Officially named the "Arts District" in 2000, the area includes galleries, restaurants, grocery stores and about 450 live–work lofts. However, the city authorities were in no hurry to change the area's industrial status. Architect Tokunaga admitted that in planning terms the Arts District is a mirage; it does not exist on zoning maps. "Our approach to the Arts District is indifference. The artists can stay there until the demand for industry becomes stronger and industry takes its place back." However, the real danger to this community is not likely to come from a future return of industry, but rather from plans for more lucrative uses of this downtown area. Maintaining the industrial designation of the area means that the resident artists have no rights and no say in future planning decisions.

These two examples, and others that I covered in my research, can be considered archetypal dead zones (Borret 1999). They are mainly former industrial areas or nineteenth-century infrastructures such as slaughterhouses, abandoned barracks, dysfunctional harbors, and train yards. The zones usually have strong boundaries that render access to them somewhat restricted and make the sites look inward. Emptied of their former official uses, they were overtaken, sometimes temporarily, by myriad informal activities. Arising from decisions by landlords or local authorities to suspend any new development the result is, on the one hand, degradation of the area and its buildings, and, on the other, if the area is not completely sealed off, an infiltration of informal activities. In turn, when developers are ready to re-colonize the site, it will be portrayed as dead, void, dangerous in efforts to persuade the authorities and the public to approve more lucrative uses and structures (Doron 2000a).

Edges

Some characteristics of dead zones can be found in much smaller urban sites. "Edge places" are situated besides roads and railway tracks, pavements and riverbanks. Due to their size and setting, they are impervious to re-development and receptive to informal activities. For example, on the edge of a San Francisco highway, inside a series of buttresses supporting the cliff, I was introduced to a community of homeless people who had settled there. I encountered a similar homeless settlement on the unkempt banks of the Tiber in central Rome where immigrants had created makeshift shelters and food gardens. More extensive linear villages are common along railway lines in Thailand and Malaysia (Doron 2000d). A different edge that gained more publicity was the no man's land along the former Berlin Wall which was occupied after the fall of the Wall by hundreds of wagon dwellers (Berg 1998).

Other urban communities inhabiting the edges of streets engage in myriad activities such as begging, vending, busking and selling sex. Although entirely dependent on the traffic of passers-by, these communities need a solid edge from which they can operate. The dense vegetation of edges of parks and gardens, in places such as Royal Park in Brussels, the Independent Park in Tel Aviv and Russell and Bloomsbury Squares in London enabled public sex to take place by concealing it from the public eye.

Since it is difficult, if not impossible, to implement redevelopment projects in these edge spaces, they are often sanitized, cleansed of their dilapidated and unkempt appearance and the informal activities that take place there. These cleansed zones effectively become no man's lands. From being a "lived space" (de Certeau 1988), these edges, in a violent act (Wigley 2002), are returned to their former status as a one-dimensional line drawn on a planning map.

Overlapping spaces

Dead zones are spaces in which the formal program has been suspended and replaced by informal activities; edge spaces contain these same activities alongside formal ones. A third distinct kind of space is where the formal and informal overlap, existing simultaneously with no clear physical or temporal boundaries between them (Soja 1996). This kind of condition exists in various places, but can only be located in temporal, not geographical, terms. For example, in Golden Gate Park, tourists roam the dilapidated Second World War bunkers, oblivious to the sexual activities that are taking place just around the corner or in a neighboring bush. Spaces under highway bridges, in Kuala Lumpur and Bangkok, are used simultaneously for commerce, shelters for homeless people and children's playgrounds. In Singapore, of all places, with its brutal punishment of gay sex, I visited the Han Fun Club, an established public sex/cruising area under a highway bridge. The edge of the place also had a small shrine, which I assumed was dedicated to a person who had been killed in a road accident nearby.

11.3
North bank of the Tiber, Rome. The banks of the Tiber were inhabited by homeless people, mainly immigrants, before they were (re)designed and paved.

11.4
A squatter village on a live train line and under a highway, Bangkok

11.5
World War II bunkers in Golden Gate Park, San Francisco. The space is simultaneously a tourist attraction and a public sex site.

Indeed, it is Singapore that bears the most striking examples of transgressive zones. As a "generic city," I assumed that Singapore would not have transgressive spaces or concentrations of "simultaneous presence" (Koolhaas 1995: 1250). Thinking that a *dérive* would be pointless in such city, I took a break from my restless ramble and went shopping. The shopping mall was five stories of corridors built around a large atrium. While I was standing on one of the balconies that offered a panoramic view, I noticed that the place was bugged with CCTV cameras, one of which was turning towards me.

Among the shoppers strolling along the corridors, some turned their backs to the shop windows, and as they leaned on the atrium railing, they gazed, like me, into the void. Standing there, for almost one hour, I saw that some were neither looking for a shop, nor interested in the architecture of the void. They were actually staring, across the void, directly at me and at some other men standing on the floor below. I stared back. The void enabled this play of gazes without the risk of intimacy. It prevented strangers coming too close or too soon. And this void, once the gaze was established, was cut, folded, and squeezed under the pressure of our gazes. Our gaze was an architectural tool; the void was the ground. The shopping mall was re-designed; now it became a sexual playground. The capitalist space was suspended, and transgressed. I pondered whether I should perhaps have asked the planner in the city's planning department to update the map, as the red color for commercial uses turned pink.

Urban Nomads

The examples I have given of zones, edges and overlapping spaces illustrate that transgressive space exists in recognizable and official "public space" as well as in dilapidated and marginal urban spaces. Underlying all these spaces is the lack of a definite program; in the shopping mall in Singapore the atrium is such a space. Alternatively, even if there is a concrete program for the space, the impossibility of enforcing it exclusively opens the space to informal uses, a situation that destabilizes the identity of these places. Correspondingly, the heterogeneous and changing identities of the users deny their identification as a community (Boeri 1998). For this reason, and for their transitory inhabitation of urban public space, I refer to them as "urban nomads," a term borrowed from Deleuze and Guattari's discussion of nomadism (1987).

I would argue that, in fact, we are all urban nomads the moment we step outside our homes and residential communities. We become part of a community which Alfonso Lingis (1994) describes, in the title to his book, as "the community of those who have nothing in common," a community that is formed by putting oneself in the other's place, by becoming placeless. To be placeless and to inhabit the other's place is to trespass and to transgress. And indeed, many activities carried out by urban nomads—vending, sleeping, having sex, playing music, planting, painting, inhabiting, crossing the street, and even walking on the street—are deemed transgressive. Under various laws, offenders can be imprisoned for up to three months.

By moving from a private to what is recognized as a public place, the activities become transgressive (Cresswell 1996). Activities such as drinking, painting, playing, waiting, sleeping, having sex and more can be criminal if carried out in public in certain circumstances (see such UK laws as the Anti-social Behavior Act 2003 and the Sexual Offences Act 2003). It is not only that many activities that take place in private are fine and in public illegal. Some of these activities or rather their perpetrators are considered dirt. In the seventeenth century, sex workers were portrayed as dirt that needed to be cleansed or designed out of public space (Ackroyd 2001). This portrayal has lasted until today as expressed in a few local councils' press releases, such as "Westminster supports police crime drive to clean up the West End" (Westminster City Council 2001). However, by seeing dirt as just an entity that does not fit into the established order (Douglas 1966), one can understand where this association has came from and why the authorities fear such activities. The nomadic nature of these activities derives from the fact that they do not fit into the established order and do not have a proper place (de Certeau 1988)—hence they occupy, intermittently, the margin—a no man's land that is supposed to be empty of all activity. However, these activities open a new space in the social and physical boundaries of public spaces, and at the same time reveal that these boundaries exist. And this, according to Foucault (1997) and Bataille (2001), marks the urban nomads as transgressive.

Outdoor Rooms: No Space for Urban Nomads

That public space is a void which contesting communities are fighting to re-shape is an unsettling reality that policy makers and urban planners have an almost existential difficulty accepting. Such space defies planning and design tenets and transgresses the boundaries of representative democracy. This might be why a completely different understanding of public space is put forward by the most influential British urban policy makers, the Urban Task Force (UTF), chaired by Richard Rogers. Their report, *Towards an Urban Renaissance*, conceived public space as an "outdoor room within a neighborhood" (Rogers *et al.* 1999: 91).

The association of open public space with a room, that is, with enclosure, negates the concept of public space as unbounded. The "outdoor room" metaphor implies a movement from the open, past a threshold, into an enclosure. Moreover, the use of the metaphors "door" and "room" (or "house") when describing public space, domesticates urban open space, with all the gender, political and social exclusions that the mechanism of domestication entails. Exclusiveness and confinement were expressed implicitly when the UTF classified functions that public space was supposed to serve: "from outdoor eating to street entertainment; from sport and play areas to a venue for civic or political functions; and most importantly of all as a place for walking or sitting-out" (ibid.: 57).

In imposing such a specific set of functions that supposedly reflect the needs of the public, the UTF presumed to know who the publics were and claimed to represent them in their entirety. Nonetheless, by privileging leisure as the most appropriate activity for public space, the UTF downplayed other activities—survival strategies, identity performances, and unofficial economic transactions. Common activities in urban space such as street vending, busking, soliciting, writing graffiti, cruising, lying down or sleeping were excluded, thus ignoring the people who actually use urban spaces in these ways (Amin *et al.* 2000). For urban nomads the value of a place is always its use. The purpose of evicting urban nomads from streets, squares and parks is often to increase the land value around these public spaces, generating capital out of sanitized public space.

The UTF's mistake was not in providing a partial list of activities or acknowledging only one social group. Its mistake lay in the idea that a defined list can be set. More fundamental still is the UTF's assumption that public space is positive and harmonious, that it does not by its very nature contain contestation and conflict. Such space might only be achieved in totalitarian states (Deutsche 1998) but even in Tiananmen Square, which is regulated by numerous police and CCTV, illegal street vending still occurs.

The results, directly or indirectly, of UTF's misunderstanding of public space have become evident in the past few years in various local authorities' campaigns to cleanse public spaces of "undesirable elements." Trying to gentrify inner city areas, to attract tourists, to reduce the crime rate in London, or just to beautify some spots, local authorities have adopted a zero tolerance approach. Just like the zero tolerance strategy of former New York Mayor Rudolph Giuliani, this approach has led to segregation, excessive control, and to a social cleansing of some street communities in public spaces. Examples of segregation include: the "cleaning up" around Kings Cross Station of homeless people and prostitutes who have traditionally used the area; the closure at night of underpasses under Charing Cross station to shut out the homeless; the new landscaping and closing up of Russell Square at night in order to prevent sex cruisers from meeting or engaging in sexual activities; the plan to transform Leicester Square into a "family zone" by evicting prostitutes and street vendors; and regulating performances of buskers in the square (Doron 2002a).

The local authorities' actions against urban nomads have been carried out in the name of the public or the "local community." The excluded street communities have never been considered part of the public by politicians, architects and planners, nor have they been viewed as a community of their own. The term "community" was and still is used to refer to a group of people who live in close proximity to each other and who own or rent property in a certain geographical area. In the British electoral system, as well in many others, the local residents are the ones who elect a representative for the local city council and national government. Therefore, although urban public space is used by many non-residents, especially in inner cities, the power to determine the preferred nature of this space, its by-laws, opening hours and so on is given to local residents and other property owners. This power also designates. The resident community is designated the primary, if not the only, client group for architects. The rest, namely the urban nomads, are excluded. As a result, public space, which should maintain a diffuse identity and open programs, is being eroded, becoming the equivalent of a suburbanite's backyard.

Russell Square: Erasure of the Margin

This situation is evident in Russell Square. The square, which is the largest in central London, was designed by Humphry Repton at the end of the seventeenth century, at the peak of the Bloomsbury area's redevelopment. The design of squares during that period in this area of town aimed to create a seclusion zone of gentility, uniformity, and security in the somewhat threatening regions beyond the walled city. The design of these squares "might have been derived from the example of old monastery courtyards or convent gardens with which London was once familiar" (Ackroyd 2001: 241). The "outdoor room" echoes this seventeenth-century type of secluded public space. However, before long, these supposedly new harmonious and homogeneous public spaces became the stage for a contested and fragmented social reality. They were populated by the homeless and squatters, some of whom had been living and working in and around the fields on which these "public spaces" were built (ibid.).

Russell Square did not change much until the Second World War, when the iron gates were taken away for the war effort. From then until 2002, the square was used at night for cruising and outdoor sex. In addition to being open at night, the square's location, walking distance from Soho (London's "Gay Village"), the West End and major train stations (Euston and King's Cross) was another factor in attracting cruisers and rough sleepers.

Cruising, gay outdoor sex and rough sleeping require fairly intimate spaces. Russell Square, and nearby Bloomsbury Square, also designed by Repton, had the necessary quality: areas of dense shrubs that ran parallel to the fence. Repton's reasoning was that parks and gardens should "give the appearance of extent and freedom by carefully disguising or hiding the boundary" (Repton 1795). And indeed this design feature not only gave the appearance of freedom but created spaces where freedom was exercised. As with the dead zone, elements of planning and design actually opened these spaces to informal activities.

In the mid-1990s, to clamp down on cruising and outdoor sex activities in Russell Square, the thick bushy areas were thinned out and floodlights were introduced. These actions exposed the sexual activities, causing residents to complain. Camden Council then won a Heritage Lottery Fund grant to re-design the square, which had been altered slightly in the 1950s, and restore it to its original layout. The results, however, were far from faithful to the original. The most dramatic alteration to the square's original design was the removal of 75 percent of the bordering shrubberies (CABE 2002a). This feature was not only unique to the square but also represented one of the four concepts of Repton's garden design (Repton 1795). The reason given was that the residents felt unsafe with this thick hedge. The removal of this green buffer was not only an aesthetic loss but exposed the square to the noise and pollution of surrounding traffic.

Ironically, a design prepared by the queer organization Outrage! would have been more faithful to the original, with their proposal to allocate a third of the park for cruising and outdoor sex. These activities, to a certain extent tolerated by law, would be concealed by a series of thick bushy boundaries, following Repton. This idea was modeled on the "tolerance zone for gay sex" that operates in parks in Copenhagen and Amsterdam (Outrage 1998).

Even the removal of the bushes and the introduction of harsh lighting did not stop the council closing the square at night "to protect the assets of the restored square" (CABE 2002a). The Commission for Architecture and the Built Environment's positive report about the new design states: "[the] gating of the square and the removal of dense vegetation seem to have solved the problems of anti-social behavior" (CABE 2002b). But the same report admits that "Russell Square is not sociable in the way that a smaller space might be, in the sense that conversations spring up between strangers." Ironically, it was the green margins that promoted the most noteworthy social interactions.

Transgressive Architecture

> Truly public space would defy categorization. Indeed, it would not even be recognizable as a space. Its openness to heterogeneous social transactions would be such that it would have no clear form, no definable limits.
>
> (Wigley 2002: 284)

Since 2003, Russell Square has been the site for interventions by Transgressive Architecture (TA). The group was formed in 2001 in response to the sanitization and segregation of London's public spaces (Transgressive Architecture 2005). The aim has been to introduce some of the spatial and social qualities of dead zones into prescribed public spaces, especially where such spaces have undergone extreme categorization, sanitization, and segregation. Correspondingly, the group's work creates spaces that are receptive and open to urban nomads rather than just to the immediate local residents. Finally the group, in its diverse activities, has tried to draw attention to the boundaries of spaces (academic space, urban space, personal space) and transgress them.

The group has used two working methods. On the tactical level, we have used installations and interventions inspired by the urban nomads' ways of (mis)using prescribed space. On the strategic level, we have created theoretical design proposals that negate the local authorities' ideas of public space. Some of these proposals were submitted as planning applications. These methods are a development but also a critique of Bernard Tschumi's "exemplary actions" and "counter-design" (1998).

The first of TA's projects was the *Bad Sheets*, which originated in a small exhibition at London Metropolitan University School of Architecture gallery. The exhibition combined collages and a series of ten bed sheets, printed on one side with images of urban nomads and on the other side with a planner's zoning map. Each bed sheet was folded to a size that resembled an open sleeping bag or a tombstone. The sheets were spread around the space of the gallery and the lobby of the school, partly interfering with smooth movement within the space. As part of this installation a quotation from Richard Rogers was graffitied in red marker over the entire glass wall that separated the school from the street. The text by Rogers declared that "The physical and intellectual accessibility of the public domain is a litmus test of society's values: inclusive and thriving public spaces foster tolerance and radical thought" (Rogers *et al.* 1999: 152). In addition to advertising the exhibition and communicating its main idea to passers-by, the graffiti aimed to question whether the gallery's glass wall, or any surface of an exterior wall of a building, is private or public. A day after the opening I was asked by the school to remove the graffiti. To do that I used one of the exhibition's bed sheets, which as a result looked as if it had been stained with blood.

This *Bad Sheet* and ten others were used in a series of unauthorized installations, carried out between March and June 2001 in several contested public spaces in London, including Trafalgar Square (Fig. 11.6), Leicester Square, Parliament Square, Charing Cross underpasses and Russell Square (Doron 2002a; Moertenboeck and Mooshammer 2003). During that time, these public spaces were suffering from a cleansing campaign that was sanitizing and segregating them. By installing the *Bad Sheets* in these spaces, the boundaries between public and private, art and everyday life objects, the space of politics and of architectural production were transgressed. A few of the public spaces in which the *Bad Sheets* installation had been located were later revisited by the TA's Atelier. The students of Atelier 2, at University of Greenwich School of Architecture and Construction, were asked to create alternative plans for these spaces, taking into consideration the urban nomads who had occupied them and

11.6
Transgressive Architecture, *Bad Sheets* intervention in Trafalgar Square, London. After a few minutes the sheets were confiscated by the square wardens and the void where they had been laid out was marked with the word VOID using pigeon food.
Source: From the film *The Bad Sheets* (2002)

who had been evicted by the local authorities. The students submitted three of these proposals as planning applications, transgressing the boundary between academic work and practice, and using the architectural plans as a generator of a democratic debate (Doron 2002b).

Similar tactics, installations and design proposals were used in the *Limits of Inclusiveness* project, carried out in 2005, concentrating exclusively on Russell Square. The aim of the project was to bring back and intensify some of the qualities that the square had possessed before it was sanitized and to open the square to urban nomads rather just to the local resident community. As a direct-action installation, the students of Studio 3, Interior Architecture, University of Brighton School of Architecture and Design, designed and built four life-size installations. These installations, named *Transborderline* after a similar work by the Italian group Stalker (Romito 2001; Doron 2000b) were devices designed to be used to cross the fence but also as shelters. They diffused the boundary of Russell Square and, like Repton's original design for the square, they widened the boundary and recreated it as a place to dwell. The *Transborderline* reintroduced the margin into Russell Square. The act of this illegal architecture, and other works by the group, echoed the spatial and conceptual attributes of transgression described by Bataille (2001) and Foucault (1997). For them the term is understood neither as a revolutionary act, or as an action that constitutes new space but as an act that reveals and tests boundaries and opens them without erasing them.

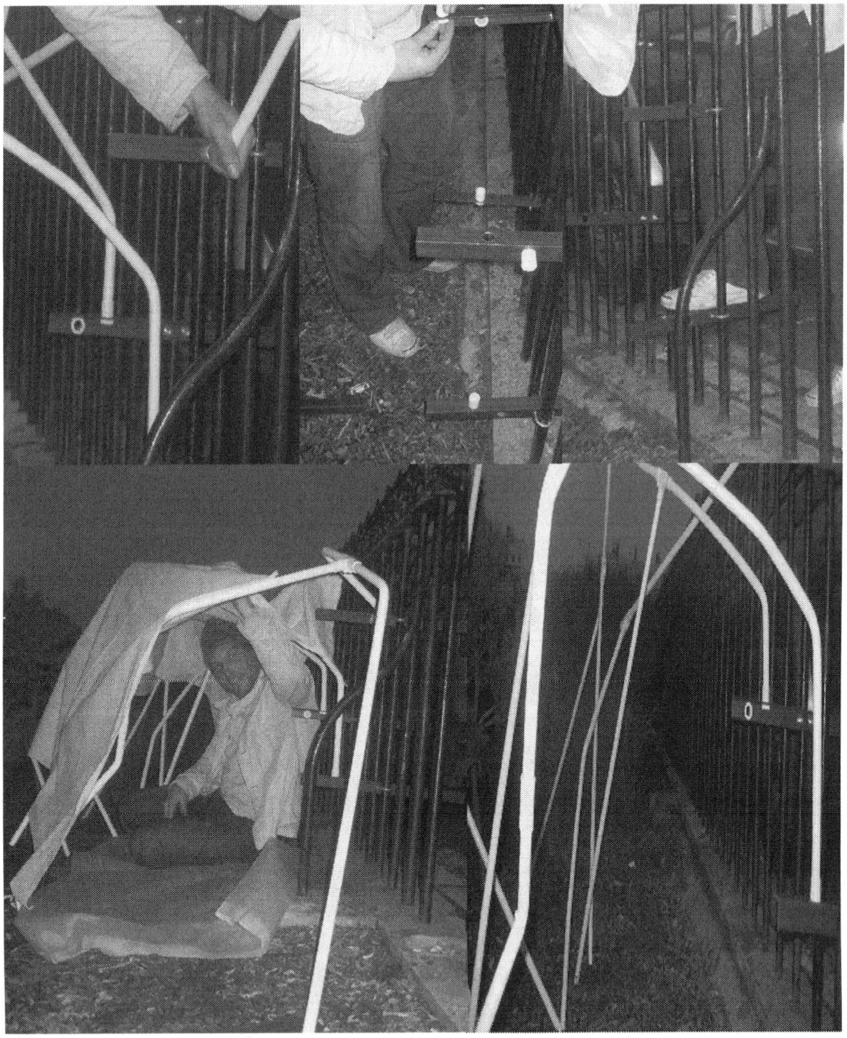

11.7
***Limits of Inclusiveness, Transborderline* project: A device to both cross and inhabit the fence, Russell Square, London**
Source: Designed by Darryl Jarvis, Studio 3 – Transgressive Architecture, Interior Architecture, University of Brighton School of Architecture and Design (2005)

The *Transborderline* projects also transgressed the boundaries between real structure and a rhetorical statement (Tschumi 1998). As such, they also became an investigatory device for examining the socio-political condition of the site of Russell Square. This last attribute was materialized when Studio 3 students asked for permission from the local authorities to install the *Transborderline* on the square's fence for a few hours. As expected, the permit was denied because, as the council official stated, the local residents opposed any project that enabled people to enter the square at night. This situation demonstrated again the ultimate priority the local council gives to local residents over urban nomads—in this case our students.

The second stage of the *Limits of Inclusiveness* project is a new planning proposal for the square to make it a more inclusive space. TA will submit the final design to Camden Council. The design seeks to accommodate, within a limited space, numerous and sometimes contested activities by increasing the surface area of the square and offering a variety of site conditions to meet the needs of different communities. Since the park cannot be extended horizontally, we folded the ground, forming hills, valleys, plains and underground places. While TA's design includes specific environments for each section of the square, it does not suggest what types of activities occur or where, offering instead a great variety of spatial conditions which people can appropriate and manipulate. We believe that as the landscape becomes more heterogeneous, so will the communities who inhabit the square.

TA's design is positioned between two very different approaches to envisioning and designing public space. One approach sees public space as a blank canvas on which users act in various unpredictable ways, as exemplified by Adrian Geuze and West 8's work, especially their design for Schouwburgplein in Rotterdam. The other approach compartmentalizes and segregates public space, designing different places for various but specific groups. TA, however, draws inspiration from dead zones and the *terrain vague* (spaces devoid of program and truly open) to propose public spaces that are spatially complex to enable heterogeneous groups of people and activities to find the kinds of places best suited to them without physical or legal ordering of the space.

The square's appearance, redesigned in the manner TA proposes, will differ significantly from the desolation, emptiness, and openness that characterize many dead zones. Dead zones at the edge of the city, which are vast in scale, can accommodate diverse and conflicting activities. However, in a fairly small inner-city square, where demand for space is much greater, the landscape needs to be diversified and densified to accommodate everyone. At the same time, with the capsularization of Western society (De Cauter 2004), the sanitization and excessive control of public space, and the suburbanization of the inner city, it is important that the dead zones (those under the category of "zones") be left alone. These kinds of spaces should be protected through simple planning regulations that suspend them from further development and from those regulations typically imposed on formal public spaces. These transgressive spaces can be models of more open hybrid space as well as places where the city can regain its urbanity.

References

Ackroyd, P. (2001) *London: The Biography*, London: Vintage.

Amin, A., Massey, D. and Thrift, N. (2000) *Cities for the Many Not the Few*, Bristol: The Policy Press.

Bataille, J. (2001) *Eroticism*, London: Penguin Books.

Berg, R. (1998) "Islands in a Coded Urban Space: Wagenburgen in Berlin," in INURA (eds) *Possible Urban Worlds*, Zurich: Birkhauser.

Boeri, S. (1998) "Les Paroles des Habitants: Où les Codes Entrent en Conflit," in Studio Open City (eds) *A Moving City*, Brussels: Studio Open City.

Borret, K. (1999) "The 'Void' as a Productive Concept for Urban Public Space," in GUST (eds) *The Urban Condition: Space, Community and Self in the Contemporary Metropolis*, Rotterdam: 010 Publishers.

Commission for Architecture and the Built Environment (CABE) (2002a) "Russell Square, London: Design Process," online. Available: http://www.cabe.org.uk/library/casestudy.asp?id=221&show=analysis &PARAMS (accessed September 5, 2005).

Commission for Architecture and the Built Environment (CABE) (2002b) "Russell Square, London: Design Process in 'CABE Library'," online. Available: http://www.cabe.org.uk/library/casestudy.asp?id=221&show=evaluation&PARAMS (accessed September 5, 2005).

Commission for Architecture and the Built Environment (CABE) (2003) *Wasted Space?* Online. Available: http://www.wastedspace.org.uk/wasted_space.pdf (accessed January 10, 2004).

Cresswell, T. (1996) *In Place/Out of Place: Geography, Ideology, and Transgression*, Minneapolis, MN: University of Minnesota Press.

de Cauter, L. (2004) *The Capsular Civilization: On the City in the Age of Fear*, Rotterdam: NAi Publishers.

de Certeau, M. (1988) *The Practice of Everyday Life*, Berkeley, CA: University of California Press.

Deleuze, G. and Guattari, F. (1987) *A Thousand Plateaus: Capitalism and Schizophrenia*, London: Athlone Press.

Deutsche, R. (1998) *Evictions: Art and Spatial Politics*, Cambridge, MA: MIT Press.

Doron, G. (1995) "The Last Palestinian Village in the City," Tel-Aviv, *H'air*, June 9, 1995: 30–32.

Doron, G. (2000a) "The Dead Zone and the Architecture of Transgression," *CITY, Analysis of Urban Trends, Culture, Theory, Policy, Action*, 4: 247–263.

Doron, G. (2000b) "Fourth Dimension," *Blueprint*, 178: 56–59.

Doron, G. (2000c) "A New Urban Paradigm: Kyong Park in Detroit," *Archis*, 09: 67–71.

Doron, G. (2000d) "Rethinking the Squat," *Archis*, 12: 68–71.

Doron, G. (2002a) "*The Bad Sheets*," *CITY: Analysis of Urban Trends, Culture, Theory, Policy, Action*, 6:.43–59.

Doron, G. (2002b) "Untitled," *Archis*, 02: 41–45.

Douglas, M. (1966) *Purity and Danger*, London and New York: Routledge.

Foucault, M. (1997) "Preface to Transgression," in D.F. Bouchard (ed.) *Language, Counter-memory, Practice*, Ithaca, NY: Cornell University Press.

Hollier, D. (1998) *Against Architecture: The Writings of Georges Bataille*, Cambridge, MA: MIT Press.

The Home Office (2002) "Protecting the Public," London, TSO online. Available: http://www.homeoffice.gov.uk/docs/ptp.pdf (accessed September 20, 2005).

The Home Office (2003) "Table of Previous Offences Comparative to Offences in The Sexual Act 2003," online. Available http://www.homeoffice.gov.uk/docs3/offences.pdf (accessed September 20, 2005).

Koolhaas, R. (1995) *S, M, L, XL*, New York: The Monacelli Press.

LeVine, M. (2005) *Overthrowing Geography: Jaffa, Tel Aviv, and the Struggle for Palestine, 1880–1948*, Berkeley, CA: University of California Press.

Lingis, A. (1994) *The Community of Those Who Have Nothing in Common*, Bloomington, IN: Indiana University Press.

Lynch, K. (1990) *Wasting Away*, San Francisco: Sierra Club Books.

Moertenboeck, P. and Mooshammer, H. (eds) (2003) *Visuelle Kultur*, Vienna: Boehlau Verlag.

Naabarro, R., Richards, D. and Chapman, H. (1980) *Wasteland: A Thames Television Report*, London: Thames Television.

National Land Use Database (NLUD) (2003) "Classification Version 4.4 2003 Land Use," online. Available http://www.nlud.org.uk/draft_one/land_use_class/pdf/NLUD_v44.pdf (accessed September 10, 2004).

Outrage (1998) "'Zone of Toleration' for Gay Sex in Russell Square?" Online. Available: http://outrage.nabumedia.com (accessed March 20, 2005).

Palestine Remembered (2005) "Jaffa Town Snapshot," online. Available: http://www.palestineremembered.com/JaffaTownsSnapshot.html (accessed September 20, 2005).

Regve, O. and Raz, Y. (eds) (1996) *The Dream Fair*, Tel Aviv: The Council for Protecting Buildings and Settlements.

Repton, H. (1795) "Sketches and Hints on Landscape Gardening," quoted in Ohio State University, History of Horticulture, online. Available HTTP: http://hcs.osu.edu/history/history/078.html (accessed March 20, 2005).

Rogers, R. and Power, A. (2000) *Cities for a Small Country*, London: Faber and Faber.

Rogers, R. and the Urban Task Force (eds) (1999) *Towards an Urban Renaissance*, London: Department of the Environment, Transport and Regions.

Romito, L. (2001) "Transborderline," *Architectural Design* 71: 23.

Soja, E. W (1996) *Thirdspace: Journeys to Los Angeles and Other Real-and-imagined Places*, Oxford: Blackwell.

Transgressive Architecture (2005) "Transgressive Architecture," online. Available: www.transgressive architecture.org (accessed September 20, 2005).

Troen, S. I. (2003) *Imagining Zion: Dreams, Designs, and Realities in a Century of Jewish Settlement*, London: Yale University Press.

Tschumi, B. (1998) *Architecture and Disjunction*, London: MIT Press.

van Dijk, H. (1996) *Colonizing the Void: West 8 Landscape Architects*, Rotterdam: NAI Publishers.

Westminster Council (2001) "Westminster Supports Police Crime Drive to Clean up the West End," online. Available: http://www.westminster.gov.uk/councilgovernmentanddemocracy/ councils/pressoffice/ news/ (accessed February 2002)

Wigley, M. (2002) "Bloodstained Architecture," in GUST (eds) *Post/Ex/Sub/Dis Urban Fragmentations and Construction*, Rotterdam: 010 Publishers.

Part IV

Discovery

For any space to be loose, people must first find it and exploit the opportunities it offers for pursuing the activities they desire. Most of the spaces described in this book are easily found as they lie within the well-traversed domains of urban life. Some, however, are leftover or abandoned spaces, more hidden and less open to public view. Whether they are on the periphery of cities or in their centers, they are by and large detached from most people's daily routes through the city. The loose spaces created in abandoned buildings and adjacent outdoor areas are the topic of this final part.

Tim Edensor, Lynda Schneekloth and the research team Urban Catalyst all present examples of building sites whose earlier use is no longer present and to which no new, formal use has yet been assigned. The previous uses were predominantly industrial; now the buildings are empty, sometimes seriously deteriorated where nature has intervened. Their openness and specific physical features invite new uses and suggest new ways of occupying space, of working and recreating, of seeing and feeling the world. Discovering the site is not only the discovery of a space but the discovery of alternative ways of being and doing.

Edensor, in Chapter 12, relishes the myriad physical and sensual qualities of abandoned factories in the north of the UK, recounting the many embodied experiences and opportunities for escape and adventure they generate. In Chapter 13, Schneekloth too describes sensual pleasures and opportunities for adventure offered by a former industrial landscape of grain elevators along the Buffalo River in northern New York State, while also examining its history as a material, imaginal and conceptual place and pondering its possible future as place of wildness and wilderness. The kinds of occupancy Edensor and Schneekloth present are largely informal and momentary; the abandoned sites are not so much re-inhabited as visited. In Chapter 14, Urban Catalyst focus on longer term and more organized forms of occupancy—albeit still temporary—where large industrial or institutional buildings in the center of European cities are re-used: that is, they are appropriated by various groups of citizens for commercial, artistic, athletic, leisure and community activities, with permission from owners and planning authorities but with a limited amount of renovation.

Indeed, none of the appropriations profiled here involves permanent physical interventions to preserve or to remedy (with the exception of remedial work on the natural landscape of the Buffalo River, to restore it from its polluted state). The occupancy of the spaces is gentle; the intention is not to change them but to use them as they are. Their current features are considered outstanding assets, either for the pleasure and opportunities for adventure they afford, in the cases presented by Edensor and Schneekloth, or because they allow for new uses without extensive capital improvements, in the cases presented by Urban Catalyst. What may be regarded by others as waste, as something to be removed and replaced, becomes instead a resource, material for new and often innovative uses.

Since the authors in this part look at abandoned sites, they take a wider temporal perspective than the other chapters, looking at buildings and landscapes over a long time frame. Future conditions and longer-term consequences are also of interest to Schneekloth and Urban Catalyst. The kinds of temporary activities described range from a short duration of a few hours, on a canoe trip, to a few months for various exhibitions or cultural programs to a few years in the re-use of an existing building.

In the unruliness, decay and apparent disorder of ruined buildings, Schneekloth and Edensor see possibilities for pleasure and discovery, an escape from the controlled city of scripted ways of acting and thinking. "Messiness" stimulates the body and the senses, encourages movement, exploration and creativity—the antithesis of manicured parks and themed environments where occupants are passive consumers, following a set script. The sites Urban Catalyst has studied, empty buildings in the center of cities which are largely intact, offer a more pragmatic and practical escape from the restrictive economic order of the surrounding city since in such places initial capital investment costs are absent and ongoing costs of operation significantly reduced.

The occupancy of abandoned places involves a certain degree of risk and uncertainty. There are physical risks of injury in simply entering ruins; Schneekloth broke her arm falling into a hole. There is also uncertainty as to who or what one may encounter there. The duration of the re-use of industrial buildings is indeterminate. Those who "discover" must be brave and determined. However, none of the authors suggests the uncertainty and risks should be reduced because they are at the core of this kind of looseness. Disorder and uncertainty are both forms of openness to possibility.

Many of the activities Edensor describes are transgressive and he prefers to keep the sites secret so that they can retain the qualities that make them special. In sharp contrast, the success of the "temporary uses" Urban Catalyst has studied depends upon attendance, participation and consumption by members of the public; for this to happen, the sites must be made known. The landscape Schneekloth describes and envisions lies between these two poles: the public is invited but the more clandestine uses should continue to have a place. In all cases, what was once a site with only one use now hosts multiple uses; in the re-use of intact buildings this multiplicity is intended, recognizing that different uses support each other, that discovery can be a collective endeavor.

All the industrial sites referred to are the legacy of a top-down organization of space, often at a very large scale, employing systems that could span half a continent, as with the grain transported from the Midwest to the Buffalo River for onward shipping. This organization and these systems are now gone; in their place are much smaller organizations, if there are any at all, working from the ground up, concerning themselves with small-scale activities on delimited sites without financial investments (or risks) and often working collaboratively, rather than competitively, with each other. Urban Catalyst holds that such actions and ways of working do not have to be incompatible with conventional planning for redevelopment; planning for temporary uses of the kind they describe can be incorporated into planning for longer-term uses. Like Schneekloth, Urban Catalyst recognizes that in these re-discovered sites, conventional ways of thinking are loosened as much as conventional ways of occupying. Much can be learned from that looser thinking.

Chapter 12

Social Practices, Sensual Excess and Aesthetic Transgression in Industrial Ruins

Tim Edensor

Before they became abandoned and neglected, industrial ruins were sites of dynamic and dense activity. Flows of people, matter and energy coursed through their locale from far and wide. Following their slide into desuetude, such derelict sites are commonly regarded as "blots on the landscape," spaces of inactivity, full of potential danger. In contrast to their formerly functional, productive state, ruins may appear to be unused and entirely marginal to urban life, finished as useful sites and wholly unproductive yet new forms of life and use emerge out of this wreckage, for apparently derelict space hosts a range of "alternative," improvisational and creative practices. In contradistinction to many normative, everyday activities, usually deemed to be "appropriate," pursued in the over-designed and themed spaces of contemporary western cities, such endeavors are not subject to the gaze of police, CCTV cameras or fellow citizens. Whilst highly designed and regulated urban space can never entirely banish activities regarded as "transgressive" or encode space so as to thwart oppositional and idiosyncratic decoding, the emphasis on producing social order in a realm of commodities and spectacles undoubtedly constrains use and meaning.

Ruins are spaces where people can escape the straitjacket of self-consciousness, where no evident rules pertain about what can be done and where there are opportunities to engage in playful, creative and sensual practices. Ruins are marginal spaces (Shields 1991) that serve as spatial resources for doing things differently outside the ordinary, regulated space of the city. In addition, they provide an experiential realm in which sensual and aesthetic regulation is absent and the effects upon the body and its apprehension of space foster a different form of experience that encourages a more playful and sensual engagement. In this chapter, I identify some of the practices which surround industrial ruins in the North and Midlands of England, Wales and Scotland, and then explore the material, aesthetic and textual qualities which make them suitable venues for a wealth of practices.

Playing, Dwelling and Botanizing in Ruined Space

Ruins are typically consigned to decay by corporate and governmental decisions about relocating production and marking industrial obsolescence and are subsequently labeled by local planning authorities as "wasteland" or "derelict" space (see Doron, Chapter 11, this volume). Ruins host an abundance of matter that has been designated as "waste" but can serve numerous functions. Initially, the asset stripping of ruins tends to be perpetrated by informal scrap dealers who remove recyclable metals and stone for re-sale to builders and metal re-cyclers, weakening the structure of buildings and rendering them susceptible to the vicissitudes of the weather. As they decay and become more enduring fixtures in locales, they come to be resources for more contingent enterprises. People swarm around many ruins in search of useful materials, for the tiles, windows and doors which can be utilized to fabricate sheds, lean-tos and other structures. Ruins frequently contain items of furniture such as cupboards and tables which can be re-used to adorn domestic spaces, as well as other curios which can act as impromptu sculptures or decorations for homes and gardens. In addition to this function as a local, free, informal scrapyard, ruins also function as temporary places of shelter and abode. Homeless people are able to find refuge and a certain degree of privacy, and often make use of the scraps of furniture and other matter to construct beds, partitions, tables and chairs, and to make fires to keep themselves warm.

Most obviously, however, and partly because they possess the allure associated with no-go zones, ruins serve as spaces of fantasy, places in which illicit pleasures are enjoyed, and childish and adult adventures are played out. For children, industrial ruins contain numerous features that encourage all kinds of play and offer an opportunity to develop the useful skills of recognizing and negotiating the kinds of danger from which children are often insulated in highly risk-conscious societies (Fig. 12.1).

Derelict factories and warehouses are centers that invite curious investigation. There are empty corridors to run along, stairs to ascend, windows and other spaces through which to climb. There are trapdoors to be avoided or to drop down or through which to hurtle objects. Extensive abandoned and cleared shop floors enable the performance of spectacular and dangerous adventures. Cupboards,

12.1

store-rooms, cellars, lofts and offices provide snug, "felicitous" spaces (Bachelard 1969) which can serve as dens and hidey holes. Feats of balance, agility and bravery may be accomplished in these unsupervised playgrounds which, full of risk, clash with the regulated recreational spaces of the more ordered world outside, playgrounds that circumscribe the diversity of practices and contain a limited range of "appropriate," largely risk-free activities. Free from the safety-first instincts of parents and other adults, children can devise their own rules and give full rein to their imaginations. The signs of childish play are widely in evidence in derelict spaces. Territorial signs demarcate the dens of gangs as do the slogans of sub-cultural allegiance and popular culture. Old seats and tables are re-assembled to furnish impromptu dens which are adorned with found objects and pictures.

Besides serving as exemplary sites for children's play, ruins are sites for more illicit endeavors which may be practiced by all ages. There are abundant signs of the use of both legal and illegal stimulants by drinkers who leave empty beer cans and spirit bottles, sniffers who discard used bags of glue, smokers who drop the remnants of their spliffs and heroin users who litter areas with needles and silver paper. Moreover, ruins provide venues for small and large parties free from the prying eyes of the law. Indeed, empty industrial sites were widely used by organizers of secret, illegal raves, large dance parties that were held across Britain in the late 1980s, to escape the constraints of zealous policing. There are often clear signs of sexual activity in ruins, with discarded condoms testifying to the shelter afforded to those engaged in secret trysts and to erotic teenage exploits which are frequently recorded on wall surfaces.

These illicit and usually disparaged activities are possible because ruinous sites provide an opportunity to experiment with hedonistic pursuits, for instance, providing a private realm in which addicts can carry out their habits with little fear of interruption. For while there are usually "keep out" signs and boards, fences and other barriers at most derelict sites, these are easily transgressed. Once inside, there are rarely security guards as notices promise (these signs are presumably for insurance purposes only) and, once inside, visitors are out of sight and earshot of the forces of law and order and fellow citizens.

It is because of this absence of scrutiny that ruins are the venue for another form of activity that is more carnivalesque, that concentrates on the pleasurable destruction of buildings and objects and is negatively identified as "vandalism." In the ruin, property that is subject to destruction appears to belong to nobody, and the building has already been marked as no longer of any value and usually awaits demolition. The power of conventions that limit expressive physical performance and a more unhindered engagement with the material world, and the tendency for objects to be regarded as sacrosanct and inviolable, mean that there is a transgressive delight in contravening them in willful destruction. Such expressive practices are enjoyable and satisfying.

In most ruins, the windows and urinals have been assaulted and shattered and this testifies to the widespread pleasure discovered in throwing missiles and witnessing the splintering sound and spray of shards. Porcelain sinks are fractured with heavy boulders or iron poles or sent skittering across the floor where they shatter as they come into contact with walls. Wooden boxes are dropped from upper floors or down lift shafts and spectacularly splinter. Even brick walls may be annihilated by experimenting with improvised techniques of demolition, and lighter partitions made of plasterboard and wood can be ripped asunder with gratifying ease. Watching things clatter downstairs, deliriously tumble from assigned positions into a chaotic heap as shelving is tipped over, thick oil spill out from pierced tanks and ooze across floors and down gradients are pleasurable spectacles which reveal material properties. Setting fire to stuff—witnessing plastic coagulate and bubble, wood hiss and spark and sealed containers explode—similarly shows us the qualities of matter, the properties it possesses, and the release of unfamiliar sounds and smells.

In a similar vein are those more criminal, anarchistic practices which involve the theft of automobiles and motorcycles. Ruins provide a venue where improvised forms of joyriding may be satisfactorily undertaken, for the ruin is often replete with challenging slopes, wasteland and props around which to maneuver (Fig. 12.2). The affordances of the ruin which inhere in the expanses of concrete floor, chutes, curbs, large boards and ramps also provide a playground for skating, skateboarding,

motorcycle scrambling and mountain biking. Climbers too can be found scaling ruinous walls, practicing their holds and keeping "climbing fit." 12.2

Ruins are unpoliced spaces in which a host of artistic endeavors may take place, blurring further the distinctions between practices deemed transgressive and rational. Most obviously, they provide an extensive area of vertical surfaces for the inscriptions of graffiti artists, and indeed, graffiti is a ubiquitous presence in those ruins in which access is easy. Especially when these are concentrated on the internal walls of the derelict building where they cannot be seen by neighboring residents, there is little sanction against graffiti since it makes little difference to a site already identified as unsightly and excessive. In these favored sites, graffiti ranges from the wall-to-ceiling coverage of all planes in a riot of color, turning buildings immersed in the grey and brown hues of dereliction to spaces adorned with multi-colored effusions of names and cartoons, to the crude daubing of football and music slogans and gang names, and from the humdrum inscriptions of obscure tags and monikers to the detailed, complex works of graffiti "artists." Occasionally, the embellishments of extensive multi-colored illustrations blend with the fractured roofs, large puddles and intrusive plants to create scenes extremely rich in texture and hue. Ruins provide unsurveilled urban spaces for graffiti artists to develop their alternative aesthetics and skills, for where graffiti has been largely regarded as "out of place" in the more regulated spaces of the city (Cresswell 1996), its presence is more ambivalent in spaces of dereliction. These spaces also serve as a venue for all sorts of other impromptu artistic endeavors. The opportunity to play with objects and other forms of matter unselfconsciously is afforded by the lack of any surveillance and other onlookers and by the range of material that is often to hand. Accordingly, improvisatory sculptures suggest that they have been wrought by visitors at play.

These more radical engagements with matter contrast with the care with which space and objects are maintained in the regulated material world outside the ruin, through the polishing, replacement and repair of things. The transgressive desire manifest in these acts of destruction speaks of the restricted interaction with things and space and the concomitant bodily control that is required to maintain this state. In the ruin, released from such constraints, we may corporeally and sensually engage with material in a context in which our actions have little impact on propriety and property. These typically carnivalesque, yet often affective, acts of collective endeavor re-inscribe the disorderly in an increasingly smoothed over urban environment made fit for consumption and organized tourism.

Besides these adventurous endeavors, ruins attract an increasing range of vaguer leisure activities that perhaps can be best labeled informal tourism. For unlike the ordered spaces of most tourism and the performative conventions that they require, ruins offer disorganized spaces for visiting. Unlike the sequential purview of selective sights and forms of information, the sedate perusal of cultures, the pre-assigned photograph points, the carefully marked pathways, guided tours and the shopping stops typical of many habitual tourist performances (Edensor 2001), passage around a ruin offers a contingent visit across unpredictable space, with a host of unidentifiable objects, texts and scenes. The contrast with the highly regulated and commodified landscapes of contemporary tourism draws individuals and groups to explore ruins where they may conjecture and imagine that which they behold, from individual adventurers to more organized urban explorers equipped with torches, hardhats, climbing equipment, face masks and cameras. These latter groups record images and accounts that are placed on websites dedicated to urban exploration.

The attraction of ruins is not limited to their use for carnivalesque or usually proscribed activities for they also act as sites for more mundane, practical pursuits, for a range of habitual and unspectacular activities carried out routinely by urban-dwellers. Such practices sew ruins back into the space of the local and into the present. Most typically, ruins are incorporated into the walks of urbanites, and the often large tracts of wasteland which surround them are as close to rural landscapes as some city-dwellers may be regularly acquainted. This underdetermined land is often a desirable place to take a dog for a walk, especially when a park is not within walking distance, and such unofficial green realms also offer opportunities for people to tether grazing ponies and erect jumps for horses, as well as serving as colonizable land for gypsies and other travelers. The flower beds and landscaped lawns which previously served as the regulated surrounds of factories and offices can later serve as temporary gardens in which a range of produce from vegetables to marijuana may be cultivated. In the case of the latter plant, the absence of any obvious ownership makes the identity of the cultivators difficult to detect. The same is true for those who use ruins as unofficial rubbish dumps for they can hardly spoil a landscape which has already been identified as an eyesore. As locations for these practical uses of local space, ruined sites supplement facilities which already exist and provide a space for activities for which there is no provision.

Ruins also act as refuges for urban wildlife. As they quickly become colonized by animals and plants who seek out nesting spaces, food sources and territories, ruinous wastelands and spaces of rubble also attract birdwatchers and botanists. As Roth observes, "as things fall apart, out of their remains emerge new forms of growth" (1997: 2). While strenuous efforts are mobilized to banish all but those plants and animals which are considered desirable within urban settings, insects, birds, mammals, fungi, shrubs, flowering plants and trees expend feverish energy (Cloke and Jones 2002) in quickly colonizing any available space, making it apparent that the urban is always also constituted by non-human life forms despite their wrongly assumed absence (Fig. 12.3).

In contradistinction to the rural, urban space is normatively considered suitable for domestic pets and certain garden birds but it is the realm of neither livestock nor feral animals and plants, which are commonly labeled as pests. These "wild" plants and animals are identified with the countryside or with nature "reserves," yet in derelict space such exclusions are rebuked by the multifarious and disorderly forms of life that colonize ruins.

In ruined space, urban dwellers can satisfy a desire to see that which contravenes urban order and reveals the other inhabitants, and thereby witness the potential for the city to become a "zoopolis—a place of habitation for both people and animals" (Wolch 2002: 734). Griffiths, Poulter and Sibley (2000) show how feral

12.3

cats in Hull who inhabit derelict sites are conceived as disorderly by some, whereas for others these felines are fed and appreciated as more liberated than their domestic cousins. Similarly, many enjoy the sight of urban foxes, owls, kestrels and other birds as well as the vibrant poppies, willow herb and Himalayan balsam which quickly inhabit ruins. Ruins thus provide valuable sites for amateur naturalists, botanists and birdwatchers to seek out sightings in the urban.

Industrial wastelands can also provide rich green spaces which are equally or more ecologically valuable than rural spaces, particularly those which are intensively farmed and subject to strict control by means of weed-killers and pesticides. An apparently blighted landscape on Canvey Island in Essex, hemmed in by a superstore and a derelict oil terminal, is an "oasis in a landscape of oil refineries, new housing, massive roundabouts and drive-through McDonald's" (Vidal 2003), a terrain replete with industrial and household debris which might be considered a "wasteland." Strikingly, it has, however, been described as "England's rainforest" because of the density of its rare wildlife population, notably of insects, moths and other invertebrates (Canvey Island 2004). Created by the debris dredged up as silt and laid down over the land, full of industrial wreckage and spillage, this post-industrial landscape might not conform to conventional notions of rural beauty but it has become a Mecca for naturalists and there is a campaign to convert it into a nature reserve.

Ruins are potential sites for a wide range of social activities which differ from those usually accorded preferential status in the city for they are not regarded as "respectable" and "appropriate" in the inscription of urban norms of conduct. Such activities contrast with those practices organized around industrial production which sustained forms of sociality and social relations. Instead of being directed by prescriptive rules of comportment, practice and social engagement, the relations with space described above are forged through affective and enthusiastic desires. Social bonds may be locally constituted and consolidated by the coming together of adolescent gangs and homeless citizens, by dog walkers and gardeners or they may be formed through more extensive networks, for instance, by loose collectives of "urban explorers." All these practices constitute alternative communal uses that stitch ruins back into localities, broaching their normative separation from the smoothed over, highly regulated, de-sensualized characteristics that increasingly typify urban and suburban space.

Affordances of the Ruin

Some of the affective and expressive activities in ruins are enabled and given added pleasure and resonance because they take place in a space that is replete with rich and unfamiliar affordances (Gibson 1979). Here I am referring to characteristics such as the textures, form, weight, consistency and state of decay of objects, along with other redistributed matter and materials around and across which expressive practices take place. The qualities of space and materiality possess agency in that they constrain the operations the body is able to undertake but also enable other maneuvers. In the sensual interaction with unfamiliar affordances of ruined space, the body is coerced and stimulated to perform in unfamiliar ways.

The physical arrangement of a ruin tends towards disarray, clutter and arbitrariness. This dispersal of material according to no ordering schema but largely to happenstance means that instead of moving towards objects and objectives, bodies tend to move contingently and improvisationally. With the erasure or blockage of previous sequential routes, and often the collapse or removal of walls and doors, large ruins increasingly come to resemble labyrinths in which path-making is arbitrary and open to multiple options. This anti-structure contrasts with the partially supervised linearity which determines much movement through the city and opens up a host of spaces that normally may not be traversed and occupied. There are no temporal restrictions that legislate the length of time that is appropriately spent in a location, no surveillance or social impediments to movement and no need to adhere to the self-conscious monitoring of one's own body in a city of onlookers. All these elements thwart the tendency to habitually reproduce the purposive directionality of most city movement. Accordingly, visitors may clamber across old production lines and on top of obsolete machines, slide down chutes, climb into storerooms and attics or descend into murky cellars. Other spaces that once espoused order may now be violated. We may dance upon the boardroom table or spin round in the manager's chair. Besides this liberating of the body's movement, other spaces can seem strange and disruptive, a strangeness which is manifest in the unusually dark interiors, the sheer expanse of empty factory floor (Fig. 12.4) and the peculiar sounds and smells that assail the senses.

This sensual unfamiliarity contrasts with the frequently desensualized outside world, with its de-odorized environments and its constraints on noise, the unbroken smoothness of its pavements and floors, the prevailing textural sheen and the predictable design that effectively insulate the body against jarring sensations in its encounter with urban space. Alongside this, the structuring of movement and the strategic techniques that control pedestrian circulation in retail and semi-public spaces are absent in the ruin, as is the accompanying cajoling of the body into preferred comportment, movement and expression. Initially disruptive, the absence of these ordinary constraints can cause the body to open up before the sensory impacts that assail it and interact with space in a playful, unself-conscious fashion.

The disarrayed affordances of the ruin coerce the body to bend, crouch, clamber, slide, jump, swerve and tread carefully. Indeed, there is no opportunity to walk in a linear, uninterrupted, purposive fashion. The point of entry to the building might involve a measure of physical exertion such as climbing over an unstable wall, hacking a path through tangled vegetation or squeezing through a small window or the crack of a partially open door. Once inside, these perils might be multiplied with encountering slippery timber, loose floorboards or rickety stairs or swinging light fixtures and falling tiles. An awareness of these dangers develops a more sensually attuned body which takes account of risky space and learns how to negotiate it.

But, in addition, the moving body is forced into performing in accordance with the *ad hoc* structure presented by the ruin, and this can cause the enaction of

12.4

unfamiliar or half remembered gestures and maneuvers that jolt the body out of the complacent, habitually inexpressive and self-conscious performances played out on city streets. Moreover, instead of the self-contained bodily comportment through the city, through which a fixed stride, steady gait and minimal gestures delimit interaction with the environment and others, the body is inadvertently coerced into a more expressive, improvisatory performance, awakening performative possibilities which lie beyond that to which it has become habituated. Jolted out of its fixed composure, the adult body can move towards a more expansive physical engagement with its surroundings, a somatic disposition which recalls the long-forgotten sensual memories of childhood play.

Ruins encourage a host of expressive recreational uses not only for children but for adults who use these derelict spaces as playgrounds. Actions carried out for the pure kinaesthetic pleasure in performance are enabled through the lack of any regulation and by the affordances of ruined structures. Crawling through dense undergrowth, scrambling over walls and under fences, leaping over hurdles and across gaps, kicking debris of various qualities along the floor, throwing rubble at chosen targets and dancing and sprinting across stretches of flooring generate a rekindled awareness of the *jouissance* of gymnastic, expressive movement. Flights of fancy stimulated by mediated fantasies can be enacted by clattering along rooftops or careering down decrepit fire escapes so that bodily endeavors are entwined with the stimulus of popular cultural imagery. These opportunities for expressive and playful movement are taken up by visitors and signs of playful exercise abound in ruins. Rope swings hang over wooden beams, burst footballs and improvised goalposts litter floors, bottles are lined up in shooting galleries, wheeled vessels are utilized as impromptu forms of transport and extemporized football pitches are created. There is a return to a less self-conscious, embodied engagement with space and materials in conditions of immanence, without purposive planning or eye to efficiency or utility.

These sensual interactions with ruined space are accompanied by a radically sensual engagement with ruined matter. This sensual encounter brings to the fore an awareness of the materiality of things (Fig. 12.5). These freely available objects may be touched, thrown, picked up, stroked, pulled apart, kicked, drummed upon, squeezed or jumped on. Exciting to the touch, such artifacts and surfaces encourage the hand to run over them and explore their consistency, at variance to the more reserved interaction with objects in commercial and exhibition spaces. One may confront and experience the textures of decaying materials: the stark, hard, cold feel of a piece of industrial metal machinery, the splintery and pulpy texture of a damp wooden work bench, the delicious sheen of a wooden hand rail worn to smoothness 12.5

over decades or the moldering dampness of paper, wallpaper and plaster. And one might apprehend the weight of oil drums and steel boxes, the profusion of peculiarly shaped and tactile off-cuts and remnants of manufactures, the thick greasiness of chains and cogs, the encrusted exteriors of foundry fittings, the pliability of wires and thin metal strips, the cushioned consistency of moss and the sliminess of wet, rotting wood.

Ruinous Aesthetics

In recent years, the urban fabric has become ever more subject to aesthetic control. Particularly in those spaces which are organized around an aesthetic coding of spectacular sights, including theme parks, heritage attractions and other tourist venues, great efforts have been extended to brand space and reduce it to a few key themes or designs. These schemes also extend to those realms in which there have been partial attempts to encode preferred meanings through design—areas such as malls, heritage districts, festival marketplaces and entertainment centers whose designers have "learnt" from these themed spaces.

Ruins entirely violate such aesthetic schemes in which objects are subject to disciplinary distribution, where difference is carefully situated so as to be domesticated and contained. By contrast, in the ordinary ordered urban realm, an intensive manicuring limits the appearance of clutter which might complicate sight-lines and walkways, and there is a blend of the bright (street furniture, window displays, screens and advertisements) and the mutedly smooth (the surfaces of walls and paths), careful color coding and polished planes. In ruins, there has been no attempt to keep up appearances and the scene is one of disorder, disarray and the mingling of usually unlike categories of things. This material excess, in which objects and matter have moved away from their assigned locations, is initially disturbing to habituated aesthetic sensibilities. In the ruin we confront an alternative aesthetics which rebukes the seamlessness of much urban design and opens up possibilities for appreciating beauty and form otherwise.

In contrast to the carefully polished sheen and restricted palette of tightly controlled space, ruinous surfaces offer a random display of colors and textures. The paint on walls bubbles and blisters, flaking off to reveal combinations of earlier layers, composing a colorful mosaic which might also include strips of wallpaper, bricks, lath, timber and concrete. Other matter is similarly subject to the agents of decay. The bacteria and fungi that swiftly colonize damp derelict space produce intricate swathes of ornamentation that feature blotches, extensive tributaries and vertical splashes of green where water drips attract thicker mosses (Fig. 12.6). The mess of fixtures—the light switches, electrical boxes, shelves and pipes—becomes festooned with organic matter such as cobwebs and lichen, and small particles of falling debris. The process of decay also releases all those hidden conduits of energy and matter from their confinement behind walls. In exuberant disarray, pipes and electrical wiring produce effusive patterns across walls and floors as a building falls apart. These

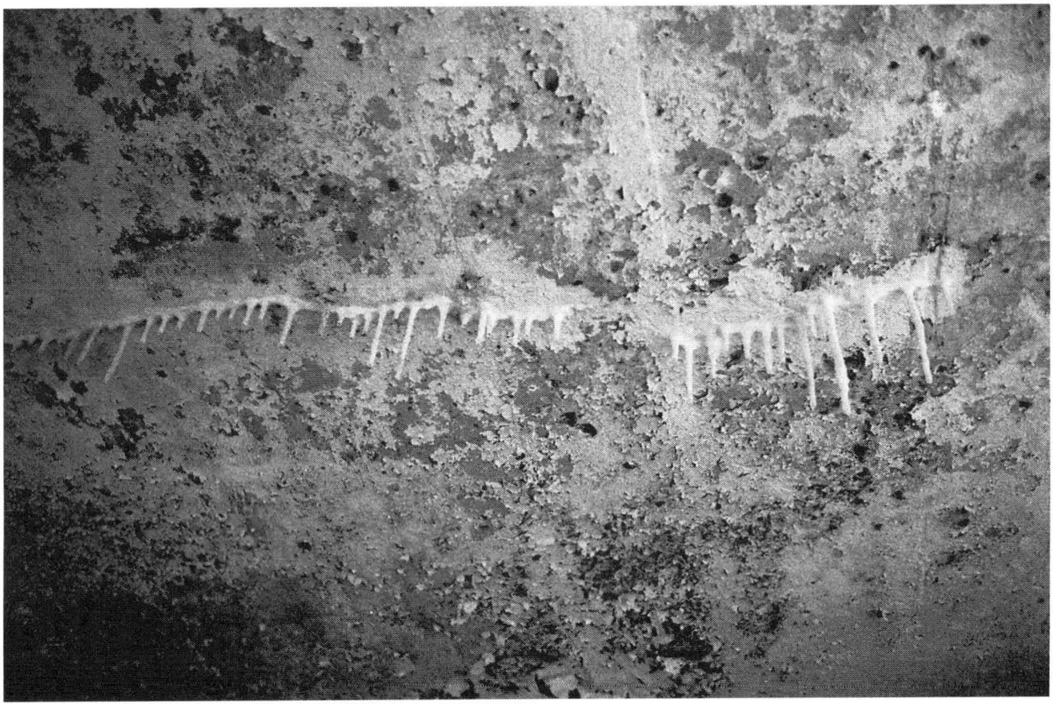

multiple and disorderly medleys of color and texture are a rebuke to the singular color and textural schemes of smoother space. They possess an aesthetic charge of their own, which foregrounds both the materiality of substances and the deliciously variegated patterns that accidentally emerge, provoking both pleasure in confronting unfamiliar compositions and a heightened awareness of the contrastingly stringent aesthetic control exercised elsewhere. 12.6

Inside ruins, objects fall out of their previously assigned contexts to recombine in arbitrary and often dreamlike combinations, a random dis-ordering which is shaped by where things land or have been thrown. The rules which determine that objects should be kept apart, and belong to particular categories and positions, no longer pertain for the material divisions between the rural and the urban, the inside and the outside; the past and the present are dissolved.

Two aesthetic effects are associated with the happenstance of this dis-ordering. First, such processes produce a vast, mingling mass of stuff in which discrete entities are often difficult to identify. The admixture of heterogeneous materials can result in a mulch of matter where objects and other kinds of matter usually kept apart meld to constitute "strange new products, changed compounds" (Yaeger 2003: 112). These chance arrangements also produce peculiar juxtapositions; objects stand close together and seem associated with each other in new and unfathomable ways. Released from their former function and position, objects in such assemblages are enchanted with different associations, strike different chords of meaning. Unlike artistic and commercial montage which deliberately arranges objects to provoke associations of meaning, these fortuitous combinations entirely disrupt the ways in which objects are supposed to relate to each other for they follow no such scheme but constitute an alternative aesthetics of dissonance and peculiar associations. We are free to conjecture and infer wildly about these material relationships.

Second, ruins feature more discrete, accidental sculptural forms that emerge from processes of decay and the collapse of ordered placement. In their recontextualized individuality, such objects possess a powerful aesthetic resonance, particularly because of their location or altered stance. Leaning sideways or positioned upside-down, squashed into a confined space, crushed and bent out of shape, splayed out or simply left in isolation by the clearance of surrounding matter, these ruined things appear odd (Fig. 12.7). Shattered drainpipes tilt away from their formerly vertical positions, drawing attention to their texture and metallic qualities. Neat, conical piles of tiles which have cascaded through gaps in the ceiling cluster on floors. Congregations of fallen beams seem to act as the structure for some primitive dwelling. These new arrangements express a shapeliness and materiality or reveal the separate parts out of which they are comprised. Instead of confronting objects that are separated from each other at appropriate distances, these artifacts contravene our usual sense of perspective, rebuke the way things are supposed to assume a position in regimented linearity. Reframed by their situatedness in ruined space, in which doors, walls and other dividing barriers have often been demolished, such objects are striking because of their surrealistic and sculptural qualities: mighty girders that have been twisted in the violence of disintegration, a splintering box that now spills its contents, a solitary metal machine stranded in isolation on a shop floor, a weakening shelf sagging in the middle as its contents weigh it down, an array of multi-colored paperwork composed into a pile, and buckled and warped flooring.

The happenstance montages of ruined space comment ironically both on the previously fixed meanings of their constituent objects and the ever-so-carefully arranged montages of commodified space. These assemblages are pleasurable because of the ways in which objects that carry different semiotic charges relate to each other and because of surprising, unpredictable meanings that emerge from these conjoinings. Similarly, there is a host of arbitrary relationships between different forms, shapes, textures and materialities that produces ineffable sensations stimulated by the variable materiality and tactility of the world. The aesthetics of ruins are arbitrary; the distribution of objects in space shows a lack of design. It is difficult to describe such scenes and to recoup them back into dominant systems of representation.

The forces which have dis-located objects in ruins can be completely obscure. For instance, certain things seem to be too large and weighty to have been moved without cranes or hydraulic machinery or may appear to be located according to a logic that defies the nature of the space in which they newly reside. It may be that other visitors have moved things around as part of illogical schemes or with creative ends in mind. The collective patterns of brick piles and the tight constellations of

12.7

disparate debris suggest artistic endeavors, and other attempts to clear space and order matter perhaps testify to the usage of space for play or accommodation. Alternatively, non-human agents could be responsible, through home-building or hunting, or maybe this resisting of things occurs through the agency of wind or rain or chemistry. Where either of these agents seems unlikely, out-of-place artifacts and unfamiliar amalgamations provoke conjectures about how they came to be positioned thus and may conjure up fantastic scenarios, in which uncanny entities and energies have turned order into chaos.

Factories rarely accord with ideas of beauty but are deemed functional spaces in which aesthetic qualities are subordinated to utility and efficiency. Yet ironically, the ruination of industrial space instigates an appreciation of the previously disregarded material and formal qualities of machines, other objects, decorative schemes and spatial organization. This aesthetic recharging can take on a surrealist perspective when the oddness of disparate and unidentifiable objects and the unusual location of more familiar things confound the normative ordering of the object world. Yet the textural beauty and the shapeliness of objects, the queer perspectives and the evocative relationships between things also challenge the normative aesthetics of urban space. This aesthetic dis-ordering and re-ordering challenges visitors to play, to rearrange things according to whim and creative impulse, and it allows more interventionist practices that involve the augmentation of interiors by graffiti, the assembly and reassembly of artifacts in different form, the creation of tottering mixed media sculptures and the daubing of floors and walls with industrial substances. These acts of creation can never be out of place because there are no aesthetic conventions to follow. Yet even without any active artistic interference in ruined space, a journey through the reconstituted and fluid aesthetics of ruins can re-enchant the world outside, making it look peculiar and arbitrary; ordinary things become recharged with strangeness, the mundane is haunted by sculptural attributes and the normative order of things appears most peculiar.

Illegible Textual Space

The uses and meanings of ruins are wholly undetermined. Upon entering a ruin, one can see that it has been assigned no function other than to be assigned as useless space that will at some time in the future be "useful" once more. Yet this lack of evident purpose or meaning possesses enormous potential and scope for visitors to utilize ruined space and construct meanings, allowing their imaginations to interpret uncontrollably and contingently.

Ruins are almost impossible to read in the same way that the pre-determined spaces of the commercial and public world outside might be decoded for they are no longer encoded with any pre-assigned or preconceived meanings and much depends upon the interpretive disposition of the onlooker. The hierarchical arrangements, sequential order of production, timed activities, channeled movement and regulated flows of people, material, information and energy might now only be faintly traced out, if they are visible at all. Now that material disarray has redistributed the machines, fixtures, supplies, stationary, tools and containers, their original purpose is trumped by peculiar recontextualization or remains altogether obscure. The use for which particular specialist, obsolete tools and machines were once put is now a matter for conjecture.

However, such scenes and objects are not always completely strange; they may be strangely familiar. They might be, as Raphael Samuel puts it, the "sleeping images which spring to life unbidden, and serve as ghostly sentinels of our thought" (1994: 27), those involuntary memories which rudely interrupt passage through space by hurtling us back to a long-forgotten past. Such memories are, however, never articulate because they are invoked by sensual impressions and sensations which lie beyond language. Rekindled by noises, atmospheres and aromas, these diffuse recollections are nonetheless powerful and very often recall the sensual experiences of childhood. In childhood, sense-making was not central to encountering the world and hence experience was never recorded or subject to reflection but part of a non-reflexive and immediate immersion in space and time. Recalling the loss of these powerful experiences disrupts the adult apprehension of the world and can throw us back to a pre-cognitive realm in which purpose and meaning were unclear and contingent. The sublimated stories and fantasies of childhood can be involuntarily resurrected in the welter of movement, sights, sounds and smells that emerge out of the encounter with the unfamiliar affordances of the ruin, and this, in turn, can loosen the bonds of propriety and monitored, self-conscious performance. The long-lost sense of being dirty, of sensually moving through an environment full of obstacles, of picking up and playing with an obscure object can be re-discovered in an encounter with ruined space, and lead to a more expressive and playful engagement with space and matter.

This triumph of the sensual over the logocentric is one of the ways in which the values of inarticulacy can be indulged. The disconnected fragments, peculiar juxtapositions, obscure traces of the past, involuntary memories, inferred meanings, uncanny impressions and peculiar atmospheres cannot be woven into an eloquent narrative. Rather like the nature of a ruin, the stories about it must similarly be constituted out of a muddle of assembled forms of matter, occurrences, shafts of momentary insight and sensations. Ruins are dis-articulated spaces, and language can only hesitantly capture their characteristics, merely gesturing towards their impact and significance. There are numerous scraps of stories that wait to be told. But any story-telling must be open-ended and improvisatory, full of non-sequiturs, irrelevances and inconsistencies. In contradistinction to the potted and exemplary narratives that seamlessly relate histories of places and people, recounting preferred forms of heritage for tourists and potential investors, these stories are loose and can trail away into silence or incoherence. Clues about the people, their characteristics and the activities that formerly centered upon now-ruined spaces are multiple, yet often ambiguous or unintelligible, although these ghostly, enigmatic traces invite us to guess at their meanings and purposes, to make up extemporized narratives. Such incoherent and illegible stories have a material parallel in the decaying notice-boards and instructions for use which, though partially erased, retain scraps of words and incomplete sentences and in the poetic inscrutability of product labels and technical terms that are no longer part of an industrial vernacular language.

This inarticulacy might appear to be an impediment for those who want to consume packaged narratives and decode smoothly encoded spaces, but it can also be conceived as an opportunity to escape predictable and formulaic accounts. Instead, we can make up stories out of the scraps and intimations about previous life that we come across, improvised and rambling tales that are not hemmed in by form or convention. This encounter with the past and the attempt to infer and deduce what happened reveal the impossibility of capturing it in some "official" or "expert" fashion. The numerous chanced-upon fragments and traces map the erasure of memory in their dramatic partiality; they also evoke "what in memory is lost when language intervenes—the sensation left by the unfindable" (Klein 1997: 10), revealing the limitations of narrating the past. All stories are always selective and partial although they masquerade as singular and authoritative, and this is glaringly the case with historical accounts. In the loosened space of the ruin, opportunities are rife to narrate the world contingently, providing an opportunity for creative interpretation, fantastical imaginings and wild speculation.

The Transgressive Excess of Ruins

The fostering of different ways of interacting with space and matter contrasts with the disciplined pursuits commonly followed in more tightly regulated spaces. Much contemporary urban space follows the logic of the "machinic episteme" (Lash 1999), through which an overarching, grid-like pattern can confine things and people to specific places and thereby achieve social and spatial order. The disjointed, dis-articulated mess of the ruin contrasts with the array of adjoining single-purpose, often bounded spaces in which only preferred activities occur, creating what Berman terms "a spatially and socially segmented world—people here, traffic there; work here, homes there; rich here; poor there" (1982: 168).

These disciplinary processes contribute to what Sibley terms the "purification of space," which is born out of "a distaste for or hostility towards the mixing of unlike categories" and manifests "an urge to keep things apart" (1988: 409). These "purified" or "strongly classified" spaces contrast with other "weakly classified spaces" that possess blurred boundaries, are associated with "liberation and diversity" and in which activities, objects and people mingle, allowing a wide range of encounters and greater self-governance and expressiveness (1988: 414).

While in Western cities such impure spaces appear to be becoming rarer, the tendency to achieve a seamless spatial order which facilitates the efficient, rationalized circulation of commodities, money, information and people is thwarted by the massive over-production of things and information, the vast surplus that a system of endlessly new fashion and planned obsolescence must generate. This excess of matter and meaning reveals the limited capacity of the over-designed, commodified, over-coded city of thematic spaces to persuade citizens to follow preferred meanings and practices. As John Tagg (1996: 181) observes:

> [urban] regimes of spectacles and discourses do not work . . . they are never coherent, exhaustive or closed in the ways they are fantasized as being . . . they cannot shed that ambivalence which always invades their fixities and unsettles their gaze.

Instead, they are "crossed over, graffitied, reworked, picked over like a trash heap . . . plagued by unchanneled mobility and unwarranted consumption that feeds, unabashed, on excess in the sign values of commodities." Industrial ruins are exemplary spaces of disorder which produce this semiotic and material excess. They contain manifold unruly resources with which people can construct meaning, stories and practices. Far from being waste spaces in which nothing happens, industrial ruins are thickly woven into local practices ranging from the carnivalesque to the mundane, from the artistic to the eccentric. These sometimes dissident, transgressive pursuits can survive because of the lack of surveillance and regulation that centers upon ruins, by their aesthetic and semiotic chaos and by the unfamiliar or long-forgotten sensations they provoke through their sensual affordances. Underdetermined and provocative, industrial ruins are spaces in which the urban is practiced otherwise.

References

Bachelard, G. (1969) *The Poetics of Space*, Boston: Beacon Press.

Berman, M. (1982) *All That Is Solid Melts into Air*, London: Verso.

"Canvey Island: England's Rain Forest," available: http://www.buglife.org.uk/html/project_canvey_island_more.html (accessed August 20, 2004).

Cloke, P. and Jones, O. (2002) *Tree Cultures*, Oxford: Berg.

Cresswell, T. (1996) *In Place/Out of Place: Geography, Ideology and Transgression*, London: University of Minnesota Press.

Edensor, T. (2001) "Performing Tourism, Staging Tourism: (Re)producing Tourist Space and Practice," *Tourist Studies*, 1: 59–82.

Gibson, J. (1979) *The Ecological Approach to Visual Perception*, Boston: Houghton Mifflin.

Griffiths, H., Poulter, I. and Sibley, D. (2000) "Feral Cats in the City," in C. Philo and C. Wilbert (eds) *Animal Spaces, Beastly Places: New Geographies of Human–Animal Relations*, London: Routledge.

Klein, N. (1997) *The History of Forgetting: Los Angeles and the Pleasure of Memory*, London: Verso.

Lash, S. (1999) *Another Modernity: A Different Rationality*, Oxford: Blackwell.

Roth, M. (1997) "Irresistible Decay: Ruins Reclaimed," in M. Roth, C. Lyons and C. Merewether (eds) *Irresistible Decay*, Los Angeles: Getty Research Institute.

Samuel, R. (1994) *Theatres of Memory*, London: Verso.

Shields, R. (1991) *Places on the Margin*, London: Routledge.

Sibley, D. (1988) "Purification of Space," *Environment and Planning D: Society and Space*, 6: 409–421.

Tagg, J. (1996) "The City Which Is Not One," in A. King (ed.) *Re-presenting the City: Ethnicity, Capital and Culture in the 21st Century Metropolis*, London: Macmillan.

Vidal, J. (2003) "It Doesn't Look Much, but this Bleak Corner of England Is Being Hailed as England's Rainforest," *The Guardian*, May 3, 2003: 4.

Wolch, J. (2002) "Anima Urbis," *Progress in Human Geography*, 26: 721–742.

Yaeger, P. (2003) "Trash as Archive, Trash as Enlightenment," in G. Hawkins and S. Muecke (eds) *Culture and Waste: The Creation and Destruction of Value*, Lanham, MD: Rowman and Littlefield.

Chapter 13

Unruly and Robust

An Abandoned Industrial River

Lynda H. Schneekloth

We put the canoe in at the Ohio Street Boat Ramp, less than a mile from City Hall in downtown Buffalo. This small park, one end of the Buffalo River Urban Canoe Trail, was constructed on the site of a barely active rail siding next to an historic warehouse building. Across the river are two enormous grain elevators and the ruins of a former industrial building, now filled with trees and grasses. The park is the first reclamation of the industrial river landscape after the completion of the Remedial Action Planning Process in 1989 and the first time in a century that the Old First Ward neighborhood of 100- to 150-year-old cottages has had access to the water.

The 10-mile canoe trail along the Buffalo River winds through a landscape that both reveals and conceals layers of history. The river meanders through a flat land that hints of its former life as the bottom of a large glacial sea. One paddles through the abandoned industrial fabric that is returning to wilderness, along the unruly river shoreline adjacent to the city's early urban housing. The last 200 years of settlement are evident but nothing speaks to the presence of native peoples who lived along this river before Joseph Ellicott laid out the plan for Buffalo in 1804.

The hollow grain elevators, dying industries and ghostly structures are the remains of the technological utopian vision that gripped Buffalo between the opening of the Erie Canal in 1825 and the closing of heavy steel plants in the 1980s. The landscape we see from the river is the landscape of that dream—a dream in disarray, visible in the ruins of the artifacts and buildings and in the overgrown wild landscapes. The quarter-mile-long Concrete Central grain elevator sits abandoned on a peninsula, surrounded by railroad tracks and grasses and shrubs that are home to deer, foxes and hawks. In spite of being so close to the central city, one hears very little except the periodic trains. The place is void of urban sounds. The apparent solitude conceals the fact that this space is still one of the busiest rail corridors on the east coast.

13.1
The Buffalo River Urban Canoe Trail passes the rusted marine legs of the Concrete Central grain elevator

The technological dream has also left an invisible legacy in the contaminated sediments and polluted waters. The Buffalo River may no longer be flammable as it was in the 1950s and 1960s, but it is not clean. There are advisory warnings against swimming and eating fish caught in the river, yet old men sit and fish from the concrete bunkers that house combined sewer overflow outlets, and young children jump into the waters to swim. The railroad bridges are covered with graffiti, announcing the presence of the kids who use this abandoned landscape as their playground. This is a landscape of marginal activities, illegal dumping and drug deals.

The Buffalo River area, like many former industrial sites scattered across the land, is a palimpsest; the power of natural processes and the lives of the people who have lived here have been etched on it. Sometimes these marks remain; sometimes they are erased by succeeding activities. Across eons, the region has been molded by the geological and meteorological forces of water, wind, ice and snow. But the greatest transformations have occurred during the past 200 years with the complex power humans have to make places "with hands, tools, and machines, through law, public policy, and actions undertaken hundreds, even thousands, of miles away" (Spirn 1998: 17).

Human actions along the river emerge from different and often contradictory perspectives about what rivers and land mean, how they might be used and what importance they have. During recent history, people with various ideologies and imaginations have interacted with this 100 sq miles watershed, attempting to transform it into a world in their own image, whether that image is a bountiful land, a technological utopia or an intact ecological system. Each view struggles to bring a place type into being that reflects what they believe the world should be.

Through the onslaught of conflicting intentions and physical changes, the land and river remain a silent but not inactive witness to the passing years, work, stories, lives and deaths. The Buffalo River is today a landscape of contradictions and tensions, a contested place between official positions, worldviews, advocacy work and unrestrained activities. And in this unruly and robust space, there is an unsettling looseness of definition, of boundary and of meaning.

Coming Undone: Coherence and Degeneration

Places like the Buffalo River industrial landscape not only exist in their material and physical manifestation but are structured by our imaginations and concepts about them (Schneekloth and Franck 1994). Three aspects—material, conceptual and imaginal—frame a recognizable place type such as an urban river, a factory or a park. As with all place types, an industrial landscape, such as that which existed on the Buffalo River, was composed of artifacts and a spatial order that reflected its use as a port, railroad transfer station and site of production. A conceptual order was overlaid on this physical world and it, in turn, facilitated the reproduction of that space through laws, regulations, and standard operating procedures that ensured that industry remained its primary use. Moreover, the imagination of industrialized landscape and port framed what people believed happened there—productive work that supported the families of the city sat alongside images of the dark and illicit activities that accompany ports as transient spaces.

When the three aspects of place type—material, conceptual and imaginal—are coherent, as they were during the height of the industrial era, they uphold our expectations and ideologies through their physicality, our use of them and the meanings we assign to them. But when there is a slippage among the three attributes, the space becomes loose and unsettling. As Lynch says, "[W]hen customary boundaries are lacking, we lose our grip on things" (1990: 12).

The Buffalo River has shifted in and out of material, conceptual and imaginal coherence. To the native peoples who fished and hunted along the river, in its marshes and wetlands, it was a resource that sustained them both through the provision of food and through its manifestation as the world that was considered "home." To the industrialists and capitalists who used the river as a different kind of resource, the river and its lands were again materially, conceptually and imaginally integrated. The vision that generated the transformed river and reconstructed landscape was premised on the newly acquired power over natural processes: people were enthralled with the capacity of their makings and believed that the new technologies would create a better life. Within 25 years of the opening of the Erie Canal in 1825, Buffalo had emerged as the center of transshipment and industrial development in the rapidly expanding nation (Goldman 1983; Boyer 2002). At the beginning of the twentieth century, Buffalo was the sixth largest port in the world. By the time the Buffalo River caught fire in 1968, the river had been so totally reconstructed that it was no longer even imagined to be a "river" but rather a component in the production process, an externality to be consumed. In slightly more than a century, the riverine habitat of native peoples had been transformed into an

13.2
A print of the mouth of the Buffalo River in 1797. The land was given to Captain William Johnson, Buffalo's first white settler, by his Seneca Indian wife's relatives.

industrial cesspool; the same river that had been a participant in the lives of the First Nations had been re-imagined as a blank slate on which to write the story of the Industrial Revolution.

The deindustrialization of the Buffalo River in the late twentieth century through global restructuring, ageing industrial processes and more stringent environmental regulations undid the landscape of production, removing people, work and things from the land and the river until what had been a world of bustling activity slipped into quiet absence. The industrial stranglehold on the Buffalo River fueled by the technological utopian vision loosened as the material world of innovative factories and production centers degenerated into ruins and a wasteland.

Their goal was the concrete central grain elevator—the largest of all those built along the Buffalo River and abandoned in 1966. To reach the elevator, they crossed the railroad bridge and walked through a regenerating grassland past a few burnt out cars to the center of the quarter-mile elevator, where you could still enter the space under the silos. The purpose was to photograph the structure.

The massive concrete elevator, over 100 feet tall, sits silently next to the Buffalo River. Well, not so silently that day. The space was filled with shouts and shots as teenage boys playing paint-ball scurried through the endless open spaces among the columns.

The startling light streaming in through the openings created stark contrasts, rendering the space as breathtaking as any cathedral. It was this contrast that made the hole invisible. She took a step into the blackness and fell four feet to the bottom of the pit. "Where are you? What happened?" asked the photographer. After a wave of pain, she managed to stand up in the hole but knew that there was no way she could climb out. Her arm was likely broken or at least, badly sprained. "What should I do? How can I help?" She said, "Go get the boys." They came in their fatigues with paint-ball rifles in hand and gently lifted her out; they made a sling out of the scarf. The wild and unruly boys are gracious and proud as they tell the story in the lunchrooms of South Buffalo high school about "the old lady" who fell into the hole and how they rescued her.

The area is still zoned for heavy manufacturing, but the Buffalo River area is no longer the industrial center of the city because there is so little industry. The land is "vacant" even though filled with empty buildings, littered with rusting artifacts and overrun by unruly flora and fauna. The in-between status of the deserted industrialized landscapes and the lack of coherence among their material, conceptual and imaginal aspects are the basis of the "rustbelt" designation of regions such as Buffalo (Cooke 1995). The imagination of places becomes self-fulfilling as negatively charged place names such as "rustbelt" and "brownfield" discourage engagement and redevelopment. "[V]acant land not only affects the physical form of the city; it also affects the image of the city" (Bowman and Pagano 2004: 90).

The river, once a central part of people's working lives, has become nearly invisible—its presence slipping out of the city. This has freed it to become itself again in ways that have generated new uses, meanings and imaginations. As the artifacts crumble and rust and traces of human activity disappear, the river has started to clean itself and the land has begun to grow plants, an amazing feat in the toxic and inhospitable soils left as the legacy of heavy manufacturing.

Wildness and Wilderness

The disinvestment and degeneration of the industrial Buffalo River revealed a crack in the technological utopian vision and represented a significant typological and ideological shift in the modern industrialized world. This is seen not only in the burning waters, abandoned factories and loss of commerce; it is also evident in the late twentieth-century environmental movement in the United States that challenged a set of practices codified in property rights and regulations. That this movement has been somewhat effective probably owes as much to the moving of many industrial jobs overseas and to more sophisticated science and new technologies as it does to the strength of its collective action. Nevertheless, in a relatively short period of time, as citizens organized the first Earth Day in 1970, the United States took action and passed the federal National Environmental Protection Act (NEPA) in 1969 and pollution control laws such as the Clean Air Act (1970) and the Clean Water Act (1972).

The Buffalo River and the Great Lakes of which it is a part are not only the responsibility of local, state and federal governments, they are also within the jurisdiction of the International Joint Commission (IJC), a US/Canadian body charged with oversight of the Great Lakes. In the 1980s, the IJC identified 42 toxic hot spots—areas that were contributing the greatest pollution load to the lakes. The Buffalo River and the Niagara River into which it flows were both identified as Areas of Concern that would require a Remedial Action Plan (RAP). The Buffalo River RAP was completed in 1987 and the Urban Canoe Trail Park was one of its first projects.

New York State's Department of Environmental Conservation is charged with implementing the Buffalo River RAP. To include those citizens who had participated in developing the RAP and also to advocate for the river, we formed a non-profit organization in 1989, The Friends of the Buffalo River "to promote, preserve and protect the Buffalo River, its natural and cultural heritage." A new image of the Buffalo River was articulated in the RAP and by its citizen advocates, a vision that challenged the paradigm of river-as-resource so evident in the technological vision of business and industry. The mission of the Friends expanded in 2001 to include the Niagara River and its RAP.

It is understandable that the governmental bodies responsible for public health would be taking action here, but why would a group of citizens commit their time and energy to a wasteland, over and over again, and not just in Buffalo but in many other places throughout the world? The Buffalo River is not a pristine wilderness area; it is still a seriously impaired body of water surrounded by a landscape of ruins and weeds. There are many reasons given by individuals for their involvement in place-based, watershed and preservation organizations: the public good, preservation of

13.3
A view of the naturally regenerating Buffalo River from the Smith Street Habitat Restoration site with the permanently raised railroad bridge in sight. The boat visible in this pastoral scene is EPA's Research Vessel *Mudpuppy*, taking core samples of the riverbed to determine the extent of historic contamination as the basis for sediment remediation.

heritage, access to recreation, and environmental health. But there is an overarching pull toward engagement beyond an intellectual rationale. Like many wastelands, the Buffalo River is seductive in its wildness, its looseness and the majesty of its ruins. A canoe ride down its waters, a walk through the tall grasses or a quiet moment in the coolness of an abandoned structure thicken the experience of life and deepen an awareness of the local place we inhabit (Lippard 1997). There is a wildness and an unruliness about this place yet also a connection to a robust wilderness that engages and envelopes anyone who comes within its reach.

Unruly and Wild

Wasted places generate their own kinds of activities, meanings and imaginations in part because they have slipped out of legitimate conceptual structures such as ownership patterns and maintenance responsibilities. "In abandoned places, the release from a sense of immediate human purpose allows freer action as well as free mental reconstruction" (Lynch 1990: 25). These spaces are unruly and disordered; they defy human intent and control.

In the absence of adult activities such as "work," places like the Buffalo River become the playgrounds of the young, the *terrains vagues* (Jackson 1984) onto which adolescents write their own meanings and stories. Like the industrialists before them, the young are often unaware that the river may have a life of its own and they use it as a blank page on which to make their own marks—whether that is through legitimate activities as simple as getting out of the house and engaging in extreme

13.4
The Buffalo River is still classified as a water body to be used for waste and discharge, a class "C" stream. This means that it is not safe for swimming or fishing; nevertheless, young people swim in the waters in rather dangerous industrial areas.

sports or as a setting for illicit activities such as stripping stolen cars and trespassing on private property. Unattended spaces not only attract the young and their activities, but accumulate waste; illegal dumping continues to litter the landscape, increasing the appearance of disorder.

There is a wildness in the Buffalo River and its messy shoreline. This is a wildness that attracts and repels because it is a reflection of those parts of human culture that we repress and seek to eliminate. But we need spaces for illicit and unsanctioned activities; many people need to break out of socially accepted norms, especially young people and those on the margins of legitimate society. The spaces of disorder not only permit a kind of retreat, recklessness and abuse, they sanctify it in their own state of wildness.

The Buffalo River is generous and permissive; its unruliness is an important condition for human life. This is the imaginal "away" of a highly controlled society, of parents and institutions (Lynch 1990). It is a place to meet friends for a secret rendezvous, where youngsters catch snakes and build forts, where adolescents light fires in the darkness of the late hours, where drug deals are conducted away from watching eyes and where homeless men create small dwellings and caches for their meager belongings. Even without condoning many of these activities, we may find it important to protect this disordered wildness. Advocacy for the preservation of ruins, tacit support of the use of these wild spaces by the homeless and the young without owner harassment and a willingness to leave spaces untidy, un-improved and without easy access are ways to ensure that there are left over, loose spaces in our landscape.

Robust Wilderness

But there is another wildness along the Buffalo River that approaches wilderness, the word meaning originally "the lair of the wild beast." The apparent disorder is deceptive unless one knows how to read a naturally regenerating landscape. Understanding this unchecked profusion and participating in its order is one of the lures for those who have come to take action on behalf of the Buffalo River.

The structure and order of human settlements and spaces such as factories and industrial work spaces demand continual maintenance. And in the absence of that care, an older order erupts as it has on the Buffalo River, one based on the interrelationship between complexity and order, health and functioning of the system. In much of the temperate world, this means that pioneer and weedy species colonize the bare land, generating fields of dense grasses that are almost impenetrable, sprouting on unattended roofs, through the cracks in former parking lots and between abandoned railways. Over time, in places with sufficient water and adequate soil conditions, the fields are replaced by successive shrubs, grasses and even trees. Next to the river, wetlands and lowland forests re-appear, shading out the weedy species and diversifying the habitat. Animals return to take advantage of new habitat and food sources.

In its relentless flow the river scours the contaminated sediments. Without new pollutants, it is now able to sustain invertebrates and fish, although their health is still impaired. The damage to the ecosystem of this river has been extensive; it is still degraded. Yet at the same time, we are witnessing a powerful transformative act by the earth itself: the river is no longer dead.

13.5
The Buffalo River basin, historically a marshy delta, was channelized to accommodate industry such as grain transshipment. The abandoned Cargill Elevator and its rail yards are located between the Buffalo River on the north and a wetland remnant on the south.

In our post-industrial and highly suburbanized landscapes, areas like the Buffalo River are precious because they embody both wildness and wilderness. Ruins and the remains of human artifacts are spaces of wildness, especially for adolescents who use them to play paint-ball, smash bottles, experiment with their sexuality and light illegal fires. In a less crowded world, one might argue that the unruly wildness and robust wilderness might be the same place, leaving room for marginal and intrusive activities within diverse and productive habitats. But it is not clear that over time this same space can be both wild and wilderness because natural regeneration processes work best if there are relatively large tracts of land free to self heal without abusive and reckless behavior. The Buffalo River former industrial landscape is a relatively small space from the perspective of a natural system. Within this space, it is not apparent how to balance the needs for unruly wildness with the requirements of a robust wilderness. Perhaps this tension is more easily resolved through time as places move in and out of control and care, and spaces for both wilderness and wildness travel across our landscape as areas are reclaimed and new ones slip into abandonment.

It is possible to envision a complex and diverse Buffalo River that continues to bear the marks of its industrial heritage, maintains its sense of looseness and, at the same time, becomes a more intact and healthy ecosystem, a green infrastructure for urban life. To affirm the many lives of the river requires multiple approaches and interactions. To date, this has included attending to the material world with cleanups, habitat restoration projects, cultural preservation, and pollution abatement. This vision demands planning and legal structures that leave space for the river's own agency, protecting it from further abuse even while meeting the needs of surrounding communities and young people and possibly again contributing to the economic well-being of the city.

Late one summer afternoon, we met at the river to plant some native seedlings. We saw smoke coming from the edge of the river: a lone man, shaggy and dirty, was sitting, stirring a fire and drinking a beer. We let him know what we were doing so he would not be startled. As we began our digging, he approached and started to talk to me about the plants. I was surprised that he knew the names of most of them. Jake (his name was Jake) told me he lived in these woods during the summer but he had to hide his things because he was afraid of the boys who came sometimes—especially the boys who had painted the three trunks red in the little clearing, marked by their gang's symbol. He hid when they came. As we talked, Jake spotted the only horse chestnut of the bevy of plants. "What a beautiful tree. Will you plant that over here?" We finished and left for our homes. Jake and the horse chestnut tree stayed by the river.

Like most places on the face of this earth, the Buffalo River has been remade many times, most recently by human hands, minds and imaginations. In its current state of typological looseness, there is an uneasy yet open space within which to construct new relationships among the physical, conceptual and imaginal aspects of the unbounded type. The abandonment of the region by industry has provided a small space within which to address this landscape type, to explore the implications of alternative visions and to struggle with the issues of power over who gets to make decisions regarding new uses and meanings.

Environmental organizations such as the Friends of the Buffalo Niagara Rivers are demanding a place in that conversation, albeit without formal power. They bring a perspective that differs from the capitalist resource-based worldview by articulating that the transformation of an urban river includes purposefully re-imagining it in a way that conjoins the evolving "natural" world and the emerging environmental policy/legal frameworks of our culture. This requires a shift of the imaginal view of the Buffalo River from wastelands or "vacant" lands to a space of natural processes—a productive landscape. "[T]he rules by which times, things and persons are placed within or without a productive realm are crucial assumptions" (Lynch 1990: 162) because the imagination regarding productive activity is used in actual making and unmaking. If the Buffalo River landscape is perceived as vacant land, it will be up for grabs. If it is perceived as a natural area, it may well be conserved and protected as a slice of wilderness in the city. And if we can begin to see marginal places as critical to the well being of our society, then perhaps, if we are fortunate, it can also be a place of wildness.

Places like the Buffalo River need friends who attempt to bring alternative perspectives into the cultural discourse, conservative in their efforts to preserve the ecological and cultural integrity of the river landscape and radical in their purposeful attempt to change the imagination of the place. Only with new eyes is it possible to canoe the Buffalo River and to see not devastation but monuments and ruins that speak to the lives of our parents and their grandparents. An informed mind and a new imagination are required to see beyond fields of weeds to recognize successive communities of vegetation and productive wetlands that are the incubators of life. And it takes a tolerance and willingness to appreciate the shadows and the importance of the *terrains vagues*, to leave some spaces of disorder in a cultural and natural landscape. The incoherence that comes when the material, conceptual and imaginal aspects of a place slip may be uncomfortable. However, the incongruity may not be a condition that demands a "fix" but rather a special time to reconsider how looseness can be maintained.

Loose Thinking

It is early fall and we have brought the canoe over to the shore near one of the railroad bridges. The trees are beginning the process of throwing their leaves away in preparation for the winter. The leaves are brittle; the wind rattles them and in gusts pulls them off the trees so that they float down, creating a carpet of yellow and red on the water's surface. The air is moving about us, rippling the water, causing small waves to lap the shoreline. The river is alive and stirring; we feel it under us as we feel the wind caressing the land, the trees and us.

Sitting on the derelict industrial shoreline of the Buffalo River, the sense of self loosens and one experiences and imagines a different way of being in the world. However, like the landscape itself, this imagination of a less bounded self has been denigrated, abandoned, discarded; it is wasting away. Not only do we seldom experience an intense intimacy with the world, we do not even have an appropriate language to speak of these experiences. And yet they exist. Michael Brill (1994) would call these moments of connectiveness "charged," and the places that inspire this sensibility of being extraordinarily attentive and at one with the world "charged places."

Even environmental groups like the Friends, who struggle to re-name a relationship to the given world, find it difficult to understand sufficiently the radical implications of their work or the disconnect between their aspirations for this place and the world of words and meanings we inhabit. Because we are so immersed in our culture we do not understand it as a set of beliefs that envelopes us and we are restrained from seeing how "reality" is a story constructed and reified in our daily lives, struggles, and discourses. But there are spaces in which we can, as Hillman (1982) says, "see through" the imaginal and conceptual landscape of our culture that is so carefully guarded to remember that these cultural stories are "quaking bridges built out of yearning" (Hoeg 1998: 278). When things fall apart, as along the Buffalo

River, the looseness of the place opens a crack in the edifice of dominant paradigms, creating a space for the restructuring not only of the place but of the culture that made and abandoned it.

It is hard practical work to protect abandoned buildings and contaminated landscapes. And it is hard practical work to generate a new fiction by recognizing that the world we are living in is itself "made-up" (Scarry 1985). The constructed culture of the modern West has encapsulated and manipulated the world so that we live almost exclusively inside our own makings and our own minds, supported by "institutions of dislocation in every dimension of social and cultural existence" (hooks 1992: 199). These conditions lure us farther from the sensual earth into the *logos*, the unique but isolated human habitat.

In spite of the power behind this dominant perspective, an increasing number of scholars, philosophers, poets, artists and citizens are seeking both to unmake the technological utopian fantasy and to offer re-visions of who human beings are and might become. The literature that confronts the modern sensibility of rationality and the isolated self is vast. Some of the most disciplined and provocative writers are: Abrams (1996), who suggests that we have transferred our sense of wonder at the world to wonder of the word; Eisenberg (1999), who explores the premise of nature as an active agent; Harrison (1992), who uses the history of our relationship to the forest to explore the emergence of Western thought and its consequences; and Solnit (2000), who explores the power and consequence of walking as a loose space for re-conceptualizations of the world. Evernden (1993) speaks of humans as the "natural aliens," and archetypal psychologists Hillman (1982) and Sardello (1992) have recovered the alchemic discourse on the soul of the world, replacing humans into a sacred world.

These writings and makings suggest that the kinship experienced amid the regenerating fabric of vegetation and disintegrating industrial ruins was the human condition as experienced by our species for millions of years. It is the world that we have constructed in modernity—of humans as an isolated and disconnected species disassociated from the sensual world—that is an aberration. The human evolved as a member of the earth community and, for most of its existence as a species, lived with a "participatory consciousness" in an alive world (Berman 1984). Sardello (1992) reminds us that it as plausible to believe that the world is alive as it is to believe that it is dead, although if one lives in a culture that is structured around an inanimate world, it is hard to recognize this isolative sensibility as a belief.

It is all too easy to dismiss the notion of a participatory consciousness as hopelessly romantic, primitive, or a form of animism. It does not fit our models of rationality and objectivity. The condition of interactivity and dependency has been rendered invisible, and the edifice of technology is so distancing that we neither recognize nor appreciate our total dependency on things as basic as water and air, sun and plants, culture and each other.

Yet, there are spaces in our lives where the grip of the modern sensibility is loosened. A moment at the Buffalo River in the fall amid waving grasses that cast off the smell of late summer reminds us that there are others on this earth and that we are not trapped solely in the human-made world. If we loosen our "psyche from its confinements within a strictly human sphere, freeing sentience to return to the sensible world that contains us . . . we come to feel as if there is a presence, an intelligence beyond our own" (Abrams 1996: 262). Each place, as each person, has its own unique psyche and being. Even the distressed Buffalo River and wasting artifacts have a presence; they literally "present" themselves to us. Sitting quietly in the canoe watching a hawk soar, listening to the waves lapping the shore, we experience the "lure of the local," an attachment to this place (Lippard 1997). It is easy to ignore or romanticize these responses unless we remember that to do so only confirms how deeply embedded we are in the cultural stories we inhabit and how well we have learned the lesson we were taught: to denigrate our connectivity with the earth.

"That's where Frankie drowned," said one young boy, pointing to a place under the silver railroad bridge. "Right here." Scrawled across an adjacent railroad abutment in large letters is the name FRANKIE, spray-painted one dark night by the young boy's older brother and his friends.

The young people were participating in an environmental education program in which two schools (one from an old Irish working class neighborhood downstream, and the other from an upper middle class suburban neighborhood upstream) met to talk about their parts of the Buffalo River. Each class had drawn a map. The 4th and 5th graders from the suburbs drew their school, the park, the animals they saw and their river activities, such as fishing. The Buffalo group not only included Frankie's memorial on their urban river but also located the burnt cars, railroad embankments, their pond, a skeleton of the jaw of a small mammal, and marked where they swam and their fathers fished. Each school created a small aquarium of a "healthy" river to study the ecology of riverine habitats that they nurtured. At the end of the year, the small aquarium was emptied back into the river with a small ceremony. "I hope the animals can live here," said one young girl from the urban Buffalo school. "I'm afraid the water is too polluted." She was probably right.

Postmodern constructivist theorists such as Borgman (1992), Haraway (1988) and Hayles (1995), among others, have opened a new space for re-imagining the place of humans in the world by unveiling our "truths" as positions or perspectives. The proposition that our world is constructed has freed us from many such truths: uncritical assumptions regarding the facts of science, ideologies of the political economy, the culture of everyday life, gender relations and identity politics, views on nature and epistemological positions. The difficulty with a constructivist view is that it leaves no room for the existence of the world and the earth outside of our fabrication of it. The debate about essentialism and constructivism is particularly fierce within the environmental sciences and cultural studies because the position that one takes here determines the imagination of the universe (Soule and Lease 1995; Cronon 1996). And yet, the belief in a constructed vs. a given world is itself a making and a false choice.

13.6
A tribute to a fallen friend, Frankie, who drowned in the Buffalo River

In her discussion of "interactivity" and "positionality," Hayles (1995) suggests a way of understanding how both the "given" and "made" worlds co-exist. The earth and its universe are not "real" in the sense that what we see and experience is really there. We can only perceive the world with the sensory capabilities and prosthetics of our species; the earth and its universe are more vast and complex than we can imagine. Hayles suggests that we might imagine the world as a "flux," organized and given meaning by our experience of it. This same flux is organized very differently by other species such as trees or viruses, even though they use the same material and energy we do. In this alternative conception of everything, the world is both given (energy/matter) and constructed by the position and interactions of each species. If one accepts this conception of the world, then it is easy to see how humans, with their recent power over the flux, are dangerous to the others. The more we reorganize the flux to meet our needs, the less able other beings and conditions are able to organize it for their needs.

This brings us back to the Buffalo River wasteland—the remains of a great unmaking of an already existing world that was replaced by a constructed technological order that fed us grain grown in the Midwest and made steel with which we built our cities. Humans, like all creatures, interact with the world; we must make and unmake things. The issue is not that we interact but *how* we do these things. It makes a difference how we use and care for the spaces of the world we transform and the artifacts we fabricate and later unmake when they are no longer useful. If our attitude toward the earth and its own processes is consumptive without regard for the requirements for the flux by the others, then we will continue to devour the world without regard for its own agency and constructive purposes.

But there is another way to be in the world, grounded in the imagination of a participatory consciousness, an attitude that pulls us out of ourselves to take into account others in the world. This is not a return to some form of unselfconscious animism, but rather the conscious construction of an imagination that puts concern and interest in the other equal to interest and concern in self, what Bishop (1990) calls an "ecological imagination." To live in an ecological world that coheres materially, conceptually and imaginally demands a responsible restraint on the alteration of everything. It requires that we encourage looseness as a legitimate part of our world, not just as a condition of those places we have abandoned such as industrial landscapes.

The Buffalo River once ended in cattail marshes along the shoreline of Lake Erie and supported an array of wildlife, soils, vegetation and microscopic creatures. We made it a channelized waterway of uniform depth. Because of the constructed shoreline, it no longer supports diverse wildlife, nor can it flood and restore the cyclical sedimentation of the land. It is trapped by *our* version of the world—conceptually, materially and imaginally—unless we find a way to free it, and us, again.

It is important to re-connect with the river and abandoned places through our interactions with them and through the mindful practical work of organizations such as the Friends. It is equally important to recognize our responsibility to embrace

13.7
A boy fishes on the wall of a combined sewer overflow (CSO) along the Buffalo River across from the grain elevators

looseness in the constructed ideas, worldviews and visions that we inhabit, more freely making and unmaking our conceptions of the world itself. This standpoint is a new loose space—an opening in which to question the very foundation and epistemology of modern Western culture and its belief in an isolated self in a dead world.

An ecological imagination challenges the dominant worldview of an insensate world, a belief that has been destructive to the web of beings who share this small planet in a profusion of places, bioregions and cities. A participatory consciousness makes room for a world of subjects and agents, pulling us to understand how we may be able to co-exist and co-evolve in a respectful and chaotic manner. Embracing a space that does not so sharply differentiate between humans and the rest of the earth welcomes the hybridity of new makings, including ours, while respecting the requirements of each species for its own interactions with and construction of the flux. This more open imagination is fed by places like abandoned but regenerating industrial landscapes. If we can better understand our attraction to, need for and desire to protect an unbounded landscape such as the unruly and robust Buffalo River, we may become more able to construct and inhabit diverse imaginations of the physical, conceptual and imaginal spaces of this world and our place in it.

References

Abrams, D. (1996) *The Spell of the Sensuous*, New York: Vintage Books.

Berman, M. (1984) *The Reenchantment of the World*, New York: Bantam Books.

Bishop, P. (1990) *The Greening of Psychology: The Vegetable World in Myth, Dream and Healing*, Dallas, TX: Spring Publications.

Borgman, A. (1992) *Crossing the Postmodern Divide*, Chicago: The University of Chicago Press.

Bowman, A. O. M. and Pagano, M. A. (2004) *Terra Incognita: Vacant Land and Urban Strategies*, Washington, DC: Georgetown University Press.

Boyer, B. (2002) "A Polluted River Comes Back," *Clearwaters* (New York Water Environment Association), 32: 10–12.

Brill, M. (1994) "Archetypes as a 'Natural Language' for Place Making," in K. Franck and L. Schneekloth (eds) *Ordering Space: Types in Architecture and Design*, New York: Van Nostrand Reinhold.

Cooke, P. (ed.) (1995) *The Rise of the Rustbelt*, New York: St. Martin's Press.

Cronon, W. (ed.) (1996) *Uncommon Ground: Rethinking the Human Place in Nature*, New York: WW Norton & Company.

Eisenberg, E. (1999) *The Ecology of Eden*, New York: Vintage Books.

Evernden, N. (1993) *The Natural Alien: Humankind and Environment*, 2nd edn, Toronto: University of Toronto Press.

Goldman, M. (1983) *High Hopes: The Rise and Decline of Buffalo, New York*, Albany, NY: State University of New York Press.

Haraway, D. (1988) "Situated Knowledges: The Science Question in Feminism and the Privilege of Partial Perspective," *Feminist Studies* 14: 575–600.

Harrison, R. P. (1992) *Forests: The Shadow of Civilization*, Chicago: University of Chicago Press.

Hayles, N. K. (1995) "Searching for Common Ground," in M. Soule and G. Lease (eds) *Reinventing Nature: Responses to Postmodern Deconstruction*, Washington, DC: Island Press.

Hillman, J. (1982) "Anima Mundi: The Return of the Soul to the World," *Spring (1982)*: 71–93.

Hoeg, P. (1998) "Reflections of a Young Man in Balance," in *Tales of the Night*, trans. B. Haveland, Toronto: Doubleday.

hooks, b. (1992) *Black Looks: Race and Representation*, Boston: South End Press.

Jackson, J. B. (1984) "The Origin of Parks," in J. B. Jackson (ed.) *Discovering the Vernacular Landscape*, New Haven, CT: Yale University Press.

Lippard, L. (1997) *The Lure of the Local: Senses of Place in a Multicentered Society*, New York: The New Press.

Lynch, K. (1990) *Wasting Away: An Exploration of Waste: What It Is, How It Happens, Why We Fear It, How to Do It Well*, M. Southworth (ed.), San Francisco: Sierra Club Books.

Sardello, R. (1992) *Facing the World with Soul*, Hudson, NY: Lindisfarne Press.

Scarry, E. (1985) *The Body in Pain: The Making and Unmaking of the World*, New York: Oxford University Press.

Schneekloth, L and Franck, K. (1994) "Type: Prison or Promise?" in K. Franck and L. Schneekloth (eds) *Ordering Space: Types in Architecture and Design*, New York: Van Nostrand Reinhold.

Solnit, R. (2000) *Wanderlust: A History of Walking*, New York: Penguin Books.

Soule, M. and Lease, G. (eds) (1995) *Reinventing Nature: Responses to Postmodern Deconstruction*, Washington, DC: Island Press.

Spirn, A. (1998) *The Language of Landscape*, New Haven, CT: Yale University Press.

Chapter 14

Patterns of the Unplanned

Urban Catalyst

(Philipp Oswalt, Philipp Misselwitz, and Klaus Overmeyer)

Directly behind Berlin's Ostbahnhof railway station lies a wide expanse of wasteland. The investment projects for this site, planned during the second half of the 1990s, can be found in glossy brochures under the ambitious-sounding name "Spreeraum Ost" (Eastern Spree River Area). The cranes are missing, the cityscape is falling apart, and wild growth proliferates between disused tracks. The regional and urban rail route, which divides the site, appears to lead through a lifeless prairie.

But the view from the train is deceptive. Visitors and even many locals would never guess that this prairie is alive. Hidden behind the gray silhouettes of the apparently empty industrial façades, in inner courtyards and old warehouses, there is a vital laboratory of all kinds of different uses. Young graphic designers, artists, architects, and filmmakers can be found behind the old façade of the head office of *Neues Deutschland*, the former East German ruling party newspaper, and in the adjacent barracks. At night, the gray area south of the rail track, which appears empty, becomes an interesting cluster of sub-cultural night clubs. In order to build a planned, but yet not financed large sports arena, a series of buildings were demolished in 2004. Most of the temporary users of those buildings found new spots in the same area, to the west or the north, while the plans for the start of the ground breaking for the large investment project have now been delayed several times.

A walk through the former RAW (railway improvement works) to the north, on Revaler Strasse in the Berlin neighborhood of Friedrichshain, brings unusual

14.1
Abundance of vacant space near the former Wriezener Station, Berlin, 2002. Several now famous nightclubs and start-up companies originated in the surrounding area at the end of the 1990s.

encounters. Railway cars were still being repaired here until 1994. In 1998, after the site had remained unused for four years, local residents took the initiative to revive the wasteland. They founded the RAW-Tempel e.V. and initially leased four RAW buildings for three years. Within a few months, a platform for over 30 alternative cultural and social projects had been established. For most of those involved, the RAW represents a niche in which new ideas can be tried out free from pure market economy cycles and with minimum investment. Unlike traditionally developed service centers, the different people involved work together. They do all they can, without pay, to arrange community projects such as public discussion forums, a children's circus, and even workshops with citizens to develop their part of the city. The emergence of the RAW is a typical example of grass-roots urban development. In 2001 and 2002, the owner of the site commissioned urban planners and tried to develop the site, but due to lack of demand no investment took place and further temporary use as an indoor bike park was established.

Comparable to RAW-Tempel e.V. is a former silk factory on the banks of Lake Zurich, run by an interest group since 1980 as a collective with 19 permanent employees. Known as the Rote Fabrik (Red Factory), over 300 events are now held there every year. In addition to a theater and rehearsal rooms, the factory houses a restaurant, a kindergarten, a bicycle workshop, a local meeting place, a sailing school, 50 studios and a free art school. Eighty permanent jobs have been created within the milieu of the individual projects. Over 200 musicians, artists, and actors have their workplaces here. The originally informal, intermediate usage has mutated into a profitable, permanent use (Wolf 1998).

Many other examples demonstrate that the phenomena of derelict sites caused by de-industrialization, abundance of infrastructure or political faults are not Berlin-specific phenomena, but represent a common part of the urban fabric in nearly all European cities (deadline and Urban Catalyst 2006; Oswalt *et al.* forthcoming). Post-industrial change in Europe has generated very different social, economic and spatial conditions in urban centers: a polarized map where certain cities enjoyed unprecedented boom and regeneration while others failed to absorb vast, often centrally located areas left abandoned after the closure of industries decades ago. Commercial development in cities like Helsinki (Hentilä *et al.* 2001) continues to profit from a strong real estate market while economic crisis and collapsed property markets in Berlin have led to a slowdown and virtual standstill in property development. In a context of an over-supply of space and high vacancy rates many developers resign themselves to apathy and "wait for better times." However, the success and failure of urban transformation processes cannot be measured by short-term growth alone. A booming economy with an over inflated real estate market can banish all creative energy from the city, making it impossible for young and weaker economies to thrive, potentially endangering a "sustainable mix" of activities and actors, a criticism raised, for example, in Amsterdam some years ago, when the city experienced an economic boom. One could argue that, in both scenarios, temporary use can thrive while, to a certain degree, traditional planning tools fail to provide an energetic, vital and humane city.

Over a period of two years (2001–2003), Urban Catalyst, composed of an interdisciplinary team of architects, planners, lawyers, sociologists and representatives of local municipalities, has researched the potential of temporary use and the apparent crisis of classical planning. This research was based on two main hypotheses: (1) spontaneous, temporary uses can have positive long term effects; and (2) the unplanned phenomena of temporary uses can be successfully incorporated into the planning and management of cities. Philipp Oswalt and Klaus Overmeyer initiated and directed the research project that was funded by the European Commission within the Key Action 4 City of Tomorrow and Cultural Heritage program of the European Union. The project, with 11 partners in six countries, was coordinated by the Technische Universität Berlin.

The research took place in five European cities, which represent the spectrum between economic success and crisis: Helsinki, Amsterdam, Berlin, Vienna and Naples. Case study sites were characterized either by a time gap—a moment of standstill between the collapse of a previous use and the beginning of new commercial development—or by the problems of gentrification and social exclusion created by a thriving real estate market. In all cases, temporary use became a vehicle that provided opportunities for new, unplanned activities, transforming banal and everyday spaces into breeding grounds for new forms of art, music, and pop culture, as well as for economic development, technological inventions and startups.

In the context of these developments, a re-evaluation of the role that temporary use plays in our cities seems both relevant and timely. Temporary use could

14.2
Indian electronic music concert as part of the Goa Festival, Club Freischwimmer at Arena Berlin, Landwehrkanal, Berlin, 2004

become a new tool for a strategic planning process that triggers change where traditional planning tools such as the master plan fail. While traditional state-financed urban development is no longer affordable, the radical shift to neoliberal planning policies has failed to offer inclusive models (Harvey 1989). Boom and gentrification can lead to social exclusion and an increasingly divided urban society, while the failure of market-driven development to adapt in the context of economic collapse has led to apathy and stagnation. Both gentrification and neglect are symptoms of a crisis, which should be considered as an opportunity to critically examine and question the existing planning procedures and consider alternative models of development.

The research project Urban Catalyst investigated the potential of temporary uses for long-term urban development. In order to discover the potential of the temporary, it was necessary to develop a precise understanding of the tactics and networks that make it possible.

What and Where is Temporary Use?

The range of temporary uses is vast and diverse, including fashionable leisure activities, theatre projects or concerts in disused warehouses and on former industrial sites or weekday bars in empty shops or stores, commercial markets and businesses, fairs and even housing projects. The following categories offer some broad differentiations: cultural activities, sports and leisure, commercial activities, migrant economies, gardening and (urban) agriculture as well as social projects. Temporary uses do not develop in isolation. Often, an initial use attracts others, generating use clusters over a short period of time. Such clusters may also include programs very different from the initial use and can develop extensive-informal and formal networks of exchange. Especially in the initial phase of setting up a temporary use, such clusters can grow rapidly, like fast dividing cells. Given easy and cheap access to vacant space, the bonus of a creative and inspiring environment and mutual support needed while dealing with the property owner or municipal bureaucracies can lead to tightly knit micro-communities.

In the research project, a use was defined as "temporary" if those initiating it and the other actors involved expected it to be of limited duration. This time period can be set by a contractual arrangement with the owner of a specific building, space or plot. In most cases, however, the temporary uses do not have a formal basis at all. They are either tolerated by the owner (who can decide to cancel this arrangement when he chooses) or simply be illegal or semi-legal; or they might lack necessary building permission. Following this definition, uses can lose their classification as "temporary" as soon as this status changes and they consolidate into an established use based on regular contractual arrangements or ownership.

Temporary uses often emerge in in-between spaces or gaps, on former industrial or infrastructural areas, in vacant shops, businesses, office spaces, as well as in empty housing areas. All are typologies that are an integral by-product of urban development processes, triggered by deindustrialization or other structural economic or social changes. Or they might be caused by legal, political or environmental conditions. In moments of high demand, such areas can quickly be re-planned, built and put to a new use, despite the characteristic high costs for demolition of old structures, decontamination of pollution and new construction. Yet traditional development patterns struggle or fail to absorb urban residual sites if initial investment costs are too high due to ground pollution, building contamination or lack of an appropriate infrastructural context. In other cases, planning restrictions, lengthy and complex processes to obtain building permits or political sensitivities rule out large-scale, fast-track speculative development. Alternatively, a weak or even shrinking real estate market increases the risk of development. These are only a few of the factors that may create a pause or moment of standstill between a former use and new, planned use. It is within this time gap that temporary use manifests itself. But not all spaces are appropriate. Temporary use also relies on the condition of the available infrastructure, which will reduce the initial investment costs, easy access, an attractive locality and the presence of a network pool of potential users.

Although, by definition, temporary uses are activities limited to a certain duration, they do leave traces and often influence further development of the site. A disused space may have become invisible to potential developers. Temporary users

14.3
and
14.4
Opening of the installation "Badeschiff," a swimming pool floating in the Spree River, as part of an art exhibition in 2004, from a concept by Susanne Lorenz, artist, and AMP Architects. The pool has since remained open as a public venue under the management of Kulturarena, a popular Berlin arts venue.

then become "pioneers," discovering the space and making it publicly known through their temporary use initiatives, resulting in various outcomes. In many cases, temporary use functions only in the interim, eventually being replaced by higher-value land uses; at these sites temporary users and their specific agendas do not have a sustainable influence on the future development of the specific site. Along a different path of development, the presence of a temporary use can give a specific

14.5
Horse riding on vacant strip of the former Berlin Wall

stimulus to future development of a site. It can influence the future programming of the site by setting an example of a possible use or it may influence the site's future physical appearance by saving buildings that would otherwise have been demolished. Within the worldwide squatter movement, many examples of this can be found.

The temporary use may also remain on a specific site, consolidating and transforming into a permanent use. Or a path of symbiosis may be followed where the temporary use remains even after the site has been re-developed, albeit in a reduced form. Established and temporary uses co-exist side by side to mutual advantage. For example, a temporary use can attract public audiences to a temporary event staged at a site while relying on a stable support infrastructure.

Who Is Involved in Temporary Use?

The motivation to become a temporary user varies, but all temporary users have at least one characteristic in common: they are on a threshold, on the way into or out of mainstream society and regular activities. In this sense, they are not yet established in the urban landscape either because they have recently migrated to the city or they are entering a new phase in their lives (e.g. leaving their parents' home for university). Three main kinds of initiators can be identified: drop-outs, start-ups and switchers.

Some citizens become temporary users from a desire not to conform, creating niches for an alternative and independent lifestyle. Since the 1960s, sub-cultural milieus have developed in almost all European cities. Squats, trailers, caravans and houseboats still provide an alternative environment in urban surroundings. In some cases, such environments are not voluntarily chosen but provide the only alternative for survival after social or economic collapse.

A nearly opposite motivation drives a different and often much more privileged social group: the desire to realize the dream of an independent business. Setting up a bar, gallery or sharing an office in an inspiring and creative environment may be the first step towards a lucrative business. A makeshift and low-rent environment can therefore become a jumping-off board into an established economic cycle. Entrepreneurs of a different kind are also immigrants, legal or illegal, excluded from the social and legal system, where the milieu of informal and semi-legal uses provides opportunities to work and, if successful, integrate into the established society.

Other temporary users may be ordinary citizens in search of an alternative part-time occupation or a thrilling experiment. Through doing that, they escape the routine and boredom of regular lifestyles. Temporary use can provide an exciting playground and an alternative universe, e.g. a student running a weekday bar once a week or a businessman practicing cross-golf or *Volxgolf* (golf played in disused or underused parts of the city).

Informal economies become reception and integration thresholds into society for new arrivals and penniless immigrants. Other temporary users take refuge from conventional lifestyles and enjoy the openness and freedom offered by the claimed spaces. The virtually cost-free access to these spaces gives financially weak players the opportunity to grow in a protected but unsubsidized environment and become active participants in the shaping of their city. It gives them the opportunity to contribute to the shaping of the city and its public spaces beyond the classical mode of high-investment urban development. The city is no longer shaped only by high-capital investors. A second group of actors, with few financial resources but with high levels of creativity and social ambition, is entering the arena.

In most cases, temporary users do not act in isolation but rely on an intensive formal and informal support structure. Often, a precondition for the successful initiation of a temporary use project is the presence of agile and capable individuals or "key agents." At times, key agents can be found in the municipality, as representatives of the owner or they act as temporary users themselves. Such agents have access to resources, relevant experience or specific skills such as dealing with the bureaucracy or writing funding applications. At the same time, they have an idealistic social motivation beyond "business as usual" and are able to act as negotiators, building bridges between conflicting parties. Their most crucial input is often given in the initial phase of a temporary use when a support network or internal organizational structure needs to be constructed.

In many cases, the realization of temporary use depends on the agreement of the legal owners of a specific vacant building or open area. Many owners are persuaded by the promise of non-monetary gains without significant, if any, investment on their part. Raising the property's profile or generating a specific and recognizable identity often translates later into higher sales or rental prices. Alternatively, the presence of temporary users on the site can ensure a certain degree of free-of-charge security and protection against possible vandalism and further decay. Sometimes owners just enjoy enabling other people's activities for their own philanthropic reasons. Although the fear of not being able to get rid of temporary programs once they are installed still prevails among most owners, the harsh reality of economic stagnation and over-supply of space increasingly leads to a recognition that if temporary uses become permanent, reliable and stable tenants will be present and income will be generated.

An owner's sustained resistance is one of the most important reasons for failure to take over a site. Clashes of interest are frequent. The owner might decide to "wait for better times" for fear of temporary users blocking development options and effectively decreasing the real estate value of the property. Alternatively, the owner simply might not want to get involved in an unfamiliar "temporary use experiment" with its time-consuming negotiations and reduced income which might not justify the administrative effort involved.

The temporary nature of many programs, offering reliable services in the fields of gastronomy, cultural events, flea markets, art and education programs or self-help skill training programs to name but a few, does not necessarily relieve consumers or program initiators of the typical dynamics of ordinary buyer–seller relationships. Here, temporary programs need to develop the skills to attract specific audiences as a customer base. In other cases, however, activities are offered without the selling of a specific service—creating access to otherwise closed sites for leisure activities such as sports, walking, picnicking, etc. In the sub-cultural milieus, which frequently surround temporary use, non-monetary exchange flourishes with much more ease.

European planning law generally does not allow for the flexibility needed when dealing with temporary uses, which are subject to the same rules and planning regulations as ordinary uses. But, as many examples show, municipalities do hold the power to be pro-active. Through the pragmatic and non-bureaucratic initiatives of individual employees, the municipality can become an enabler, removing hurdles and obstacles and acting as an arbiter in situations of conflict between temporary users and property owners. The municipality can also directly initiate temporary use by legally backing financial risks such as loans, by giving access to its vast and often vacant premises or by formally involving temporary users in urban planning processes. However, in most cases, bureaucratic, compartmentalized thinking and lack of initiative prevail and municipalities often fail to recognize the potential of temporary uses as engines of inclusive urban development (Schäfer and Lau 2003). Often, temporary users do not have the financial resources or are not prepared to invest in order to meet the legal requirements that pertain both to ordinary and temporary uses. If they cannot get by or find a legal loophole, many prefer to leave the site in search of a more convenient location.

How Does Temporary Use Succeed?

Initiating a temporary use is risky. Despite the advantages a site may possess, many of the conditions are uncertain and the kinds of rules and criteria temporary users follow are necessarily different from those of conventional developers and tenants.

In order to transform and appropriate a found space, temporary users are generally prepared to invest a high degree of self-initiative, as the Austrian sociologist Peter Arlt (forthcoming) describes:

> A decision over a location is made not so much in accordance with the existing conditions, but more in accordance with the kind of inspiration it might trigger. The original idea for a use can completely transform in accordance with the found qualities of a place. Place is here understood as a totality of urban context, the spatial qualities and its changing atmospheres themselves as well as objects found or in possession of the temporary user, the owner or neighbors, and many other criteria. Not everything is equally relevant but place and program are developed and sharpened in a step-by-step process. The crucial step is the process of blending idea and space to the point where both become synonymous with each other and something new has emerged.

Temporary users employ a pioneer strategy of development. Not only are they more tolerant of the different and at times extreme conditions of a found space but they make the best of these conditions for their purposes. Through the pragmatic and low-cost appropriation of existing physical and infrastructural elements, temporary uses can be realized with comparatively little financial capital. In many cases, only small or no alterations are made to the basic physical structure of a found space. The most obvious reasons for such low key appropriations include the often limited financial means available and the legal uncertainty of the new use. The high degree of adaptability of temporary users generates more flexibility, speed and reduces operational costs. If essential, furniture or technical infrastructure such as electricity, water or heating can be repaired, adjusted or developed.

Temporary users have almost no capital to invest. Money is replaced by self-initiative, social networks and the re-use of existing materials, space and conditions. Temporary users are groups of people with a shared goal and agenda, who invest enormous amounts of unpaid work into the achievement of their common aim. In a creative way, they invent new ways to bypass obstacles, to help each other and to convert the existing into the newly desired.

Long-Term Effects of Temporary Use

The research project conducted by Urban Catalyst confirmed that spontaneous, temporary uses have positive long-term effects, both at the sites where they were originally located and well beyond. Some temporary uses become permanent; often these are self-organized cultural and social institutions that continue to benefit the cities where they are located. Even when the temporary use at a given site disappears (mostly because the site owner is using his real estate in a classical way), quite often it is re-established at a different site. A prototypical example of this is the Berlin nightclub WMF, which has moved more than six times since 1990. The change of location mostly transforms the activity. The initiative might also split into several parts but these transformations mostly have a positive effect, updating and refreshing the character of the activity. For example, after two years of very successful temporary use, the lease for the Haus des Lehrers in Berlin was cancelled. The temporary users fought to stay, unsuccessfully. They also tried to move together to a new location. Finally, they found two new appropriate locations. Both buildings offered more space than needed and therefore allowed the two clusters to grow by absorbing new uses. On the other hand, through moving and splitting, the identity and integrity of the original cluster were lost.

Often a temporary use has an ongoing effect on the location itself. Temporary uses often make formerly rather unknown sites publicly known; this is sometimes strategically used by site-owners (e.g. Galerie Loop in Berlin, KDAG in Vienna, Club Hacienda in Manchester). The temporary uses can also contribute substantially to the symbolic and programmatic redefinition of sites, mostly from former industrial or infrastructural use to postindustrial types of programs (culture, services, leisure). In the case of Manchester in the UK, the activities of a music sub-culture in combination with a gay culture and an Asian community transformed the image of an entire city. Spaces that have dropped out of the cycle of the market economy often suffer from a negative image. Through temporary use such spaces are often made accessible again for the first time. If successful (e.g. clubs), abandoned sites are "re-discovered" and made known to a wider public and, thus, generate the necessary preconditions for a commercial re-development. In a temporary use context, unconventional activities and new use concepts are being tested that can develop into commercially viable and lasting programs and specific use profiles of the site, as is the case with the arena and its adjacent activities in Berlin-Treptow. Through temporary use and gradual appropriation, a former bus depot was converted into the arena, consisting of a large concert and event hall. An entire cluster of uses has been established around it, partly as commercial development and partly as temporary use. These include a flea market, a temporary pool and sauna, a restaurant, a youth club and offices for startup companies.

Independently of their individual lifetimes, temporary uses make a strong impact on the cultural and social capital of cities. Due to their innovative character, they very often establish new cultural and social practices and lifestyles, which are then incorporated into everyday life and popular and high culture. Temporary activities are also an incubator for the development of new types of professionals. The people involved in temporary use projects gain new professional experience which often totally changes their personal professional perspectives. Formerly unknown but needed professions (and professionals) emerge.

Temporary Use as a Catalyst for Urban Change

Intermediate uses can play a role in the development of cities. In many places, economic crisis and recession have led to real estate market slumps, leaving buildings that have been vacant for a long time still empty and producing vacancy in many recently occupied buildings. Ambitious, large scale project developments are becoming increasingly difficult. The competition for tenants is hard fought. Cases from Berlin and Amsterdam may be signs of new strategic thinking in the heads of several investors. Local authorities, urban planners, and project developers can learn from these examples. Intermediate uses show us new ways of achieving urban change—alternatives to impotence, lethargy and waiting for better times.

It is necessary to critically examine planning practice. If an urban site is to be developed, a customary basic process is initially assumed. An owner or investor commissions a planner to develop a concept for building on the site or a local authority has such a draft drawn up to attract investors. The main players are the owner, the investor and the local authorities. A desired end status is drawn up, which is then translated into a master plan. However, sometimes this procedure functions poorly: either the local real estate market is going through a bad phase, the local residents object to the plans, contamination is found on the site or old buildings are protected by preservation orders. Buildings left vacant for a period of years are evidence of the weaknesses of such an approach. The current economic crisis makes the situation even worse. Private investments are not forthcoming and public coffers are empty so they cannot fill the gap. Considered in this way, there is hardly any room to act.

This crisis can be used as an opportunity. Alternative scenarios for action can show us ways out of this situation. It is not the ideas of present-day urban development that are instructive here but spontaneously occurring processes that initially take place far from architecture and urban planning. Nevertheless, they have clear effects on urban development and urban culture. Temporary uses are a neglected potential; they can play a strategic role as an addition to capital-oriented urban development. It is often the sites that fall through and fail from a traditional planning viewpoint that become breeding grounds for new ideas. New fields of experimentation are created precisely there, where the model described above fails or is delayed for years or even decades. An urban wasteland is not only an oasis for rare species of plants and animals and several eccentric urban ecologists; it is also the nucleus of a different type of urbanism.

What can planners learn from processes that take place without planning and whose essential characteristic is spontaneity, and what role can they play in this process? Can inherently dynamic processes be controlled at all? Can temporary uses be initiated or cultivated? What happens when the economic situation does not permit conventional project development or when an overheated real estate market banishes all creative energy from the city? A case in Amsterdam offers some answers to these questions.

Amsterdam has experienced an enormous economic boom in recent years, although this has primarily affected the core city south of the IJ River. While the southern part of the harbor pier was developed by ambitious residential projects, the enormous northern part, only a few hundred meters away, was left empty. Paradoxically, development pressure from the growing metropolis even led to new

14.6
Temporary use of NDSM Hall, Amsterdam Noord, 2003. This former wharf, owned by the municipality, is currently managed by the group Kinetisch Noord.

and expensive land reclamation for 18,000 apartments despite the unused space adjoining them immediately to the north. To counteract this trend, the city administration of Amsterdam North, as the planning authority and landowner, developed a new type of development concept for an 8.6 ha dockland site, the core of which is the initiation of temporary cultural uses. These users are intended to help make the area known to the public and, in the medium term, to create a living, mixed-use neighborhood. A 20,000-sq m hall and large outdoor areas of the former NDSM dockyard were made available for this purpose. A competition was held at the beginning of 2000 to find a suitable organization for the temporary use of the areas. The Kinetisch Noord Group, an initiative especially founded for this purpose originating in Amsterdam's former house-squatting scene, won the competition and received a 10-year contract and a grant of 6 million Euros. Kinetisch Noord's idea integrates existing craft uses with cultural activities, sports and leisure. The 20,000-sq m hall is divided into numerous small plots used by various groups. Implementation of the overall concept is determined through panel discussion. The NSDM hall provides a critical mass of activities stimulating the further development of the surrounding abandoned harbor. The plans involve mixed use: a theater, small firms, craftsmen, artists, traders, entrepreneurs, boat builders, recycling firms, etc. The community provided approximately 7.5 million Euros in total for the construction of the hall. The project forms the nucleus for the development of a roughly 2 sq km part of the city, in which it is intended to create over 3 million sq m of developed space during the next few years (see Stealth Group 2002/2003).

Intermediate uses not only function as pioneers in urban development projects but also fulfill an important socio-political and cultural role. The former Palast der Republik (Parliament building and cultural center of the GDR) was closed in 1990 after asbestos was found. Beginning in 1997, the Palast has been gutted to its basic structure in an expensive asbestos removal program. In recent years, an increasingly controversial debate on the future of this site developed. In the end, the demand for the demolition of the Palast building and reconstruction of the former old palace façades, torn down in 1950, was able to gain the political upper hand. Cost reasons (estimated construction costs of 670 million Euro), content gaps in the use concept, and the start of a renewed competition, etc. make immediate reconstruction unrealistic. Thus, there was a time gap which allows a conscious parting from a building that held social significance for the GDR society like no other. Its unavoidable asbestos rehabilitation is seen by many as being a symbolic act of cold demolition. A critical and innovatively experimental examination of the history and future of the location is to be held in order to rejuvenate the site and its environment in the short term, to prepare for its future use, and to enable a societal re-evaluation process of the disputed location. After two years of struggle, the organization Zwischenpalastnutzung—a group of potential users— and Urban Catalyst managed to realize a 100-day-long temporary cultural use under the title of "Volkspalast" in 2004. Many additional activities followed until the end of 2005, attracting over 600,000 visitors to more than 900 events, ranging from experimental dance, music and art programs to the annual meeting of German industries and the anniversary party of McKinsey, a large consulting firm (see Zwischenpalastnutzung e.V. and Bündnis für den Palast 2005; Deuflhard *et al.* 2006).

14.7
Volkspalast 2004, Fassadenrepublik, an interactive performance installation in the partly-flooded ground floor of the Palast der Republik, Berlin

14.8
Volkspalast 2004, modern dance performance "Sascha Waltz" by Dialoge, which moved through three different parts of the Palast der Republik

14.9
Volkspalast 2005, Der Berg. Temporary installation of an artificial mountain both inside and outside the building. Three paths lead through the mountain: one for philosophers, one for pilgrims, and a climbing route. The pool (bottom) was a site for interactive performance, but could also be used by guests staying overnight in an adjacent "hotel."

Planning the Unplanned

In addition to formulating models of action to support temporary uses and to use them as catalysts for sustainable urban developments, it is necessary to reflect upon the basic ideas of planning and to explore how other modes of action might be combined with classical methods and aims.

Classical planning is based on ideas of permanence and stability, of linearity and control. It proceeds on a series of assumptions and rules. To plan is understood to mean defining both a final vision and built structures (including infrastructure and open spaces) with fixed programs and uses. The entire area is fully designed and controlled and the owner of the site is viewed as the only party to carry out actions. The time period between the present and the start of the project is generally marked by waiting until the desired conditions for development arise (planning, economic and legislative circumstances) and is often considered "dead" time for the site. This approach might be successful for certain tasks but the problems of urban development today demonstrate the deficits of these methods. Among other problems, classical planning has no means of developing areas that are not commercially exploitable right now. It does not provide space for active users who do not have sufficient funds to purchase or rent market-priced spaces. And it is unable to adapt quickly to changes in user needs.

This critique of traditional planning processes is not directed toward urban planning alone but also toward policies of cultural and economic subsidization that often are based on a hierarchical top-down approach. It often appears ridiculous that huge sums of financial aid are poured into "official" culture while much more effective and successful sub-cultural programs survive and flourish with comparatively little subsidy. This phenomenon also occurs in relation to the support given to small-scale start-ups and inventions.

To address these questions, Urban Catalyst aims to include temporary use and temporary users in urban planning. To this end, it is necessary to think of planning as a process that occurs over time and to think not only in terms of a desired end result, but rather in development steps from very early on, which might unfold in several directions, where the end result is never defined. In the past decade interest in process-based urban planning has grown among some advanced planners (e.g. Alvaro Siza with his housing development in Evora, Portugal; Rüdiger Lainer with Flugfeld Aspen in Vienna; Florian Beigel with Brikettfabrik Witznitz, and several projects by Kees Christiaanse, including an urban design for RAW-Berlin Friedrichshain in cooperation with Urban Catalyst in Berlin (Oswalt *et al.* forthcoming)). In all these projects the aim is to define a spatial framework that can absorb different forms of appropriation and emerging uses over time, which cannot be foreseen and should not be defined from the very beginning of the project but which would unfold.

It is also necessary to realize that spatial developments result from the interplay of different actors. While in the regular market economy sufficient financial resources are the main engine of development, ensuring that owners realize their aims, the development of temporary uses depends upon the successful interaction of different (local) players. Finally, temporary use demonstrates the importance of values beyond monetary ones. To incorporate temporary use into the planning of cities depends upon a critical stand towards the all-prevailing domination of market-driven thinking with its inherent over-estimation of financial capital and monetary exchange and its underestimation of social capital.

Urban Catalyst aims to introduce financially weaker parts of the population into the active creating and shaping of the city. At the same time different types of urban spaces (wastelands, low-standard neighborhoods) that normally do not appear on the radar screen would again be considered in urban planning. State institutions (like the municipality) would become a stimulating force, while the real action is undertaken by temporary users. A positive interaction with financially powerful parties to undertake investment projects and even partnerships with them seems possible. Urban Catalyst promotes the return of financially weaker sections of society to a more active role within processes of urban change, which would lead to the inclusion of a more varied spectrum of interests, individuals and spaces. Again, the state could assume a stimulating role that would include extensive interaction with commercial investors.

This approach has to question existing regulations and power structures. A key question is how real estate property is legally and culturally regulated within society. In order to enhance temporary use and support the sustainable development of cities, it is important to limit the control the owner has over a site. In several countries (e.g. the Netherlands), laws allow third parties to occupy sites and buildings that are unused. Such regulations can provide important pressure to make space available, which otherwise would be frozen over long periods of time (Kantzow and Oswalt 2005).

While innovation often arises in informal contexts (e.g. the PC was invented in a garage, a typical location for informal, bricolage activities), it is formal contexts that normally ensure long-lasting, sustainable effects. Given the research by Urban Catalyst, it is crucial to integrate the informal and the formal more effectively. This means, on the one hand, to formalize the informal: to analyze and understand the unplanned patterns behind self-organized activities, to develop prototypes, models and tools from these investigations, to formalize them and to make them available for other contexts and people. On the other hand, formal procedures of planning, administration and management have to be examined critically and an attempt has to be made to de-formalize and deinstitutionalize existing practices, changing and adapting them to more informal approaches. At the same time, the informal will open new perspectives for participatory models. Uncertainty and unplanned conditions will provide new opportunities for citizens to have a greater influence on how and by whom the city is used.

References

Arlt, P. (forthcoming) "What Urban Planners Can Learn from Temporary Users," in P. Oswalt, K. Overmeyer and P. Misselwitz (eds) *Urban Catalyst: Strategies for Temporary Use*, Barcelona: Actar.

deadline and Urban Catalyst (2006) Templace.com, online. Available : http://www.templace.com

Deuflhard, A., Krempl-Klieeisen, S., Oswalt, P., Lilienthal, M. and Müller, H. (eds) (2006) *Volkspalast: Zwischen Aktivismus und Kunst*, Berlin: Theater der Zeit.

Harvey, D. (1989) "From Managerialism to Entrepreneurialism. The Transformation in Urban Governance in Late Capitalism," *Geografiska Annaler* 71 B (1): 3–17.

Hentilä, H. L., Kopomaa, T. and Nagy, D. (2001) "Urban Catalyst, Work Package 3: Analysis, Helsinki Case Study," unpublished research report, Helsinki University of Technology, Centre for Urban and Regional Studies.

Kantzow, W. and Oswalt, P. (2005) "Property," in P. Oswalt (ed.) *Shrinking Cities*, vol. 1, Ostfildern, Germany: Hatje Cantz.

Oswalt, P., Overmeyer, K. and Misselwitz, P. (eds) (forthcoming) *Urban Catalyst: Strategies for Temporary Use*, Barcelona: Actar.

Schäfer, R. and Lau, P. (2003) "Legal Framework and Regulations as Instruments for Strategies of Temporary Uses within the Development of Urban Residual Areas in European Cities," unpublished research paper, Berlin, Stadt und Dorf.

Stealth Group (Milica Topalovic, Marc Neeln, Ana Dzokic) and City Administration Amsterdam Noord (Rob Vooren, Con Vleugel, Ted Zwetering) (2002/2003) *Urban Catalyst at Amsterdam Noord: Research Report Amsterdam Noord, Work Packages 3+4, 5*, Amsterdam: Stealth Group and City Administration Amsterdam Nord.

Wolf, R. (1998) "A Star is Born – Rote Fabrik Cultural Centre," in R. Wolff, A. Schneider, C. Schmid, P. Klaus, A. Hofer and H. Hitz (eds) *INURA: Possible Urban Worlds. Urban Strategies at the End of the 20th Century*, Basel: Birkhäuser.

Zwischenpalastnutzung e.V. and Bündnis für den Palast in cooperation with Urban Catalyst (eds) (2005) *Zwischennutzung des Palast der Republik: Bilanz einer Transformation*, Berlin: Zwischenpalastnutzung e.V. and Bündnis für den Palast and Urban Catalyst.

Annotated Bibliography

Contributors to *Loose Space* have recommended the following works that are connected to themes and issues discussed in their chapters.

Alexander, C. ([1965] 1996) "A City Is Not a Tree," in R. LeGates and F. Stout (eds) *The City Reader*, London: Routledge.

This is a seminal piece that describes the city in terms of overlapping networks, narratives and paths. It rewards re-reading because the attempt to organize and control public space with "tree-like" thinking returns in many guises. It is also useful to counter the hegemony of the grid or any other formularized permeability. Alexander describes the city as a "semi-lattice" wherein cul-de-sacs are never eliminated and the order of the lattice or grid is never complete.

Altman, I. and Zube, E. H. (eds) (1989) *Public Places and Spaces*, New York: Plenum.

This collection of papers offers scholars and practitioners rich and varied perspectives on public space and public life that continue to provide a valuable perspective on this topic. A broad range of places is covered and the inclusion of spaces for children and the impacts of the public domain on women make this a particularly useful overview.

Appleyard, D. (1976) *Planning a Pluralist City: Conflicting Realities in Ciudad Guayana*, Cambridge, MA: MIT Press.

Appleyard raises a much ignored point that cities are sometimes "planned without planners." Planners attempt to design a city according to professional ideals and formal spatial organization while urban dwellers form inferences of the city based on their personal territories, regular use and personal memories. The author introduces a paradigm to understand how inhabitants structure the city by introducing the concept of an "educational city." The knowledge gathered from these communications can help the planning policies.

Augé, M. (1995) *Non-Places*, London: Verso.

Augé argues that stability is illusory. The geometries of anthropological place (axes, crossroads, monumental centers) have dissolved and along with them traditional conceptions of identity and social relations. He critiques the increasingly fleeting and fragmented nature of supermodernity as a disappearance of place through a phenomenological exploration of what he calls "non-places"—freeways, transit lounges, aircraft cabins, supermarkets, hotel rooms, leisure parks and large retail stores, as well as the informational spaces of telepresence. A work that leads us to rethink the study of place and place experience.

Berman, M. (1982) *All That Is Solid Melts into Air: The Experience of Modernity*, London: Verso.

A highly inclusive and integrative view of modernism, delving into artistic, intellectual, religious and political activities, considering leading figures and ordinary people, with a focus on cities and urban experience. Starts with Goethe's *Faust*, moving through Marx, Baudelaire, Dostoevksy, a history of St Petersburg and ends with Robert Moses and Berman's own experience of observing his Bronx neighborhood lost to the Cross-Bronx Expressway. Berman gives a compelling portrayal of modern environments and experiences with all their disintegration and renewal, promise and disappointments, hope and uncertainty. Insightful, revealing, never abstract.

Annotated bibliography

Betsky, A. (1998) "Nothing but Flowers: Against Public Space," in M. Bell and S. T. Leong (eds) *Slow Space*, New York: Monacelli Press.

This essay is almost a treatise on issues of public space and identity within the context of modernity and postmodernity, using as examples specific sites in American iconography such as the boulevard and the open road. Combining elements of existentialism and a critique of capitalism and the way cities have developed, Betsky offers an intriguing reading of contemporary meanings of public space.

Boddy, T. (1992) "Underground and Overhead: Building the Analagous City," in M. Sorkin (ed.) *Variations on a Theme Park*, New York: Noonday Press.

A critical account of the design and management of quasi-public walkway systems and atria in downtown commercial areas, primarily in North America. Boddy notes that these new spaces generally present a highly sanitized version of public life; they have a controlling influence on the behavior of users and a negative impact on both the vitality and the quality of real street life outside. He also highlights ways these spaces help define new social roles and to generate new, subversive forms of activity.

Borden, I (2001) *Skateboarding, Space and the City: Architecture and the Body*, Oxford: Berg.

This detailed examination of skateboarding draws upon a wide range of Lefebvre's theoretical concepts. Borden uses the behavior, perceptions, values and imagination of the skateboarder to lead us through an "interrogation" of the functions and meanings of built space, opening up many new questions. The book combines a general theorization of contemporary urban society with attention to subtle details of human behavior, symbolism, and spatial design. Skateboarding is presented in positive terms as a re-appropriation of parts of the city.

Bowman, A. and Pagan, M. (2004) *Terra Incognita: Vacant Land and Urban Strategies*, Washington, DC: Georgetown University Press.

This book explores and problematizes urban "vacant" land. The question explored is whether or not the existence of this type of loose space is a liability for communities or a resource. The authors based their work on a national survey sent to all US towns with more than 50,000 inhabitants and addressed issues of meaning, policy, regulation, strategies and opportunities. It is a pragmatic book with case studies on Phoenix, Philadelphia and Seattle.

Bridge, G. and Watson, S. (eds.) (2002) *City Reader*, Cambridge, MA: Blackwell.

This reader is an interdisciplinary volume containing the most influential writings concerning the city with key questions, debates and analysis. It includes classical texts on city imagination, urban economics, division and difference, city publics and urban interventions. Included are Simmel, Le Corbusier, Jacobs, fiction writers like Dickens and Joyce, but also Harvey and Castells, Sassen, Soja and Zukin, Sennett, Neil Smith and Mike Davis. Go back to Benjamin, moving on to Lefebvre, de Certeau, Foucault, Virilio all in the same reader.

Burayidi, M. A. (ed.) (2000) *Urban Planning in a Multicultural Society*, Westport, CT: Praeger.

Chapters cover a range of topics related to insightful planning in culturally diverse cities. Some theoretical approaches discuss critical as well as pragmatic approaches and point out recent changes in the planning theory resulting from increased multi-culturalism. Also included are different viewpoints on the degree of inclusiveness in culture-specific urban planning, educating urban designers and how various planning institutes take on the responsibility of planning for multi-cultural cities.

Carr, S., Francis, M., Rivlin, L.G. and Stone, A.M. (1992) *Public Space*, New York: Cambridge University Press.

This analysis of people's public space needs, rights, meanings and connections offers an overview of the role of parks, plazas, squares, streets, found spaces and other public domains in people's lives. Includes detailed descriptions of specific, illustrative cases in the US and Europe. It uses observed qualities of public spaces and their use to address issues of design and management.

Carter, P. (2002) *Repressed Spaces: The Poetics of Agoraphobia*, London: Reaktion.

The issue of agoraphobia is examined from many different perspectives: psychoanalytic, urban and feminist. Agoraphobia, or the fear of open space, has been translated into the fear of crowds that contemporary urban areas trigger. The book offers a thorough reflection on those practices that trigger agoraphobia and contextualizes and even justifies agoraphobia within the context of late capitalism and the culture of consumption that distances people from each other.

Copjec, J. and Sorkin, M. (eds) (1999) *Giving Ground: The Politics of Propinquity*, London: Verso.
Essays reassert the possibility of an urbanity that critically examines the forces of uniformity present in the globalized public realm as well as the opposite forces of differentiation emerging from a particularist politics of identity. If the city is to remain the "privileged place of a politics of freedom," as the editor M. Sorkin proposes, then a re-thinking of a "politics of propinquity" is necessary. In such a prospect, public space becomes the locus of encounters and negotiations of concrete men and women and not a "social abstraction" to be confused with spaces of mediated communication or fantasized collective identities. This book is useful in locating theoretical problems connected with the use and concept of public space.

Cresswell, T. (1996) *In Place/Out of Place: Geography, Ideology and Transgression*, Minneapolis, MN: University of Minnesota Press.
Through three case studies—graffiti in New York City, attempts to hold a free festival at Stonehenge and the Greenham Common Women's Peace Camp in England—Cresswell explores the designation of certain acts as transgressive. These cases shed light on the ways that space and place are used to create a "normative landscape": of what may be "right" in one place but not in another. Useful for its succinct exploration of transgression and the spatial/ideological mapping of the landscape.

Cupers, K. and Miessen, M. (2002) *Spaces of Uncertainty*, Wuppertal: Muller und Busmann.
This book offers a very good conceptual treatment of and challenge to the concept of public space. It focuses on marginal spaces in Berlin and the spaces of instability, movement, creation and destruction within which the history of Berlin is characterized. The residual and the margin as spaces of uncertainty lie at the edge of traditional public space. The authors argue that this is a more accurate example of issues of development and identity regarding contemporary cities.

de Certeau, M. (1993) "Walking in the City," in S. During (ed.) *The Cultural Studies Reader*, London: Routledge.
De Certeau celebrates the importance of everyday practice as a form of resistance to the dominant ideologies of urban life. Focusing on one everyday form of practice, he presents a phenomenological interpretation of space as the very medium through which the personal and the local re-assert themselves, continually subverting the rationality and discipline of established social practice and the physical order of urban space. He notes that social life is continuously being produced and reshaped by everyday movements of thousands of individuals.

Deleuze, G. and Guattari, F. (1987) *A Thousand Plateaus: Capitalism and Schizophrenia*, Minneapolis, MN: University of Minnesota Press.
This is one of the least accessible of books around but one that rewards those who approach it like a keen traveler approaches a city—in no particular order and without seeking a singular narrative thread. Some favorite threads include: rhizome, body without organs, faciality, segmentarity, the refrain, the war machine and smooth/striated space.

Deutsche, R. (1996) *Evictions: Art and Spatial Politics*, Cambridge, MA: MIT Press.
In these essays, Deutsche, an art historian and critic, reveals the connections between art, architecture, urban planning, urban development and the politics of public space. In a thorough and detailed manner, using examples from New York City, she demonstrates how urban ideologies and interests combine to legitimize forms of urban development that claim to benefit all but, in fact, work to exclude the working class, the poor and the homeless. Also analyses cases of public art that pose critiques of urban real estate interests and exclusionary forms of urban redevelopment.

Dovey, K. and Dickson, S. (2002) "Architecture and Freedom: Programmatic Innovation in the Work of Rem Koolhaas," *Journal of Architectural Education*, 55: 268–277.
Rem Koolhaas has been the most skilled of architects in seeking to undo the programmatic strait-jacketing of the architecture–behavior relationship and the reproduction of social ideology through architecture. This

article is a critique of his programmatic surgery; it argues that despite significant achievements, the work is less successful in this regard than it seems.

Edensor, T. (1998) "The Culture of the Indian Street," in N. Fyfe (ed.) *Images of the Street*, London: Routledge.
This is a celebration of the practices and sensory qualities of the Indian street, partly based on de Certeau. Edensor argues that that the street is more than just a text and that discursive analysis is not enough. Contrasts the Indian street with the increasingly regulated, desensitized and over-determined Western street.

Edensor, T. (2005) *Industrial Ruins: Space, Aesthetics and Materiality*, Oxford: Berg.
The book develops in greater detail themes that Edensor addresses in this volume. Illustrated with over 80 photographs of British industrial ruins, he explores the ordering processes shaped on urban organization, materiality and normative aesthetics and develops an argument that ruins can confound orderly and official forms of commemoration and memory, that can be supplemented by more sensual, contingent and exploratory forms of remembering.

Ferrell, J. (2001) *Tearing Down the Streets: Adventures in Urban Anarchy*, New York: Palgrave.
A fascinating account of Ferrell's adventures with a range of "urban anarchists" across the US and in Amsterdam: street musicians, graffiti artists, bicycle activists, homeless youth, skateboarders and outlaw radio operators. A motorcyclist, professor of criminology and urban anarchist himself, Ferrell combines lively stories and evocative descriptions of places and people with a discussion of both historical and recent struggles over public space. Takes the side of the underground groups he has observed, arguing for the value of a disorderly urban culture.

Foucault, M. (1986) "Of Other Spaces," *Diacritics*, 16: 22–27.
This short essay is a splendid critique of notions of space. Instead of assuming a definition of space as a void, Foucault sees space as heterogeneous, stating that we can describe a site according to the set of relations that define it. Introduces the notion of heterotopias which are counter-sites, "a kind of effectively enacted utopia in which real sites, all the other real sites that can be found within the culture are simultaneously represented, contested and inverted" (p. 24).

Frykman, J. and Lufgren, O. (eds) (1996) *Forces of Habit: Exploring Everyday Culture*, Lund: Lund University Press.
A fascinating introduction and a series of interesting essays on the role of habit. Habit is shown to be entrenched in so much of what passes for normative social order, and is powerful precisely because it generates non-reflexive practices that remain non-amenable to critique.

Gehl, J. (1987) *Life Between Buildings: Using Public Space*, New York: Van Nostrand Reinhold.
First published in 1971 in Denmark, this inspirational work both celebrates and analyses everyday life and needs in urban streets and squares. With detailed observations from Denmark, Gehl distinguishes between necessary, optional and social activities, noting their interconnections and how they are affected by the quality of the physical environment. Gehl pays careful and insightful attention both to urban planning and to micro-features of public space and their impact on people's actions and sensory experiences. A classic work on daily life in public spaces.

Gilloch, G. (1996) *Myth and Metropolis*, Cambridge: Polity.
This is a comprehensive, easy-to-read theoretical examination of Walter Benjamin's diverse writings on cities, extensively referenced to its primary sources. Particularly strong on different ways in which people perceive and use space, including Benjamin's accounts of different cities he lived in and visited (Paris, Moscow, Naples, Berlin), and his examination of how a child views the city and space in general in a non-instrumental, non-domineering fashion through all the five senses. Drawing on Marxist, surrealist and psychoanalytic concepts, Gilloch shows how Benjamin's analyses unlock different ways of interpreting city life.

Habraken, N. J. (1998) *The Structure of the Ordinary: Form and Control in the Built Environment*, Cambridge, MA: MIT Press.
Habraken creates an interesting link between formal design and the everyday life experiences of people, declaring that this combination can define place-making. He illustrates how the "common fabric" of environments, those that are intimately linked with people, can be sustained in formal architecture. Introducing three orders—physical, territorial and cultural—Habraken produces many examples to support this concept.

Heckscher, A. and Robinson, P. (1977) *Open Spaces: The Life of American Cities*, New York: Harper and Row.
This classic analysis offers an in-depth view of public spaces in the United States. The historical perspective presented is particularly valuable for an understanding of the evolution of public life, especially the functions of the public square.

Jacobs, J. (1961) *The Death and Life of Great American Cities*, New York: Vintage.
While working for an architectural magazine in the 1950s, Jacobs was shocked by the impact and deceptions of urban renewal. In this now classic work she describes successful urban districts as those where people are safe on the streets and sidewalks among a diversity of uses and strangers, and interesting cities as those with interesting streets, because streets are the vital organs of cities. In short, cities are found in the streets. This book has helped re-shape urban planning and leads us to think about each element of a city—sidewalk, park—as a synergistic unit, both encompassing structure and going beyond it to the functioning dynamics.

Kayden, J. S. (2000) *Privately Owned Public Spaces: The New York Experience*, New York: John Wiley.
A meticulous study of all the indoor and outdoor spaces private developers in New York City have provided for public use in order to receive floor area bonuses. The book presents a systematic classification of all the types of spaces and a thorough history of the related zoning and design regulations, with complete information on the location, design, status and functioning of every case of such privately owned public space in all five boroughs. Excellent for its detail and comprehensiveness and its consideration of the dilemmas posed by the emergence of quasi-public spaces.

Kohn, M. (2004) *Brave New Neighborhoods: The Privatization of Public Space*, New York: Routledge.
Kohn examines the increasing privatization of public space in the US as evident in interventions in the built environment (malls and gated communities) and in constraints on the right to free speech in quasi-public spaces. Very useful for: its dissection of the difficulties of categorizing a given space as public or private, a history of the court fights by the IWW for political street speaking, and a recent history of Supreme Court rulings on the right to free speech in shopping malls. Other chapters explore the political impact of gated communities and residential associations, the history of Battery Park City in New York, and critiques of a proposal to zone out homeless people from downtown areas.

Lash, S. (1999) *Another Modernity: A Different Rationality*, Oxford: Blackwell.
Lash highlights the disorderly, disruptive, affective and ever-changing dimensions of modernity in contradistinction to that side of modernity which foregrounds science, rationality and systematics.

Lefebvre, H. (1996) *Writings on Cities*, ed. P. Kofman and E. Lebas, Oxford: Blackwell.
Lefebvre criticizes the "functional" understanding of both cities and urban spaces, counterposing it to the diversity and creativity of everyday "use value." He notes that throughout history, city centers were not only commercial but also concentrations of religious, intellectual, political and economically productive activity. It is in urban spaces that people meet their needs for socialization, representation and play. The diversity of social needs inevitably leads to tension, to the confrontation and negotiation of difference, and also to disequilibrium and unpredictability. This is part of what attracts people to urban space. The book's introduction provides a digestible overview of Lefebvre's ideas and his influence on a later generation of US scholars.

Lippard, L. (1997) *The Lure of the Local*, New York: The New Press.
Lippard reveals the relationship among land, history and culture in the everyday sense of living in the world. She avoids romantic and universal determinations of "place" and embeds her explorations in daily life of a

multi-cultural society that so often depends on loose space for its performance. Her focus on activist art as a way of seeing through the veneer of place reveals the tension of "longing for home" and the condition of alienated displacement so prevalent in modern cultures.

Lofland, L. (1998) *The Public Realm: Exploring the City's Quintessential Social Territory*, New York: Aldine de Gruyter.
A sociologist's examination of being out in public and interaction among strangers, spelling out various pleasures and benefits. Lofland examines the conditions under which public face-to-face interactions between strangers occur, describing different levels of unfamiliarity and engagement. One fascinating insight: what makes strangers in the city exciting is that they are at the same time both close up and distant and mysterious—and this leads to fantasy. Lofland provides a well-argued critique of recent anti-urban shifts in both design and social life. Also provides excellent illustrations and a comprehensive set of references on existing approaches and knowledge.

Low, S. (2000) *On the Plaza: The Politics of Public Space and Culture*, Austin, TX: University of Texas Press.
An historical and anthropological account of two plazas in San Jose, Costa Rica, looking at both the long history of plazas, going back to Europe and indigenous practices, and the shorter history of these two plazas as Low observed changes in their design, use and management in recent years. Combines ethnography, personal narrative, history and literature. Detailed, well-illustrated presentation of the widely varied uses and users of the plazas is paired with considerations of the wider cultural and political context.

Lynch, K., with contributions from M. Southworth (ed.) (1990) *Wasting Away*, San Francisco: Sierra Club Books.
Wasting Away is a comprehensive overview of many aspects of waste to include what it is; how it happens, the taboo of waste; and how we might waste better. It covers waste things, waste places, and waste people, drawing on the literatures of planning, design, anthropology and sociology. Lynch confronts the shadow side of making by provoking us to think about unmaking and its consequences.

Mitchell, D. (2003) *The Right to the City: Social Justice and the Fight for Public Space*, New York: The Guilford Press.
A scholarly, geographically-based and detailed history of the struggles for the right to dissent in public space in the US. Starts with the earliest court cases over political speaking on the sidewalk and extends to the Free Speech Movement at the University of California in Berkeley in the 1960s, the struggle for People's Park in Berkeley, and the anti-homeless campaign in various cities. Excellent for its understanding and presentation of court decisions and transformations in the law and, simultaneously, its attention to the specific spatial contexts of these struggles.

Sennett, R. (1973) *The Uses of Disorder: Personal Identity and City Life*, Harmondsworth: Penguin.
Sennett argues that the true task of planning is not to solve its mundane mechanical problems, such as transport, but to provide a setting where young people can explore, engage with others, and thereby develop fully into adults. The value of the book lies in its reasoning as to why it is important to mix with people who are different. The diversity and anarchy of the city provide a necessary setting for growth into mature adulthood. Sennett describes some ways physical planning can facilitate this engagement, as well as providing a sociological/psychological critique of the "purified community" of the nuclear family in the suburban home and community.

Sennett, R. (1996) *Flesh and Stone*, London: Faber & Faber.
Flesh and Stone is an historical account of the relationship of the body to urban space in the Western city. It is based on a thesis that certain master narratives about the body and identity take on urban form. It is a wonderfully written book that is at once about the disciplining of the body in public space and the quest for emancipation.

Shields, R. (1991) *Places on the Margin: Alternative Geographies of Modernity*, London: Routledge.
An anthropological, sociological, geographical and historical reading of natural landscapes which we regard as "marginal" and thus unimportant although also dangerous and exciting. The determination of particular spaces as marginal is part of the process of defining culture and self-identity. Chapters examine leisure at the

seaside resort of Brighton, honeymooning at Niagara Falls, and the concept of "the North" in Canadian and UK contexts. Shields provides well-theorized analyses of the social construction of these spaces: as they have been physically built up, but also through film and postcard views, and through contemporary ritualistic forms of behavior and language.

Solá-Morales, M. (ed.) (2004) *Ciudades, Esquinas. Cities, Corners*, Barcelona: Forum Barcelona/Lunwerg Editores.

This is a bilingual book with contributions by well-known authors from a wide range of countries writing about the city as a place of meeting and exchange and an instance of cultural diversity. Focuses on the intersection of cultures and the space of social life and adopts street corners as a metaphor for the city as a whole. The texts are organized into several sections entitled "stone corners," "people's corners," "more and more corners," and "corners of the world." Includes contributions by Jean Louis Cohen, Hans Ibelings, Rosa Feliu, Mirko Zardini, Felipe Leal, Charles Correa, Saed Akhtar, Minoru Mori and Richard Sennett.

Soule, M. and Lease, G. (eds) (1995) *Reinventing Nature? Responses to Postmodern Deconstruction*, Washington, DC: Island Press.

The nine chapters in the book represent some of the most critical thinking regarding the relationship of humans and nature. In modern, technologically based society, the very concept of nature appears to be a human construction. What is it? Where is it? Who controls the dominant representation of this relationship controls the dominant acceptance of reality? The comprehension and representation of the world reside in a fertile loose space at this transitional time and the authors, who include P. Shepard, A. Borgman, K. Hayles and others, explore the nature of the cultural struggle.

Stewart, K. (1996) *A Space on the Side of the Road: Cultural Poetics in an 'Other' America*, Princeton, NJ: Princeton University Press.

A fabulous, poetic account of the people and decaying, neglected culture of West Virginian mining towns, which utilizes a series of spoken narratives to convey the pain and helplessness of an exploited working-class community, bypassing ordinary anthropological methods and ways of telling.

Whyte, W. (1988) *City: Rediscovering the Center*, New York: Doubleday.

A detailed analysis of public space based on his earlier (1980) book, *The Social Life of Small Urban Spaces*. Whyte's research draws on extensive field observation to reveal complexities in the uses of various public spaces in Manhattan and other North American cities. A main focus is design elements which make plazas and other public spaces popular with users. This volume adds an expanded discussion of the design problems of urban development in the 1960s and 1970s, suggesting management strategies and planning regulations which help expand the usefulness of such spaces.

Young, I. M. (1991) *Justice and the Politics of Difference*, Princeton, NJ: Princeton University Press.

Political philosopher Young critiques theories of democracy that do not develop an inclusive participatory framework. Their ideals of a unified and homogeneous public assume the universality of the identities and perspectives of privileged groups, requiring the assimilation or suppression of minority identities and experiences. From an eloquent feminist perspective, Young proposes a theoretical approach and a public policy that would affirm rather than suppress group differences. She celebrates experiences of contemporary city life that are characterized by variety of activities, social differentiation without exclusion and encounters with difference.

Zukin, S. (1995) *The Cultures of Cities*, Cambridge, MA: Blackwell.

Zukin shows that cities have multiple cultures that are constantly being produced in their central spaces, mainly in the streets but also in parks, shops, museums and restaurants. She analyzes how different notions of urban culture reshape urban politics and conflicts over revitalization. Looking at Manhattan and learning from Disneyworld, she talks about the symbolic economy where new public spaces are produced by the intertwining of cultural symbols and entrepreneurial capital. This book is a penetrating analysis of urban daily life with plenty of original thought on urban culture.

Index

Page numbers in *italics* denotes an illustration

abandoned sites 8, 18, 21, 23, 231–2, 259; industrial *see* Buffalo River; industrial ruins
Abaza, M. 108, 109
Abrams, D. 265
Abramson, D. 148
actual territories 195, 209
aesthetics: violation of by industrial ruins 245–9
aesthetics of order 94, 154–5, 156–7; and Central Park 154–69; creation of in public space 156–7; and privatization of public space 160–2
affordance(s) 51; concept of 40; and found spaces 40, 51; and industrial ruins 241–5
Akcan, Esra 208
alana 181, 189
Alexander, C. 116, 129
Alexanderplatz (Berlin) 80, 85
Alexandras housing complex (Athens) 172, 180–91, *184*, *186*; during German occupation and civil war 182; heterotopic moments 181–2; memories of porosity 189–91; prison on side of 181–2; resisting decay 183–8, *188*
Amsterdam: temporary use in 273, 282–3, *283*
anonymity: and found spaces 44–5; of urban public space 5
Antonioni, Michelangelo 198
Appadurai, A. 207
appropriation 29, 35–7, 93; concept of 99–100; and found spaces *see* found spaces; and spontaneous memorials 136–9
architecture 175
Arlt, Peter 280
Art District (Los Angeles) 215–16
Asian city 114
Asphalt Rundown 199
Athens: Battle of 182; Olympics (2004) 183; refugee housing complexes and separation from rest of city 171, 180–1; refugees from Asian Minor 179; *see also* Alexandras housing complex
Augé, M. 106
authority 94
Azad 202

Bad Sheets project 224–5, *225*
'Badeschiff' *276*
balconies: as threshold site 85
Ban Panthom (Bangkok) 117–30; building types 120; car parking 120–1; class and ethnicity 127; as confluence of flows 129; day/night activities 122–4, *123*; disruptions in 118; homeless people 124–5; public/private 120–2; sacred/secular space 125–7; sex industry 124; site of illegal activities 124–5; slippages 127–8; smooth and striated space 128–9; street hierarchy 117–18, *117*, *119*, 128, 129; tensions between globalization and local tradition 128; urban morphology 117–20, 129
Bangkok 93, 113-15 *see also* Ban Panthom
Bataille, J. 220
'Battle of Athens' 182
Bauhaus School 180
beautification: and aesthetics of order 154, 155, 156, 163
Beigel, Florian 286
Belgrade 18
Benjamin, Walter 106, 129, 130, 175, 177, 181
Berlin 77, 273; Alexanderplatz 80, 85; Europacentre shopping centre 79–80, 80–1; Marlene-Dietrich-Platz 77, *78*, 79; Palast der Republic 283–4, *284*; RAW-Tempel e.V. 271–2
Berlin Wall, former 217, *277*
Berman, M. 251
Bishop, P. 7–8, 268
Bloomsbury Square (London) 222–3
Boddy, T. 24
Bogotá 97
bonus plazas 38–9, 44, 46, 51
Borden, I. 14
Borja, J. and Castells, M. 97
Bourke Street Mall (Melbourne) 86–7, *87*
bridges: spaces under 7–8

Brill, Michael 264
Brooklyn (New York) *16*, 42; flea market *42*, 44, 45
Brown, D.F. 67
Bruegel the Elder, Peter 38
Bryant Park 50
Buddhist processions 66–7
Buffalo River 231, 232, 253–69, *259*, *260*, *262*, *267*, *268*; coherence and degeneration 255–8; deindustrialization of 257, 258; and loose thinking 265–9; playground of the young 259–61; Remedial Action Plan for 258; robust wilderness of 261–4; shifting in an out of material, conceptual and imaginal coherence 256–7; wildness and unruliness of 259–61
Buffalo River Urban Canoe Trail 253, 258
building thresholds 9, 73–91; and convergence 75–9; as distinct spaces in own right 82–4; emergence from private spaces into public realm 75, 81–2; and liminality 73–5, 87; negotiation of 89–90; and passage of time 75, 79–81; and playful behaviour 74, 79, 80; ritualistic forms of behaviour 81; softening of distinctions between inside and outside 86–8; as space apart from wider public realm 75, 84–6; spatiality of social relations 77; variety in people's uses of 89–90; and wedding photographs 74–5, 81, *82*, 86, 90
Business Improvement Districts 24
Butzer, Hans and Torrey 147

cafés: Little Italy 62–3
Campo Boario 201–3, *202*, *203*, 204
Canvey Island (Essex) 241
car parking: Ban Panthom 120–1
Carnivale 15
Carr, S. 15, 20, 22
cars 100, 106–7
Central Park (New York) 94, 154–69, *158*, *159*, *167*; aesthetics of order 154-69;
contrasting aesthetics and accommodated serendipity 162–5; design of and elite 157–60; disciplining of looseness through aesthetics of order 165–7; looseness in 157, 163, 168; major events 165; and notion of beauty 156; political demonstrations debate 162; privatization of public space and aesthetics of order 160–2, 168; reliance on private sector/individuals for funding 160–1; rules and regulations 156
Central Park Conservancy 156, 160–2, 164, 168
chaos theory 200
'charged places' 264
Charter of Athens 180
Chicago 69
childhood 250
Chinatown (New York) 35, 56–62, *57*, *59*, *60*, *61*, 67–70; architecture of buildings 56–7; diverse retail uses of streets 58; multiple uses of a building at street level 57; and shopkeepers 60; social activities on streets 58; street vendors 58, 59–60, *60*, 68
Christchurch (New Zealand) *11*
Christiaanse, Kees 286
Christiania (Copenhagen) 214–15
circulation loops 6
cities: conditions encouraging looseness 4; variety of place types 2–3; variety of public spaces in 4–6
city of thresholds 173, 174, 177
Clark, Gordon Matta 200
classical planning 286
Clean Air Act (1970) 258
Clean Water Act (1972) 258
Colombo (Sri Lanka) 64–7, *65*
colonization 214
Colonizing the Void 214
colonnades 73
Columbine memorial 133, 135, 137, 143, 144, 146
commercial possibilities: and loose space 18, 93; *see also* retail activities
'community', term of 222
community gardens 18
'community' needs 171
communities of the 'other' 171
constructivism 266
controls 29
Copenhagen: Christiania 214–15
corners: duality of local appropriation and global disappropriation in Guadalajara 100–6, 111
counter-paradigm 178
Crawford, M. 6, 24, 108
crime 22, 26
Critical Mass 15, *23*, 166, 168
curb space 68

'datascapes' 207
De Carlo, Giancarlo 208
de Certeau, M. 103, 114
De La Vega 164
de Lauwe, Chombart 99
dead zones 172, 224, 227; Art District (Los Angeles) 215–16; Christiania (Copenhagen) 214–15; defining 211–12; depiction of Ha'Yarkon Estuary as 210–11, 213; 'edge places' 217; finding of 214–19;

need for protecting 227; overlapping spaces 217, 219
Debord, Guy 198; *The Society of the Spectacle* 168
Dedrick, J. and Kraemer, K. 98
Deleuze, G. and Guattari, F. 113, 115, 127, 128, 199, 220; *Mille Plateaux* 199
demonstrations 18–19
derelict sites 15, 16–17, 273; defining 212; *see also* industrial ruins
dérive 198, 214
descansos 133
designed public spaces 39, 51
development of urban sites 282
Diana, Princess: memorials 135, 143, 145
Dijk, Han van 214
dirt 220
disappropriation 99–100
discovery 30, 231–3
Disneyland 24
disorder: and loose space 21–3
disruptive behaviour 18–19
diversity: and loose space 19–21
Dizengoff, Meir 213
doorways 73, 79, 84
drug dealing 50

Earth Day 258
East Village (New York) 42
eating and drinking: and found spaces 43; *see also* street vendors
eclipse watching 80, 85
ecological imagination 268, 269
Edensor, T. 55, 114
'edge effect' 89
'edge places' 217
Eisenberg, E. 265
Ellicot, Joseph 253
emotions, private: expression of in public settings 12, 14
Engler, E. 151
entrepreneurship, local 18
environmental movement: in United States 258
essentialism 266
ethnoscapes 207
Europacentre shopping complex (Berlin) 79–80, 80–1
Evernden, N. 265
everyday activities 29, 36
'everyday urban space' 6
experimentation: and loose space 18

factories, abandoned *see* industrial ruins
farmers markets 18
fences 8, 41
festival market places 7, 11
flâneur 114, 177
flea market (Brooklyn) *42*, 44, 45
Flinders Street railway station (Melbourne) 75–6, *76*, 84, *85*
Florence 21
flowers: as expression of grief and commemoration 143
flows of desire 116
flux 267
Flying Carpet, The 204–5
'folk assemblages' 142
Fonda la Santa Cruz (restaurant) (Guadalajara) 101–3, *102*
Foucault, Michel 114, 177, 199, 220
found spaces 35, 38–52; and affordance 40, 51; and anonymity 44–5; essence of 40; features 39–40; and freedom of choice 35, 40, 46; freedoms of 50–2; identifying 41–3; and New York Public Library steps 42, 43, 44, 46–50, *47*, *48*, *49*; and 9/11 40; qualities of 44–6, 52; and safety 46, 51; stimulation of open-mindedness 45; uses of 43; viewed as safe 46, 51
freedom: and loose space 17, 20
freedom of choice: and found spaces 35, 40, 46
Friends of the Buffalo River 258, 263

garbage dumps 15
gated communities 109, 176; Guadalajara 98
gay men 20
Gehl, Jan 12, 45, 58, 108
gentrification 274
Geuze, Adrian 227
Ghent Urban Studies Team 207
Gibson, J.J. 40, 51
Giuliani, Rudolph 221
global business: tensions with local citizens in Latin America 93, 96–7, 128
globalization 110, 206; and Latin America 96, 97
Golden Gate Park 217, *219*
graffiti 14; and *Bad Sheets* project 224; and industrial ruins 238 ; at Rabin's memorial site 139, 147;
Gran Plaza, La (Big Plaza) (Guadalajara) 107
Greece 207; collective experience of urban porosity 178–9; refugees 179; *see also* Athens
Greek Popular Liberation Army (ELAS) 182
Greek Refugee Rehabilitation Committee 180
Greenacre Park (Manhattan) 46
grid 100

Grider, G. 142
Griffiths, H *et al* 240–1
'Gruen transfer' 88
Gruen, Victor 108
Grundman-Brigtmann, Claude 147
Guadalajara 93, 96–111; appropriation of space for food venues 101–6, *104*, *105*, 111; appropriation of space in shopping malls 107; buying in the *tianguis* 109–11, *110*; duality of local appropriation and global disappropriation in corners 100–6, 111; electronics industry 98; growth of urban dualization 98–9; and illusion of Silicon Valley 98–9; inequality 98
Guattari, F. 113, 115, 127, 128, 199, 220

habitus 160
Han Fun Club (Singapore) 217
handrails 28
'hard architecture' 2
Harrison, R.P. 265
Harvey, D. 176
Haskins, E.V. and DeRose, J.P. 151
Hawks and Sparrows (film) 199
Ha'Yarkon Estuary (Tel-Aviv) 210–11, *211*, 213
Hayles, N.K. 267
Helsinki 273
heterotopias 174, 177–8
heterotopic moments 174; during German occupation of Greece 181–2
'heterotopias of illusion' 209
Hillier, B. and Hanson, J. 116
Hillman, J. 264, 265
history: and memory 148
Hogarth, William 38
homeless people 12, 14, 18; in Ban Panthom 124–5; and dead zones 217, *218*; and ruins 235; and Russell Square 222
Hong Kong: Filipino maids in *3*
houses: contrasted with monuments 191; *see also* Alexandras housing complex

identity: exploring of and loose space 20
immigrant communities 206–7; and *Transborderline* project 203–6
in-between spaces 35, 172
incentive zoning: New York City 38–9
'Indian street' 114
industrial ruins 8, 231, 234–52; absence of constraints and security 237, 242, 243; affordances of 241–5; and artistic endeavours 238; functions of 'waste' and re-use of materials 235; and graffiti 238; hosting of alternative creative practices 234–5; and informal tourism 239; lack of evident purpose 249; liberating of bodily movement 242–4; as refuges for urban wildlife 240–1; resurrection of childhood memories 250; sensual engagement with ruined matter 244–5; site of illicit activities 236–7; site of mundane and practical pursuits 239; as spaces of fantasy and adventure 235–6; spaces of wildness 262; transgressive excess of 251–2; and vandalism 237; violation of aesthetic schemes 245–9; *see also* Buffalo River
Innocenzi, Aldo 199
International Conference on Modern Architecture (CIAM) 180
International Freedom Center 151–2
International Joint Commission (ICJ) 258
invisible communities 172
Israel 207
Istanbul 208
Italy 208
Iwama, Asako 202

Jacobs, Jane 51, 81, 116, 129
Jaffe 213
Jemaa e Fna (Marrakesh) 21, *21*
July bombings *13*

Kandy (Sri Lanka) 64–7
Key Action 4 City of Tomorrow and Cultural Heritage program 273
Kinetisch Noord Group 283
Kings Cross Station (London) 221
Koolhaas, R. 207
Kowinski, W. 108
Kurdish exiles: helping of by Stalker 201–2

La Cecla, Franco 200
La Varra, G. 8
Labini, Francesco Sylos 199–200
labyrinth 116
Lainer, Rüdiger 286
lampposts 8
Lash, S. and Urry, J. 97
Latin America: and globalization 96, 97; imposition of automobile-centred urban model 106–7; reshaping of cities 97–8; tensions between global business and
local citizens 93, 96–7, 128
learning: differences as resource of 19–20
Lefebvre, H. 4–5, 10, 106
leftover spaces 7–8
Leicester Square (London) *5*, 7, 76
leisure-oriented facilities 80

Ligis, Alfonso 220
liminality 35, 36, 73–5, 87, 88, 89, 90–1
Limits of Inclusiveness project 173, 225–7, *226*
Lin, Maya 149
Little Italy (New York City) 35, 62–4, *63*, 67–70
Lofland, L. 19, 22
London: cleansing of public spaces 221–2, 224; Leicester Square *5*, 7, 76; Russell Square 222–3, 225–7, *226*
loose living 12
'loose parts' 40
loose space/looseness: activities generating 12–14; apparent 24–5; benefits and risks of 17–23; creation of 10–15; as a dialectical process 26; and different social groups 15–16; factors contributing to 2, 4; indeterminacy of 17; locations and types of 6–8; and movement 14–15; people and creation of 10–12, 28; physical features of 8–10; and possibility 17–19; relationship with tight space 23–8; as relative and adjustable 25–6; simulations of 24; temporal variability of 25; and urban layouts 6; variation across time 15 17
loose thinking: and Buffalo River 265–9
Los Angeles: Art District 215–16
Lynch, K. and Carr, S. 15, 20, 22
Lynch, Kevin 6, 51, 212, 256; *Wasting Away* 212

Maas, Winy 207
'McDonaldization' 103
'machine episteme' 251
maintenance: and aesthetics of order 154, 156
Malchei Israel Square memorial 94, 133, 135, 136, 137, 139, 142, 143, *144*, 146, 147, 151
malls *see* shopping malls
Manchester 281
Manhattan 42, 44
mapping: and Stalker 200
marginality 171–2
marketplaces 7, 9, 11, 38
Marlene-Dietrich-Platz (Berlin) 77, *78*, 79
marquees 73
Marrakesh 21, *21*
master plan 274
Melbourne *25*, 79; Bourke Street Mall 86-7, *87*, convergence and building thresholds 75–6; Flinders Street railway station 75–6, *76*, 84, 85; Parliament House 24, 81–2, *82*
Memorial to the Murdered Jews of Europe (Berlin) *19*
memorials 94; differences between official and vernacular 148–9; official 147–9; spontaneous *see* spontaneous memorials
memories 190, 249–50; and history 148
'memory fence' 135, *136*, 137
Merleau-Ponty 199
messiness 232
Mexico City 97
Middle East 108
Milner, Lord Alfred 213
mixed-use neighborhoods 6
Modern Movement 180
Monger, G. 133
Montevideo 97
monuments 190, 191
movement: liberating of in industrial ruins 242–4; and loose space 14–15
'movement economies' 116
municipal authorities 30
Mutations 207
MVRDV 207

Nager, A.R. and Wentworth, W.R. 50
Naples 175, 181
National Environmental Protection Act (NEPA)(1969) 258
National Land Use Database (NLUD) 212
National Technical University of Athens (NTUA) 185
negotiation 94
New York 18, 35; bonus plazas 38–9; Central Park *see*Central Park; Chinatown *see* Chinatown; found spaces 41–3; incentive zoning 38–9; Little Italy 35, 62–4, *63*, 67–70
New York City Department of Parks and Recreation 160, 162
New York Historical Society: 'Missing: Streetscape in a City of Mourning' 133
New York Public Library staircase 42, 43, 44, 46–50, *47*, *48*, *49*
Niagara River 258
Nicholson, S. 40
Nielsen, T. 8
nighttime 15, 122-4
9/11 40; and found space 40; memorials 94, 133, 135, 136, *136*, 137, 140, 141–2, *141*, *142*, 143, 144–5, 146, 151, *151*; official memorial 148, 151–2
no man's land 217, 220
nomads, urban *see* urban nomads
non-places 106, 108, 109
Norberg-Schulz, C. 73
Northland shopping mall (Detroit) 108

Ocalan 201
Oda Projesi 208

official memorials 147–51
Oklahoma City: memorials at site of bombing 94, 133, 135, 137, 139, 143–4, 145, 146
Oklahoma City National Memorial 147
Oldenburg, R. 15
Olmsted, Frederick Law 156, 157–60, 161
'open persons' 6
open-ended streets 35, 54–72; adaptability to different uses 67–8; characteristics of 67–70; and Chinatown 35, 56–62; Colombo and Kandy (Sri Lanka) 64–7; diversity of uses 67; fixed and semi-fixed elements 69; Little Italy 35, 62–4, *63*, 67–70; multi-sensory qualities 69–70; significance of 70–2; socio-cultural identity 70
open-endedness: concept of 55
Orientalism 114, 129
Oswalt, Philipp 273
otherness 176, 177, 178, 185, 191
outdoor rooms 220–2
Outrage! 223
Overmeyer, Klaus 273
Oxxo 100–1, 103

paksoi 118, *121*
paktrok 118
Palast der Republik (Berlin) 283–4, *284*
Panopticon: Foucauldian model of the 128
Pantera, La 196–7
Paradigmata 207–8
Park, Kyong 208
parks 15, 38, 39, 44; and aesthetics of order 155; as 'pleasure grounds' 157; *see also* Central Park
Parliament House (Melbourne) 24, 81–2, *82*
participatory consciousness 265, 268, 269
partitioned city 176, 177
Pasolini, Pier Paolo 198, 199
Pataki, Governor 152
people: and creation of loose space 10–11, 28
people-watching: and found spaces 45
perching places 42
Philip II, King of Spain 100
physical recreation: and loose space 12
place types: variety of in cities 2–3
planning 286–7; classical 286
Platform 208
playful behaviour: and building thresholds 74, 79, 80; and industrial ruins 243-4
playgrounds 39
plazas 7, 8, 24, 38; bonus 38–9, 44, 46, 51; main function of public 55
political activities: and loose space 12, 17–18
porches 73
porosity, urban 130, 174, 175, 178–9
possibility: and loose space 17–19
postmodernity 106
Pred, A. 69
prisons 2
privatization of public space 70, 96, 108; and aesthetics of order 160–2; *see also* shopping malls
process-based urban planning 286
'public good, the' 171
public/private: in Ban Panthom 120–2
'purification of space' 251

Queen Elizabeth Hall (South Bank, London) 27

Rabin, Yitzh: assassination of 94, 133; memorial at site of assassination 135, 136, 137, *138*, 139, 142, 143, *144*, 146, 151
railway improvement works *see* RAW
railway sheds, former 8
railway stations 84; thresholds of 78, 84
Rapoport, Amos 55
raves: industrial ruins as site for 236–7
RAW (railway improvement works) 271–2
RAW-Tempel e.V. 271–2
refugees 172, 179
regulation of public space 8, 25, 30, 54
religious belief 93
religious rituals 14; on Sri Lankan streets 66–7
Remedial Action Planning Process 253
Repton, Humphrey 222
research, urban 207–8
resistance 30, 171–3
restaurants: Little Italy 62, 68
restrictions: on people's use of public space 20, 71
retail activities: adapability of building spaces at street level 68; open-ended streets 58, 60, 67; *see also* street vendors
'right to the city' 5
ritual liminality 73–4
roadside memorials 133, *134*
Rogers, Richard 221, 224
Rojek, C. 91
Rome: and Stalker *see* Stalker; transformation of banks of Tiber 196–7
Romito, Lorenzo 194, 198, 199
Rote Fabrik (Red Factory) 272
Roth, M. 240
ruins 8, 232 *see also* industrial ruins
rules 29

Russell Square (London) 222–3; *Limits of Inclusiveness project* 225–7, *226*

sacred space: and secular space in Ban Panthom 125–7
safety 20; and found spaces 46, 51
Said, E. 114
Samuel, Raphael 249
San Gennaro festival 64
Santiago de Chile 97–8
Santino, J. 142
Sardello, R. 265
School of Architecture (Rome): protests (1990) 196
Segal, R. and Weizman, E. 207
segregation, spatial 172
semi-fixed elements: and open-ended streets 69
Sennett, R. 100, 129; *Uses of Disorder* 22
Seoul: Noryangjin fish market *9*
Seven-Eleven 101, *102*, 103
sex activities 14, 220; clamping down on in Russell Square 222–3
sex industry: Ban Panthom 124
Shields, R. 15, 82
shopping malls 15, 28, 106–9, 111, 162, 219; appropriation of space in 107–8; functions of in Middle East and Southeast Asia 108–9; and 'Gruen transfer' 88; as non-spaces 106; simulations of looseness 24; transforming of urban spaces into 108
Sibley, D. 251
Sica, Vittorio de 198
sidewalks 7, 14, 15, 29, 35, 36; adaptability for varying uses 67–8; as found
spaces 41, 42; need for not too many permanent fixtures 71; privatization of 54, 70; Sri Lanka 65–6; use of in Chinatown 58
Simmel 175, 176
Singapore 217, 219
Situationist movement 198
Siza, Alvaro 286
skateboarders 14–15, 27, 28, 75–6; and thresholds 82–4, *83*
slippages 114–15; Ban Panthom 127–8; co-existence with poverty 130
smell 36, 69–70
Smithson, Robert 199
smooth space: and striated space 115–17, 127, 128
social groups: and loose space 15–16
socializing: at thresholds 77; in found space 43
socio-cultural identity: open-ended streets 70
'soft architecture' 2
sois 118, *119*, 120, 125, 128
Solá-Morales, Ignasi de 8
Solnit, R. 265
Sommer, Robert: *Tight Spaces* 2
Sorkin, Michael 208
sounds 36–7, 69
South Bank Centre (SBC) 27
'spatial syntax analysis' 116
spillover places 41, 42
'spontaneous malling' 108
spontaneous memorials 94, 133–52; and appropriation 136–9; attracting of commercial activities 137, 139; clearing up of by authorities 139, 143; designing and curating 141–3; duration 139; expression of opinions at 145–7, 150–1; location 135; objects left at 143–5; and official memorials 149, 151–2; physical and emotional participation 140; as places of pilgrimage 137; roadside 133, *134*; as temporary 139
squares 38, 39, 41
Sri Lanka 35, 67–70; Colombo and Kandy 64–7
staircases/stairs 8, 29; as found space 42; and refugee housing complexes in Athens 181; and skateboarders 84–5; as threshold site 86
Stalker 171, 172–3, 193–209; approaches 195; attitude towards landscape 198; commemoration of Pasolini 199; contribution 208; development of new language of mapping 200; early development 196–8; environmental philosophy and influences 199–200; field research 198; helping of Kurdish exiles and establishment of Campo Boario 201–3, *202*, *203*; involvement with marginalized communities 201; Manifesto (1996) 199; and migrant communities projects 203–4; *modus operandi* 198; reanactment of *Asphalt Rundown* 199; *The Flying Carpet* project 204–5; *Transborderline* project 173, 204–6, *205*; use of multi-media 200–1; Walk about Rome 193–6, 198
Stalker (film) 193, 196, 212, 214
Stalker/ON 208
State Library (Melbourne) 83
steps 36, 41, 81, 82, 83
stigmatization 171, 172
strangers 5
street, open-ended *see* open-ended streets
street blocks 6
street corners *see* corners
street performers 12, 36, 40, 43, 45; and theater-on-the-threshold 76–7, *77*, 90

street vendors *9*, 12, 18, *21*, 22–3, 36, 42, 45, 49; in Chinatown 58, 59-60, *60*, 68; in Colombo and Kandy 65-6; and found space 45-6
streets 6, 7, 36, 106; hierarchy of in Ban Panthom 117, 117–18, *119*, 128, 129; and thresholds 79
striated space: and smooth space 115–17, 127, 128
strolling 108
sub-cultural milieus 277
surveillance 8, 20; and aesthetics of order 154, 156
symbolism 10

Tagg, John 251
Taiwan 207
'Take Back the Memorial' 152
Tan, Pelin 208
Tarkovsky, Andrei 193
teenagers 20, 28
Tel Aviv 213; portraying as a void in order to regenerate 213–14
temporary use: as a catalyst for urban change 281–4; definition and sites of 274–7; long-term effects of 280–1; and municipalities 279; people involved in 277–9; and planning 286–7; potential of 273–4; strategies for success 279–80
tension 29, 93–5
terraces 73, 82
terrains vagues 227, 259, 264
texture 37
Thailand 114–15; ethnic differences 127
theater-on-the-threshold 76–7, *77*, 90
theme parks 162
themed environment 3, 11, 26
third world cities 108
threshold moments 190
threshold spaces 174
thresholds 176–7; recognizing urban 175; regulating passages 176; *see also* building thresholds
Ti-Nan Chi 207
Tiananmen Square 18, 24, 221
tianguis (street market) 109–11, *110*
tight space: relationship with loose space 23–8
time: building thresholds and passage of 75, 79–81
Tokunaga, Jim Y. 216
tolerance: learning of through disorder 22
Tompkins Square Park (New York) 163
Transborderline project 173, 204–6, *205*, 225
Transgressive Architecture 172, 223–7; *Bad Sheets* project 224–5, *225*; *Limits of Inclusiveness* project 173, 225–7, *226*
transgressive space 219–20
Troen, S.I., *Imagining Zion* 213
troks 118, *119*, 120, 124, 128, 129
Tschumi, Bernard 224
turnstiles 73
types 2

Urban Catalyst 231, 232, 233, 271–87
urban corners *see* corners, urban
Urban Flashes 207
urban layouts: and looseness 6
urban nomads 219–20, 224; local authorities' actions against 221–2
Urban Task Force (UTF) 221
urbanity: key features of 7

vandalism: and industrial ruins 237
Vattimo 199
Vaux, Calvert 157–60
Veblen, T. 160
vendors *see* street vendors
video game arcade 87–8, *88*
Vienna: vegetable gardens *7*
Vietnam Veterans Memorial 149, *150*
Villagio Globale 202
Virilio 199
Volkspalast 284, *285*

Walk about Rome 193–6, 198
walls 8, 41
wat 118, 120, 125–6, 128
wedding photographs 74–5, 81, *82*, 86, 90
Westin, A.F. 44
Whyte, William H. 39, 45; *Street Corner Society* 100
WMF nightclub (Berlin) 280–1
World Trade Center attacks *see* 9/11

Young, Iris Marion 19–20, 140

zero tolerance approach 221
zoning 71
zoopolis 240
Zukin, S. 87, 106
Zwischenpalastnutzung 284